"A detailed, almost day-by-day account of political debates that preceded Japan's surrender in World War II. . . . A nonrevisionist, reflective, opinionated, intensely researched WWII history." —*Kirkus Reviews*

"Historian Barrett debuts with an impressively researched chronicle of the months leading up to the atomic bombing of Hiroshima. . . . By capturing both sides of the conflict, Barrett generates drama despite the inevitability of the book's conclusion. Military history buffs will be riveted." —*Publishers Weekly*

"David Dean Barrett's detailing of the ruling militarists' iron grip on Japanese decision-making—even after two atomic bombs and the Soviet entry into the Pacific War—should finally put to rest any notion that the Japanese were trying to surrender. As *140 Days to Hiroshima* clearly shows, it was the bomb that influenced the Emperor to make his historic interventions forcing his government to finally surrender. Yet even then, Japan's military almost derailed Hirohito's decree to end the war." —D. M. Giangreco,
author of *Hell to Pay: Operation Downfall and the Invasion of Japan, 1945-1947*

"*140 Days to Hiroshima* utterly destroys the revisionist fictions that Japan would have surrendered months earlier if only they had been notified that they could retain their emperor, and that Truman dropped the bombs to awe the Soviets rather than to defeat an already-defeated Japan. It is an important book and a gripping read." —Robert James Maddox,
author of *Weapons for Victory: The Hiroshima Decision,* and editor of *Hiroshima in History*

"The interplay between the leaders of Japan and America during the conclusion of the Pacific War—when some leaders in Japan did their best to lead their country to surrender—is a narrative of human drama that still challenges minds around the world. David Dean Barrett's work is an important contribution to an in-depth understanding." —Kazuhiko Tōgō,
professor at Kyoto Sangyo University;
former Ambassador of Japan to the Netherlands;
grandson of former Japanese Foreign Minister Shigenori Tōgō

"David Dean Barrett's *140 Days to Hiroshima* offers a comprehensive and definitive account of the events and decision making that culminated in the American use of atomic weapons against Japan in August 1945. Barrett's meticulous and balanced review of the evidence makes it clear that the circumstances at the time justify Truman's decision to use atomic weapons. He convincingly demonstrates that the Japanese government was not prepared to surrender on terms acceptable to the United States and its allies prior to the attacks on Hiroshima and Nagasaki, that President Truman and his top advisors understood this, and that Truman's sole objective in resorting to atomic weapons was to end the war as soon as possible and thereby save American lives. Barrett further demonstrates that there were estimates for American casualties in the projected invasion of Japan that exceeded 500,000 and that the use of atomic bombs against Hiroshima and Nagasaki was the key factor in bringing about Japan's surrender."   —Michael Kort,

professor of social science at Boston University
and author of *The Columbia Guide to Hiroshima and the Bomb*

140 DAYS TO HIROSHIMA

THE STORY OF JAPAN'S LAST
CHANCE TO AVERT ARMAGEDDON

DAVID DEAN BARRETT

DIVERSION
BOOKS

For more information, email info@diversionbooks.com

Diversion Books
A division of Diversion Publishing Corp.
www.diversionbooks.com

Book design by Janine Suarez for Neuwirth & Associates

First Diversion Books edition April 2020
First Diversion Books trade paperback edition May 2021

Paperback ISBN: 978-1-63576-752-0
eBook ISBN: 978-1-63576-580-9

Printed in The United States of America

Library of Congress cataloging-in-publication data is available on file.

Dedicated to all the American veterans who served during World War II

CONTENTS

AUTHOR'S NOTE

The common way for Japanese names to be displayed is first name last and last name first. I've chosen to follow the more universal method of first name first and last name last.

PROLOGUE

By the summer of 1944, U.S. military power in the Pacific Theater had grown spectacularly. Beginning nine days after the D-Day invasion in France, American forces launched their largest attacks yet against the Japanese-held islands of Saipan on June 15, Guam on July 21, and Tinian on July 24. Situated 1,200 to 1,500 miles south of Japan, the crescent-shaped archipelago known as the Marianas was strategically important to the defense of the Empire, protecting vital shipping lanes from Asia and a widened aerial attack of the homeland.

Over the next sixty days, each of the three islands fell to the Americans. During grueling land and sea campaigns, U.S. forces killed 60,000 Japanese soldiers, sailors, and airmen, while the Japanese inflicted just under 30,000 total casualties on the Americans, killing 5,500.

On June 19 and 20, west of the Marianas in the Philippine Sea, the American and Japanese Navies fought one of the greatest air-sea engagements of World War II, the Battle of the Philippine Sea—also known as "The Great Marianas Turkey Shoot." In the course of the two-day battle, American aviators decimated their Japanese counterparts, shooting down nearly four hundred aircraft. The additional destruction of three Japanese fleet aircraft carriers forever prevented Japan from using carriers to conduct offensive operations in the war.

The losses also made clear to Japan's military leaders that there was no chance of victory; their only remaining options would lie within the terms of peace, if the Allies were willing to negotiate. With Japan's failed defense of the Marianas, the war journal of Imperial Headquarters concluded in July of 1944:

> We can no longer direct the war with any hope of success. The only course left is for Japan's 100 million people to sacrifice their lives by charging the enemy to make them lose their will to fight.

In judging the situation…there is unanimous agreement that henceforth we will slowly fall into a state of ruin. So it is necessary to plan for a quick end to the war."[*][1]

In the aftermath of battles, American Seabees (Naval Construction Force) transformed Saipan, Tinian, and Guam into some of the largest airfields in the world. By Thanksgiving, those bases were mated with the United States' newest four-engine, long-range heavy bomber, the B-29 Superfortress, putting Japan squarely in the crosshairs of America's strategic bombing campaign.

The fall and early winter of 1944 saw the fall of Peleliu, which was six hundred miles east of Mindanao; the invasion of the Philippines; the Battle of Leyte Gulf, the largest naval engagement in history; and the relocation of the strategic bombing campaign against mainland Japan from China to the Marianas.

As 1945 opened and the War in the Pacific entered its fourth and decisive year, the United States had fought its way across the vastness of the world's largest ocean and had begun its assault on Japanese territory, but at an ever-greater cost. From the summer of 1944 to the war's end in August of 1945, America suffered nearly two thirds of its total Pacific War casualties, including over half of the men killed in action.

---

* Japanese propaganda persistently referred to the nation's population as 100 million, whereas the actual count in the 1944 census was about 72 million.[2] The 100 million figure included twenty-four million Koreans, who had been under Japanese rule since 1910.

1

TOKYO BURN JOB

More than 70,000 men in the 3rd, 4th, and 5th Marine divisions invaded Iwo Jima on February 19, 1945. In anticipation of the most intense ground fighting of the war—what the U.S. knew would be a fiercely determined opposition—the assault was supported by 800 ships and 220,000 naval personnel.[1]

Located midway between the American B-29 bomber bases in the Marianas and the main islands of Japan, the tiny speck of volcanic earth was invaluable amid the vast Pacific Ocean, its runways representing salvation for crippled B-29s returning from bombing missions. Taking the island and eliminating its enemy radar station also deprived the Japanese of an early warning system for attacks on the home islands and eradicated the risk of any further attacks by Japanese planes against Guam, Saipan, and Tinian as well.

In the thirty-six days of combat it took to wrest the eight-square-mile island from its 20,000-plus defenders, 19,217 Americans were wounded and a further 6,822 killed—853 men for every square mile. Japanese losses were nearly total.

The new air offensive from the Marianas—which began in late November 1944—was a huge logistical improvement over the India-China operations, but it remained ineffective. To take advantage of the newest, most sophisticated, and expensive heavy bomber in America's arsenal—the B-29—the bombs were being dropped from over 25,000 feet during the day. The bombs were often miles off target, primarily due to the persistent existence of the jet stream and cloud cover over Japan.

Things quickly changed when, on January 20, 1945, a rising star in the United States Army Air Forces, thirty-eight-year-old Curtis LeMay, nicknamed "Old Iron Pants," took control of the XXI Bomber Command headquartered at Harmon Field on Guam. A veteran of nearly two years of aerial combat with the Eighth Air Force in England, LeMay had helped develop the "combat box" formation used over Europe. The configuration protected heavy bombers against fighter attack by maximizing the defensive firepower of all the .50 caliber machine guns of the planes in the formation, while at the same time concentrating the bomb pattern on the target. Future Secretary of Defense Robert McNamara described LeMay as "the finest combat commander of any service I came across in the war."

Sent to the Pacific to produce results, throughout February and into the first week of March LeMay and his staff worked on plans that radically altered the XXI's bombing tactics. No longer would the B-29s bomb from high altitude. Instead they would fly at less than ten thousand feet, under the cover of darkness. The lower altitude reduced the amount of fuel required for missions while also easing the stress on the plane's finicky R-3350 engines. And in an extreme effort to reduce all possible weight, all the B-29s' .50 caliber machine guns were removed, except for the twin .50s in the tail of the plane. Less weight translated into bigger bomb loads.[2] To minimize the exposure of aircrews to flak and fighters, LeMay introduced a concept he called "compressibility," the bombers "forming up and concentrating over the target in minimum time to overwhelm defenders."[3] LeMay, who had flown a number of missions in Europe, had wanted to lead this attack using the new tactics with his men, but he had been grounded for the sake of security after being briefed about the atomic bomb.[4]

The B-29s' primary weapon would be the M69 incendiary bomblet. Nicknamed *Tokyo Calling Cards*, M69s were hexagonal steel cylinders three inches in diameter and twenty inches long, weighing 6.2 pounds. Each bomblet contained Napalm-B encased in cheesecloth as its incendiary filler. The improved version of napalm included newly added polystyrene and benzene, which yielded a longer-burning fire at temperatures up to 2,000 degrees Fahrenheit. Thirty-eight of the bomblets were enclosed in a finned E-46 aimable cluster. The cluster opened at a designated altitude, typically 2,000 feet, and would spread its munitions across a 500 feet by 2,500 feet swath. Each of the M69s had a three-foot-long cotton streamer, resembling the tail of a kite, to orient its fuse downward, control the velocity of descent, and spread the munitions as they dropped to the target. After hitting a building or the ground, the timing fuse burned for three to five seconds before detonating a white phosphorous charge. The explosion propelled flaming globs of napalm up to a hundred feet, instantly starting intense fires. A typical bombload for a B-29 included forty cluster bombs or 1,520 M69 bomblets.[5]

Tokyo, the first target for LeMay's ten-day mini blitz, would be the recipient of half a million such bomblets.

MARCH 9–10, 1945

In the lead-up to the raid on Japan's most populous city, 13,000 men on three Pacific islands toiled nearly non-stop for thirty-six hours to ready the fleet of planes for its mission. At 5:36 p.m. on March 9, 1945, the first B-29 crews started rolling down Guam's runways and continued, one at a time, in fifty-second intervals.[6] At the same time, planes began taking off from Saipan and Tinian.

After six hours of flight, at about 11:40 p.m., the lead elements of 325 B-29 Superfortresses from the 73rd, 313th, and 314th Bombardment Wings approached the coast of Japan. The crewmen donned flak vests and helmets and strapped themselves into their seats as tightly as possible. Only the dim light of a crescent moon and the stars above brightened the dense blackness.

Spread out over more than two hundred miles,[7] the planes looked like giant roller coaster hills horizontally staggered left and right of a center line and vertically in steps at altitudes from 5,000 to 7,900 feet.[8] Short, blue flames burned from the two superchargers on the back side of each of the B-29s' four engines.[9] Ironically, crewmen from the 73rd Bombardment Wing listening to Radio Tokyo on their flight to the city heard, among other selections, "Smoke Gets in Your Eyes," "My Old Flame," and "I Don't Want to Set the World on Fire."[10]

Just south of the Chiba peninsula, the great armada split in two. From there the 314th flew parallel to the coastline of Tokyo Bay. The 73rd and 313th soared past the eastern side of the Chiba peninsula and then turned northwest.[11]

At 12:07 a.m. on March 10, the lead pathfinders, sweeping in low and fast at nearly 300 miles an hour and at right angles to each other, unleashed their white phosphorous M47 bombs to mark the primary target. With superlative navigation, the crews managed to ignite a fiery cross on the ground to literally show "X" marks the spot. The part of downtown Tokyo chosen for the attack measured about three by four miles, and was located between the southwest corner of the city's main rail station and the Sumida River. Despite the evacuation from cities of great numbers of Japanese, including children, a huge population of essential laborers remained. The target area "teemed with life: an estimated 750,000 workers crammed into the twelve square miles of low-income housing and family-operated factories. It may have been the most densely populated place on earth."[12] As more pathfinders flew over the target and released their payload, searchlights pierced the night sky and succeeding planes quickly encountered both beams of light and anti-aircraft fire. One of the lead aircraft was hit almost immediately and plunged "like a ball of fire" into the ground at 12:16 a.m.[13] With the target area now clearly marked, planes from the main group commenced dropping their E-46 clusters onto a swiftly growing fire. From the ground, Father Gustav Bruno Maria Bitter said the M69 bomblets reminded him of "a silver curtain falling, like the lametta, the silver tinsel that we hung from Christmas trees in Germany…And where these streamers…touch[ed] the earth, red fires would spring up."[14] Houses and buildings flared like the fuses of a firework as they were hit.[15] Smoke rising from the city quickly infiltrated open bomb bays and crewmen picked up an uncharacteristic odor—the sickening, sweet smell of burning flesh.

The thick smoke also created the potential for midair collisions. In one such instance, two B-29s had begun their bomb runs at almost the same time, but at two different altitudes. As they converged on the city, the distance between them had become dangerously close. As the lower of the two planes was making final preparations, the co-pilot looked up and saw catastrophe in the making—a B-29 emerging from the smoke directly above them, its bomb bay doors already open. The co-pilot screamed the warning to the pilot, who immediately pushed the throttle forward and accelerated out from under the second B-29.

About an hour into the assault, the number of planes over the city had grown significantly, and the drone of their radial engines had become ever present.[16] The scene greeting these airborne crews was beyond anything they could have imagined. A wall of flames stretched across the horizon; it looked like Hell on earth,[17] a city engulfed in fire rising hundreds of feet into the air.

Powerful thermals belched from the ground, some as high as twenty thousand feet. One collided with a plane, suddenly pushing it upward a thousand feet. Just as abruptly, the plane hit an invisible wall of cold air, shoving it back down. The twin shocks produced a thunderous clap that reverberated throughout the cabin like two boards being slapped together.[18] The violent shaking of the aircraft broke loose floorboards and threw the crew's personal belongings and equipment everywhere and caused numerous cuts and bruises.[19]

Another black column of billowing smoke rose from the surface and hit the right wing of one of the B-29s, completely flipping the plane into a three-hundred-sixty-degree aileron roll, plunging it toward the burning city. Miraculously, the pilots managed to regain control seconds before the plane would have hit the ground.[20]

Searchlights endlessly swept the sky looking for the massive bombers. Japanese crews manning the searchlights attempted to get multiple lights onto a single plane. When successful, the effect created what looked like an inverted cone above the plane. B-29s unlucky enough to get caught in the illumination cones were quickly subjected to concentrated Japanese machine-gun fire. The red, green, and yellow tracers streaked across the sky in long arcs, most falling below the planes.

Anti-aircraft batteries joined the torrent of fire, spewing flak shells that sent deadly shards of steel into the paths of the incoming B-29s. Shrapnel from the exploding flak shells sounded like pebbles rolling off the plane's aluminum skin. [21] The lethal barrage also included sporadic phosphorus shells that created blinding white flashes which momentarily incapacitated pilots in the night's darkness. By far the most numerous were the more common flak shells often seen in the European air war that looked like puffs of black smoke as they burst.

However, the Japanese added a fascinating variant to their flak shells. In an apparent effort to more rapidly establish the altitude of aircraft, the shells were chemically treated to burn green, red, and purple. The effectiveness of the practice, when paired with the illumination cones, proved fatal for at least one unfortunate B-29 and its crew.

Already trapped between two searchlights, a purple flak shell exploded just in front of the nose of one of the B-29s. Anti-aircraft crews quickly spotted the proximity to the bomber and followed it with several more rounds of purple flak. The next tore into the cockpit, instantly killing the pilots. More of the purple shells ripped into the crippled bomber. Seconds later the plane rolled over and began a slow death spiral to the earth, crashing and exploding in a huge fireball.

While not in large numbers, Japanese aircraft attempted to defend the city against the B-29 crews, darting in and out among them. Occasionally, the inexperienced and ill-trained Japanese pilots adopted kamikaze tactics. In one such attack, a Zero pilot rammed his plane into the middle of a B-29. Suddenly, the entire sky seemed to explode as the high-octane gas in the wings and second bomb bay detonated along with the bomb load in a colossal thunderclap. Still flaming, parts of the two planes cartwheeled in the air and slammed into the ground. The tail section of the B-29 blazed across the sky before smashing into a field. One of the engines crashed into a hillside and disintegrated; the other three bounced and rolled, tearing up large swaths of earth. One massive piece of the wing, with flaming gas tanks inside, slowly circled like a spent and twisted red and orange boomerang, finally plummeting into undergrowth. The bodies of some of the crew, still strapped in their seats, lay scattered amongst the twisted wreckage.[22]

AN ENTIRELY DIFFERENT STORY UNFOLDED at street level. The city had become a mass of flames, smoke, and explosions that rocked its inhabitants. The crescendo of air raid sirens blared in groans and wavering high-pitched whines, mixing with blood-curdling screams.

A few of the better-off inhabitants fled to the concrete shelters that they had buried in the ground around their homes.[23] The fire's roar sounded like a great freight train. Walls collapsed and large piles of rubble that once were buildings and homes burned out of control. Charred, blackened bodies lay everywhere. Thousands of firemen battled in vain to extinguish the inferno, in some cases using static water tanks. Rubble in the streets made it even more difficult for the fire crews to move equipment between the city's crowded buildings.[24]

Whipped by stiffening winds, fires spread quickly. Enormous balls of flame jumped from building to building with hurricane force, creating a tidal wave of flame.[25] As historian Barrett Tillman noted, "In those frightful hours humans watched things happen on a scale that probably had never been seen. [As] superheated ambient air boiled the water out of ponds and canals while rains of liquid glass flew, propelled by cyclonic winds. Temperatures reached 1,800 degrees Fahrenheit, melting the frames of emergency vehicles and causing some people to erupt in spontaneous combustion."[26] Exploding gas tanks blew structures apart.

People "were momentarily paralyzed by the awesome sight of the planes blanketing them like huge dragons—greenish from the searchlight beams, crimson from the glare below."[27] Most people had no protection and ran around frantically to escape the heat, smoke, and flames; many were on fire, some writhed on the ground in torment, others ran naked through the street, their clothing burned off. Some jumped into small containers of water intended for firefighting, only to be scalded to death.[28] Thousands more crouched terrified in their wooden shelters, where they roasted alive. Large numbers attempted to flee to the great Buddhist temple in Asakusa; it became their tomb.[29]

One mass of people crowded together in the street, staring at the flames. Firemen shouted to them to make for the bridge across the Kanda River, but a wall of fire blocked their path. Suddenly a young man leapt up and led the way, jumping over tree trunks that burned like logs in a mammoth fireplace. Soon others followed in a single file. Momentarily blinded by the intense light, he gasped for breath and stumbled, near the end of his endurance. Through the roiling smoke he finally spotted the concrete bridge, crowded with squatting people. He ran to them and to his salvation.[30]

The center of Tokyo glowed incandescent like the sun.[31] Billowing clouds of smoke surged up, illuminated from below by orange flames. Scorched trees and telephone poles lay strewn across streets like giant matchsticks, their warped lines snaked out along the ground.

Not even the *Gobunko*, a bunker complex built into the hillside near the Fukiage Gardens within the Imperial Palace compound, primarily for the protection of the royal family, escaped harm completely. Shortly after midnight, as the raid was just beginning, the Emperor was still on duty in his underground command post, half-asleep and awaiting two important phone calls—one about the Japanese Army's final take-over of the puppet government in Saigon (today Ho Chi Minh City), Vietnam, the other about the birth of his first grandchild.[32] Unable to sleep due to the horrifying sounds of the raid, Hirohito remained safely sequestered inside the *Gobunko*. Eventually, the firestorm's high winds reached the palace, dropping burning embers on the shrubs and camouflage surrounding the bunker and starting several fires. Palace guards and staff had only pails of water and branches to put out the flames; and as they struggled to do so, its acrid smell infiltrated the space where the Emperor's family took refuge.[33]

Sometime after 3:00 a.m., the hum of B-29 engines and the sound of air raid sirens ended. Scattered clouds continued to glow, reflecting the flames of the burning city. Searchlights dimmed. As dawn broke, the light of day spread over the city and revealed a blackened and ashen landscape. Smoke curled into the sky as fires punctuated the now practically barren panorama.

Some of the worst killing grounds were the schools, according to Hidezo Tsuchikura, who, along with his two children, took refuge on the roof of the Futaba School. For ninety minutes they took turns dousing each other's clothing from a tank of water as their garments caught fire. Finally, after consuming the surrounding neighborhood, the fire receded. But by then only Tsuchikura, his children, and twelve other people remained alive. He observed,

> The entire building had become a huge oven three stories high. Every human being inside the school was literally baked or boiled alive in the heat. Dead bodies were everywhere in grizzly heaps. None of them appeared to be badly charred. They looked like mannequins, some of them with pinkish complexion…
>
> But the swimming pool was the most horrible sight of all. It was hideous. More than 1,000 people…had jammed into the pool. The pool had been filled to its brim when [they] first arrived. Now there wasn't a drop of water, only the bodies of the adults and children who had died.[34]

People ran to the Sumida River and leapt through walls of flame to dive into the water and onto the riverbanks. Layer upon layer of people all attempting to escape to safety crushed the early arrivals, and when the torrent of flames came, anyone holding their head above water risked being choked by smoke or seared by flame. The all-consuming fire sucked up the oxygen, suffocating thousands.[35]

The captain of one Fire Company was stunned by the scene he found on the Ryōgoku Bridge, "'a forest of corpses' packed so closely that they must have been touching as they died. They had returned to humanity's carbon existence, crumbling at the touch."[36]

In the river below:

> The entire river surface was black as far as the eye could see, black with burned corpses, logs, and who knew what else, but uniformly black from the immense heat that had seared its way through the area as the fire dragon past. It was impossible to tell the bodies from the logs at a distance. The bodies were all nude, the clothes had been burned away, and there was a dreadful sameness about them, no

telling men from women or even children. All that remained were pieces of charred meat. Bodies and parts of bodies were carbonized and absolutely black.

As the waves along the riverbanks receded, more bodies revealed themselves:

> stacked in neat precision, as though by some machine… row upon row of corpses. The instrument was the tide, which had come and gone since the firestorm passed by, leaving rows of bodies like so much cordwood cast up on the beach…How many bodies had washed out to sea was impossible to tell, but they must have been in the thousands, for there were tens of thousands in the river.[37]

Incendiary bombs had rained down on Tokyo for nearly three hours. The raid caused an urban conflagration, a fire storm much like the one that had destroyed Dresden, Germany, just a few weeks earlier, and it resulted in greater loss of life than any aerial assault in any theater during World War II. Approximately 84,000 people perished while 261,000 buildings and homes were destroyed, leaving 1.15 million homeless. Nearly sixteen square miles of Tokyo had been turned to ash—about eighteen percent of the industrial area and sixty-three percent of the commercial area. In the explicit ten-square-mile targeted area, eighty-two percent had been destroyed.[38]

While American bomber crews sustained losses, a little less than five percent of the force, casualties were slightly lower than expected and deemed acceptable. LeMay's new tactics were an unmitigated success in terms of damage. They also exposed the vulnerability of Japanese air defenses and the inadequacy of their firefighting facilities, which were totally overwhelmed dealing with the effects of the massive incendiary attack.

Three and half years earlier, General George Marshall, Chief of Staff of the United States Army, told news reporters in an off-the-record briefing on November 15, 1941, three weeks before Pearl Harbor, that "If war with the Japanese does come, we'll fight mercilessly. Flying Fortresses [B-17s] will be dispatched immediately to set the paper cities of Japan on fire. There won't be any hesitation about bombing civilians—it will be all-out."

Marshall may have been off with his timing and the plane causing the destruction, but his prediction had now been seared into the fabric of the war against Japan (and with Germany well before March 10). And by 1945, the military had the concurrence of the American public. *Time* magazine, for example, "described LeMay's firebombing of Tokyo as 'a dream come true' which proved that 'properly kindled, Japanese cities will burn like autumn leaves.'"[39]

In the aftermath of the attack that morning, Tokyo Radio broadcast the following message: "During an air attack on the city of Tokyo last night, Imperial forces destroyed over one hundred American planes. It was a great victory for our forces, who will continue to fight for the honor of our Emperor and until our enemies are driven away."

The actual number was just fourteen. The bombing also precipitated an exodus from the capital with more than a million people leaving on their own accord in the weeks following the raid.[40] And regardless of the positive spin Japanese propaganda attempted to put on the event, no one living in or visiting Tokyo could fail to recognize the attack for what it was—a catastrophe greater than the city had ever seen. They also knew if the Americans were able to project such a powerful force, it meant they would be back, likely soon.

MARCH 19, 1945
140 DAYS TO HIROSHIMA

Nine days after the firebombing of Tokyo, Emperor Hirohito decided to see for himself the destruction wrought by the air raid. That morning his small entourage of just two cars drove slowly through the remains of Tokyo. The first car was flanked, front and rear, by two motorcycles, each with sidecars. The second car, occupied by the Emperor, was a large, two-toned, crimson and black, armored Mercedes-Benz 770 adorned with his gold chrysanthemum pennant. As the vehicles moved through the ruins, the view in every direction was of a vast, flattened wasteland dotted by stone statues, concrete pillars and walls, the skeletal steel frames of buildings, and a scattering of telephone poles.[41] Nearby, small groups of civilians in ragged clothing dug through the rubble for anything of value, most with empty expressions on their faces. They watched the visitors with reproachful eyes as the tiny motorcade passed.[42] Occasionally, the cars pulled off to the side of the road and the Emperor, carrying a cane, got out with his doctor, chamberlain, and several men in military uniforms, to speak with local officials. In one ward alone, only fifty of 13,000 homes remained intact, and more than 10,000 residents were either dead or injured. Ultimately, it would take four weeks to dispose of all 84,000 corpses.[43]

By the time Hirohito visited the devastation brought to his capital by LeMay's new tactics, the American general had already conducted a mini blitz against Japan, also hitting the cities of Nagoya (twice), Osaka, and Kobe. In a period of just ten days, the Americans flew 1,595 sorties and dropped 9,373 tons of bombs, destroying thirty-one square miles at a cost of just twenty-two airplanes.[44] The pace, scale, and ferocity of the attacks shocked the Japanese. And LeMay was just getting started. By war's end he would obliterate forty percent of Japan's sixty-six largest cities, destroy 2.3 million homes, and *dehouse* approximately thirty percent of the entire urban population of the country.[45] After another attack on Tokyo in late May, the Emperor and his family would be forced to move from their residence to the *Gobunko*.

Still, during the final months of the war, Japan's leaders would never leave their capital, which would be bombed several more times before the end of the conflict. It would have been seemingly incomprehensible to ignore the magnitude of and relentlessness of LeMay's aerial assaults and harbor any doubt about how powerful their enemy had grown or what its intentions were as long as they refused to surrender.

2

A THIRD PRIME MINISTER
IN LESS THAN A YEAR

The genesis of the 1931–45 Japanese government dated to the end of the Meiji Restoration in 1868. In an effort to unify a fragmented people against the perceived threat of colonization by Western Powers, in 1869 "a small group of samurai from Satsuma, Chōshū, Tosa and Hizen," who dominated the newly formed government of Japan, chose the path of least resistance and opted to link their power and right to rule to the Emperor.[1] From that moment, their objective and that of their successors was to use their divine Emperor as a mechanism to bestow power onto the real leaders. The approach morphed over time into a military oligarchy.

By the time of the Russo-Japanese War, 1904–1905, the army had begun popularizing the concept of death before dishonor, connecting it to the ancient practices of *bushidō* (the way of the warrior) and *Yamato-damashii* (Japanese spirit).[2] The hero system marking this new era, which extolled individual self-sacrifice—especially death for the benefit of the whole and their godlike Emperor—earned immortality for the individual. It would prove an exceptional ideological mechanism for mobilizing a country for total industrialized war.

With the "resurgence of Shintō ideas, carrying with it a new emphasis on the Emperor's divine descent,...it became clear that any regime succeeding the Tokugawa [Period 1600–1867] would have to act in the Emperor's name."[3] As historian Ian Buruma put it, Shintō, Japan's ancient ethnic religion, "would be transformed from a nature cult with many gods to a national faith that welded all Japanese together under one imperial roof."[4] Infusing the marriage of Shintō with the divine Emperor into every element of life, Japanese leaders went so far as to make the religion part of their new constitution in 1868–69.

Fifty years later, the ascension of Hirohito—the slightly built, five-foot six-inch, bespectacled, mustached, and shy prince—marked the pinnacle of the Emperor myth in Japanese history. Buruma writes:

> The enthronement [of Hirohito] was staged as a huge media event. Day and night, newspapers and radio broadcasts reported rice-growing ceremonies, flag-waving and parades, lantern festivals, award ceremonies, and Shintō rituals of various kinds, some of which had been quite recently invented. Many books were written, and lectures delivered, on the essence of Japaneseness and the *kokutai* [their sovereign Emperor], and many warnings were given about the dangers of dissent. Reverence for ancestors, unity of the monarch and the people, and the unity of rites and governance were presented by learned men not just as Japanese, but as "scientific" principles.[5]

> The climax of all this came on November 14, 1928, or rather the following morning, when Emperor Hirohito was formally reborn as a living god, after having spent the night in the holiest of holy shrines at Ise, communing with his progenitor, sun goddess Amaterasu Omikami.[6]

The years' long buildup to Hirohito's enthronement, as well as the fantastic spectacle of it, had unintended consequences for Japan's leaders and the new Emperor. They now had to face the monster they had created. Because just a few years later, as historian Tsurumi Shunsuke explains:

> The people [now]…demanded that the government follow a literal interpretation of the national myth, [and] the majority of the officials in power did not dare to refuse openly. The Emperor himself…did not say publicly that he disapproved of this new policy. On the contrary, he was influenced by the development of the war against China [which began in 1931 after members of the Japanese army staged a bombing near a railway line and subsequently blamed the Chinese army as an excuse for the invasion of northeastern China, known as Manchuria at the time], and he did not support those politicians who sought to put a stop to it by evacuating the expeditionary forces.[7]

Hirohito's willingness to withhold backing from officials seeking to end the war with China were not the actions of a monarch sitting idly by while others led. Instead, the Emperor clearly made a choice to use his power to influence the course of one of the most important issues facing Japan, its war with China. Indeed, Hirohito's behavior was indicative of someone who wanted an active voice in the country's decisions. And it is difficult to imagine how a man brought up to believe he was divine, designated as the sovereign of the state, ranked as commander in chief of the Imperial forces, told the people of Japan were his children, and instructed that his decisions were sacred and inviolable, could *not* believe he had an obligation and a right to be directly involved in the leadership of his country.

But that did not mean the Emperor wanted to make decisions without the aid of counsel. Like most leaders, Hirohito sought information and advice to make important choices. In November of 1937, coinciding with a major escalation of Japan's war with China, he decided to bring the chiefs of Army and Navy General Staff into closer consultation with his government by establishing a body known as the Imperial General Headquarters-Government Liaison Conference. From senior officers in this body, he received daily updates and frequent briefings on the status of military campaigns. During these sessions, Hirohito often challenged his commanders with insightful questions that revealed more than a casual understanding of the material presented. Nevertheless, a sizable gap remained between his display of knowledge and his actual influence, since Imperial Headquarters still controlled the flow and accuracy of information shown to the Emperor. Both surreptitiously assured Hirohito saw events the way his military chiefs wanted, which facilitated their ability to obtain his support for their strategies and operations.[8]

In the political arena, advice also came from many sources, but here the Emperor could use his judgment to evaluate options less prone to distortion.

> On June 1, 1940, the Emperor exercised his own discretion in choosing a new Lord Keeper of the privy seal. Ignoring *genrō* Saionji [Kinmochi's] qualms about [Marquis Kōichi] Kido's right-wing bent, expressed through the former's refusal to recommend a candidate, Hirohito decided to heed [former Prime Minister and Prince, Fumimaro] Konoye and [Kurahei] Yuasa's positive recommendations and appoint Kido, the revisionist bureaucrat and class-conscious leader of the hereditary aristocracy, to succeed the ailing Yuasa as his most

important political advisor. The youngest man ever to hold the post, Kido was nearly fifty-one; Hirohito was thirty-nine.[9]

BORN TO A NOBLE FAMILY—GRANDSON to Takayoshi Kido, one of the leaders of the Meiji Restoration—Kido graduated from the prestigious Kyoto University. His first major posting within the Japanese government had been as Konoye's Minister of Education in 1937. Two years later, Prime Minister Baron Kiichirō Hiranuma tapped him to become the Home Minister in his Cabinet. During his time in the Konoye and Hiranuma Cabinets, Kido's right-wing politics emerged in his advocacy of complete military and political dominance over China and East Asia and in a single-party system in Japan. After becoming Lord Keeper of the Privy Seal (a non-Cabinet advisory post to the Emperor, nevertheless quite powerful as the Privy Seal controlled who and what information reached the Emperor), he recommended to Hirohito both Prince Konoye for a second term as Prime Minister in 1940 and Hideki Tōjō in 1941. However, by the time Japan launched her war of conquest, starting the Pacific War in late 1941, Kido had become fearful of the Western Powers.

Slight of build, Kido had short, thinning hair, wore round, wire-rimmed glasses, and donned a toothbrush mustache. To his friends he was known for his debonair grooming, and his "hunted animal look," a disarming expression of puzzled astonishment regardless of the circumstances. To those who were not his friends, Kido was known for melodramatic hysterics, during which he would scream threats. But whether friend or foe, Kido was known as one of the coolest, shrewdest, and soundest advisors in the government. Emperor Hirohito had known Kido all his life and had worked with him closely since 1922.[10]

By the summer of 1944, Hirohito, by his own creation, was constantly surrounded by a military that had been waging a war of aggression for seven years. He had been involved in all of Japan's major decisions, including the selection of the warmongering Hideki Tōjō as Prime Minister in the fall of 1941.

During the Battle of Saipan, the United States created a prisoner encampment capable of holding the 25,000 Japanese civilians on the island. By June 23, 1944, a week into the battle, the camp had more than a thousand inmates. Word of the defections reached Japan and Hirohito, who found them disturbing. In response, he issued an imperial order on June 30, encouraging civilians to commit suicide and empowering Lieutenant General Saito Yoshitsugu, the commander of the Japanese forces on Saipan, to promise those who did commit suicide that they would receive "equal spiritual status in the afterlife with that of soldiers perishing in combat."[11] July 8, the day after Japan's largest Banzai charge of the war, as Marines moved north to the tip of the island unopposed through the stench of the thousands of dead Japanese soldiers, they found 1,000 civilians in the throes of destroying themselves, "dashing their babes against the rock, hurling their children and wives into the sea, jumping from the cliffs."[12]

Amidst the suicidal wave, Saipan had fallen. Emperor Hirohito withdrew his support and then accepted the resignation of Prime Minister Tōjō and his entire Cabinet. After nearly three years of rule, the man who had taken his country to war with the United States, the British Empire, and the Netherlands was gone, replaced by former Lieutenant General Kuniaki Koiso, the man partially responsible for the invasion of Manchuria in 1931.[13] He was a less notorious choice. Historian David Bergamini described Koiso as "wizened and narrow-eyed. The new prime minister looked more like a Chinese opium den proprietor than a Japanese head of state. He was known in Japan as a man of guile, a specialist in counterespionage rather than combat."[14]

Changing Prime Ministers was nothing new to Hirohito. In fact, Tōjō's tenure had been one of the longer ones. From his ascension to the throne on November 15, 1928, until the Japanese surrender on September 2, 1945, Hirohito would appoint nineteen of them, including one twice and one three times, ultimately sixteen different men.

Koiso received the post only because the *Jūshin* (senior advisors to the Emperor, comprised mostly of former Prime Ministers) and Kido could not come to a consensus on a better alternative. The appointment came with an "Imperial admonition to give Japan's situation a 'fundamental reconsideration' looking to the termination of the war."[15] Whatever the intention behind the Emperor's phrase, Koiso's Cabinet changed nothing, restating "a decision to continue the war with renewed vigor and further sacrifice."[16]

APRIL 5, 1945
123 DAYS TO HIROSHIMA

The Koiso Cabinet lasted barely eight months, ending April 5, 1945, brought down by the Emperor, who blamed Koiso for defeats at Leyte and Iwo Jima.[17]

Shortly before the termination of the Koiso government, Hirohito told an aide, "I believe the war is certainly winnable if we make our best efforts, but I am anxious about whether or not the people will be able to endure until then."[18] Thus, in spite of the devastation being created by LeMay's strategic bombing offensive and the continuing losses on Pacific battlefields, Hirohito's greatest concern was whether the growing unrest among his people could lead to the termination of the monarchy, before the war could be won.[19]

About the same time, despite having previously labeled the Soviets "untrustworthy" years earlier, the Emperor chose to ignore his intelligence forecasters on February 15, 1945, and Tōjō on February 26, who both told him the Russians were likely to abrogate the Soviet–Japanese Neutrality Pact, signed in April of 1941, joining the war against Japan whenever it judged its power to have weakened sufficiently. On April 5, 1945, the Soviet Union denounced the pact.

The same day Koiso's government fell, the Emperor called to the Imperial Palace a trusted friend, a man of unquestioned integrity and loyalty to the Emperor and the current president of the Privy Council, seventy-seven-year-old Kantarō Suzuki. (The Privy Council of Japan was an advisory group to the Emperor that operated from 1888 to 1947.) Early in his naval career, Suzuki had led fearless torpedo attacks during Japan's wars with China and Russia, forever etching his name into the prominent circles within the country.[20] Suzuki had served as Grand Chamberlain from 1929 to 1936 and was one of many targeted for assassination during the *February 26 Incident*, a 1936 coup attempt by middle-grade army officers. Scarcely escaping with his life, Suzuki was shot in the head, chest, shoulder, and groin.[21] Suzuki would remember that during this event, while the Prime Minister and other Cabinet members hid, fearing for their lives, the Emperor "ordered Japanese troops to attack the revolutionaries barricaded in Tokyo because the Government had more or less split up."[22]

Now, according to Grand Chamberlain Hisanori Fujita, who attended Suzuki's audience with the Emperor, Hirohito urged the reluctant former admiral to accept the appointment as Prime Minister with extraordinary language, "You are my one and only hope" and "I beg you to accept it."[23]

After the war, Suzuki told the U.S. Strategic Bombing Survey (USSBS) that after accepting the Prime Minister position from the Emperor, Hirohito expressed his "desire to make every effort to bring the war to a conclusion as quickly as possible, and that [became Suzu-ki's] purpose."[24] The new Prime Minister was left in a dangerous spot, in which "on the one hand he had instructions from the Emperor to arrange an end to the war; on the other hand, any of those opposing this policy who learned of such peace moves would be apt to attack or even assassinate him."[25]

Perhaps out of concern for his own safety—after all, he had nar-rowly survived an attempt on his life in 1936—shortly after taking over as Prime Minister, Suzuki's "comments at [a] conference of senior statesmen gave no hint that he favored an early cessation of the war, [and he] promptly signed a pledge presented by a delegation of gener-als from Imperial Headquarters committing himself to prosecute the war to the bitter end."[26]

By the onset of World War II, Japan's military had so eroded civilian influence in government that the country had become fundamentally a military oligarchy. It was comprised of three components: the divine Emperor and commander in chief of the Japanese military; the Prime Minister, appointed by the Emperor, who could also dismiss him at his sole discretion at any time; and the Prime Minister's Cabinet, par-tially chosen by him and in part by the Chiefs of the General Staff of the Army and Navy. The Chiefs of the General Staff typically placed the most hawkish members of their services into the army and navy war ministry Cabinet positions. Furthermore, decisions made by the Prime Minister and his inner Cabinet, the Big Six, had to be unani-mous. Thus, any dissenter either by vote or resignation had the effect of a veto. Once a unanimous decision had been made, it was presented to the Emperor merely for his ratification. Failure to reach a unani-mous decision could even cause the Prime Minister and his Cabinet to resign. Resignation by either the Army or Navy War Minister automati-cally caused collapse of the government. Thus, the wartime Japanese government was incredibly flawed.

In practice, since its creation by Prime Minister Koiso on August 5, 1944, the country was run by a superset of the Cabinet, known as the Supreme Council at the Direction of War (SCDW), the Supreme Council or the *Big Six*. Its members included the Prime Minister, the Army and Navy War Ministers, the Army and Navy Chiefs of Staff, and the foreign minister, who was the group's only civilian.

A holdover from the Koiso Cabinet, Army Chief-of-Staff General Yoshijirō Umezu had already had a lengthy and distinguished military career, commencing with a citation for gallantry at Port Arthur, during the Russo-Japanese War. As Vice Minister of War, Umezu had denounced the perpetrators of the *February 26, 1936, Incident.* In its wake Umezu had assumed the task of cleaning out the conspirators involved and restoring discipline.

Umezu was thoroughly committed to the war with China, beginning in 1937. He served as the long-term (1939–44) Commander-in-Chief of the Kwantung Army in Manchuria and as His Majesty's ambassador to Manchukuo, essentially ruling over 1,000,000 square kilometers and 80,000,000 people. During this period, Umezu doubled the size of the Kwantung Army and prepared for war with the Soviet Union.[27]

In mid-1944, Tōjō ordered Umezu to report to Imperial General Headquarters (IGHQ) as chief of staff. Umezu said of the post, "since [1941] from the very beginning I have opposed war against the U.S., I hate to accept this appointment. Moreover, the war conditions are unfavorable. There are no measures which I can take as chief of staff… It is necessary to end this war as soon as possible. For that, diplomacy or other techniques will be required."[28]

Most viewed Umezu as the army's outstanding moderate, a circumspect, efficient, bureaucratic soldier.[29] The Vice Chief of Staff of the Imperial Army General Staff, Lieutenant General Torashirō Kawabe, described Umezu as "'complex' and a 'very politically minded' character who kept his personal views concealed even from his closest staff. His nickname was the 'Ivory Mask.'"[30]

For his War Minister, Suzuki chose General Korechika Anami. Suzuki and Anami had first met when they were serving Emperor Hirohito in 1929, Suzuki as Grand Chamberlain and Anami as aide-de-camp. Both men liked and respected one another. Suzuki wanted the general, as his War Minister because he believed Anami could control the army,[31] an imperative to terminate the war successfully when it was time. However, as historian Richard B. Frank has pointed out, "this left those seeking to end the war with the problem of controlling Anami."[32]

Kawabe described Anami as a "man of willpower rather than of resourcefulness." Anami flunked the entrance exam to the military academy four times. But where he fell short academically, he excelled in his ability to relate with his men, often with trademark adages such as, "simplicity represents strength" and "morality is a fighting strength."[33] Anami's secretary, Colonel Saburo Hayashi, described him thus, "He was not a person who thought and thought, and examined the data and then arrived at a conclusion. Rather, something would strike his mind and he would make an instant decision…He was a very admirable person, rare among military men. Since he had no political sense, it was unreasonable for him to be war minister." Colonel Masahiko Takeshita, Anami's brother-in-law, characterized him as "not the brilliant type, not one you would expect to become a general or war minister. He did not belong to what might be called the 'cult of success.'"[34]

In 1910, Anami met General Umezu, five years his senior, and from that moment on Umezu greatly assisted in the advancement of Anami's career. Umezu had been responsible for Anami's 1929 appointment as aide-de-camp to the Emperor. In 1937, Umezu made him Chief of the War Ministry's Military Administration Bureau, and during his tenure in this position, on three occasions Anami lent help to Tōjō in his ascension to Prime Minister of Japan. During his time as commander of the Kwantung Army, Umezu brought in Anami to command a division. Six months after Tōjō appointed Umezu to chief of staff, Umezu brought Anami back from New Guinea, where he had been in command of Japan's forces since November of 1943, to be chief of army aviation, one of the pinnacles of the army establishment and the same post Tōjō held before taking over the war minister slot and the premiership four years earlier.[35]

By mid-1945, the extremely popular and gregarious fifty-eight-year-old Anami had become the most powerful man in Japan. A practitioner of archery, kendo, and judo, Anami projected a powerful physical presence. Although Anami respected the Emperor, he did not approach him with trepidation, behavior which made Hirohito uncomfortable. Instead, to the very end, Anami would attempt to wean the younger man from the influence of the liberals and pacifists.

Anami held deep convictions, none stronger than his philosophy of warfare, which he viewed as a brutal affair of pain and suffering that ultimately came down to a clash of wills and the human spirit, or *seishin*, a trait he believed outweighed any material factors and could turn the tide of battle.[36]

Another holdover from the Koiso Cabinet whom Suzuki inherited was Navy Minister Admiral Mitsumasa Yonai. No stranger to the highest levels of military and civilian service, Yonai had enjoyed a long and notable career in the Navy, holding some of its top offices, including Commander-in-Chief of the Combined Fleet, 1936–37, and Minister of the Navy from 1937–39. Before Japan's entry into World War II,

Yonai served as Prime Minster for one of the shortest terms on record, from January–July 1940. His Cabinet was brought down after just seven months by army leaders, among them General Anami, over Yonai's unwillingness to join an alliance with Germany—a stance that earned him lasting resentment from the army.

His successor, second-time Prime Minister Konoye, rectified the situation barely a month later on September 27, 1940. The timing was extremely advantageous for Japan to join the Axis alliance—Poland, France, Belgium, and the Netherlands had already been defeated by Germany, Britain was clearly focused on surviving Germany's onslaught, and the United States remained neutral.

Yonai had not wanted to see the Japanese blunder into a war with the United States. Four years later, in the political upheaval caused by the loss of the Marianas and the ouster of Tōjō, Yonai believed the loss to be so great that Japan should have made peace.

In Koiso's Cabinet, he became not only Navy Minister but also *co-Prime Minister*. Shortly after assuming those positions, Yonai directed Rear Admiral Skichi Takagi, a brilliant researcher, to resume the secret work he had previously begun at the behest of Admiral Shigetarō Shimada, a member of Tōjō's Cabinet, to investigate the mistakes made in the war as explicated in top-secret files. His analysis of Japan's air and shipping losses led him to the conclusion that Japan could not win the war—the only solution was Tōjō's assassination or dismissal, the latter of which had just taken place, and an immediate effort to obtain a peaceful end to the war regardless of the consequences.[37]

On May 20, 1945, at Yonai's contrivance, Admiral Soemu Toyoda replaced Admiral Koshirō Oikawa as Navy War Minister in the Big Six, as part of a push by Yonai to supposedly add a persuasive voice for peace to the group.[38]

Toyoda came from the same area in northeastern Kyūshū as Anami and Umezu. Born to an impoverished samurai family, he had attended the Naval Academy and Navy War College and served with the Supreme Military Council during World War I. Considered brilliant, he was also so meticulous and sarcastic that more than one subordinate had suffered a nervous breakdown.[39] In appearance he was plodding and pie faced. He was considered a moderate, a capable officer, primarily an administrative sailor who had held most of the top jobs in the Japanese Navy.[40]

Known for his integrity, Toyoda also had a reputation for being well-informed, outspoken, stubborn, and intransigent.[41] In 1941 he had opposed the war against the West. As Navy Chief-of-Staff, Toyoda had commanded Japan's Combined Fleet during the catastrophic defeats in the Battle of the Philippine Sea, known as "the Great Marianas Turkey Shoot," in June of 1944, and in October of that year during the largest naval battle in world history, the Battle of Leyte Gulf. The routs virtually destroyed the remainder of Japan's surface fleet.

The last office, that of Foreign Minister, had originally been assigned to Prime Minister Suzuki himself by the Emperor. Suzuki recognized immediately that he was ill-prepared to handle it. Kido suggested the retention of Mamoru Shigemitsu; however, Koiso vetoed that choice. Suzuki then sought to gain the services of sixty-two-year-old Shigenori Tōgō, which Kido endorsed. Suzuki knew "Tōgō as the foreign minister at the time of Pearl Harbor who could neither abide Tōjō's judgement to seek war nor truckle to Tōjō's autocratic manner, [and that] by now [Tōgō] was a clear disciple of peace."[42] Tōgō was also known for being a blunt individualist,[43] a strong-willed man and a talented negotiator; he was thought of as "arrogant [and]…inclined to be contemptuous of other people's opinions [and]…was far more outspoken than… Suzuki."[44] Tōgō's contemporary, Shigeru Yoshida, described him as "taciturn, expressionless and singularly bereft of anything that could be described as personal charm."[45]

Born as Park Shigenori in Kagoshima, a southwestern city in Kyūshū, his family of potters had been forced to come to Japan from Korea in the sixteenth century. His father, a successful businessman, purchased the Japanese family name of Tōgō when his son was five.[46] Shigenori graduated from Tokyo University, where he majored in German literature. Tōgō had begun his career as a diplomat in 1913, as a consular officer in Mukden, Manchuria. During World War I Tōgō had a "well-varied" experience in Switzerland, Scandinavia, France, and England. He was a member of the Japanese delegation at Versailles following the war, and he served in the newly opened embassy in Berlin from 1919 to 1921, where he met his wife, German-born Edita. He finished his initial overseas duties as first secretary to the Japanese Embassy in Washington for four years, where—he remembered—he felt "an exhilaration of the spirit at coming to the country which stood for freedom."[47]

In 1937, Tōgō performed a short stint as Japan's ambassador to Nazi Germany, but he quickly discovered his efforts to thwart an expansion of the Berlin Tokyo Anti-Comintern Pact (anti-communist pact) into a full-fledged military alliance was being circumvented by secret negotiations between General Hiroshi Ōshima of the Imperial Army and Joachim von Ribbentrop, Germany's Foreign Minister.

Tōgō's last overseas posting, as ambassador to the Soviet Union, lasted from 1938–1940. During that time, he negotiated the settlement to the Battles of Khalkhin Gol, which ended September 16, 1939, and the Soviet–Japanese Neutrality Pact, which was consummated April 13, 1941.

Less than two months before Japan's attack on Pearl Harbor, Tōgō joined Prime Minister Hideki Tōjō's new government as its Foreign Minister. Tōgō adamantly opposed the war with the United States, and during the final two weeks of October 1941, he and Finance Minister Okinori Kaya became extremely pessimistic about the chances of success in a war with the US. Yet, neither Tōgō nor Kaya was willing to make any one-sided concessions to the Americans that could have secured continued peace, nor did they openly threaten to resign and bring down Tōjō's Cabinet.[48] And after a seventeen-hour marathon meeting of the Liaison Conference on November 1, 1941, Tōgō gave in to the argument from Tōjō, the army, and the navy, which was to set a cutoff date for negotiations with the US, November 29, 1941. The deadline was followed by Tōgō's denial of all of Ambassador Kichisaburō Nomura's requests to offer the Americans a meaningful compromise.[49]

After serving a little less than a year, Tōgō left the Tōjō Cabinet on September 1, 1942, during a dispute with the Prime Minister over a change in the administration of the countries under Japan's Greater East Asia Co-Prosperity Sphere. Tōgō claimed the people in those nations were no longer the masters of their fate.

That was Tōgō's outward justification for his resignation; in reality, he had known all along that Japan's Co-Prosperity Sphere had never been a mutually cooperative alliance. It had always been a military occupation by force for the benefit of only one party, the Japanese. In March 1941, the Imperial Rule Assistance Association had published *Basic Concepts of The Greater East Asia Co-Prosperity Sphere*, which openly acknowledged this fact, stating:

> Although we use the expression "Asian cooperation," this by no means ignores the fact that Japan was created by the Gods or posits an automatic racial equality. In other words, some Asians were more equal than others. In fact, the assumption of Japanese superiority permeated relations with the rest of Asia.[50]

In the years following his resignation from the Tōjō Cabinet, leading up to the invitation to join Prime Minister Suzuki's government, Tōgō threw himself into an all-consuming research of the history of defeat, focusing on the plight of Germany and Russia after World War I. He concluded:

> The morale of the people is high at the start of the war and while it continues favorable. Dissatisfaction develops as shortages of food, clothing and fuel are felt. Unless dealt with, the conditions lead, when defeat comes, to political and social revolution. With the end of the war, the masses experience liberation, whether in victory or defeat. At that stage, surviving remnants of futile listed customs, institutions and prerogatives are drastically curtailed and the power of the common people enlarged.[51]

By the spring of 1945, Tōgō saw Japan in the same light as Germany in 1918. As such, in order to preserve the Imperial system, he believed the war needed to be concluded at the earliest possible time.

APRIL 7, 1945
121 DAYS TO HIROSHIMA

On the morning of April 7, the governor of Nagano Prefecture called on Tōgō first by phone and a little later in person. The governor told Tōgō that Admiral Kantarō Suzuki was assembling his Cabinet and wanted him to come to Tokyo at once to discuss becoming the foreign minister; he then asked what reply he should give the Prime Minister. Tōgō informed the governor that he would need to meet with Suzuki to see if there was an agreement of views before he could say for certain whether he would be willing to accept the post.

That evening, Tōgō traveled by train to the capital from his home in Karuizawa, a resort town in the mountains near Nagano about a hundred miles away. As he arrived in the ashen ruins of Tokyo that night, it's possible his thoughts harkened back to a comment made by his wife Edita three years earlier at a dinner party on the evening of April 7, 1942. She told the wife of a neutral diplomat that she needn't "worry about sending her furs and jewels and wines out of Tokyo or go to the expense of building an air-raid shelter, since the Americans could never bomb Tokyo."[52] At about 10:30 p.m., Tōgō reached the Prime Minister's Official Residence, a two-story Art Deco-style mansion influenced by the architecture of Frank Lloyd Wright.[53] Tōgō knew Suzuki from his time as foreign minister in the Tōjō government as the two occasionally met at the Privy Council.

Given the lateness of the hour, Suzuki got right to the purpose of the meeting, stating that he was *just a sailor* not qualified for the political office; however, the weighty responsibility as Prime Minister had been requested of him by the Emperor which made it impossible for him to refuse. He also said he had no experience in diplomacy and would like Tōgō, without fail, to join his Cabinet as foreign minister.[54]

In response Tōgō queried Suzuki about his position, asking if he had taken office with some fixed course of action, since the present circumstances would make it anything but easy to manage national affairs with the war effort reduced to the last extremity. Tōgō then reminded the Prime Minister that he had done all he could to avert this war, and he would be very gratified to end it as soon as possible. But before he accepted the invitation to become a part of Suzuki's new Cabinet, he wanted to hear the Prime Minister's opinion of the prospect of the war.[55]

Suzuki replied, "I think we can carry on the war for another two to three years."[56] Likely stunned by the response, Tōgō answered "that in view of the fact that the decision in a modern war turns predominantly on consumption of materials and the ability to increase production, [he] was convinced that continuing the war would be exceedingly difficult, and that Japan could not carry it on for as long as another year."[57]

Suzuki's response to Tōgō was odd because he had been given a mandate to "make every effort to bring the war to a conclusion as quickly as possible" by his Emperor just days earlier, and Tōgō was considered the best option as foreign minister to make that happen. Whatever Suzuki's motivation, Tōgō interpreted it as a significant divide in their respective views and subsequently declined the appointment as foreign minister, saying that even if he felt able to accept the grave responsibility for Japan's diplomacy, he would be unable to cooperate effectively with the Prime Minister as long as the two of them held views so juxtaposed. The discussion continued a short time longer but went nowhere.

Since it was getting very late and Suzuki seemed tired, the two men agreed to end the meeting. As Tōgō readied to leave, he asked the Prime Minister to reconsider his views on the war.[58]

The following day, Tōgō visited several loyal contemporaries, beginning with Admiral Keisuke Okada, a man he had previously discussed ending the war with and one he believed had played a considerable role in the formation of Suzuki's Cabinet. In response to Tōgō's description of his conversation with Suzuki the previous night, Okada told him, "We can't suppose that Admiral Suzuki's policy for prosecuting the war is necessarily fixed, and you should join this Cabinet and help to mold it. Besides, the Suzuki Cabinet will be in very difficult straits if you don't join it."[59] On his return home, Tōgō also called on two of his seniors in the Foreign Service, Imperial Household Minister Tsuneo Matsudaira, and former Prime Minister Kōki Hirota, who both advised him to take the Foreign Ministry and overcome the impasse.

Later that afternoon, Suzuki's Chief Cabinet Secretary Hisatsune Sakomizu called on Tōgō and echoed the earlier comments. Sakomizu believed the Prime Minister's views were not inflexible and that Tōgō should meet with him again to see if an accord could be struck. Further, he thought it was impossible for the Prime Minister to speak of an early peace—such language coming from one in the Prime Minister's position, and the circumstances, might have undesirable repercussions; but [Tōgō] should, he thought, read the Prime Minister's real intention and take the post.[60]

Tōgō did not see Sakomizu's comments as convincing. "…If the Premier was of the same opinion as [Tōgō], there was no reason he could not have confided the fact to [Tōgō] in a tête-à-tête. And if [the Prime Minister] had not that much confidence in him [Tōgō believed they] could hardly …expect to achieve the co-operation which the critical days ahead would demand."[61] The following day, Marquis Matsudaira, chief secretary to Kido, called on Tōgō. Matsudaira told Tōgō, "I don't think that Premier Suzuki's views on the war are unalterable, and you should correct them after entering the Cabinet. Anyway, I believe that you needn't worry, because it seems that the Emperor is considering ending of the war."[62]

After receiving so much encouragement from trusted colleagues, Tōgō agreed to speak with Suzuki a second time and met with him April 9, 1945, once again at his official residence. This time, obviously counseled, Suzuki took a much more conciliatory approach with Tōgō, stating, "So far as the prospect of war is concerned, your opinion is quite satisfactory to me; and as to diplomacy, you shall have a free hand."[63] The change in behavior and language sealed the deal for

Tōgō, who immediately swung into the role and began making suggestions to Suzuki who quickly approved them all.

Unfortunately, Suzuki's recruitment of Tōgō, with his shifting positions, was a portent of things to come as the new Foreign Minister sought to bring the war to an end.

3

A NEW PRESIDENT GETS UP TO SPEED

APRIL 12, 1945
116 DAYS TO HIROSHIMA

Just four weeks before the defeat of Nazi Germany and the end of the war in Europe, the man who had led America for twelve years, longer than any other president in the history of the United States, through the Great Depression and the dark days of World War II, died in Warm Springs, Georgia, from a massive cerebral hemorrhage. For many Americans, it was a shocking loss. For those close to President Franklin Delano Roosevelt, it was obvious his health had been failing for some time—and his recent trip to Yalta to meet with Churchill and Stalin had exacted a terrible toll on his already declining strength.

On the news of Roosevelt's death and Vice President Harry S. Truman's elevation to president, some of the nation's most senior military leaders—Generals Dwight Eisenhower, Supreme Allied Commander Europe; Omar Bradley, commander in chief of the American ground forces; and George Patton, commander of the US Third Army—speculated about Truman's ability to lead the country. Bradley wrote that Patton was bitter and emphatic: "It seems very unfortunate that in order to secure political preference, people are made Vice President who [were] never intended, neither by Party nor by the Lord to be Presidents."[1] Patton's reflections were indicative of West Point elitism. Perhaps he would have tempered his comments had he known the commoner now about to occupy the White House was the very same thirty-four-year-old National Guardsman from Missouri who had commanded Battery D, 2nd Battalion, 129th Field Artillery Regiment in the final days of World War I. Truman's battery of four 75mm guns fired a thousand rounds an hour from Hill 290, half a mile west of Neuvilly, France, just a short distance from Patton's command post on

September 26, 1918, in support of the Meuse-Argonne Offensive, the largest attack by the Americans in WWI.[2]

Truman's military experience had begun with the Missouri Army National Guard from 1905–1911. He rejoined the Guard in 1917 when the United States entered World War I and was discharged as a major in May 1919, six months after it ended. With the demobilization of American military forces following the war, Truman rejoined the Reserve Officer Corps a year later, achieving the rank of colonel in 1932. He continued to serve even after being elected senator in 1934, and by 1936 he received his second regimental command. During his term as the junior senator from Missouri, Truman got to know an enormous number of the officers who would lead the country in the next World War.[3] Senator Truman volunteered for active service during World War II, but was rejected primarily because President Roosevelt wanted senators and congressman who belonged to the military reserves to support the war effort by remaining in Congress.

Truman was Roosevelt's third vice president, succeeding John Garner and Henry Wallace, and FDR could not have been more indifferent toward him. The feeling was mutual. Truman's response through intermediaries when first approached about joining the ticket at the 1944 Democratic Convention had been, "Tell him to go to hell." Upon hearing Truman's response, Roosevelt snapped back on a call to the Chairman of the Democratic National Committee, Robert Hannegan, loudly enough so that all gathered in the room could hear, that he had made his decision and Truman had no choice in matter. "If he wants to break up the Democratic Party in the middle of a war and maybe lose that war, it's up to him," Roosevelt said. Truman acquiesced and accepted the nomination.

After both men were sworn in on January 20, 1945, they met just twice before FDR's death. Truman hated both meetings, claiming the president did all the talking and only spoke about what he wanted. The reality was, as Truman entered Speaker of the House Sam Rayburn's office for one of their regular, late-afternoon sessions of relaxed conversation, scotch, bourbon, and/or branch water, he had been privy to almost nothing about the issues facing the president or the current state of the war.

Moments before Truman arrived at Rayburn's office, the Speaker had received a call from Steve Early, Roosevelt's Press Secretary, asking him to have the vice president call the White House immediately. Rayburn relayed the message, Truman called the White House, and asked the operator to connect him with Steve Early. Seconds later, Early told Truman, "Please come right over, and come through the main Pennsylvania Avenue entrance." Truman hung up, turned to Rayburn and said, "Sam, I've been summoned to the White House; I'll be back shortly."

At about 5:25 p.m., Truman arrived at the White House and was quickly ushered into Mrs. Roosevelt's study on the second floor. The First Lady was sitting with Colonel John and Anna Roosevelt Boettiger. Truman instantly sensed something significant had taken place. Mrs. Roosevelt was graceful, dignified. She stepped forward, placed her arm gently about Truman's shoulder and said, "The President is dead." For a moment Truman could not speak. The last news he had heard from Warm Springs was that Roosevelt was recuperating nicely. In fact, he was apparently doing so well that no member of his immediate family or his personal physician was with him. All this flashed through Truman's mind before he found his voice.

"Is there anything I can do for you?" Truman said to the widowed First Lady, to which she said, "Is there anything we can do for you; for you are the one in trouble now?"

Truman struggled to maintain his composure.

The momentary silence in the room was interrupted with a knock at the door before Secretary of State Edward Stettinius, Jr. entered, his handsome face sad and drawn, followed by Les Biffle, Secretary of the Senate, and Steve Early. Truman asked Stettinius to call a meeting of the Cabinet and then turned back to the First Lady. "Is there anything you need?" Mrs. Roosevelt told the vice president, "I would like to go to Warm Springs. Would it be proper to ask for a government plane to take me there?" Truman responded, "Yes, it is, and on behalf of a grateful nation we are honored to do so."

Outside the privacy of Eleanor Roosevelt's study, preparations were well underway for the swearing-in ceremony for the new president. The West Wing throbbed with activity as reporters, photographers, White House staff, the Secret Service, and a few of Truman's own staff converged from several directions, crowding corridors and offices. Voices were hushed and tense. Telephones rang incessantly. In the twilight outside, across Pennsylvania Avenue, in Lafayette Square, thousands of people gathered in silence.[4]

Truman walked into a room filled with people. There was a discussion among a few members of those gathered about the need to find a bible for the oath. Truman looked dreadful as he sat down for a moment in a brown leather chair; he appeared absolutely dazed. Looking up, he spotted his wife Bess and daughter Margaret on the other side of the room. Bess was holding a handkerchief that she repeatedly dabbed at her eyes to wipe away tears. The three didn't say anything to each other; they simply looked at each other and then embraced. Bess, Margaret, and Secretary Frances Perkins were the only women in the room.[5] Suddenly a man entered the chamber holding a bible and announced, "Found one!"

Truman looked briefly at the man and then the bible; it was an inexpensive Gideon edition with garish red edging on the pages. Howell Grim, a short, stooped, bald-headed White House head usher, took the bible and dusted it off.

Another man walked over to break up the Truman family hug and motioned that they were ready to begin the ceremony. In attendance were Edward Stettinius, Secretary of War Henry Stimson, Secretary of Commerce Henry Wallace, Secretary of the Interior Harold Ickes, Attorney General Francis Biddle, Secretary of Agriculture Claude Wickard, Secretary of the Navy James Forrestal, Chairman of the War Production Board Julius Krug, Treasury Secretary Fred M. Vinson, Speaker Sam Rayburn, House Majority Leader John McCormack, Robert Hannegan, Secretary of Labor Frances Perkins, and House Minority Leader Joseph Martin. Only two uniformed officers attended the ceremony, Chief of Staff (today Chairman of the Joint Chiefs of Staff, the most senior military position in the United States) Admiral William Leahy and Major General Philip Fleming.

Truman walked into the Cabinet Room with Bess and Margaret and stepped in front of Chief Justice Harlan Stone beneath the portrait of Woodrow Wilson. Bess and Margaret stood to Truman's left. The nine members of the Cabinet filed in around them. A few reporters, photographers, and newsreel cameramen were then allowed in, and milled around in confusion. Truman picked up the bible from the end of the table that dominated the room and held it in his left hand while he and Stone waited a moment for the group to settle.

Chief Justice Stone began: Raise your right hand and repeat after me.

Truman looked at the clock on the wall; it showed 7:09 p.m. He then looked at some of the faces in the room, placed his left hand on the bible and raised his right hand.[6]

STONE: I, Harry Shipp Truman

Truman paused momentarily; he then corrected Justice Stone. Truman responded, I, Harry S. Truman. Ninety seconds later, Truman concluded with So help me God, and became the 33rd president of the United States.

Truman looked straight ahead through his thick, round glasses, his sharp features taut. Then suddenly he snapped the bible up to his face and kissed it, which impressed everyone in the room. Truman then shook hands with Justice Stone. The ceremony was over in little more than a minute.[7] The new president turned away from Justice Stone and addressed the room full of people:

"Boys, if you ever pray, pray for me now. I don't know whether you fellows ever had a load of hay fall on you, but I feel like the moon and the stars and the planets have fallen on me. Don't expect too much of me."

As the group began to disperse, several people stepped up to President Truman and shook his hand; most said nothing, caught up in the emotion of the former president's passing. One of the reporters called back to Truman, "Good luck Mr. President."

Truman countered, "I wish you didn't have to call me that."

He then asked the members of the Cabinet to remain.

The men took their seats around the table and listened as Truman began by thanking them for the service they had already rendered to their country and President Roosevelt. He said he would be very pleased to have them all remain in their posts. The president then told them it was his intention to continue both the foreign and domestic policies of the Roosevelt administration. However, he was now the president, and as such, he was responsible for the final decision—and he accepted that responsibility along with the consequences. Truman concluded by saying, "please do not hesitate to give me your advice; I will always listen to what you have to say, even if you disagree with me."

Truman has been depicted by some historians, especially during the first months of his presidency, as inexperienced, ill-prepared, and a weak leader whose decisions were heavily influenced by his senior political and military advisors. It was true that Roosevelt had kept Truman in the dark, and in the minutes immediately following his swearing-in ceremony Truman acknowledged the shock of the moment. Yet, those words of distress had barely left his lips when he sat down to inform his Cabinet where the buck stopped.

However, choosing to follow FDR's policies was not always a simple task. It soon became apparent to Truman that it was far easier for him to determine Roosevelt's military views—where he had the Joint Chiefs of Staff (JCS), who he trusted, to confirm them—than it was to determine the deceased president's thoughts on domestic and foreign policy. President Roosevelt had always been very careful to keep his real sentiments masked, often only giving people the impression that he agreed with them. As such, Truman faced the difficult task of comparing the differing opinions of multiple advisors in an effort to determine FDR's true thoughts.

Undeterred, the self-educated Missourian from the Show Me State "prided himself on how many pages of documents he could chew through per day—he was a champion reader."[8] An early riser with a powerful work ethic, Truman devoted himself to understanding the issues confronting his administration and the country.

And long before Truman became president, he had proven himself a capable and decisive leader during his combat experience in the First World War and throughout his time in the United States Senate, where he was considered anything but a novice to Washington's power politics.

By 1945, he had served in the Senate for ten years and chaired what many now consider the most productive investigative committee in the history of the Senate, the Senate Special Committee to Investigate the National Defense Program—or as it came to be known, *The Truman Committee*.

Begun in March of 1941 to identify and correct problems of waste, inefficiency, and war profiteering in US war production, the committee was led by Truman until August of 1944, when he accepted his party's nomination as vice president. Members of Senator Truman's committee traveled the length of the country visiting war plants and conducting hearings in local hotels. The committee conducted hundreds of hearings over the next three years and earned Truman nearly universal respect for his thoroughness and determination. It also thrust him into the national limelight, a prime reason for his selection as vice president in the 1944 election. By some estimates, the Truman Committee saved the government and taxpayers ten to fifteen billion dollars (ten times those numbers today).[9]

One program whose expenditures caught Truman's eye was the Manhattan Project, managed by the Secretary of War, Henry Stimson. And at the conclusion of the post-Oath-of-Office Cabinet meeting, as the other members filed silently past, Stimson remained. "The

Colonel," as he liked to be called, told the president he needed to speak with him about an urgent matter.

Born just two years after the end of the Civil War to a wealthy New York family, Stimson had attended two of the most prestigious schools in the country, receiving his bachelor's degree from Yale and a law degree from Harvard.

Stimson began his public service (1906–1909) as a US attorney for the southern district of New York. That was followed by an appointment to the Cabinet of President William Howard Taft as Secretary of War from 1911–1913. Like Truman, Stimson joined the army during the First World War and experienced combat as a colonel in the field artillery. After the war he returned to the private sector for several years before President Calvin Coolidge recalled him in 1927 as a special commissioner to Nicaragua. Two years later, Stimson was made Governor General of the Philippines. In 1929, President Herbert Hoover named Stimson his Secretary of State, during which he led the US delegation at the London Naval Conference in 1930. By the onset of World War II, Stimson had a reputation, in opposition to many in the United States, for being an outspoken interventionist. In 1940, Franklin Roosevelt chose him as his Secretary of War.

From 1940–1945, Stimson oversaw the enormous buildup of American military forces, the management of the Manhattan Project, and the selection of Lieutenant General Leslie Groves, a United States Army Corps of Engineers officer, to head it. By the evening of April 12, 1945, Stimson was a frail seventy-seven, ground down by a lifetime of service, but unwavering in his determination to see the war through to victory.

Truman closed the door and sat down with Stimson. The Colonel told the president that an immense project had been underway for some time, the purpose of which was to develop a new explosive of unbelievable destructive power. He asked for an opportunity, as soon as practicable, to brief the president on the details of the project. Stimson concluded saying, "the device will likely have enormous significance in our foreign affairs." Truman consented to the meeting immediately.

About two years earlier, staff investigators from the Truman Committee had begun picking up puzzling hints of a secret project and huge unexplained expenditures, identified only as The Manhattan Project. On June 17, 1943, Truman had called Stimson and asked about it.

STIMSON: The other matter is a very different matter. It's connected with—I think I've had a letter from Mr. Hally, I think, who is an assistant of Mr. Fulton of your office.

TRUMAN: That's right.

STIMSON: In connection with the plant at Pasco, Washington.

TRUMAN: That's right.

STIMSON: Now that's a matter which I know all about personally, and I am one of the group of two or three men in the whole world who know about it.

TRUMAN: I see.

STIMSON: It's part of a very important secret development.

TRUMAN: Well, all right then—

STIMSON: And I—

TRUMAN: I herewith see the situation, Mr. Secretary, and you won't have to say another word to me. Whenever you say that to me, that's all I want to hear.

STIMSON: All right.

TRUMAN: Here is what caused that letter. There is a plant in Minneapolis that was constructed for a similar purpose and it had not been used, and we had been informed that they were taking the machinery out of that plant and using it at this other one for the same purpose, and we just couldn't understand that and that's the reason for the letter.

STIMSON: No, no, something—

TRUMAN: You assure that this is for a specific purpose and you think it's all right; that's all I need to know.

STIMSON: Not only for a specific purpose, but a unique purpose.

TRUMAN: All right, then.

STIMSON: Thank you very much.

TRUMAN: You don't need to tell me anything else.

STIMSON: Well, I'm very much obliged.

TRUMAN: Thank you very much.

STIMSON: Goodbye.

TRUMAN: Goodbye.[10]

The fact that the chairman of the Senate Special Committee to Investigate the National Defense Program would temporarily halt any investigation into uncounted millions of dollars in defense spending on Stimson's word alone was a tribute to the secretary's reputation.[11]

APRIL 13, 1945
115 DAYS TO HIROSHIMA

At 11:00 a.m., sixteen hours after Truman's swearing-in as president, America's military leaders gathered in the White House study to brief him on the status of the war in Europe and the Pacific. Present were Secretary of War Stimson, Secretary of the Navy James Forestall, Army Chief of Staff General of the Army George Marshall, Chief of Naval Operations Fleet Admiral Ernest King, Lieutenant General Barney M. Giles of the Army Air Forces, and Admiral William Leahy.[12]

In stark contrast to Roosevelt, who was almost always evasive and rarely stated what was truly on his mind, Admiral Leahy recalled Truman that day as "using the simple and direct language that soon was to be familiar with all [and]said he was proud of what already had been accomplished by the American Navy and Army."[13]

The report of the Joint Chiefs of Staff to the president was succinct. They told him Germany would not be overcome for another six months; Japan would not be defeated for another eighteen months.

General Giles was the first to speak. He told the president he would be dividing his comments by the two major theaters of operation, rather than jumping back and forth. Giles began with the Pacific. On the night of March 9–10, three hundred twenty-five B-29s, flying out of Guam, Tinian, and Saipan from the XXI Bomber Command, carried out the first low-level incendiary attacks against Japan. The bombing destroyed an estimated sixteen square miles of Tokyo. With the end of the Battle of Iwo Jima, the Army Air Forces had begun to base P-51 fighters on the island to provide bomber escort for attacks on the Japanese home islands, and on March 27, a contingent of 125 Superfortresses laid mines in Japan's Shimonoseki Strait in an effort to further disrupt Japanese merchant shipping. Shifting to the European Theater, Giles highlighted only one operation, an attack on Berlin by 1,250 bombers and 670 fighters on March 18, the heaviest to date on the Nazi capital.[14]

General Marshall was next up. He too began with a discussion of the Pacific Theater, stating that on March 2, airborne troops recaptured Corregidor in Manila Harbor. Units of the 8th Army landed on Mindanao on March 10, and the Brits liberated Mandalay on March

12. D-Day for the Okinawa campaign began April 1, with the first real opposition to the 10th Army and the 24th Corps beginning on April 4. On March 6, the IX Corps completed its drive to the Rhine River. Cologne, Germany's third largest city, had fallen to the First Army on March 7. The First Army had also taken the Ludendorff Railway Bridge at Remagen and began the first crossings of the Rhine the same day. On March 15, the VII Corps of the First Army crossed the Rhine River in strength. On March 18, the Third Army took Coblenz, and on March 20, the Seventh Army broke through the German West Wall defenses and the Third Army began crossing the Rhine. Soviet forces now occupied Danzig, Poland, and had entered Austria on March 30, entering the suburbs of Vienna on April 5. On April 11, the Ninth Army's Second Armored Division reached the Elbe River, south of Magdeburg, approximately fifty miles southwest of Berlin.[15]

Truman listened intently to the rapid-fire pace of Marshall's presentation and was very pleased with the Army's progress.

The sixty-five-year-old Marshall was one of the most decorated and respected military leaders in American history, yet he had never commanded troops in battle. Graduating from Virginia Military Institute in 1901, Marshall began his career in the United States Army a year later as a second lieutenant. Over the next decade and half, he served in the US and overseas in positions of increasing rank and responsibility. A year before America entered World War I, he had become the aide-de-camp to Major General J. Franklin Bell, commanding the Department of the East. Assigned to the staff of the 1st Division, Marshall assisted in the division's mobilization and combat operations in France, and coordinated operations, including the huge Meuse-Argonne Offensive. Immediately after the war, Marshall became aide-de-camp to John J. Pershing, the Army's Chief of Staff. A little more than twenty years later, by the outbreak of World War II in 1939, Marshall had become Chief of Staff for the Army and was the primary architect for exponentially increasing its size, along with Stimson.[16]

When Marshall sat down, Admiral King began his presentation and stated that hostilities on Iwo Jima had ended March 26. Repair and expansion of the existing airfields had begun even as the fighting continued. In fact, emergency B-29 landings on Iwo Jima had commenced in early March while the battle was still in full swing. The 1st, 2nd, and 6th Marine Divisions of 3rd Amphibious Corps had been engaged in the Okinawa campaign since the beginning of April. On

April 6, fast carrier forces off Okinawa were discovered by Japanese scout planes. In the ensuing fighting, the Japanese first attacked with about 100 fighters and bombers and later in the day with 200 kamikazes.[17]

King was once asked if he had said, "When they get in trouble they send for the sonsabitches." King replied he hadn't, but that he would have said it if he had thought of it. Admiral King

> regarded exceptional performance of duty as the norm and evinced insensitivity or even callousness to his subordinates...But if King proved harsh with subordinates, he was no toady to superiors. Those who fell short of King's standard found he could be hostile, tactless...or even insubordinate.[18]

King commanded the respect of everyone who knew him. Born in Lorain, Ohio, in 1878, he had entered the Naval Academy in 1897 and, while still attending, served in the Spanish-American War aboard the cruiser *USS San Francisco*. King graduated in 1901 and spent the next ten years at sea as a junior officer on five different ships. During World War I, he was a staff member for Vice Admiral Henry T. Mayo, the Commander in Chief of the Atlantic Fleet. By the end of the war, King had risen to the rank of captain. Between the wars King spent time first in the submarine service and then in aviation, the latter duty beginning in 1926. There, in 1927, he received his aviation wings at the age of forty-eight, as the only captain in his class. By 1930, King had become captain of the carrier *USS Lexington*, then one of the largest carriers in the world. In 1933, as Chief of the Bureau of Aeronautics, King worked with Chief of the Bureau of Navigation, Rear Admiral William Leahy, to increase the number of naval aviators. During this period, in 1938, King corroborated earlier findings of the vulnerability of Pearl Harbor, by successfully simulating a naval air raid on the base. Unfortunately, his results were not taken seriously.

A few months before the start of the Second World War, it appeared King's career was headed for the navy's graveyard, only to be resurrected by his friend Admiral Harold "Betty" Stark in 1940. On December 30, 1941, three weeks after the attack on Pearl Harbor, King was named Commander in Chief of the United States Fleet and Chief of Naval Operations. During the early stages of America's entry into the war, King's unbending will, decisive character, incredible work ethic, and keen mind allowed him to overcome the staggering obstacles he faced in fighting a two-ocean war. A member of the Joint Chiefs of Staff and the Allied Combined Chiefs of Staff, King left his imprint on every important war conference from Casablanca to Yalta. While supporting the Allied strategy of defeating Germany first, King's insistence on sending adequate resources to the Pacific paid huge dividends in the Japanese defeats at Midway and the Battle for Guadalcanal, victories that prevented Japan from consolidating its early gains.[19]

After King concluded the briefing, Truman told the group he felt it was urgent that he send some word to the country's armed forces as to what they should expect from him. But he first wanted to address Congress. He also felt he needed to assure the American public and their armed forces, as well as its Allies, that the United States would continue its efforts in prosecuting the war.[20] As the men left, Truman asked Leahy to remain.

Truman told the Admiral, as he liked to call him, that he wanted him to continue in his current capacity.[21]

Leahy responded, "Are you sure you want me, Mr. President? I always say what's on my mind."[22]

To which the President said, "I want the truth. I want you to stay with me and always to tell me what's on your mind. You may not always agree with my decisions, but I know you will carry them out faithfully."[23]

The Admiral replied, "You have my pledge Mr. President. You can count on me."[24]

A man of experience, frankness, and independence, Leahy had been one of Roosevelt's most trusted advisers. The son of a Civil War veteran who had graduated from West Point, William Daniel Leahy had grown up in the Midwest and, after being refused admission to West Point, begrudgingly entered the Naval Academy. Graduating in 1897, he saw his first action as an ensign in the Spanish-American War. In World War I, during the proving trials for the battleship *USS New Mexico*, Leahy gained a reputation for making quick and direct decisions. At around the same time, Leahy met then Assistant Secretary of the Navy Franklin Roosevelt. The two men shared a friendship that lasted until FDR's death.

In 1937, Leahy was promoted to Chief of Naval Operations. He immediately began campaigning to increase the strength of the Navy to counter the rise in power of Imperial Japan and to prepare for the potential of a global war. Later that same year, after the Marco Polo Bridge Incident—a small border crossing by Japanese forces into

China that became the catalyst for the start of the Second Sino-Japanese War—Leahy advised Roosevelt to go to war with Japan. Leahy saw a military response to the attack as an opportunity to show Japan, Germany, and Italy there was a nation willing to stand up to them and fight for peace.[25] Regrettably, the prevailing political climate in the United States kept Roosevelt from acting on Leahy's counsel.

Retiring from the Navy at the age of sixty-four and becoming the Governor of Puerto Rico in 1939, Leahy was called back into active service in late 1940 by Roosevelt, who stated, "Bill, if we have a war, you're going to be right here helping me run it."

A little more than two years later, FDR appointed Leahy to the newly created position of Chief of Staff to the Commander in Chief. In this position, Leahy had two functions. In the first, he represented the president to the entire American military, and reciprocally he carried information and questions from the armed services back to the chief executive. In the second, Leahy sat at the junction point for communication from both the army and navy, making him the only advisor to the president with complete knowledge of nation's military state. The job brought the two men into very frequent contact, as Leahy kept Roosevelt up to date on not only current crucial issues, but also future strategic questions.[26]

In his role as Truman's Chief of Staff, as with FDR, Leahy had a daily meeting with the president, and it did not take long before he began forming opinions about his new boss. To Leahy, it became evident immediately that Truman was "amazingly well-informed on military history...from the campaigns of the ancients...to the great global conflict into which he suddenly had been thrust in virtual supreme command. He absorbed very quickly the gist of the dispatches brought to his attention at our daily conferences and frequently we were going to the map room to discuss some particular development."[27]

Even in the area of international relations, where Truman recognized he had a lot to learn, the president showed himself to be a quick study. To assist his Commander in Chief, Leahy selected summary papers from the Joint Chiefs of Staff for Truman to review, which turned out to be a sizable stack of documents. In a few days, Truman had absorbed the material and was showing an understanding of those "strands of the business of war."[28] And at a personal level, Leahy said that Truman was "one of the nicest people I have ever known."

APRIL 16, 1945
112 DAYS TO HIROSHIMA

"The day was clear," President Truman remembered, "and the temperature had moderated somewhat since morning, the warmth of summer had not yet come to Washington. Tulips were blooming in the White House garden."[29]

Four days after the death of Franklin Roosevelt, Truman entered the House Chamber of the Capital to address Congress for the first time. As he walked toward the main podium, everyone in the chamber rose to their feet and gave him a standing ovation. The room was filled with senators, congressmen, justices of the Supreme Court, members of the Cabinet, other high-ranking government officials, and members of the Diplomatic Corps. The president stopped frequently to shake hands as he walked down the aisle. Once at the podium, Truman looked up and caught a glimpse of Mrs. Truman and Margaret. Truman was visibly moved by the response of the audience and completely forgot to allow the Speaker of the House, Sam Rayburn, to introduce him, as was protocol.

Truman began his speech with "Mr. Speaker." As he did, Rayburn immediately interrupted him and leaned over from the rostrum just behind the president and whispered to him, "Just a minute, Harry, let me introduce you." Rayburn spoke softly, but the microphones that stood before him had been turned on, and he was heard all over the chamber and all over the country via radio. Rayburn straightened up and in a full voice said, as a few muffled chuckles were heard in the audience and Truman smiled, "The President of the United States." Truman turned back to face his listeners and began again.

> Mr. Speaker, Members of the Congress: It is with a heavy heart that I stand before you, my friends and colleagues, in the Congress of the United States.
>
> Only yesterday, we laid to rest the mortal remains of our beloved President, Franklin Delano Roosevelt. At a time like this, words are inadequate. The most eloquent tribute would be a reverent silence.
>
> Yet, in this decisive hour, when world events are moving so rapidly, our silence might be misunderstood and might give comfort to our enemies.
>
> In His infinite wisdom, Almighty God has seen fit to take from us a great man who loved, and was beloved by, all humanity.
>
> No man could possibly fill the tremendous void left by the

passing of that noble soul. No words can ease the aching hearts of untold millions of every race, creed and color. The world knows it has lost a heroic champion of justice and freedom.

Tragic fate has thrust upon us grave responsibilities. We must carry on. Our departed leader never looked backward. He looked forward and moved forward. That is what he would want us to do. That is what America will do.

So much blood has already been shed for the ideals which we cherish, and for which Franklin Delano Roosevelt lived and died, that we dare not permit even a momentary pause in the hard fight for victory.

Today, the entire world is looking to America for enlightened leadership to peace and progress. Such a leadership requires vision, courage and tolerance. It can be provided only by a united nation deeply devoted to the highest ideals.

With great humility I call upon all Americans to help me keep our nation united in defense of those ideals which have been so eloquently proclaimed by Franklin Roosevelt.

I want in turn to assure my fellow Americans and all of those who love peace and liberty throughout the world that I will support and defend those ideals with all my strength and all my heart. That is my duty and I shall not shirk it.

So that there can be no possible misunderstanding, both Germany and Japan can be certain, beyond any shadow of a doubt, that America will continue the fight for freedom until no vestige of resistance remains!

We are deeply conscious of the fact that much hard fighting is still ahead of us.

Having to pay such a heavy price to make complete victory certain, America will never become a party to any plan for partial victory!

To settle for merely another temporary respite would surely jeopardize the future security of all the world. Our demand has been, and it remains—Unconditional Surrender!

The entire audience rose to its feet and gave Truman the loudest applause he received during the entirety of his speech.

By the time of Truman's address, the demand for unconditional surrender had been the foundation of Allied policy for more than two years. It had also become a major point of contention with Germany and Japan and how the war would eventually end.

Unconditional surrender meant quite simply that the defeated nation would accept whatever the victor decided. It was the equivalent of a revolution for the vanquished, because its objectives included the removal of the government and its leaders (both political and military), disarmament, and the trial of war criminals. To enforce those objectives also required military occupation. Thus, temporarily, the conquered country would no longer have sovereignty over its people and resources. Most wars had ended by negotiation and the establishment of mutually agreed, if not desirable, terms. While the Allies' demand for unconditional surrender was not unprecedented, it was certainly atypical. And for American military leaders, unconditional surrender was not merely a political slogan—it was a war aim infused into all strategic planning, as military historian Richard Frank put it, for an "…enduring postwar peace. Unconditional surrender afforded a legal authority—well beyond established international law of military occupation—that would permit a profound internal reorganization of the Axis nations. Thus, dropping the goal of unconditional surrender would have produced a very different postwar transformation of Japan" and Germany.[30]

The genesis for the unconditional surrender demand from the Axis powers went all the way back to Roosevelt's experience as the Assistant Secretary of the Navy under President Woodrow Wilson in the final years of the First World War and the subsequent armistice agreement with Germany.

Even before the United Stated had entered World War I, President Wilson had attempted numerous times to help bring the war to an end, the last instance on January 22, 1917. In that final appeal the President coined a phrase that ultimately gained a measure of notoriety, specifically that there must be "peace without victory." The wellspring of Wilson's statement, according to historian Raymond G. O'Connor, came from the belief that

> Victory would mean peace forced upon the loser, a victor's terms imposed upon the vanquished. It would be accepted in humiliation, under duress, at an intolerable sacrifice, and would leave a sting, a resentment, a bitter memory upon which terms of peace would rest, not permanently, but only as upon quicksand. Only a peace between equals can last.[31]

Considering World War I had been going on for nearly two and half years, with millions of lives already lost and no end in sight, Wilson's belief was not surprising, in particular after factoring in his country's desire to stay out of the war.

Initially, FDR publicly endorsed Wilson's motives for mediating the war. But by the time the first German armistice proposal reached Washington on October 7, 1918, more than a year and half later, Roosevelt now, along with many others, rejected the idea of a conditional peace and a secession of combat that looked anything like "peace without victory."

Their attitude may very well have reflected the change in the fortunes of war, which by then had swung decisively against Germany, but it was one now shared by the Allies, members of Congress, and the American press.[32] Many in Congress were especially vocal in expressing how the war should be concluded. Senator Henry Cabot Lodge stated unequivocally, "no further communication with the German government upon the subject of an armistice or conditions of peace, [should take place] except a demand for unconditional surrender."[33] And Senator Lodge was hardly the only American advocating unconditional surrender; even more prestigious leaders lent their voices to the debate, including former President Theodore Roosevelt, who insisted Americans should "adopt as our model unconditional surrender," and General John J. Pershing, in overall command of the American Expeditionary Forces, who declared that "complete victory can only be obtained by continuing the war until we force unconditional surrender."[34]

Nevertheless, WWI did not end with Germany's unconditional surrender. Then, only three years after the armistice ending war and the signing of the Treaty of Versailles, its enforceability was being questioned among Allied military leaders. In 1922, General Tasker Bliss, the American representative on the Supreme War Council and a cosigner of the Treaty of Versailles, commented, "The one great error in armistice, as now admitted by thinking men generally in Europe, was in the failure to demand complete surrender with the resulting disarmament and demobilization."[35]

The failure of the Treaty of Versailles, a negotiated coalition peace necessitated by the conflicting ambitions of the various Allies, to convert Germany into a permanent democracy and prevent it from becoming a threat to world again in just twenty years, served as the quintessential lesson learned by FDR. Peace should not simply be the end to the current hostilities. Rather, it ought to be the creation of circumstances that facilitates a lasting peace between those combatant nations after the war. [36]

There can be little doubt that Roosevelt's experiences in World War I had a lasting effect on the views he carried into World War II. In response to a direct question at a press conference in 1944 about the armistice ending of WWI and how the war would end this time, Roosevelt firmly rejected a repetition of 1918. "No," he said, "nothing like last time. That is out."[37]

As the chief architect of unconditional surrender in the Second World War, FDR always demurred from specific discussions about the objectives under the policy, other than his assurances from its onset in January of 1943, subsequently restated by both Churchill and Stalin, that the Allies drew a distinction between the leaders and governments of the Axis powers and their people, and they had no wish to destroy or enslave those peoples after the war.

On the other hand, what Roosevelt didn't want was very clear: discord among the coalition. The most likely source of dissension was disagreement over war aims.[38] Achieving victory, complete military victory, over its enemies was the most important goal of the Allies, for without it nothing else was possible. Deferring peacetime specifics until near the end of the war kept a tenuous coalition together throughout a long military campaign until final victory, and it created a postwar environment with the greatest flexibility and the fewest possible established commitments.

APRIL 23, 1945
105 DAYS TO HIROSHIMA

In two days, Truman was to meet with Stimson to discuss the specifics of the Manhattan Project. On this day, Truman met with Soviet Foreign Minister Vyacheslav Molotov at the White House to discuss the attitude of the Soviet government toward Poland, which the US considered in violation of the agreements made at the Yalta Conference. Also attending the meeting were Secretary of the State Stettinius, Ambassador to the Soviet Union Averell Harriman, the American interpreter Charles (Chip) Bohlen, Leahy, Soviet Ambassador Andrei Gromyko, and the Soviet interpreter Vladimir Pavlov. According to Leahy, who had also attended the summit of the Big Three in the Crimean in February:

[President Truman] lost no time in making very plain to Molotov our displeasure at the Soviet failure to carry through the agreement made at Yalta about the character of the new Polish government.

Using blunt language unadorned by the polite verbiage of diplomacy, Truman said that (1) Failure to agree on the Polish problem would offend the American people and might adversely affect or prevent post-war collaboration that would be so advantageous to both nations and the world; (2) He [Truman] was determined to carry through to success the United Nations Conference in San Francisco despite any disagreements between individual members. This was a clear intimation that he would accomplish a union of peace-loving nations whether or not Russia became a member.[39]

...The President's strong American stand at this meeting, expressed in language that was not at all diplomatic, left to the Soviet Union only two courses of action: either to approach closely to our expressed policy in regard to Poland, or drop out of the United Nations. I did not believe they would take the latter course. Truman's attitude in dealing with Molotov was more than pleasing to me.[40]

Truman's language and attitude may have been pleasing to Leahy, but Molotov was clearly offended, stating, "I have never been talked to like that in my life."

Truman retorted, "Carry out your agreements and you won't get talked to like that." However, over the coming months, the tough talk—which had in part been prompted by Britain's Foreign Secretary Anthony Eden, after he and Stettinius had failed to reach accord with Molotov on the makeup the new Polish government—would become more cooperative on the advice of Marshall and Secretary of Commerce Harry Hopkins. Both Marshall and Hopkins believed the Russians would be necessary to tie down Japanese forces in Manchuria and China in advance of the American invasion of Japan.

Nevertheless, Molotov reported Truman's treatment and language to Stalin, and two days later Truman received what historian Richard Rhodes called "one of the most revealing and disquieting messages to reach [him] during [his] first days in office."[41] Stalin flatly rebuffed Truman and his demands relative to Poland, telling him the Russians had paid in blood to liberate the country and they were going to create a government that aided Soviet security. Truman had over-played this hand; Stalin held all the aces, although Truman should be forgiven for believing in the agreements struck at Yalta a mere sixty days earlier.

The atomic bomb was another matter, and Stimson had already alerted Truman the night of April 12 to the political potential of it, when he stated that "the device will likely have enormous significance in our foreign affairs."

APRIL 25, 1945
103 DAYS TO HIROSHIMA

Shortly before noon on April 25, Stimson and his choice to head the Manhattan Project, General Leslie Groves, entered the White House for their meeting with the president. So concerned about preserv-ing the secret of "S1," Stimson and Groves entered through different entrances to avoid being seen together by the press. General Marshall stayed away entirely.[42]

Stimson's choice of General Groves to lead the project had proven to be of great importance. Groves was a shrewd judge of talent, and his no-nonsense manner had swiftly moved the project toward completion by the spring of 1945. Meeting Groves at the president's office, Stimson asked the general to wait in the outer office until he called for him.[43]

At long last, Truman was going to hear the details of the project he had no doubt been wondering about for years. Stimson entered the Oval Office adorned with a heavy gold watch chain across his vest, his hair parted in the middle, the bangs combed forward over his fore-head. He walked over to the front of President Truman's desk and stood there holding a file covered in leather. After an exchange of pleasantries, the two men sat down.

Stimson opened the file, handed the president a memorandum, and waited for Truman to finish reading it.[45] The first sentence was intended to shock: "Within four months we shall in all probability have completed the most terrible weapon ever known in human history."[46] Stimson's next statement added a chilling warning: the world "in its present state of moral advancement compared with its technical devel-opment would be eventually at the mercy of such a weapon. In other words, modern civilization might be completely destroyed."

On one hand, Stimson's admonition about the future of the world could not have failed to cause Truman to pause; on the other hand, perhaps unintentionally, his reference to the future had opened a window of opportunity in the present. Because as frightening as potential of this weapon was for the future, Truman lived in the present, and he had a war to win. If a decisive weapon existed that might cut short that ghastly war, could he really choose not to use it?

Truman told Stimson that James Byrnes had said the weapon might be so powerful as to be theoretically capable of wiping out entire cities and killing people on an unprecedented scale. Stimson replied, "That is correct. That potential exists."

Byrnes had also informed the president the bomb might well put the United States in a position to dictate its own terms at the end of the war. Stimson, conversely, expressed as much concern over the role of the atomic bomb in the shaping of history as in its capacity to help end the war[47] and influence the conditions of peace.

Stimson abhorred the idea of using the bomb. He would have preferred to push a decision on its use into the future, in the hope that with time and under different circumstances it would never be employed.

Truman next asked whether the British had been a part of the project. Stimson told him they were, but at this time the United States was the only country in a position to construct and manufacture such bombs, and that would likely remain so for some years, and probably the only nation which could enter into production within a few years was Russia.

With that, the briefing turned to the technical aspects of the bomb. Stimson told the president he would like to have General Groves join them. Truman had first met and locked horns with Groves nine years earlier in a 1936 conflict over issuing Army contracts to small arms manufacturers in St. Louis. The two crossed paths again in 1941 during a Congressional hearing over the movement of an army base hospital. At that time Truman stated, "Rumor has it that the commanding officer moved the hospital to make way for a golf course." Groves dryly replied, "I don't know, I'm not a golfer myself, so I wouldn't hesitate to put the hospital right in the middle of the eighteenth green."[48]

As Groves entered the Oval Office that afternoon, he was concerned about Truman's reaction to the project given the acrimony of their past conversations. So, when the president quickly dismissed Stimson's introduction of Groves, saying, "I've known General Groves for years," and then proceeded to laud the general's accomplishments, Groves thought "typical politician," but he was more than a little relieved.[49]

After the unexpected reaction to the general's introduction, Stimson handed Truman a highly condensed, twenty-five-page version of Groves' report on the bomb. But the president was looking for something quicker to provide the salient points, saying, "I don't like reading long reports." But after Stimson explained the report had already been reduced "to a degree that we couldn't possibly duplicate verbally," Truman relented and read the document.[50]

When the president finished, he looked up at Stimson and Groves, the general bracing for the inevitable disapproval. Instead, the president simply said, "I'm all in favor of it. I hope you'll be successful."

His part in the meeting over, Groves looked for the door through which he had entered but could not remember which one. He turned to Truman in confusion and said, "Mr. President, how on earth do I get out of here?" Truman pointed the way.

Groves gone, Stimson concluded with a final comment and a request. He told the president the bomb had not yet been tested, but confidence in its success was high, and he believed the United States would have a few bombs within the next couple months. The colonel then requested authorization to create a special select committee to investigate the potential consequences of "this new force" and advise the president on associated decisions. Truman gave Stimson the ok.[51]

Truman remembered that when he "saw [Stimson] to the door [he] felt how fortunate the country was to have so able and so wise a man in its service."[52]

Stimson's civilian advisory committee, comprised of prominent political, scientific, and industrial figures, became known as the Interim Committee. The unusual name derived from the temporary nature of the body. Under normal circumstances the oversight would have been handled by Congress, but many of its representatives were still being kept in the dark about the secret. The members of the Interim Committee included Stimson as Chairman; Ralph Bard, Under Secretary of the Navy; Dr. Vannevar Bush, Director, Office of Scientific Research and Development (OSRD); William L. Clayton, Assistant Secretary of the State; Karl Compton, Chief, Office of Field Service; George Harrison, Special Consultant to the Secretary of War; and Alternate Chairman, James Byrnes, Special Representative of the president and soon to be his new Secretary of State.

James Byrnes was born in Charleston, South Carolina, in 1882. At the age of fourteen he had left school to work as a clerk at a law firm. Four years later, Governor Miles McSweeney appointed Byrnes to clerk for Judge Robert Aiken in 1900. To meet the age requirement of twenty-one, Byrnes changed the year of his birth to 1879. Over the next three years, having apprenticed for a number of lawyers and judges, Byrnes was admitted to the bar as a self-taught lawyer.[53]

By the age of twenty-nine, Byrnes began the first of six terms in Congress as the representative from the Third Congressional District of South Carolina, serving there until 1925. After an unsuccessful bid for a senatorial seat in 1924, he ran a second time in 1930 and won, eventually serving two terms. In 1941, President Roosevelt appointed the South Carolinian to the Supreme Court. Byrnes became the last justice admitted by reading law rather than studying it at law school.[54]

With the outbreak of World War II, Byrnes resigned from the high court to become head of the wartime Office of Economic Stabilization and later the Office of War Mobilization (OWM) in Washington, D.C. He had such sweeping powers as head of the OWM that some referred to him as the "Assistant President." His leadership was instrumental in the successful buildup of the wartime economy, and among the construction he oversaw was the Manhattan Project.[55]

In the summer of 1944, Byrnes had hoped to be FDR's vice-presidential nominee. Worried about his conservatism, as well as the negative reaction of Catholics to his abandonment of that faith and of liberals to his open support of segregation, the Democratic National Convention instead chose Truman.[56]

But Byrnes was not finished with his service to the presidency. In February of 1945, he accompanied Roosevelt to the Yalta Conference of The Big Three, and his attendance ultimately proved valuable to FDR's successor. Two weeks before Truman's first meeting with Churchill and Stalin at Potsdam as the newest member of the Big Three, the president would make his former senatorial colleague his new Secretary of State on July 3, 1945.[57]

PLANNING FOR THE INVASION OF JAPAN

MAY 8, 1945
90 DAYS TO HIROSHIMA

Shortly after 9:00 a.m., President Truman read an announcement from the Radio Room in the White House. The world had been waiting, hoping, and praying for this for five years. In his statement the president told the American people that Germany had finally surrendered, but he quickly tempered the joyous occasion by reminding Americans of the sacrifices so many of their families had made to win the war.

Truman next cautioned his countrymen, asserting that while the end of the war with Germany was a great victory, Japan had not capitulated, and it would likely take much more work and loss of national treasure to defeat them. He warned the Japanese people that they had experienced only a fraction of America's military might and that was about to change. Truman concluded by reinforcing for the second time in his short presidency the country's determination to impose unconditional surrender on Japan, after which he clarified exactly what that meant to the Japanese—specifically the end to the war and the elimination of the influence of the military leaders who had carried them to the present threshold of disaster.

Significantly, the president only demanded the unconditional surrender of Japan's "military and naval forces" and the termination of "the influence of [its] military leaders." Truman had departed from the broadly interpreted definition of unconditional surrender, which meant that there were no terms offered prior to the loser's capitulation.

MAY 11–14, 1945
87 DAYS TO HIROSHIMA

Three days after the war in Europe ended, the Supreme Council—and only the members of the Supreme Council—met in the Cabinet Room of the Prime Minister's official Tokyo residence, the Kantei, a two-story Art Deco mansion. Although the men comprising the Big Six were the most senior and powerful leaders in Japan, since its formation under Prime Minister Koiso eight months earlier, the group's decisions had largely been those of eleven military and civilian aides known as the secretaries and assistant secretaries.[1]

In practice, the assistant secretaries met twice a week to discuss and draft war policy resolutions in response to the developing military situation. Their decisions were reported up to the secretaries. They in turn met and rehashed the work and made changes they believed appropriate. The final step was to pass the secretaries' recommendations on to the Big Six. Since the members of the Supreme Council were not always able to stay abreast of the intricate details their aides were laboring over, they found it expeditious to bring these aides to their meetings.[2] Within a short time, an unintended consequence emerged.

The roster of military secretaries and assistant secretaries was comprised of field grade officers who, beyond their responsibilities to their direct superiors, were committed to furthering the imperialistic aspirations of Japan—and most possessed a fanatical do-or-die commitment to achieve them. Their presence in the Big Six meetings came with a thinly veiled coercion of their superiors, to either acquiesce and accept their decisions or risk assassination.

The fact that officers of a lower rank were consistently allowed to force decisions that should have been made by their superiors seems inconceivable to anyone familiar with accepted military discipline and the chain of command. But it had been a part of Japan's military culture for centuries, and from the 1930s on, as long as subordinates were "motivated by moral principles," the behavior had largely been condoned.

The practice had been commonplace for so long that the Japanese created a word for it, *gekokujō*, which meant, "overpowering the higher ranks by the lower ranks or the manipulation of superiors by subordinates." The sway of these field grade officers extended all the way to the most powerful men in Japan, the members of the Big Six.

Gekokujō had been responsible for numerous political and military assignations, including the *February 26 Incident*. In the aftermath of the "Incident," General Umezu had been instrumental in restoring military discipline. But nine years later, it was patently clear his reforms had only temporarily mediated the problem.

The question then becomes, why? Why would the senior officers condone this ongoing breach of the command structure? A reasonable explanation could be that they agreed with many of the ideas and actions these officers proclaimed and undertook, and by allowing this conduct, it provided senior leadership with convenient scapegoats if an outcome manifested negatively.

There was also the threat of assassination. From the time of the Meiji Restoration in 1868, it had become commonplace in Japan. In just the twenty-seven years from 1909 to 1936 leading up to the war, eight of the country's political and military leaders had been slain, including five Prime Ministers, two generals, and an admiral. Prime Minister Suzuki had himself been a target during the *February 26 Incident* in 1936, when he was shot multiple times. Even the Emperor was not immune; in 1923, when he was prince regent, a young anarchist and civilian named Nanba Daisuke attempted to assassinate him.[3]

As such, the members of the Supreme Council found it increasingly difficult to speak their minds freely whenever their secretaries were in attendance.[4] The situation was finally brought under control at Foreign Minister Tōgō's insistence: the Big Six would meet occasionally in closed sessions without the knowledge or influence of their ever watchful and virulent staff.[5]

The secret meeting of just the Supreme Council on May 11 was the first time a discussion by Japan's top leaders broached the topic of peace. But in no way did that mean these men were prepared to consider unconditional surrender, even when confronted with the country's unending defeats on the battlefield, the ongoing naval blockade of the homelands, and the systematic razing of Japan's cities by aerial bombardment.

On the contrary, the leaders were still looking for a decisive victory that would improve their bargaining position; only the location of that battlefield continued to change. Three years earlier, it had been more than 3,000 miles to the east at Midway Atoll; in June of 1944 it had been 1,500 miles away at Saipan in the Marianas; a month before, 350 miles to the southwest on Okinawa. On May 5, 1945, while the battle of Okinawa raged on, the Emperor had personally radioed the 32nd Army on Okinawa imploring them, "We really want this attack to succeed."[6]

Two days before the Emperor's desperate radio message to Okinawa, Suzuki, in anticipation of Germany's surrender, had released a defiant statement emphasizing the loss of their European ally altered nothing.

> We firmly believe that there will surely come in our grasp a golden chance. Although the present changing situation in Europe has in no respect been unexpected on our part, I want to take this opportunity to make known once again at home and abroad our faith in certain victory.[7]

Whether Japan's people believed the loss of their once powerful ally was grounds for anxiety mattered not. Their opinions and suffering were irrelevant.

Now, two months after the start of the ongoing and devastating fire-bombing campaign against the Japanese homeland, and one month after soliciting Tōgō into his cabinet on the basis of agreeing to support his moves toward peace, Suzuki's bellicose statements disregarded the plight of his country and contradicted his pledge to Tōgō.[8] Such were the circumstances as the members of the Big Six met on May 11, 1945.

Chief Cabinet Secretary Sakomizu spoke first. He reported that every part of civilian and military life was being affected by a short-age of raw materials. Steel production had declined by two thirds, as had aircraft production; munitions had dropped by fifty percent. The entire transportation network had been crippled for lack of fuel and people to handle cargo. The rail system and production of steel ships and chemicals were on the verge of complete collapse. The rice crop was the worst since 1905, and people were living off 1,500 calories a day, two thirds of the Japanese standard, if they could get them. The country had resorted to converting acorns to food. Every weekend, city dwellers left for the country, where they sold anything of value they had for sweet potatoes, vegetables, and fruit.[9]

But from the onset of the discussions it became clear that the For-eign Minister stood alone among the members of the Big Six in his willingness to concede Japan's dwindling military, economic, and political power. But rather than giving any consideration to Tōgō's con-cerns, detailed in Sakomizu's report, and engaging in a conversation about the need to bring the war to an end at the earliest possible time, the rest of the Supreme Council brushed away all worries over Japan's rapidly growing plight.

Instead, after ruling out Switzerland, Sweden, China, or the Vatican as potential facilitators in peace discussions, they decided their best opportunity for a suitable outcome in the war, and peace, rested on improved relations with the Soviet Union. General Umezu was the first to suggest the Soviet option, positing that its power and prestige made it the most suitable prospect as a go-between to the Anglo-Americans. Anami agreed, believing "the Soviets prefer a strong Japan to emerge from the war as a buffer between their Asian possessions and the United States."[10] Tōgō countered that any notion of using the Russians was unrealistic, stating:

> The matter of Japan must have been discussed at the Yalta conference, so it is probably hopeless to try and get the Soviets on our side now judging from past Russian actions, I think it's even going to be difficult to keep her from joining the war. It would be better, in my opinion, to negotiate directly with the United States for a cease-fire.[11]

Tōgō continued by reminding his peers that Japan had already, on three previous occasions during the war—twice during Tōjō's administration, and once under Prime Minister Koiso—offered to send a special envoy to Moscow, with the idea of negotiating an end to hostilities, only to be rejected by the Russians.[12] The alliance between Russia, the United States, and Great Britain had gained too much traction. From Tōgō's perspective, it was too late.[13]

The rest of the members of the Big Six disagreed. At a minimum, General Anami wanted the Russians kept out of the war[14]; he did not want to duplicate the folly of the Germans and fight on two fronts. Yonai believed even more might be possible; he wanted Tōgō to explore the possibility of purchasing petroleum, aircraft,[15] and other supplies Japan needed from the Soviets, and he cited Tōgō's predecessor as believing in the potential to do so.[16] Tōgō dismissed Yonai's view and that of the previous foreign minister by stating that "the holder of such an opinion could only be one who had no understanding of the U.S.S.R."[17]

Tōgō's admonition about Japan's need for reconciliation with the Soviet Union was hardly an inconsequential comment. The other members of the Big Six were all conveniently overlooking both the recent history of the two nations and the current circumstances. It was politically naïve to believe the Russians, too, would disregard both, especially when enticed with only vague territorial inducements, and act on behalf of or in collusion with the Japanese in defiance of their alliance with the US and Great Britain.

The recent history of the two nations included the Russo-Japanese War in 1904–1905, from which Japan emerged victorious, and a series of battles along the Manchurian–Soviet border from 1935–1939, where they did not fare nearly so well. The latter led the Russians and Japanese to sign the five-year Soviet-Japanese Neutrality Pact on April 13, 1941, just months before Germany attacked the Soviet Union and Japan shocked the United States by bombing Pearl Harbor. Twenty months earlier, the Russians had entered into the German-Soviet Nonaggression Pact, signed August 23, 1939. It fundamentally consummated an alliance between those two countries that included mutually carving up Poland, permitted an attack by the Soviet Union on Finland—which ultimately forced Finland in March 1940 to yield the Isthmus of Karelia—and ceded the Baltic republics of Latvia, Lithuania, and Estonia to the Soviet Union in August 1940. On the other hand, the Soviet-Japanese Neutrality Pact's primary purpose, albeit executed in advance of either nation's entry into World War II, was to forestall the risk of a two-front war for each party—for the Soviets, against Germany and Japan; for Japan, against the Soviets and the Anglo-Americans.

Toward the end of 1943, Tōgō began to harbor concerns that the U.S.S.R. might abjure its neutral relations with Japan. A year later, his fears received further credence from a commanding source. Tōgō said, "In his speech on the 1944 anniversary of the November [communist] Revolution, Stalin branded Japan as an aggressor state, side by side with Germany, an unmistakable warning that Japan must exercise great caution."[18]

In February of 1945, in the aftermath of the Yalta Conference and Germany's impending conquest, Soviet Foreign Minister Molotov had been asked about his country's relationship with Japan. In response, he evaded questions about their bilateral Neutrality Pact and refused thereafter to receive Japan's ambassador, purportedly because he was too busy.

The same month, former Prime Minister Konoye had delivered a grim assessment of Russian intentions to the Emperor on Valentine's Day. He told Hirohito, with Kido listening in, that the Soviets saw the Japanese as their biggest threat in East Asia. That belief had caused them to link up with the Chinese communists, the largest communist party in Asia. The Russians also had been allied with the United States and Britain for more than three years and had been cooperating with them to expel Japan from China. If the war continued, he believed Japan's defeat was inevitable. When that happened, he feared the *kokutai* would be destroyed along with it, because the war was releasing forces—specifically the rise of communism within Japan—that endangered the Imperial House.[19]

A little more than a month later, on April 5, 1945, the Russians formally informed the Japanese they would not renew the Neutrality Pact, since Japan was giving aid to Germany. At almost the same time, General Kawabe, Vice-Chief of the Army General Staff, called on Tōgō. Kawabe informed him of the large Red Army concentration now in Siberia and asked him to do everything possible to prevent Russian participation in the war. The Vice-Chief of the Naval General Staff, Admiral [Jisaburō] Ozawa, made a similar request, as did Army Chief of Staff, General Umezu.[20]

The refusal to renew the Neutrality Pact coupled with the Soviet troop movements east should have been obvious and ominous signs of future Soviet intentions. However, the Supreme Council, save Tōgō, chose to ignore them in May when they opted to rely on the Russians to aid them in bringing the war to an end. The Emperor was also counted among those who agreed to disregard Russia's actions, according to historian Herbert Bix, "because it conflicted with his goal of negotiating an end to the war that would guarantee an authoritarian Imperial system with himself and the empowered throne at the center."[21]

Given the unmistakable signals from Moscow, the idea that at this stage in the war the Russians could have been engendered to provide critical war materials and possibly become an ally was more than wishful thinking; it was fanciful. The Soviets were in fact preparing for war against Japan, and in their lucid moments Japan's leaders knew it.

Why then did the Supreme Council pursue this course with the Soviet Union? Because so long as the Emperor and members of the Big Six were unwilling to admit defeat and accept unconditional surrender, they had to concoct a conduit through which their terms for ending the war could be heard. The Russians only became this option because the Japanese needed them to be.

How the Emperor and the members of the Big Six (excluding Tōgō) managed to draw a distinction between the British, Americans, and Soviets on the issue of unconditional surrender is also puzzling.

Unless somehow they believed because they weren't at war with Russia in January of 1943, when the policy was established by the Allies, the Soviets would treat them differently. Because as already noted, Britain, the US, and Russia had been allied for more than three years. Yet the Japanese eschewed approaching the United States and Great Britain about ending the war because they believed both would simply demand unconditional surrender; they pinned everything on the belief the Soviets would behave differently and mediate "terms" favorable to Japan.

Perhaps because if the roles had been reversed, the Japanese would not have hesitated to undercut or abandon their ally. After all, what had Japan really ever done of consequence to assist Germany or Italy during the war? The Japanese epitomized the definition of a self-serving ally. Even Tōgō, the only diplomat among the Supreme Council, admitted as much when he said, "The Russian victory over Germany [Japan's ally] was owed in no small measure to Japan's maintenance of neutral relations with the U.S.S.R., whose hands were thereby freed in the East. Despite this, the attitude of Japan—and especially of the Japanese Army—had caused the Russians over a long course of years to be extremely suspicious of Japan and firmly determined to neutralize her."[22]

But even with such history, Tōgō was the only member of the Big Six willing to accept the fallacy of Soviet intercession, and told his colleagues on May 11 that he believed there was no longer any opportunity for utilizing the Soviet Union militarily, economically, or diplomatically.[23] He said, "Wartime diplomacy is dependent entirely upon the military situation; thus, barring an immediate Japanese victory in Okinawa, no diplomatic overture [with the Soviets] stands a chance of success."[24] Regarding Anami's previously mentioned request to keep the Soviets out of the war (yet another indication of the strained relations between the two countries), Tōgō said, "of course, it was desirable that we prevent Russia from attacking us... However...to achieve this purpose we must be prepared to pay a price, now that our power to fight ha[s] diminished—and, naturally, to pay all the more if we ha[ve] any hope of persuading the U.S.S.R. to act to our advantage."[25] Rather than assuming what the Soviet position might be, Suzuki saw no reason to not to feel out the attitude of the Russians.[26]

The group finally settled on three topics for potential negotiation with the Soviets: 1) preventing the Russians from entering the war against Japan, 2) seeing if the Soviets would consider adopting a favorable attitude toward Japan, and 3) requesting the assistance of the Soviet Union in the development of a path to peace.[27] As a means of achieving point three, mediation through China, Switzerland, Sweden, and the Vatican was discussed. However, the group mutually agreed that each of these avenues would lead only to the Allies' demand for unconditional surrender; therefore, they deserved no further attention. General Umezu stated that only the Russians "would be able to mediate for a peace with the United States and Great Britain on terms at all favorable to [Japan]."[28] Anami added a somewhat prophetic comment, stating, "the U.S.S.R. would find itself in confrontation with the United States after the war, and therefore would not desire to see Japan too much weakened, the Soviet attitude toward us need not be severe."[29] Tōgō once again voiced caution, saying, "we [cannot] be optimistic about the U.S.S.R., as she [has] acted always realistically and ruthlessly…[and there is] danger [in] setting a course on the basis merely of Japanese way of thinking."[30] Tōgō could not have been more explicit in his warning about Soviet intentions and the likelihood of a positive outcome by pursuing a diplomatic solution to Japan's problems through them. Yet, that's exactly what the unanimous decision concluded to do. Tōgō's comments exemplified the disconnect between the thinking and actions of the military members of the Big Six and the reality of the circumstances they faced throughout the remainder of the war. They repeatedly sought and believed they could achieve military and political objectives beyond their grasp.

Before negotiations with the Russians could begin, the issue of compensation had to be considered. Primarily at Tōgō's recommendation, the Supreme Council agreed to abrogate most of the Treaty of Portsmouth that had ended the Russo-Japanese War. That agreement, signed in September of 1905, affirmed the Japanese presence in Manchuria and Korea and ceded the southern half of the island of Sakhalin to them. Now, in an effort to gain the good graces of the Soviets, the Japanese were willing to return their half of Sakhalin, northern Manchuria, and potentially turn South Manchuria into a buffer state,[31] subject to arbitration, keeping only Korea. Since the Big Six knew Japan would have to pay some price for peace, no one took particular exception to the proposal.

The issue of Soviet concessions tentatively dealt with, Tōgō told the Big Six he planned to have former Prime Minister Kōki Hirota launch the negotiations with the Russian Ambassador Jacob A. Malik.

The discussion then turned to the terms for peace with the Allies.

But even now, after an unabated succession of defeats on the battlefield and the methodical razing of Japan's cities by America's strategic bombing campaign, there was only defiance from the army's war minister and chief-of-staff. Anami reminded everyone that Japan still held extensive enemy territories, while the enemy's occupation of its territories remained negligible. He believed any peace terms should reflect that fact.[32] Supporting Anami, Umezu conceded a willingness to say that Japan had no further territorial ambitions.[33] Tōgō attempted to temper Anami and Umezu's bravado. He reiterated the reasonable method of approach to such an effort took into consideration the trend of the entire war and the military and political prospects for the future.[34]

Tōgō managed lukewarm support from Admiral Yonai, who seconded him.[35]

But once again Anami took issue, repeating his previous statement that Japan still controlled vast areas and she certainly had not been defeated.[36] Seeing a potential breakdown in the discussion and the risk of accomplishing nothing, Yonai suggested tabling their discussion over peace terms until a later time.[37] Tōgō, however, believed time was of the essence; walking away from this gathering of the Big Six with no peace initiative was tantamount to failure and something his country could ill afford. He needed to leave these talks with at least a starting point[38] from which his country could move forward.

But it was not to be.

Suzuki proposed going ahead with points one and two, attempting to prevent Russian entry into the war, and if possible, getting the Soviets to adopt an attitude favorable toward Japan—to which the group finally agreed.[39]

MAY 25, 1945
73 DAYS TO HIROSHIMA

Inside the Pentagon, at the end of a long rectangular table, sat General Marshall and Admiral Leahy; the two men were flanked by eight officers on each side.[40] Also in attendance were Admiral King, General and Chief of the Army Air Forces Henry (Hap) Arnold, and the members of the Joint Staff Planners. The meeting's purpose was to finalize the plans for the invasion of Japan.

In advance of the invasion, preparation had already begun, in the European Theater, to redeploy hundreds of thousands of men to the Pacific on the assumption that the war with Germany would end no later than June 1, 1945. In the SUMMARY OF REDEPLOYMENT FORECAST, dated March 15, 1945, just for army replacements from dead and evacuated wounded in the Pacific during the eighteen-month period associated with the redeployment, the average requirement was estimated at 40,000 men per month, or a total of 720,000.[41]

General Marshall opened the discussion by reminding the group of Truman's commitment to impose unconditional surrender on Japan. He went on to state that such surrender was a completely unknown concept to the Japanese, and that to date throughout the totality of the Pacific War not a single organized "Jap" unit had surrendered to any American forces. As such, the Joint Staff Planners (JSP) and Marshall did not believe the continuing blockade and bombardment of the Japanese home islands would achieve that objective. An invasion, however, could be carried out to utter defeat, and the Army recommended it as the soundest strategy.[42]

The Navy was not as convinced. Admiral Leahy stated, "Before we move on to the discussion of the invasion plans, I'd like to express my personal belief that we have not reached a point where this is the only or best option." He remained concerned that the most recent experiences with the Japs, on Iwo Jima and Okinawa—slow, grinding assaults—could be indicative of the kinds of losses the US could expect during an invasion. While the second of these battles was not yet over, the American casualty rate on Iwo Jima was one in three, and Okinawa appeared headed in the same direction.

Admiral King also voiced reservation, stating that kamikaze attacks had made American naval losses off Okinawa the worst of the war, exceeding even the 4,911 killed at sea during the Battle of Guadalcanal by a small margin.[43] In the event of an invasion of the Japanese home islands, kamikaze pilots would no longer have to fly more than three hundred miles to reach American ships. And troop transports during an initial landing assault of Kyūshū would be especially vulnerable to kamikazes.

Leahy further noted that he knew the president was apprehensive about the potential casualties connected to an invasion, and he thought alternatives like strengthening the blockade against the Japanese home islands, and maybe the coast of China, coupled with the continuation of the strategic bombing campaign, could ultimately force Japan to surrender.[44]

After Leahy finished, Marshall asked if there were any other comments, and seeing no one, he shifted the group's attention to the details associated with the invasion.

The invasion, codenamed Downfall, contained two phases: Olympic, to be launched against the southern third of Kyūshū on November 1, 1945, and Coronet, scheduled for March 1, 1946, with the Tokyo Plain as the slated objective. For the first time in the war, all US resources in the Pacific would be devoted to a single objective.[45] Admiral Chester Nimitz would have overall command of the naval forces, while General Douglas MacArthur would lead the ground troops once ashore. The invasion was planned to be much larger than the landing in Normandy a year earlier.[46]

A member of the Joint Staff Planners then took over the briefing. He stated that intelligence supported the plans for the invasion based on three factors: first, the Japanese fleet had been rendered incapable of more than a suicidal defense; second, their material resources necessary to conduct war had been severely diminished; and third, potential reinforcements to Japan from Asia were being limited to an estimated one division per month.[47] Further, the continuing destruction wrought by the strategic bombing campaign would have, by December of 1945, produced circumstances suitable for invasion.

The alternative strategy of a complete blockade and ongoing bombardment required twenty-eight divisions, only eight fewer than the thirty-six needed for both Olympic and Coronet, and it would not be completed until the fall of 1946—whereas the two-phase invasion strategy was expected to wrap up by the end of June of 1946.[48] The planners were making the argument that because blockade and bombardment would require just eight fewer divisions (approximately 120,000 to 160,000 fewer men based on the size of divisions at the time) than both phases of Downfall, and would not be fully implemented until the fall of 1946 and even then did not assure a definitive timeline to gain Japan's capitulation, that invasion was the best strategy.

But while the planners hoped Coronet could deliver a "knock-out blow" to Japan, they couldn't say for sure it would. Both the JCS and General MacArthur said Allied military operations would continue until all organized resistance by the Imperial Army and Navy ended. In other words, neither knew if Coronet would end the fighting.[49]

In preparation for the invasion option, the planners recommended the following courses of action:

1. Apply full and unremitting pressure against Japan by strategic bombing and carrier raids to reduce its war-making capacity and demoralize the population,
2. Tighten the blockade by means of air and sea patrols, to include blocking passages between Korea and Kyūshū and routes through the Yellow Sea,
3. Conduct only such contributory operations as are essential to establish the conditions prerequisite to invasion,
4. Invade at the earliest possible date, preferably no later than November first of this year, and
5. Occupy such areas in the industrial complex of Japan as are necessary to bring about unconditional surrender and establish absolute military control.[50]

US leadership had the following expectations for this campaign:

1. The Japanese will continue the war to the utmost extent of its capabilities, and US troops will confront not only Japan's armed forces but also a fanatically hostile population,
2. US forces will encounter three Japanese divisions in southern Kyūshū and three in northern Kyūshū,
3. The Japanese will only be able to reinforce Kyūshū to a total of no more than ten divisions, and
4. No more than 2,500 Japanese aircraft will operate against Olympic.[51]

At that point the Joint Staff Planner deferred back to Marshall, who continued the briefing. He told the group that ground elements for Olympic included both the Sixth Army and the Marine V Amphibious Corps. Their mission would be to seize and defend roughly the southern third of Kyūshū. The total projected commitment of forces was 767,700 men, 134,000 vehicles, and 1,470,930 tons of material.[52]

Admiral King next described the naval forces that would be involved. The Third and Fifth Fleets would operate jointly for the first time to support the invasion. The Third Fleet was assigned strategic support while the Fifth Fleet would directly conduct the amphibious operations. Carriers would be the principal striking weapon. King indicated the Navy, both American and British, planned to utilize a total of thirty-two carriers, twenty-two fleet, and ten light, with a combined air arm of 1,914 aircraft. Additionally, CINCPAC would be deploying 1,315 major amphibious vessels to back the ground forces.[53]

At the conclusion of King's remarks, Marshall brought up the issue of "first use" of poisonous gas, something he believed needed to be discussed. Large-scale stockpiles of gas had been in the Pacific Theater for some time, but US policy had always been that America would not be the first to use such weapons. Given the nature of the brutal, close-quarter fighting that had been so commonplace during the various island campaigns, Marshall wanted to take the temperature of the group to see if they'd recommend a change in policy.

"I'd like to raise an issue that we have prepared for but to date have stayed away from," he said, "and that is the use of gas against the Japs. I see gas as no more inhumane than phosphorous and the flame throwers, which we have already used and plan to make even more extensive use of in the battle to come."

Marshall was clear: he did not advocate the use of gas against dense populations or civilians—merely against the last pockets of resistance which had to be wiped out but had no other military significance. He stated that "it might even be possible to saturate an area, possibly with mustard gas and just stand off, thus avoiding the attrition caused by such fanatical but hopeless defense methods of suicidal Japanese."[54]

Hearing no support for the change in policy Marshall switched back to the topic at hand, a vote on the invasion plans. He asked if there was an acceptance of the Downfall plan. It would be a decision of huge magnitude, and while the navy clearly had expressed its reservations, they and their counterparts in the army all gave their approval[55] to Downfall and its objective—the unconditional surrender of Japan.

Despite mutual support for Downfall, behind the scenes, disagreement over how to achieve unconditional surrender from Japan remained between the two services. The Navy, specifically, King and Nimitz, continued to favor blockade and bombardment. Both men believed the casualties from an invasion would be so massive as to erode American public support for unconditional surrender. It was a belief hardened by decades of study of Japan coupled with battlefield experience throughout the war, driven home most recently in the ghastly battles for Iwo Jima and ongoing battle for Okinawa. In an invasion of Japan proper, naval planners believed despite America's efforts to interdict the flow of Japanese defenders to the battlefield, inevitably the enemy would outnumber any force the Americans could land, and the terrain, as it was on Okinawa, would counteract American advantages of firepower and mobility.[56] On May 25, Nimitz informed King he no longer supported the invasion.

In contrast to the Navy's maximum effort to study a war with Japan, the army had done comparatively little. Marshall and the army preferred invasion because they were convinced it would produce a Japanese surrender far sooner than the blockade and bombardment option. Marshall also believed that the longer the war went on, the more likely leadership would lose the American public's support for unconditional surrender.

His opinion on the need to end the war as quickly as possible was rooted in his experience as aide-de-camp to General John J. Pershing in World War I. As soon as Germany asked for an armistice, and before it had officially surrendered, Congress and the American public demanded a shift to demobilization. With Germany defeated, Marshall believed without a near-term victory over Japan, the mandate for partial demobilization could lead to a compromise settlement, one in which Japan could retain the core empire it still occupied in Formosa (modern day Taiwan), Manchuria, and Korea, and with no change to its political institutions. That kind of end to the War in the Pacific would have fallen well short of the sweeping political and military changes that would come from unconditional surrender and would leave Japan in a position to once again become a threat to peace.

MAY 28, 1945
70 DAYS TO HIROSHIMA

At the urging of Secretary of War Stimson, who had also been Secretary of State under former President Herbert Hoover, President Truman met with the former president to discuss, among other things, Hoover's thoughts on ending the war with Japan. Included in the conversation were Hoover's estimates of the human costs if the United States invaded Japan, a subject of great interest to Truman, especially in light of the recent terrible losses of life on Iwo Jima and Okinawa. Hoover offered a sobering assessment.

The source for Hoover's estimates most likely came from the "Smart Colonels" at the Pentagon. Even though Hoover had been relegated to the "political wilderness" by his own party and the Roosevelt administration, Hoover continued to provide frequent, low-key assistance to congressional committees. Papers discovered in the Herbert Hoover Presidential Library by senior archivist Dwight M. Miller revealed a link between Hoover and the group comprised of: Peter Vischer, Joseph A. Michela, Percy G. Black, and Truman Smith; the latter an intimate of General Marshall. Also involved in preparing the numbers were: Major General Clayton I. Bissell, Colonel Ivan D. Yeaton, and William LaVarre.[57]

Hoover told Truman, "There can be no American objectives that are worth the expenditure of 500,000 to 1,000,000 American lives."[58] The number had to have shocked the president.

At the conclusion of the meeting, Truman asked Hoover to recap his comments in a memorandum. Sent to the president on May 30, 1945, Hoover's paper twice more reiterated his estimate for loss of life. It needs be emphasized that the numbers Hoover gave were for deaths, not total casualties, which would likely be in the neighborhood of four times the number of men killed in action—or two to four million total casualties.

Confronted with such astounding figures, in a few days Truman sought further consultation on the matter.

MAY 29, 1945
69 DAYS TO HIROSHIMA

A day after the Truman-Hoover meeting, Under Secretary of State Joseph Grew met with Stimson, Marshall, and Forrestal to discuss an end to the Pacific War. Was a peaceful solution possible? At the time, Grew was considered the most knowledgeable diplomat in the president's administration on the subject of Japan, having spent nine years as the U.S. Ambassador to the nation. Grew told the group that he had met with the president the day before to discuss the topic and that the president was open to it but wanted to know their thoughts before proceeding any further. Grew had specifically proposed to the president that the US modify its call for unconditional surrender to allow for the continuation of the Emperor.

Stimson was the first to respond, saying, "On the surface I don't believe you'd get any disagreement from us on this point. There could be some real benefit in keeping the Emperor in gaining the compliance of the Japanese military to lay down their arms and cease hostilities. Conversely, if we don't permit them to keep the Emperor, the war may continue much longer and with ever greater costs to us."

Marshall thought there could be benefit, as well; but he also believed it was the wrong time to make such an overture. Forrestal explained why, stating that "the Japanese militarists would likely seize upon any such initiative in the midst of our campaign on Okinawa as proof of crumbling American resolve."[59] Stimson then added, "the real feature that will govern the situation is the atomic bomb."[60] Grew was disappointed by the feedback, but thanked the men for their comments and said he'd pass them along to the president.

Stimson's comment about *the bomb* was telling. Less than a week after the Joint Chiefs had approved the plans for Downfall, the Secretary of War was already hoping the invasion would not be necessary—that the atomic bomb could prove decisive. He and very likely all of his peers did not believe the loss of Okinawa, the tightening blockade, and bombardment of the Japanese homeland or the knowledge of an imminent invasion would cause Japan to surrender. Only a real and successful invasion, or perhaps an unimaginable weapon, the atomic bomb, had the potential to do that.

JUNE 6, 1945
61 DAYS TO HIROSHIMA

In the Cabinet Room of Prime Minister Suzuki's official residence, the Big Six and other key officials in the Japanese government and military met and discussed the rapidly deteriorating state of affairs in Japan, substantially worse than just a month earlier. Chief Cabinet Secretary Hisatsune Sakomizu read from a prepared document entitled *The Present State of the National Power*:

> The ominous turn of the war and the increasing tempo of Allied air raids have resulted in a serious disruption of land and sea communications and essential war production. The food situation has worsened and it has become increasingly difficult to meet the requirements of total war. Although morale is high, there is dissatisfaction with the present regime, and criticism of the government and the military is on the ascendancy. The people are losing confidence in their leaders, and the gloomy

omen of deterioration of public morale is present. The spirit of public sacrifice is lacking and among leading intellectuals there are some who advocate peace negotiation as a way out. We are faced with insurmountable difficulties in the field of transportation and communication, and if we lose Okinawa, we cannot hope to maintain planned communication with the Asian mainland after the end of June. (This turned out not to be true; it only cutoff communications through the China Sea.) Our total production of steel, at present, is about one-fourth of our output during the same period last year. The construction of steel ships, therefore, cannot be expected to continue after the middle of this year. There is also a strong possibility that a considerable portion of Japan's various industrial areas will soon have to suspend operation for want of coal. From midyear on, there will be a shortage of basic industrial salts, making it difficult for us to produce light metals, synthetic oil, and explosives. Henceforth, prices will rise sharply—bringing on inflation. This, in turn, will seriously undermine our wartime economy.

Sakomizu could not have painted a worse picture. But the military had prepared for this news and pressured an official to downplay the statistics. On the day of the meeting he composed two explanations, entitled *Conclusions*, to whitewash the patent contradictions between the report's findings and the "Fundamental Policy." However, his prose did little to suppress the obvious effort by the army to avoid reason and mask their unwillingness to accept the facts.[61] As a result, there was no thoughtful evaluation of the wartime consequences by the Vice-Chief of Staff of the Army General Staff and commander of the Central Honshu and Shikoku defenses, Lieutenant General Kawabe. He swept the report aside and calmly stated, "it shall be the Fundamental Policy of this government, to be followed henceforth in the conduct of the war to prosecute the war to the bitter end; that the Japanese people would fight to extinction rather than surrender."

The phrase "Fundamental Policy" originated from the partial title of a document that had been authored by the Supreme Command— *The Fundamental Policy to be Followed Henceforth in the Conduct of War*. It stated:

With a faith born of eternal loyalty as our inspiration, we shall— thanks to the advantages of our terrain and the unity of our nation prosecute the war to the bitter end in order to uphold our *kokutai* [national existence], protect the Imperial land and achieve our goals of conquest.[62]

Kawabe continued, stating his belief that Japan's military did not have to completely halt a US invasion, but only inflict so much damage that the Americans would be forced to regroup. After achieving this level of "success" on the field of battle, he recommended opening a path to a negotiated settlement on terms favorable to Japan.[63]

Tōgō countered that the destruction of Japan's economic capacity should be of vital concern to all. That, combined with the mounting intensity of the Allied air attacks and the inability of the Japanese air forces to defend against them, left him doubtful that Japan's situation would improve as its enemies got closer.[64]

Admiral Toyoda snapped back. Japan had reached a historic moment in its existence, one that would determine whether the nation survived. "Even if the Japanese people are weary of the war," Toyoda said, "We must fight to the last man!"

A furious Anami then bellowed, "If we cannot fulfill our responsibility as advisors to the Throne, we should offer our sincere apologies by committing hara-kiri Seppuku."[65]

Vice-Admiral Zenshiro Hoshina was next to jump on the bandwagon, stating, "Every man present should put forth his best effort, and if anyone fails, he should be prepared to commit suicide." He was followed by Suzuki, who agreed with Hoshina and added that, "There is only one way to win, and that is by determination. When the whole nation possesses this will, then we shall be able to achieve victory."[66]

General Anami then reminded the Foreign Minister that he had been tasked with making an effort to improve Japan's relations with the Soviets a few weeks earlier, including a request for war materials. Anami wanted to know what had become of that effort.[67] Tōgō, knowing little had been done, pushed back, explaining that such a maneuver was out the question—mere daydreaming. The Soviet Union was not then, and would not become later, an ally of Japan.[68]

The Army's rejoinder was a resolution that the war must continue as a matter of course, to which Tōgō renewed his objection. The discussion was heating up yet again, so Suzuki endeavored to calm things down, saying, "Oh! I think that much will be all right."[69] He then closed the meeting by asking if there were any other opinions regarding the

Fundamental Policy. Hearing only silence, he adjourned the meeting at 5:00 p.m.

JUNE 7, 1945
60 DAYS TO HIROSHIMA

In an effort to get every informed opinion on the topic of invasion casualties, Truman had sent Hoover's "Memorandum Ending the Japanese War" (aka memo 4) to his manpower czar Fred M. Vinson on or about June 4. In Vinson's response on June 7, the War Mobilization director did not contradict the casualty estimate. Further, he recommended forwarding the memo to Stimson, Joseph Grew, and former Secretary of State Cordell Hull.

JUNE 8, 194
59 DAYS TO HIROSHIMA

In Lord Keeper of the Privy Seal Marquis Kido's diary, he indicated that the first clear sign that the Emperor was considering peace occurred on June 8, the same day Kido prepared his own "Draft Plan for Controlling the Crisis Situation."[70] But like the Supreme Council, the Emperor's conception of peace did not mean unconditional surrender.

JUNE 9, 1945
58 DAYS TO HIROSHIMA

Contradicting what he had told Kido just one day earlier, the Emperor issued an imperial rescript ordering the nation to "smash the inordinate ambitions of the enemy nations" and "achieve the goals of the war." At the same time, the government-controlled press launched a daily die-for-the-Emperor campaign promoting gratitude for Imperial benevolence, and, ultimately, a movement to "protect the *kokutai*."[71]

On the same day, the *New York Times* reprinted a speech given by Prime Minister Suzuki to the 87th Extraordinary Session of the Japanese Imperial Diet:

> Having heard the gracious words of His Imperial Majesty, the Emperor, following the opening of the Diet, I am filled with trepidation and inspiration. It is my sincerest wish to be able to serve as an administrator in complete response to His Majesty's wishes.

I was filled with trepidation when the Imperial Palace and the Omiya detached palace were set afire by enemy bombings the other day. Fortunately, their imperial majesties were not harmed and I am thankful that His Majesty has been able to conduct all state affairs in his office in the Imperial Palace.

Today our empire is facing the most critical situation in the history of our nation. The war situation gradually is becoming more acute, despite the efforts made by the whole nation, and we have witnessed the advance of the enemy on Okinawa.

However, through the courageous and brilliant fighting of our land and sea forces, together with the efforts of our Government and people, we have inflicted enormous losses on the enemy on Okinawa. The unswerving loyalty and heroism and the undying exploits of our men will long remain in the pages of history. I want to pay deep respect to their noble deeds.

There are factors in the situation on Okinawa today that arouse anxiety and we have reached a stage where we can expect the advance of the enemy, at some time, to other areas of our mainland. The time has arrived when all our 100,000,000 people must look at the situation objectively and meet it with manifest determination.

From the very beginning the Greater East Asia War has clearly been a holy war. This has clearly been stated in the imperial rescript. The tyrannical attitude adopted by the United States and Britain at that time, as well as their evil designs, jeopardized the existence and safety of our empire.

Our empire had no choice but to take her stand and fight in order to assure her own existence and defense and to maintain the fruits of her many years of effort to stabilize conditions in East Asia.

I have served His Imperial Majesty over a period of many years and I am deeply impressed with this honor. As bold as it may seem, I firmly believe there is no one in the entire world who is more deeply concerned with world peace and the welfare of mankind than His Imperial Majesty, the Emperor.

The brutal and inhuman acts of both America and England are aimed to make it impossible for us to follow our national policy as proclaimed by the Emperor Meiji, who said: "Our fundamental policy is based on justice and righteousness in the past as well as at the present, and that is true and infallible both at home and abroad."

This means that Japan is fighting a war to uphold the principle of human justice and we must fight to the last.

In this present war, various participating nations have cleverly declared their reasons for becoming involved in the conflict, but in the final analysis the war was brought about by jealousy, which is the lowest of human emotions.

I hear that the enemy is boasting of his demand for unconditional surrender of Japan. Unconditional surrender means that our national structure and our people will be destroyed. Against such boastful talk there is only one measure we must take, to fight to the last.

I am thankful that Manchukuo, China and other nations of Greater East Asia are standing firm by their treaties with our empire and that they are contributing a great deal to the holy war.

In the final analysis, the current war is a war for the liberation of East Asia and should it miscarry the freedom of the peoples of Greater East Asia will be lost forever. Not only that, but world justice will be trampled underfoot.

The fundamental policy of our empire for world order is the establishment of laws guaranteeing security based on the principle of non-aggression and non-menace in order to insure the co-existence and co-prosperity of every nation and every people under a general principle of political equality, economic reciprocity and respect for the traditional culture of each nation.

From this standpoint, our empire awaits the unification of China, which will be the salvation of that nation, and desires the furthering of friendly relations with neutral countries.

Should our mainland become a battleground, we will have all the advantages of geography and the solidarity of our people. In other words, we can easily concentrate a large number of forces as well as keep them supplied, which will be greatly different from the situation we faced at the outset of the war. We certainly will be able to repulse the enemy and crush his fighting spirit.

In this critical war situation, there will be a shortage of food and difficulties in transportation. Furthermore, difficulties in the manufacture of munitions will increase. But if the whole people will march forward with death-defying determination, devoting their entire efforts to their own duties and to refreshing their fighting spirit, I believe that we will be able to overcome all difficulties and accomplish our war aims.

Judging from the trends within enemy countries and considering the developments in the international situation, I cannot help feel strongly that the only way for us is to fight to the last. With this conviction I undertook the organization of the new Cabinet under the command of His Imperial Majesty.

It is truly a critical time. I wish to be able to fulfill my desire to serve His Majesty with the support of the whole people. These are the reasons that this extraordinary session of the Diet was called, where new bills will be submitted for deliberation.

Suzuki's speech was clearly intended for global consumption. If it had only been for a Japanese audience, as a piece of propaganda to boost the morale of the masses, then its content would have been completely understandable, since the government had no interest in telling the people the truth anyway. But Suzuki's oratory was meant to be a chest-pumping statement—akin decades later to Iraqi leader Saddam Hussein's boast at the onset of the First Gulf War when he told the Allies, "The battle in which you are locked today is the mother of all battles...Our rendezvous with victory is very near." Suzuki was defiant, calling on the Japanese people three times to "fight to the last" and to do so in death-defying determination.

This was not only a call to arms but a warning to Japan's enemies, upon whom Suzuki laid the blame for the war. The Americans and British were labeled as evil, tyrannical, inhuman, and brutal, all attributes that more accurately described the actions of his own country's military.

If Japan surrendered unconditionally, Suzuki suggested, it would mean the end of the nation; as such, its only recourse was to fight on.

A factor contributing to Suzuki's rhetoric, as well as the thinking of Japan's senior uniformed officers, was that they truly believed their forces, even after losing a succession of battles, had inflicted terrible losses on the U.S. And since ultimately they regarded American morale as brittle, the notion that they had already exacted a tremendous blood price for American successes led them to believe that inflicting large casualties in a counter-invasion battle would be the tipping point to finally break American will. And despite repeated assurances from FDR and Truman to the contrary—as recently as Truman's May 8 speech— Japanese leaders chose to view unconditional surrender as tantamount to a blank check given to the victors. Historian Lester Brooks put it aptly; no self-respecting Japanese could do anything but reject this possibility.[72]

As for those Japanese civilians who may have by now grown weary of the war, former Prime Minister Tōjō had long ago strengthened and unleashed the *Kempeitai,* Japan's military police (in existence since 1881), akin to Germany's dreaded Gestapo. Known for its ruthlessness and brutality, the Kempeitai quashed any opposition by identifying, rounding up, imprisoning, and torturing tens of thousands of Japanese and endless Chinese and Korean malcontents, albeit with far fewer executions than their German counterparts. With leadership muzzled, dissenters splintered into tiny, powerless groups. "The sad fact was that there were few of them," according to Lester Brooks, "and if any of them was to exert open leadership or question government policy he could expect a prompt call from the secret thought police. There was no safe rallying point."[73] Anami, too, had made use of Kempeitai to round up four hundred well-known "end-the-war" dissidents shortly after joining Suzuki's War Cabinet.[74]

Following up on Fred Vinson's June 7 recommendation to send the Hoover Memo to Stimson, Grew, and former Secretary of State Hull, Truman had copies delivered to them along with an expression of his desire to meet with each of them "eye to eye" to discuss their individual analysis. Stimson, on his own initiative, then sent his copy to the Deputy Chief of Staff, Major General Thomas J. Handy, because he wanted to get "the reaction of the Operations Division Staff to it," and he mentioned in his diary that he "had a talk both with Handy and General Marshall on the subject."[75]

Handy's staff produced a briefing paper for Stimson which drew attention to the fact that memo 4's figure of potentially 1,000,000 American dead was fully double the Army's estimates. It was "entirely too high under the present plan of campaign" which entailed only the seizure of southern Kyūshū, the Tokyo region, and several key coastal areas. The pointed disclaimer "under the present plan of campaign" was, however, literally the only part of the five hundred and fifty word analysis, excluding headlines that carried a typed underline.[76] Also noteworthy, but unstated, was an Army estimate of 500,000 dead, if "...1,000,000 American dead was fully double" its estimates." It was a number that Truman had already heard from Hoover, both in person and in his follow-up memorandum.

JUNE 12, 1945
55 DAYS TO HIROSHIMA

On the 12th of June, Hull was the first of the recipients to review the Hoover Memo to respond directly to Truman. He branded memo 4 Hoover's "appeasement proposal" in his June 12 letter because it suggested that the Japanese be offered lenient terms to entice them to the negotiating table. However, Hull did not take issue with the casualty estimate, nor did Grew in his reply on June 13. Grew further stated that the Japanese "are prepared for prolonged resistance" and that "prolongation of the war will cost a large number of human lives."[77]

Grew's opinion would not have come as any surprise to the president since he had told Truman, ironically just hours after the meeting with Hoover, that "The Japanese are a fanatical people capable of fighting to the last man. If they do this, the cost in American lives will be unpredictable."

JUNE 13, 1945
54 DAYS TO HIROSHIMA

Hull's letter, along with Under Secretary of State Grew's response to the Hoover memorandum, arrived at the White House on Wednesday, June 13, and Truman subsequently met with Admiral Leahy to discuss the matter. Truman requested that Leahy, the president's personal representative on the Joint Chiefs of Staff, schedule a meeting with the other JCS members, as well as Secretary of War Stimson and Secretary of the Navy James Forrestal. The president wanted a conference the following Monday afternoon, June 18, 1945, to discuss "the losses in dead and wounded that would result from an invasion of Japan proper." Leahy stated unequivocally that "It is [Truman's] intention to make his decision on the campaign with the purpose of economizing to the maximum extent possible the loss of American lives. Economy in the use of time and in money cost is comparatively unimportant."[78]

The exchanges between Truman, Grew, Hull, Stimson, and Vinson not only placed the very high casualty numbers squarely on the president's desk long before Hiroshima, but, says Robert Ferrell, editor of Truman's private papers, they demonstrated that Truman "was exercised about the 500,000 figure, [Hoover had given him] no doubt about that." Historians have often pondered why Truman called the June 18 meeting, and Ferrell contends that the exchanges over the Hoover memorandum answer the question.

Hoover's estimate was validation of what Truman already knew. Casualties occurring on Pacific battlefields were mounting dramatically, and they would be on a much greater scale during an invasion of the Japanese homeland. The president was well aware of the actual casualty figures from the ongoing Okinawan campaign and the Marines' recent battle to wrest a mere eight square miles of volcanic rock from the Japanese on Iwo Jima.

To Truman, a captain of an Army artillery battery in World War I, who had experienced three months of combat that had made a lifelong impression on him, the casualty numbers were not meaningless or abstract—they were flesh and blood men, like those he had served with and commanded twenty-seven years earlier. And he had seen plenty of the dead on the battlefield. So even though the United States was already months into a steep increase in draft calls—implemented under Roosevelt to produce a 140,000-men-per-month "replacement stream"[79] for the now one-front war, a further validation of the protracted and heavy losses military planners expected from invasion of the Japanese mainland—Truman was far more worried about the lives of the actual men and the impact of their loss on their families and friends.

Evidence of this very human, emotional concern for the average American serviceman and their families was apparent in the importance Truman placed in Bill Hassett, a presidential assistant from Roosevelt's administration that Truman kept on in his administration. Head of the mail room under Roosevelt, which received thousands of letters a day from the American public, Truman elevated Hassett to the senior staff position of Correspondence Secretary, a top five White House post, and he gave him the second-best office in the West Wing, next to his own. To Truman, the ability of "the Bishop," as he was known, to keep him abreast of American public opinion was unrivaled, far superior to the polls and in Truman's view "indispensable."[80]

JUNE 15, 1945
52 DAYS TO HIROSHIMA

In reply to a request by Admiral Leahy on June 14, to the Joint Staff Planners (JPS), the Joint War Plans Committee (J.W.P.C.) wrote 369/1 June 15, 1945: DETAILS OF THE CAMPAIGN AGAINST JAPAN. The JPS made some modifications and submitted it to the Chiefs as JCS 1388.

MEMORANDUM FOR THE PRESIDENT

SUBJECT: CAMPAIGN AGAINST JAPAN...

1. *Strategy*. Throughout the series of staff conferences with the British, we've agreed that the overall concept for the prosecution of the war included provision "to bring about at the earliest possible date the unconditional surrender of Japan." We believe that the only sure way, and certainly the quickest way to force surrender of Japan is to defeat her armies on the main Japanese islands...

2. *Casualties*. The cost in casualties of the main operations against Japan is not subject to accurate estimate. The scale of Japanese resistance in the past has not been predictable.

...The best estimate of casualties for [the] possible sequences of operations follows.

	KIA	WIA	MIA	TOTAL
Southern Kyūshū, followed by Tokyo Plain, to mid-1946	40,000	150,000	3,500	193,500[81]

Albeit a substantially lower number than the other estimates, Truman now had Hoover's memo and several responses to it from his senior staff, as well as the June 15 memo above. All indicated very high casualties resulting from an invasion of Japan.

JUNE 16, 1945
51 DAYS TO HIROSHIMA

Behind the scenes, Marshall asked MacArthur for his estimate of casualties for Olympic for the first ninety days.

MARSHALL-MACARTHUR CORRESPONDENCE, JUNE 16–19, 1945

16 JUNE 1945

TO: GHQ AFPAC (MACARTHUR)
FROM: WASHINGTON...
Request by 17 June (Washington) the estimate you are using for planning purposes of the battle casualties in OLYMPIC up to D 90.

MARSHALL

JUNE 17, 1945
50 DAYS TO HIROSHIMA

MacArthur responded to Marshall on the 17th.
G-1 17 JUNE
FROM: CINCAFPAC
TO: WARCOS
Estimate of OLYMPIC battle casualties for planning purposes (C-19571) Reurad W-17477 as follows:

D to D/30:   50,800
D/30 to D/60:   27,150
D/60 to D/90:   27,100

The foregoing are estimated total battle casualties from which estimated return to duty numbers are deducted. Not included in the foregoing are non-battle casualties which are estimated at 4,200 for each 30 day [a total of 12,600].

MacArthur's estimate for the first 90 days totaled 117,650.
Marshall wrote back on June 18, and with the time difference, the message was received by MacArthur on the 19th.

URGENT
19 JUNE 1945
FROM: GENERAL MARSHALL
TO: GENERAL MACARTHUR (PERSONAL)
WAR 18528 19 JUNE
The President is very much concerned as to the number of casualties we will receive in the OLYMPIC operation. This will be discussed with the president about 3:30 PM today Washington time. Is the estimate given in your C-19571 of 50,800 for the period of D

to D/30 based on plans for medical installations to be established or is it the best estimate of the casualties you anticipate from the operational viewpoint. Please rush answer.

JUNE 18, 1945
49 DAYS TO HIROSHIMA

On June 18, 1945, at 3:30 p.m., President Truman held a meeting in the White House Cabinet Room with his Joint Chiefs of Staff to discuss the plans for the invasion of the Japanese mainland. The night before the momentous meeting, Truman had written in his diary that the decision whether to "invade Japan [or] bomb and blockade" would be his "hardest decision to date."

The fighting in the Pacific had from the outset been bitter, often barbaric, and always fiercely contested. By the spring of 1944, recognizing their failure to halt the American advance, Japan's military leaders had adopted a new stratagem. Believing American morale to be brittle, and that with enough casualties they could still win something better than unconditional surrender, the Japanese implemented the strategy of *Defense in Depth*, wherever the terrain allowed. The defense made extensive use of bunkers, pillboxes, and natural caves, often interconnected with tunnels, in some cases miles of them, as the Japanese did on Iwo Jima and Okinawa. With the majority of fortifications built behind the beaches, the battlements became increasingly dense as the attacker advanced inland. The further the invader proceeded, the greater the risk that if the attack stalled, the enemy might be enveloped.

Japanese leaders took this scheme to physical, psychological, and even spiritual extremes. Throughout training, Japanese officers indoctrinated servicemen with the belief that they would dishonor not only themselves but their family if they surrendered, and that it was their duty to die for the Emperor. Battlefield commanders were thus free to create a defense where they did not have to be concerned with their troops needing nor wanting to retreat to a safe location should a battle fail to go in their favor. Since it was virtually impossible for the attacker to bypass these fortified positions, the new strategy was proving successful, as it imposed ever higher casualties on the attacking Marines and soldiers on the island battlefields of Saipan, Tinian, Guam, Peleliu, and most recently Iwo Jima and Okinawa. Whether American morale could be broken by this means remained to be seen.

It was with this backdrop of suicidal Japanese defense strategy that Truman met with Admiral Leahy, General Marshall, Admiral King, General Eaker (substituting for General Arnold), Secretary Stimson, Secretary Forrestal, Assistant Secretary of War John McCloy, and Brigadier General A. J. McFarland who served as Secretary,[82] to decide how best to end the war with Japan. Truman opened the discussion by stating that he had called the meeting for the purpose of informing himself about the details of the campaign against Japan, after which he asked Marshall to begin the briefing.

Marshall opened by saying that the present situation in Japan was practically identical to those the US had faced at Normandy one year earlier. He then proceeded to read from a memorandum prepared by the Joint Chiefs of Staff (J.C.S 1388) for the president:

> Our air and sea power has already greatly reduced movement of Jap shipping south of Korea and should in the next few months cut it to a trickle if not choke it off entirely. Hence, there is no need for seizing further positions in order to block Japanese communications south of Korea.
>
> General MacArthur and Admiral Nimitz are in agreement with the Chiefs of Staff in selecting November 1 as the target date to go into Kyūshū because by that time:
>
> a. If we press preparations, we can be ready.
> b. Our estimates are that our air action will have smashed practically every industrial target worth hitting in Japan as well as destroying huge areas in the Jap cities.
> c. The Japanese Navy, if any still exists, will be completely powerless.
> d. Our sea action and air power will have cut Jap reinforcement capabilities from the mainland to negligible proportions. (This proved unrealistic, as significant numbers of troops were able to cross from Asia to Japan.)
>
> Important considerations bearing on the November 1 date rather than a later one are the weather and cutting to a minimum Jap time for preparation of defenses. If we delay much after the beginning of November the weather situation in the succeeding months may be such that the invasion of Japan, and hence the end of the war, will be delayed for up to 6 months.[83]

Marshall indicated he believed the Kyūshū invasion was essentially a strategy of strangulation. The basic point was that a lodgment in Kyūshū was required, both to tighten the stranglehold of blockade and bombardment on Japan and to force capitulation by the invasion of the Tokyo Plain.[84] If the Japanese were going to concede, short of complete military defeat in the field, it would happen only as a result of the continued destruction bought from our blockade and bombardment, US landings on Japan, and perhaps the real or perceived entry of the Soviets into the war against them.[85]

Regarding casualties, one of Truman's primary and stated concerns prior to the meeting, Marshall offered the following:

> Our experience in the Pacific war is so diverse as to casualties that it is considered wrong to give any estimate in numbers. But if we look at General MacArthur's experience on Luzon, because we feel our operations on Kyūshū will afford similar room to maneuver, his losses totaled 13,742 killed in action, compared to 310,165 Japanese dead or a ratio of 22.6 to 1. Therefore, for the first thirty days, we expect the casualties to be similar to those on Luzon, or approximately 31,000.[86]

Estimating casualties was hardly an exact science and ratios were commonly used. But why Marshall only provided the projected losses for the first thirty days versus the ninety days offered by MacArthur, more indicative of the expected length of the operation, remains unknown to this day.

Marshall's estimate also didn't include naval or air force casualties, or include the consequences of Japan's extensively utilized "special-attack" (suicide) forces to counter the invasion, information known to the Americans.

Perhaps even more puzzling was Marshall's own reaction to a casualty estimate for Olympic provided by MacArthur's headquarters, which told him the number could exceed 100,000. According to historian Richard Frank, "Marshall recoiled sharply at the estimates...inviting MacArthur to disavow such projections explicitly cit[ing] President Truman's sensitivities to casualties."[87]

Marshall then told Truman "it was the thankless responsibility of leaders to remain steadfast outwardly if they expected to maintain the convictions of their subordinates. Any wavering of this stance could prove costly. It was Churchill's reluctance to accept this fact that frequently stood in the way of the preparations that were critical to the D-Day operation, which in retrospect proved to be highly successful."

Marshall then quoted General MacArthur, who had stated, "I believe the operation presents less hazards of excessive loss than any other that has been suggested and that its decisive effect will eventually save lives by eliminating wasteful operations of a non-decisive character. I most earnestly recommend no change in OLYMPIC."[88]

MacArthur's words likely had minimal impact on Truman's thinking, as he was not a fan of the general, referring to him as "Mr. Prima Donna, brass hat, or five-star MacArthur."[89]

General Marshall concluded his remarks declaring that in his view the operation against Kyūshū was the only course to pursue. He said he believed that air power alone would not be sufficient to put the Japanese out of the war any more than it had been capable of doing so with Germany, an opinion also shared by General Eisenhower. The operation would be difficult, he conceded, but no more so than the assault in Normandy. Marshall concluded by saying he felt every individual moving to the Pacific should be indoctrinated with a firm determination to see it through to the end.[90]

Truman then turned to Admiral King, who concurred with Marshall. Having analyzed the situation, King believed in not only the strategic location of Kyūshū, but that taking it would be the "key to success of any siege operation." He stated that Olympic made sense as the next logical operation, and at its conclusion it would be possible to better judge the value of both China's and Russia's contributions in the defeat of Japan. King also briefly made a recommendation on the second phase of Downfall. Because of the scale of the Tokyo Plain operation (Coronet), tentatively planned for March 1, 1946, King said he felt the planning must continue in order to be ready in time. If the invasion proved unnecessary it could always be cancelled.[91]

Admiral Leahy reminded the group that the president had asked for a specific estimate of the casualties related to the Kyūshū offensive. He went on to state that in his view it would not be unrealistic to see numbers similar to what the US had just experienced on Okinawa, where the casualty rate amounted to thirty-five percent of the invasion force. Leahy then asked King if he did not believe that to be the case, why not?[92]

King responded that on Okinawa the US had been forced into a straight frontal attack. The proposed Olympic operations included three simultaneous landings with room to maneuver. In King's opinion, the casualties should be somewhere between what MacArthur experienced on Luzon and what the US saw on Okinawa. Avoiding specifics, King had just indirectly raised the casualty estimate to something greater than Marshall's.

Perhaps King's comments were intended to be the beginning of a hedge with the president. Privately, he and Admiral Nimitz had become very leery of the idea of an invasion, based on the horrendous losses on Iwo Jima and Okinawa. Both men felt an invasion of the Japanese homeland—with many times the number of defenders on Okinawa—could be catastrophic. A confrontation over whether the invasion of Kyūshū should proceed or a continuation and expansion of blockade and bombardment was looming between the US Army and Navy. That option remained open to Truman to the very end of the war.

King's remarks had also not directly addressed the issue of potential naval casualties during the invasion. The Navy had experienced some of its worst losses of the war in the seas surrounding Okinawa, and King had already acknowledged as much during the meeting with the Joint Planners in May. The losses came primarily from the 2,000 kamikaze sorties flown against the American fleet that had been forced to remain in place to support the ground troops over the course of the eighty-two-day battle. At its conclusion, the Navy had sustained damage to well over three hundred ships, thirty-six of them sunk, and almost 10,000 casualties—nearly half of them killed in action.

The discussion reverted back to General Marshall, who pointed out that the total assault troops for the Kyūshū campaign were shown as 766,700 in the memorandum prepared for the president. In response to the president's question about Japanese opposition, Marshall told Truman he expected there to be eight divisions, or 350,000 men, defending Kyūshū.[93] Always wanting to ensure he had as complete a picture as he could before making a decision, the president asked about the possibility that the Japanese could reinforce the number of troops on Kyūshū prior to the US invasion.[94] Marshall answered that the destruction of Japanese communications should foreclose that threat, but divisions were still being raised in Japan and that reinforcement from other areas, though increasingly difficult for the Japanese, was possible. King and Leahy lent additional support to this notion.

The President, knowing Olympic would only be the first phase of the assault on Japan, followed by the even larger Operation Coronet, expressed the view that it was practically creating a larger-scaled Okinawa closer to Japan, to which the Chiefs of Staff agreed. Thus, despite Marshall's, and to a lesser extent King's, efforts to drastically downplay the potential casualties, as the meeting progressed so did the implied level of losses, something Truman surely took note of as he continued to listen.

Lieutenant General I.C. Eaker, representing General Arnold, spoke next at Truman's request. He and General Arnold agreed completely with the statements already made by Marshall. He added that "any blockade of Honshu [where Tokyo was located] was dependent upon airdromes on Kyūshū." The air plan against Japan called for the use of forty groups of heavy bombers flying from airfields on Kyūshū, so without an invasion the air plan as conceived could not be accomplished. He countered advocates of a solely air-powered strategy as a means of defeating Japan, pointing out that losses to air power were as a matter of fact much greater until the ground forces came in. He ended with a warning that "delay favored only the enemy."[95]

Having heard from each member of the Joint Chiefs, the president said that, as he understood it, the JCS were still of the unanimous opinion that the Kyūshū operation was the best solution under the circumstances. The Chiefs of Staff agreed that this was so.[96]

Continuing his tour around the table, Truman next asked Secretary Stimson to lend his opinion. The Colonel said he too believed invasion was the only option that kept with America's wartime objective of unconditional surrender and the sacrifices the country had already made. He said he felt personally responsible to the president more for political than for military considerations. In that regard, Stimson believed there was a large submerged class in Japan who did not favor the present war, and whose full opinion and influence had not yet been felt.[97]

Hearing what he thought could be a possible alternative to the slaughter on the battlefield, Truman acknowledged he was always looking for and open to other means to end the war that would meet their objectives. "Do you think the invasion of Japan by white men will have the effect of more closely uniting the Japanese?" Truman asked.[98] Stimson answered that there was every prospect it would, which was why he remained hopeful some other solution would present itself before the US had to resort to an invasion.[99]

On the night of March 9-10, 1945, General Curtis LeMay, in command of America's Twentieth Air Force on Guam, implemented low-level night-time bombing using incendiary bombs. The raid laid waste to one quarter of Tokyo, sixteen square miles, killing more than 84,000. It was the single most destructive aerial attack of World War II, including the atomic bombings of Hiroshima and Nagasaki. (*Wikimedia Commons*)

The urban conflagration turned thousands of Japanese, caught in the inferno, into carbonized corpses.

(*Wikimedia Commons*)

The E-46 Aimable Cluster, containing thirty-eight M69 incendiary bomblets, was the weapon of choice by LeMay's Twentieth Air Force. Nearly half a million rained down on Tokyo early in the morning of March 9-10, 1945.

(*James Madison University Center for International Stabilization and Recovery*)

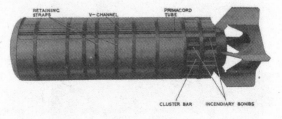

Ten days after the catastrophic attack on Tokyo, Emperor Hirohito and his small entourage walked through the ruins of the Capitol. He and Japan's leadership never left Tokyo. *(World History Archive / Alamy Stock Photo)*

Japan's divine leader, Emperor Hirohito, in his dress uniform.
(Wikimedia Commons)

Retired Admiral Kantarō Suzuki was held in high esteem by the Emperor. Becoming Japan's third Prime Minister in eight months on April 7, 1945, he would be the last of the war. Suzuki—along with Umezu, Anami, Yonai, Toyoda, and Tōgō (all pictured on the following pages)—formed Japan's Supreme Council for the Direction of the War, a.k.a. the Big Six. These men held the reins of power in Japan during the Pacific War's final months.
(National Diet Library)

Army Chief of Staff General Yoshijirō Umezu was a holdover from Prime Minister Kuniaki Koiso's cabinet, which fell on April 5, 1945. By this point in the war, the Japanese navy was largely at the bottom of the ocean. As such, the army commanded much greater influence within the government. *(Wikimedia Commons)*

Army War Minister General Korechika Anami was the most powerful man in the Army, and therefore arguably Japan, during the final months of World War II. *(Wikimedia Commons)*

Navy Minister Admiral Mitsumasa Yonai was also a holdover from Prime Minister Kuniaki Koiso's cabinet, and a former Prime Minister, albeit for merely six months. He was a hated rival of General Anami.
(*Wikimedia Commons*)

Navy Chief of Staff Admiral Soemu Toyoda was the last addition to the Big Six, at Yonai's recommendation. Expected to be a moderate in the war cabinet, he proved otherwise.
(*Naval History and Heritage Command*)

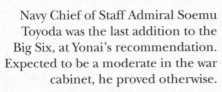

Foreign Minister Shigenori Tōgō was the only civilian among the Big Six. Tōgō had been the Foreign Minister at the beginning of war under Hideki Tojo, although he opposed war with the US and Britain. Tōgō would be Japan's leading peace proponent during the final days of the empire.
(*Wikimedia Commons*)

Upon the death of Franklin D. Roosevelt earlier in the day, Vice President Harry S. Truman was sworn in as the thirty-third President of the United States at 7:09 p.m. on April 12, 1945. *(National Archives and Records Administration)*

President Harry S. Truman was hardly a novice politician prior to becoming Commander in Chief. As a second-term senator from Missouri, he had been in office for nearly ten years and chaired one of the most powerful committees, the Senate Special Committee to Investigate the National Defense Program—or as it came to be known, the Truman Committee. *(National Archives and Records Administration)*

Secretary of War Henry L. Stimson had served his country for most of his adult life, joining FDR's cabinet in 1940. He played a key role in the buildup of American armed forces during the war, as well as the Manhattan Project and the development of the atomic bomb. Truman asked him to remain in his new administration after the death of FDR. *(Library of Congress)*

Truman had known Secretary of State James F. Byrnes for many years in the U.S. Senate. Byrnes had served in the highest positions in the American government, including a stint as a Supreme Court Justice. Byrnes was considered, then dropped, as a possible Vice-Presidential running mate for Roosevelt in 1944 because of his conservative leanings.

(US Department of State)

Army Chief of Staff General of the Army George C. Marshall is still one of the most highly respected Americans in the nation's history. During the war Marshall presided over the exponential growth of the army and was a member of the Joint Chiefs of Staff. After the war, Marshall became Truman's Secretary of State in 1947 and author of the European Recovery Program or, as it became known, the Marshall Plan. For his efforts he was awarded the Nobel Prize for Peace in 1953.

(Library of Congress)

One of Roosevelt's closest confidants and friends, Admiral William D. Leahy had known FDR for over forty years by the time the president appointed him Chief of Staff to the Commander in Chief in 1942. Known as a man who spoke his mind, he attended every significant conference during the war at the side of FDR and Truman.
(US Navy History and Heritage Command)

In overall command of the U.S. Navy's combined fleets, Chief of Naval Operations, Fleet Admiral Ernest J. King was a member of the Joint Chiefs of Staff and the Allied Combined Chiefs of Staff and left his imprint on every major war conference. And even though he supported the Germany first policy, he nevertheless made sure significant military strength went to the Pacific Theater.
(US Navy History and Heritage Command)

Secretary of the Navy Forrestal then offered his views to the proceedings. He asserted that even if the US wished to besiege Japan for a year or year and a half, the capture of Kyūshū would still be essential. Therefore, the sound decision was to proceed with the operation now. There would still be time thereafter to consider the main decision (whether to proceed with an invasion of the Tokyo Plain) in light of subsequent events.[100]

Apparently believing everyone had been heard, some of the attendees began putting their papers away in folders and briefcases, at which point Truman remembered he hadn't heard from McCloy. Truman looked at him and said, "Nobody leaves this room until he's been heard from." McCloy said he felt that the time was propitious now to study closely all possible means of bringing out the influence of the submerged group in Japan, which had been referred to by Stimson.[101]

The president stated that one of his objectives in connection with the coming conference [at Potsdam] would be to get from Russia all the assistance in the war that was possible. To this end, he wanted to know all the decisions that he would have to make in advance in order to occupy the strongest possible position in the discussions.[102]

Wanting to raise one other area of discussion before the conversation ended, Leahy stated he did not believe unconditional surrender was necessary, as Japan posed no menace for the foreseeable future. Truman said that it was with that thought in mind that he had left the door open for Congress to take appropriate action. However, since it had not, he did not believe he could yield on this point to change public policy at the present time.[103]

In concluding this part of the meeting, Truman told the group he had called the gathering because he was "hopeful of preventing an Okinawa from one end of Japan to the other." Based on the information presented and the unanimous support for it by the assemblage, he too was now in agreement that Olympic should proceed. Regarding Operation Coronet, Truman said he wanted to reserve that decision for a later time.[104] The president also said he would attempt to reconfirm Stalin's pledge, made at Yalta, to enter the war against Japan within ninety days of the surrender of Germany when he saw him at the upcoming summit in Potsdam.

As the men began leaving, Admiral King walked up to Truman and confided that in his opinion, regardless of the desirability of having the Russians join the fight against the Japanese, he did not see them as indispensable and said, "we should not go so far as to beg them to come in." He acknowledged that the cost to the US would be greater without them, but he was confident that America could handle it alone. King wanted Truman to understand this prior to meeting with Stalin.[105] The president thanked Admiral King and said he would keep it in mind.

King's comment seemed curious considering the Navy's concern over casualties. Conceivably, it was an oblique acknowledgment that any Russian involvement would necessarily come outside Japan, primarily in Manchuria, since the Soviets possessed no ability to conduct a major amphibious assault necessary to invade Japan, specifically Hokkaido, Japan's northernmost island. Therefore, their entrance into the war with Japan would have little if any effect on Japan's ability or willingness to engage American forces in the battle for the homeland, and if that was the case, why covet Soviet assistance?

Leahy had expressed the same sentiment privately to Roosevelt at Yalta, stating it "was [his]...firm opinion that our war against Japan had progressed to the point where defeat was only a matter of time and attrition." [106]

What the Navy missed, or perhaps believed it had completely cut off with their blockade of the Japanese home islands, was the flow of the Japanese troops from Asia to Japan had not been entirely halted, and the implications for the American invasion were significant. Major General Charles E. Willoughby, MacArthur's top intelligence officer, estimated in his "sinister ratio" that even a poor to average Japanese division could cost an additional 20,000 American casualties.[107] A prime example of just how effective they could be when fighting largely from fixed fortifications as on Iwo Jima, where commanding General Tadamichi Kuribayashi had a hodgepodge of airmen, unhappy sailors serving as infantrymen, and ill-trained, "second string" army units. Kuribayashi said of them, "These are no soldiers, just poor recruits who don't know anything. Their officers are superannuated fools. We cannot fight the Americans with them."[108]

But those 21,000 to 22,000 Japanese managed to extract nearly 26,000 casualties from the American invaders. Thus, getting the Soviets to tie down every possible Japanese division in Manchuria saved thousands of American wounded and dead. The Army and FDR disagreed with the Navy, and Truman chose to follow their lead.

President Truman had good reasons for approving Operation Olympic at this point. His trusted military leaders and everyone at the meeting either supported the invasion plans or raised no serious objections to it.

The atomic bomb remained untested and just a possible ace up Truman's sleeve. If he knew it worked and if the Japanese had not yet surrendered, he would have to seriously consider using it in hopes of ending the war as quickly as possible and avoiding the invasion and the horrific US casualties it foretold.

The president's meeting with the Joint Chiefs and service secretaries took place before one of the recipients of the Hoover Memo, Stimson, had been able to submit his written response. Stimson's written reply stated,

> The terrain [on Kyūshū], much of which I have visited several times, has left the impression on my memory of being one which would be susceptible to a last ditch defense such as has been made on Iwo Jima and Okinawa and which of course is very much larger than either of those two areas.
>
> ...We shall in my opinion have to go through a more bitter finish fight than in Germany [and] we shall incur the losses incident to such a war.[109]

Stimson's remarks contradicted King's comment, which emphasized "room to maneuver," because once ashore the attacks consisted of a series of frontal assaults. Perhaps Stimson understood what Marshall and King omitted, which was that the Japanese ultimately decided where they wanted to fight on the battlefield, as evidenced in the battle for Okinawa where much of the island was left undefended. There, the Japanese confined the battle to places where they could take full advantage of the topographical features to build the best possible defenses, and it only made sense they would do the same thing on Kyūshū.

In the meeting just concluded, Marshall, per US Army doctrine which preferred to use ratios, had stayed away from providing a definitive invasion estimate, other than for the first thirty days, and even then chose the lowest number he could to present to the President. Army planners had other ratios that pointed to far higher numbers. In seven previous amphibious campaigns in the Pacific, the casualty

rate had run 7.45 per thousand troops per day, whereas in the protracted land warfare in the European Theater of Operations it had
been only 2.16.[110]

On August 30, 1944, several weeks after the end of the Battle of
Saipan, the JCS's Joint Strategic Survey Committee, responsible for
changes to "Operations Against Japan Subsequent to Formosa," estimated there would be 3.5 million Japanese troops available for the
defense of the home islands. For casualty and manpower estimates,
the planners concluded that "in our Saipan operation, it cost approximately one American killed and several wounded to exterminate
seven Japanese soldiers." Applying the new "Saipan Ratio" to the invasion of Japan meant as many as half a million American lives could be
lost and many times that number wounded.[111]

A measure of the validity given to the Saipan Ratio was the fact that
General Marshall chose to use it to project casualties for upcoming
operations and for determining the Army's manpower needs for 1945.
In March 1945, the ratio factored heavily in the decision to increase
levees from 60,000 men to 100,000 per month for the US Army.[112] And
that was just for the army. Historian D.M. Giangreco tells us, "The Navy
and Marine Corps counted separately and brought the total March
call up to more than 141,000—nearly every man inducted would enter
the 'replacement stream,' now oriented for a one-front war against
Japan."[113] To be clear, these draftees were to serve as replacements for
the invasion forces that were already in theater in the case of Olympic,
or the many veterans from the grim struggle to defeat Nazi Germany
who would soon be on their way from Europe for Coronet.

JUNE 19, 1945
48 DAYS TO HIROSHIMA

MacArthur's follow-up message reached Marshall the day after the
briefing with the president.

19 JUNE 1945
FROM: GENERAL MACARTHUR
TO: GENERAL MARSHALL (PERSONAL)
C–19848

Estimate of casualties contained in my C–19571 was a routine
report submitted direct by a staff section without higher reference

for medical and replacement planning purposes. The estimate was derived from the casualty rates in Normandy and Okinawa the highest our forces have sustained at 3.8 men per thousand per day. The total force involved was estimated at 681,000 with one half engaged for the first 15 days and the entire strength thereafter. The estimate is purely academic and routine and was made for planning alone. It had not come to my prior attention. I do not anticipate such a high rate of loss. [114]

Interestingly, MacArthur's purportedly high casualty ratio of 3.8 was still only half of the rate, 7.45, used in other studies at the Pentagon for casualties in the Pacific Theater.[115] Unknown to all of the men attending the June 18 meeting was the full extent of what the Japanese had in store for their American invaders.

5

KETSU-GŌ,
"THE DECISIVE OPERATION"

With the fall of Okinawa on June 22, 1945, forty-five days before Hiroshima, the United States had driven the Japanese back nearly 3,200 miles from Guadalcanal. Now only 350 miles from Kyūshū, the southernmost of Japan's main islands, the invasion of Japan gathered strength just beyond the horizon like a giant tsunami. Defeat this time would mean the permanent end of Japan's dreams of empire.

The Japanese battle plan to thwart Downfall was called Ketsu-Gō, *Decisive Operation*—a concept not unfamiliar in the nation's history. The Japanese military had been enamored with the idea of decisive, war-winning battles dating back to its defeat of the Soviets in the Russo-Japanese War and its stunning naval victories. In its war with the United States the decisive-battle concept began with Japan's surprise attack on Pearl Harbor in December of 1941. Six months later, it reappeared in the nation's failed attempt to destroy America's remaining carriers at the time in the Pacific near Midway, and a few months later in the Battle of Guadalcanal.

In the summer of 1944, it began anew in Japan's failed attempt to destroy the American invasion of the Marianas Islands and in her last great carrier offensive of the Pacific War in the Battle of the Philippine Sea. By the fall of 1944, the "decisive" battle line shifted to the defense of the Philippines and Japan's vital shipping lanes to Asia. And finally, in April of 1945, it culminated in Japan's miscarried effort to hold Okinawa. Now, after more than three years of never-ending rollback and defeat, the battle and its outcome would indeed be decisive.

In response to the unremitting destruction of Japan's Pacific empire, the first plan for the defense of the homeland, the *Shō-Go* (victory) plan, had been approved on July 24, 1944, a few weeks after the fall of Saipan. By mid-January 1945, it became clear that a new and far-reaching strategic plan was necessary to replace the now-defunct Shō-Go plan.

Realizing the invasion of Japan may be only months away, the

Imperial Army and Navy completed the first iteration of the new plan, and on January 19, when Imperial General Headquarters presented a policy directive known as the "Outline of Army and Navy Operations" to the Emperor for Imperial sanction. Hirohito approved the plans immediately, in time for them to be formally distributed to field commands the following day, clear evidence that he knew of the plans well in advance of January 19th. The document became the basis for all future planning for the defense of the home islands.

GENERAL POLICY

1. The final decisive battle of the war will be waged in Japan Proper.
2. The armed forces of the Empire will prepare for this battle by immediately establishing a strong strategic position in depth within the confines of a national defense sphere delineated by the Bonin Islands, Formosa, the coastal sector of east China, and southern Korea.
3. The United States will now be considered Japan's principal enemy. Operational planning of all headquarters will be directed toward interception and destruction of American forces, all other theaters and adversaries assuming secondary importance.

PREPARATION AND CONDUCT OF OPERATIONS

1. Resistance will continue in the Philippines so as to delay as long as possible the enemy's approach to the Homeland defense perimeter.
2. Key strongpoints to be developed within the perimeter defense zone include Iwo Jima, Formosa, Okinawa, the Shanghai district, and the South Korean coast. The main defensive effort will be made in the Ryukyus area. Preparations in the perimeter defense zone will be completed during February and March 1945.
3. Emphasis in ground preparations will be laid on Kyūshū and Kanto. Strong air defenses will be established along key lines of communication, such as the Shimonoseki and Korea Straits, and at important ports and communications centers such as Tokyo, Nagoya, Osaka-Kobe, and the Moji-Kokura-Yawata area.
4. During the delaying operations in the forward area, preparations for the decisive battle will be completed in Japan Proper by the early fall of 1945.

5. In general, Japanese air strength will be conserved until an enemy landing is actually underway on or within the defensive sphere. The Allied invasion fleet will then be destroyed on the water, principally by sea and air special-attack units.[1]

The first noteworthy statement in the plan was that the US would be considered Japan's primary enemy. This remained true even as the war dramatically ramped up in 1944 and it became increasingly probable to the Japanese that the Soviets would eventually enter the war against them. Secondly, since the United States had not yet launched its invasions of Iwo Jima and Okinawa, both strongpoints in Japan's outer defenses, the plan called for further bolstering them as part of a delaying action to buy time to complete defenses in Japan proper. While both were included in the plan, the total domination of the air and seas by American forces made it impossible to do anything to aid the Japanese defending Iwo Jima.

However, Okinawa was a different story, actually two—one fought on land, the other in the air over the seas surrounding the island. Japanese ground forces conducted a tenacious and bitter defense on Okinawa, inflicting troubling casualties on the Americans during the protracted land battle that lasted eighty-two days.

At the same time, the separate air battle raged over the waters surrounding the island, as Japan hurled nearly 2,000 kamikazes, mostly from Kyūshū, at the Allied fleet supporting the troops on shore. The battle cost the American Navy 10,000 casualties, 5,000 lives lost, over 30 ships sunk, and more than 300 damaged, greater than those suffered during the Battle of Guadalcanal.

In both areas, the fanatical and suicidal efforts of the Japanese soldiers and airmen on and around Okinawa did succeed in buying precious time to improve the defenses of the Japanese mainland.

The January 19–20 outline also revealed the top priority: the defenses for Kyūshū and the Kanto Plain around Tokyo. The nation's military, according to historian D. M. Giangreco, "had correctly deduced that the principal invasion operations would come in the fall of 1945 on the southern island of Kyūshū and in the early spring of 1946 near Tokyo."[2] As such, these two regions received the lion's share of Japan's material and manpower resources.

Meanwhile, air strength would be conserved as much as possible, overwhelmingly for special-attack units. This meant there would be very little fighter resistance to LeMay's strategic bombing offensive against Japan and the ever more powerful American fighter sweeps of up to 800 planes launched from carriers, Okinawa, and Iwo Jima.

Lastly, the strategy for Ketsu-Gō would differ from the recent battles for Iwo Jima and Okinawa, where the Americans were allowed to come ashore only to be met by intense fire from multiple directions in well-fortified defenses built into the most advantageous terrain. Ketsu-Gō instead relied primarily on the massive use of special-attack forces that would attempt to destroy much of the invasion force at sea. Then the landing forces would be contained and then destroyed by mass counterattacks.

The generic Japanese term for all suicide operations is *tokko*, whether by air, sea, or land. Most often, when history considers Japan's use of suicide tactics during the war, it's the kamikaze pilots crashing their planes into American warships that take center stage. For Ketsu-Gō, suicide attacks were to be performed on a scale beyond anything previously seen and would be conducted in the air as well as the sea and on land.

The major objective of the combined Army and Navy air forces was to locate and annihilate the American forces while still afloat. Kamikazes were to target troop ships and equipment transports to crush the invasion by inflicting overwhelming casualties. The Japanese planned to use just over half of their 10,440 special-attack aircraft during the invasion of Kyūshū.[3] The figure was more than two and half times the number launched against the Allied naval forces supporting the Okinawa invasion. Tactically, the Imperial Army envisioned dispatching waves of three to four hundred planes about every hour. The Army expected the Navy to fly an equal number. Under those projections, the Japanese believed they could saturate the invasion fleet with as many kamikazes in three hours as they had sent against Okinawa in nearly three months.[4]

Imperial General Headquarters (IGHQ) staff officers relied on reported results of the Battle of Okinawa. They calculated that they had sunk fifty percent of American's assault shipping. While those numbers were nowhere close to reality, the Japanese had caused severe damage, and this time they would not be flying 350 miles to reach their targets. For Ketsu-Gō, Japan's military believed they could destroy twenty percent of the Allied troop transports at sea, the equivalent of five combat divisions.[5]

Allied carrier task forces would also be attacked to interdict tactical air support of the Allied landings. The Japanese even believed they could provide support for their own ground troops, something they hadn't been able to do since the early days of the war. The main emphasis would be on attacking Allied surface ships engaged in shore fire support for American ground troops. These attacks were to be synchronized with the local counter-offensive activities of Japanese land forces.[6]

In addition to over 10,000 kamikazes, the Imperial Navy was in the process of deploying an array of nautical special-attack vessels and personnel. Included among these were 1,235 small high-speed boats called *Shinyo*, which exploded upon contact with an enemy ship; two types of midget submarines, the *Kairyu* and the *Koryu*; and manned torpedoes called *Kaiten*, approximately 1,000 in all.[7] The Navy had also trained several thousand men as special-attack swimmers known as *Fukuryu* (human mines). These men would lay in wait near the water's edge up to thirty feet below the surface in rubber diving suits armed with a Type 5 attack mine. The mine contained a ten-kilogram TNT charge. The diver simply pushed the mine against a boat or ship to detonate it.

While Ketsu-Gō called for the maximum destruction of the invasion at sea, the Japanese were nevertheless prepared for those Americans who made it ashore. Here, too, the plan demanded an uncompromising defense.[8] The Japanese viewed tanks as America's most effective land weapon, especially when equipped with a flame-thrower, and they expected the US to make extensive use of them in large armored formations during the invasion. The Japanese were ill-equipped to engage this menace with conventional means, such as with Japanese tanks and anti-tank weapons. However, combat operations in the Philippines and Okinawa had identified an alternative. By employing mass special attacks of men carrying mines or other explosive devices, who would most often roll under a tank and explode themselves, the Japanese had been able to destroy or disable American tanks.

Suicidal attacks by kamikazes have often been depicted by the Japanese as a glorious and supreme expression of devotion to the Emperor and of the unequaled fighting spirit of its people, who voluntarily and willingly sacrificed their lives to save the Empire. But this portrayal is more myth than reality. Japanese journalist and war correspondent Toshiro Takagi covered the special attack corps in Chiran (the principal kamikaze airbase during the Battle of Okinawa located on Kagoshima) and devoted much of his postwar life to chronicling the real kamikaze. His meticulous research, later published as the book entitled *Chiran*, became a best seller in Japan, and it was later translated into English by Roger Pineau and published by the U.S. Naval Institute as *The Divine Wind*. Takagi details the sordid reality behind this cherry blossom myth:

> "Volunteers"…joined after intensive psychological pressure or from personnel assigned to the duty. Pilots who returned to base without carrying out their mission because of mechanical malfunction were derided. They had to face ostracism and comments like "Why did you come back alive?" and "A coward who is afraid to die is a disgrace to the special-attack unit." The condemned pilots suffered terrible mental anguish. Many were so desperate that they crashed their planes into the ground or into the ocean just to end it all.[9]

In fact, the use of suicidal forces had, on January 18, 1945, been made into official government policy by the Supreme Council at the Direction of War. The Council decided to concentrate on converting all armament production to special-attack weapons of a few major types.[10]

On February 26, discussions between the Japanese High Command and War Ministry had culminated in the adoption of a substantial mobilization: the creation of forty-two new divisions, eighteen independent mixed brigades, and six tank brigades. The bulk of these forces were to be added to the one armored and eight-line combat divisions and seven independent mixed brigades already in existence. The process of mobilizing this enormous force was to be accomplished in three stages, the first from late February to early April, the second from March through the month of April, and third by the end of September and the expected invasion of Kyūshū.[11]

Providing weapons and equipment for all these men was a significant matter. Existing Army ordnance supplies coupled with the next two months' production and the movement of some supplies from the Asian continent was sufficient to allow units to at least begin training. If production could be maintained, the shortfalls could be met by September.[12]

In March, to strengthen these untested soldiers, IGHQ moved the highly experienced 11th, 25th, and 1st Armored Divisions from

Manchuria to Japan. At the same time, it also transferred three other divisions, the 111th, 120th, and 121st, from the Kwantung Army to Korea to protect against a possible attack by the Americans.[13] The depletion of the once formidable Kwantung Army only stopped when Japan reacted to the Soviets' April 5 statement that they would not be renewing their neutrality pact.[14] This massive mobilization of forty-five new divisions, sixteen of them strong mobile formations, with the remainder used for coastal defense, was far greater than what MacArthur's headquarters had predicted in March of 1945.[15]

From March 6–23, Japan's Cabinet enacted a series of measures to strengthen internal defense and increase production. The first created the National Labor Ordinance, the second suspended school classes above grade six for the next twelve months, and the third formed the Patriotic Citizens Fighting Corps, which morphed into the National Volunteer Corps by mid-April.[16]

Two months afterward, the Japanese Diet (legislature) expanded the responsibilities of the force with the enactment of the Volunteer Military Service Law. The newest law turned the aforementioned National Volunteer Corps into a paramilitary group that required service by all men from fifteen to sixty and all women ages seventeen to forty.[17] Members of the group could be called upon to perform any number of civilian activities, but could also—if needed—be required to fight alongside regular military units.

Historian Edward Drea tells of a related story about one of his former Japanese professors, stating he:

> contacted [his] professor in Tokyo, who was sixteen years old in 1945 and well-remembered the People's Volunteer Corps—he was in it. His equipment consisted of a bamboo spear and a backpack filled with two large stones. He practiced huddling in a dank, stinking foxhole, waiting for the Americans. If the enemy approached, he would exchange his stones for a land mine. His mission was to destroy an enemy tank, and himself, with it. Reflecting back, the training, indeed the whole notion, was similar to something out of a demented cartoon. But, he emphasized, the military was serious. And if the Americans landed, he is certain he would have perished.[18]

Apparently believing the age limits to be too restrictive, noted US Asian Pacific historian Timothy Maga tells of a macabre plan:

the Ikego Defense League [south of Tokyo that] went so far as to build over 10,000 [ceramic pot bombs for use by its children]. Perfectly secured from Allied bombing raids, the pots were stockpiled in caves located within the Ikego Naval Air Station itself. Japanese Imperial Army and Navy personnel willingly participated in this arrangement, promising to pass out the bombs to the children shortly after the Americans hit the beach.[19]

Nationwide, 28,000,000 civilians fell under the control of the new laws.[20] Their weapons included: single-shot muzzle-loading muskets, longbows, sharpened bamboo spears, and pitchforks.[21] According to the 1944 Japanese census, the three prefectures over which the battle for the lower one third of Kyūshū (Olympic) would have been fought contained a population of nearly 4,000,000 people, a large percentage of whom would have been forced to participate in its defense.

Manuals and directives distributed for Ketsu-Gō stressed the use of suicide tactics. Military personnel as well as civilians were to be trained in the use of all the types of hand-carried mines and explosives to carry out such attacks.[22] The *People's Handbook of Resistance Combat*, published by the government in 1945, read, in part:

> Should the enemy invade our homeland, 100 million of us, as the Special-Attacking Forces, must exterminate them to protect our native soil and maintain our everlasting empire…The safety pin must be removed from Molotov cocktails, which should be hurled so that the side of the bottle impacts against vehicles. In aiming against the descending enemy parachutists, allow two-and-half lengths. When engaging tall Yankees, do not swing swords or spears sideways or straight down; thrust straight into their guts. Attack from behind employing hatchets, sickles, hooks, or cleavers. In karate or judo assaults, smash the Yankee in the pit of his stomach or kick him in the testicles.

The implications for civilian casualties were frightening. During the previous two Pacific War battles where a large Japanese civilian population inhabited the island, the losses—without the now-mandated direct participation—were already horrific. On Saipan, from a population of 25,000, approximately 5,000 to 7,000 citizens perished, many encouraged by their Emperor or forced by the Japanese Army to commit suicide within the island's plentiful caves or by leaping to their death from the cliffs on the northern end of the island. On the much bigger island of Okinawa, where the civilian population numbered 450,000, estimates ranged from 50,000 to as many as 150,000 (or one third of the population) killed, and once again the majority of the deaths were anything but voluntary. And as terrible as those figures portended for the civilian population, it likely would have been even worse, as Lieutenant General Torashirō Kawabe would testify:

> While it was not the intention of the High Command that children or the sick and aged be drawn into the Homeland battle, there were, however, seemingly insurmountable obstacles to the evacuation of [all] civilians from the coastal areas. For one thing, almost all food production depended upon the labor of these non–combatants. Food could only be grown in the arable land near the coast. The physical problems of evacuation—transportation, food, shelter, and sanitary facilities for millions of people—also militated against this move. The local commanders had still not found effective measures to cope with these difficult problems by the time of the surrender.

If the American invasion managed to secure any significant piece of the homeland, Ketsu-Gō dictated the fierce loyalty of the citizenry who were not only expected to fight, but like their military brethren, sacrifice their lives by attacking the American armor in suicidal waves from every direction.

This was how Japan's leaders believed they should wage the final decisive battle to save the homeland from an enemy vastly superior in technical resources.[23] The government was deadly serious in its belief that every man, woman, and child in Japan should become human explosives and throw themselves beneath the enemy's tanks.[24]

According to historian Paul Fussell, "[An] intelligence officer of the U.S. Fifth Air Force declared on July 21, 1945, that 'the entire population of Japan is a proper military target,' and he added emphatically, 'There are no civilians in Japan.'"[25] Further, because the Japanese lacked uniforms for this mass militia, no American serviceman at any reasonable combat range would have been able to immediately distinguish combatants from noncombatants, perhaps with the exclusion of the extremely young and the very old. But everyone else would have to be regarded as a potential or real combatant.

At first, the comment may seem like an incredibly harsh view of civilians. But Japan's plan to incorporate civilians into the defense, placing them precisely in harm's way, was a grim fact not missed by American codebreakers.

As Japan prepared to sacrifice its citizenry for the cause, it also ratcheted up preparations in the two geographic areas emphasized in the January 19–20 plan: the Kanto area surrounding Tokyo (Ketsu No. 3) and Kyūshū (Ketsu No. 6), deemed the most likely first target of an American invasion. Emergency preparations on Kyūshū were to be completed by early June.[26] American military reports to senior leaders calculated "the logistics base supporting [these defenses] (excluding Korea) [was]…2,903,000 men, 292,000 horses, and 27,500 motor vehicles."[27]

Responsibility for preparing the ground defenses for Kyūshū belonged to Field Marshal Shunroku Hata, Commander-in-Chief Second General Army, and under him, Lieutenant General Isamu Yokoyama, Commander of Sixteenth Area Army assigned to Kyūshū. Even though Ketsu-Gō Operation No. 6 was considered the official guide for the Kyūshū defense, the Sixteenth Area Army prepared its own more detailed plan, known as the Mutsu Operation. It split Kyūshū into three districts and further divided those areas into seven sub-divisions. Altogether, the Sixteenth Area Army had three armies and two special forces for a total strength of fifteen divisions. Included in those were one antiaircraft division, seven independent mixed brigades, three independent tank brigades, and two fortress units.[28] And despite the emphasis placed on defeating the invasion at sea and on the beaches, the Japanese were nonetheless constructing inland fortifications, which in general were further advanced in Kyūshū than in other areas of Japan, including the Kanto Plain.

But while Japan attempted to accelerate its military defense preparation, by the summer of 1945, critical shortages were devastating the Japanese economy. In June, imports of heavy coking coal from North China had ceased, crippling heavy industry. Although the domestic production of coal held up fairly well, it proved to be almost impossible to move coal in any appreciable amount due to the American submarine and mining blockade of Japan's major ports.

The shortage of coal most deeply affected the production of iron, steel, cement, and non-ferrous metals. By the beginning of July, iron and steel production stood at a mere thirty-five percent of its wartime

peak, cement at just forty-six percent. The non-ferrous metals of cop-
per and magnesium likewise fell to barely thirty-five percent of their
peaks, with aluminum plummeting to a disastrous sixteen percent.[29]

One of the most critical resources in the decisive battle plans was
oil, which was also in short supply despite efforts to conserve or minimize its use. Military consumption of about 155,390 barrels during the
month of June had further reduced the stockpile of aviation gasoline to
508,160 barrels, of which 333,900 barrels were earmarked for decisive
battle operations. Production from all sources had declined sharply
during July to a paltry 60,890 barrels, with a total reserve of just five
million barrels.[30] One of the few bright spots had come a few months
earlier when, as historian Dennis Giangreco noted, "a dozen tankers
[docked] at the Borneo oilfields were ordered to be topped off with all
the refined fuel they could carry in March 1945. The tankers were then
rushed north before U.S. airpower choked off the shipping routes to
the home islands. This refined fuel formed a secret strategic reserve,
held back from training and ongoing tactical needs, that was to be used
solely for kamikaze operations defending Japan itself."[31] But as dire as
the situation appeared, there still would have been more than enough
fuel for the 5,350 kamikaze sorties planned for the defense of Kyūshū,
which, would have "required only about 50,000 barrels [2,100,000 gal-
lons] of aviation gasoline." According the USSBS study after the war as
well as several Japanese military sources, somewhere between 59,000
(15,586,620 gallons) and 70,000 kiloliters (18,492,756 gallons) existed
by July of 1945. All of Ketsu-Gō required 40,000 kiloliters (10,567,200
gallons) of fuel.[32]

By June, production trends clearly indicated that Japan's war industry was incapable of adequately supporting the immense structure of
the Homeland Defense Forces and the tactical and strategic plans
devised for their use. The priority enjoyed by the units in Kyūshū was
draining off almost all of the material strength of the military establishment. While this meant that preparations for the decisive battle in
Kyūshū would be almost certainly completed, it also meant that Kyūshū
would very likely be the only area in which a decisive battle could be
supported.[33]

Food was also becoming increasingly scarce. With rice—the national
staple—in short supply, people in urban areas were forced to use flour
made from sweet potato vines, mulberry leaves, pumpkins, and horse
chestnuts. In a letter to the editor of the Tokyo *Yomiuri-Hochi* newspaper

that somehow avoided the keen eyes of the censors, a person bemoaned the effects of the available food: "The number of emaciated men and women…is conspicuous. Everyone is suffering from diarrhea…No one can work properly, and production will inevitably decline. The problem is the flour…If we are to win the war, we must be supplied with food that will not make us sick."[34] Adding to the woes was a forecast for the fall rice harvest to be one of the worst in years, and with transportation breaking down, moving what there was to areas of need was becoming increasingly difficult.

By the end of June, the firebombing of Japanese cities had left thirteen million Japanese homeless.[35] Millions had fled Japan's major cities for the countryside, taking what few possessions they had left along with their labor, further reducing the country's productive capacity.

Yet, despite the calamitous economic circumstances and loss of life, Army War Minister General Korechika Anami and most of Japan's military leaders were certain their counterattack to the invasion of southern Kyūshū could achieve its objective—which did not have to mean total victory. They believed it only needed to convince Truman that the bloodletting on Kyūshū foretold an unbearable ultimate cost that would force the president to suit for a peace acceptable to the Japanese. They thought the Americans would be completely surprised and overwhelmed by their massive forces.

Commanding the First General Army, General Umezu stated:

> In concentrating the entire national strength to destroy the enemy, ten Japanese soldiers would be sacrificed to kill one enemy, if necessary. The main objective would be to annihilate every enemy soldier, leaving none alive in the homeland.

He reiterated that this was not just a simple defense; but as the final, glorious struggle to preserve the nation, the lives of the men were of no consideration—men and officers would attack relentlessly over the bodies of their fallen comrades until the invaders were destroyed.

While it may be difficult to comprehend the willingness of Japan's military leaders to shed the blood of their own people on such an incredible scale, those same leaders were confident, rightfully so, that their plans would have also extracted an extremely high toll in American blood, but only if the Americans invaded. Japan's military had no answer for the other option available to Truman, blockade and bombardment; an alternative that was about to include atomic weapons.

By the end of July, it was clear to American intelligence in the Pacific and Washington that the Japanese had correctly anticipated the location for the Olympic operation and were placing their forces accordingly.[36] Postwar calculations by American intelligence—just five days after Japan's surrender—showed that the incredible build-up of troops on Kyūshū had reached 900,000 men, with three months remaining before the commencement of Operation Olympic.[37] America's Joint Staff Planners had based their invasion plans for Olympic on a Japanese defense force of 350,000 men.

But as the summer wore on, planning issues mounted for the Japanese. There was a growing concern among the High Command over the operational emphasis on Kyūshū and the demand for so much of the country's military supplies to support it. The flow had become so great that some planners thought it might not be possible to properly defend the Kanto Plain if an attack came before the end of the year.

The severe limitations of Japan's strategic intelligence added to the apprehension. The Americans' total superiority by air and sea right up to the shores of Japan meant it was impossible to get direct observation of American forces with any degree of frequency, even by Japanese submarines. As a result, its intelligence was forced to rely on radio intercepts. However, this had critical deficiencies, too, especially in determining the direction, timing, and strength of an attack.[38]

One thing the Japanese did know, which required no intelligence gathering, was the Americans' upcoming meeting with the British and Soviets at Potsdam. The consequences of those meetings reverberate to this day.

6

POTSDAM DECLARATION, A MISSED OPPORTUNITY

On May 31, 1945, Secretary of War Henry Stimson told the members of the Interim Committee,

> It is our responsibility to recommend action that may turn the course of civilization. In our hands we expect soon to have a weapon of wholly unprecedented destructive power. Today's prime fact is war. Our great task is to bring this war to a prompt and successful conclusion. We may assume that our new weapon puts in our hands overwhelming power. It is our obligation to use this power with the best wisdom we can command. To us now the matter of first importance is how our use of this new weapon will appear in the long view of history.

In response, General Marshall, a guest at the meeting, told the committee there was no question in his mind that the bomb should be used in the war as soon as it became available. It would save American lives. However, he did not want his position to influence the members in their deliberations. He then added that his ultimate preference would not be to use the bomb against Japan because it would reveal to the Soviets the new weapon's power and lessen its deterrent effect in the postwar world.[1]

By the later part of May, the problematic nature of US-Soviet relations had become well known among the top echelons of American political and military leaders. Truman was struggling to find the right approach and was being counseled alternatively by both moderate and stern advisors. In this context, Marshall preferred to keep the atomic bomb as a future trump card.

During lunch, the conversation turned to a different but related topic when Dr. Arthur Compton turned to Stimson and asked "if some nonmilitary demonstration couldn't be arranged to impress the Japanese." A discussion over the possible options ensued. If the demonstration took place in Japan and an announcement were made in advance, the Japanese might attempt to shoot down the plane, potentially killing the crew and recovering the unexploded bomb and/or place American POWs in the location. The bomb could legitimately be viewed as an experimental weapon; as such, any number of things could go wrong, including its failure to explode. If the demonstration took place on neutral ground, Japanese observers might think it had been faked. Detonating the bomb over water would produce a huge geyser; over a deserted island it would knock down a bunch of palm trees—but neither would display the awesome destruction the bomb would cause to a city. No one at the meeting believed a bloodless demonstration could sway Japan's military leaders, and its non-military use would eliminate the shock value of the new weapon and at the same time waste a bomb that was still in relatively short supply. With only unsatisfactory outcomes, the committee concluded that the bomb should be used as soon as possible "against such a target as to make clear it's a devastating strength" and without warning. All three of the Interim Committee scientists: Vannevar Bush, James B. Conant, and Karl Compton concurred.[2]

Over the next couple of weeks several Manhattan Project scientists would weigh in on this topic. James Franck, at the University of Chicago, disagreed with the recommendation and wrote a report arguing against the bomb's use. In response to the report and after a lengthy conversation at the Los Alamos Scientific Laboratory, Compton, J. Robert Oppenheimer, Ernest Lawrence, and Enrico Fermi wrote their rejoinder to the Franck report. They agreed with the earlier findings of the Interim Committee, stating, "We can propose no technical demonstration likely to bring an end to the war; we see no acceptable alternative to direct military use."[3]

On June 6, Stimson brought the Interim Committee's recommendation to the president. It concluded:

> That we could not give the Japanese any warning; that we could not concentrate on a civilian area; but that we should seek to make a profound psychological impression on as many of the inhabitants as possible. At the suggestion of Dr. Conant, the Secretary [Stimson] agreed that the most desirable target would be a vital war plant

employing a large number of workers and closely surrounded by workers' houses.[4]

The independent Target Committee had previously provided Stimson a list of recommended Japanese cities spared from the ongoing firebombing campaign where the bomb might be used. Stimson eliminated Kyoto because of its cultural and religious significance, then four cities were shown to the president as initial targets: Hiroshima, Kokura, Niigata, and Nagasaki. The cities were ordered based on their respective military value.

Prior to giving his presidential approval, Truman reviewed the justification for each target with Stimson, Marshall, and Arnold, as well as the timing for the first bomb and final choice for the first city to be bombed.

JUNE 30, 1945
38 DAYS TO HIROSHIMA

With the all-important Potsdam Conference a little more than two weeks away, Japan's Foreign Minister Tōgō instructed Ambassador Naotake Satō to see Soviet Foreign Minister Vyacheslav Molotov and "do everything in your power to lead the Russians along the lines we desire."[5] Tōgō's message to the Soviets, to be delivered by Satō, was that Japan sought:

> Firm and lasting relations of friendship...be established between Japan and Russia and [that] they shall both cooperate in the maintenance of peace in East Asia...A treaty shall be concluded between the two countries which shall assure mutual assistance on problems involving the maintenance of peace in East Asia and relations based on the principle of nonaggression.

Tōgō then offered up a few incentives:

> We have no objections to an agreement involving Manchukuo's [Japan's name for its puppet state in Manchuria] neutralization... We have no objection to renouncing our fisheries rights provided that Russia agrees to supply us with oil...We have no objection to discussing any matter which the Russians would like to bring up for discussion.[6]

Three months earlier, the Soviets had of course already renounced the Soviet–Japanese Neutrality Pact, and Japanese intelligence had been reporting Soviet troop and military equipment movements east for several months.

Satō wasn't impressed by Tōgō's offer and made it very clear (within a day or two as his response appeared in the same MAGIC Summary as Tōgō's instructions to him did) that he believed the effort was a misguided initiative with no chance for a positive outcome:

> If the purpose of this interview [with Molotov] is merely to sound out Russia's attitude, that...is one thing. If, however, we desire something more, I cannot help feeling that we will be going against the general worldwide trend—particularly in the matter of Russia's relations with England and America...They have been steadily improving—witness, for example, the establishment of the United Nations Charter and the reform of the Provisional Government in Poland—and I personally believe that this trend will continue... [Today] Japan [is] considered by world opinion as the one obstacle to the restoration of world peace.
>
> From these facts, it seems extremely unlikely that Russia would flout the Anglo-Americans and the opinion of the entire world by supporting Japan's war effort with either moral or material means...I believe that the conference [with Molotov] will have to be limited to the settlement of issues in dispute between Russia and Japan. If it should go beyond such minor questions, the reaction of the Anglo-Americans and the entire world would be tremendous. I believe that the Russians would feel absolutely unable to consent to that.[7]

Thus began a running series of communiqués between Tōgō and Satō that lasted until two days before the bombing of Hiroshima. The exchange established a pattern between the two men—Tōgō with vague and unrealistic requests, and Satō with candid (uncharacteristic for a diplomat) rebuffs intended to drive home the harsh reality of Japan's situation.

Assuming Tōgō's message to Satō accurately represented the position of Prime Minister Suzuki's government, then its political strategy represented a denial of military and geo-political circumstances coupled with an unfounded belief in the power of repetition. If Japan repeated their request to the Soviets enough times, eventually—the thinking goes—the Russians would relent and either become an ally, a supplier of much needed war materials, and/or an intermediary to negotiate an end of the war with the Anglo-American Allies. And yet, the Japanese would stake everything on it.

JULY 2, 1945
35 DAYS TO HIROSHIMA

On Monday, July 2, President Truman met with Stimson and Secretary of State James Byrnes to discuss the Secretary of War's recommendations for an Allied declaration, to be sent during the Potsdam Conference, giving Japan one last chance to surrender. Truman said to Stimson, "I understand you have some thoughts that you'd like to discuss prior to the upcoming meeting in Potsdam with Churchill and Stalin." Stimson conveyed his belief that the Allies should warn the Japanese of what was about to happen to them; specifically, the atomic bomb (once proven), and that Russia would be entering the conflict on the Allied side. He also thought, concurring with Under Secretary of State Joseph Grew, that the United States should promise the Japanese they would be permitted to retain the Emperor.[8] He proposed the following language regarding the Emperor, to be included in Paragraph 12 of the declaration:

> The occupying forces of the Allies shall be withdrawn from Japan as soon as these objectives have been accomplished and there has been established in accordance with the freely expressed will of the Japanese people a peacefully inclined and responsible government. This may include a constitutional monarchy under the present Dynasty if the peace-loving nations can be convinced of the genuine determination of such a government to follow policies of peace which will render impossible the future development of aggressive militarism in Japan.

Byrnes, who had recently been installed by Truman as the new Secretary of State, questioned the last sentence of the paragraph, believing public sentiment weighed heavily against it. Truman wanted time to ponder it, something he and Byrnes would do during the long voyage to Europe for the conference.

As a follow-up to their conversation, Stimson wrote a Memorandum For the President, entitled "Proposed Program for Japan." The lengthy document contained six articles, but interestingly did not include any statements about preserving Japan's imperial system, perhaps because of Byrnes's pushback.

Stimson's real purpose in writing the memorandum was to convince the president to modify the demand for unconditional surrender. By making the change, he hoped the Allies could obtain Japan's surrender in advance of the American invasion of Kyūshū. In article 2, Stimson wrote:

"There is reason to believe that the operation for the occupation of Japan following the landing may be a very long, costly and arduous struggle on our part."

Once again, as was the case at the June 18 meeting to brief the president about the invasion plans for Japan, the basis for Stimson's assertion was rooted in his knowledge of the Japanese terrain where Olympic would be fought, the southern one third of Kyūshū, an area he had visited several times, saying it:

> Left the impression on my memory of being one which would be susceptible to a last-ditch defense such as has been made on Iwo Jima and Okinawa and which of course is very much larger than either of those two areas. According to my recollection it will be much more unfavorable with regard to tank maneuvering than either the Philippines or Germany.

In article 4, getting to the heart of his proposal, Stimson posed the question:

> Is there any alternative to such a forceful occupation of Japan which will secure for us the equivalent of an unconditional surrender of her forces and a permanent destruction of her power again to strike an aggressive blow at the "peace of the Pacific?" I am inclined to think that there is enough such chance to make it well worthwhile giving them a warning of what is to come and a definite opportunity to capitulate.

Also, in article 4, Stimson added:

I believe Japan is susceptible to reason in such a crisis to a much greater extent than is indicated by our current press and our current comment. Japan is not a nation composed wholly of mad fanatics of an entirely different mentality from ours.

In sub-article "b," he continued:

I think she has within her population enough liberal leaders (although now submerged by the terrorists) to be depended upon for reconstruction as a reasonable member of the family of nations…The liberals yielded only at the point of the pistol and, so far as I'm aware, there liberal attitude has not been personally subverted in the way which was so general in Germany.

Stimson's faith in the submerged liberal peace faction and its ability to influence or gain control of the government ran contrary to the intelligence garnered from MAGIC—the Allied codebreaking operation—which consistently showed the Japanese militarists firmly in control, or at minimum able to block any moves toward peace. Nevertheless, it would soon become clear that Stimson's thinking would greatly influence the Potsdam Declaration soon to come and a nuanced definition of "unconditional surrender" for Japan to consider.

JULY 7, 1945
30 DAYS TO HIROSHIMA

On July 7, President Truman departed for the Potsdam Conference aboard the *USS Augusta*, a 10,000-ton *Northampton*-class cruiser. The ship had already had a distinguished career during the war serving as the headquarters for Operations Torch, Overlord, and Dragoon, as well as performing as the flagship for Roosevelt and now Truman. Transporting the president was "like moving a circus," Truman joked. In addition to the *Augusta*, the light cruiser *USS Philadelphia* made the Atlantic crossing with members of the State and War Departments, the Army, Navy, and Army Air Forces, White House staff, and the Secret Service. Truman's immediate party, only a fraction of the total, numbered fifty-three.[9]

Truman used the eight days at sea to prepare for the conference and continue his deliberation on important matters, scheduling a series of working sessions with Byrnes, Charles "Chip" Bohlen (Truman's interpreter), and Leahy, "all of whom had been closely associated with Roosevelt and at his side at Yalta," according to historian David McCullough, "the President…'squeezed facts and opinions out of them all day,' Leahy later said. Bohlen, too, was struck by how Truman 'stuck to business,' rarely taking up time [for] small talk. Averell Harriman would later find the President 'astonishingly well prepared.'"[10]

Truman and Byrnes made the final decision to remove any specific statement in the Potsdam Declaration about preserving the imperial system.

There was to be a test of the bomb in only a few short days. The considerable momentum in favor of its use would amplify if the test proved successful. Churchill, for one, agreed it should be used as soon as it became ready. After all, the atomic bomb was a military weapon—albeit the most powerful ever developed. General Groves later wrote, "As far as I was concerned, his decision [Truman's] was one of non-interference—basically, a decision not to upset the existing plans." Nevertheless, one man had to make the ultimate decision; Truman now accepted the responsibility with confidence.[11]

At the southeastern tip of England, the seaborne presidential entourage picked up an escort of six British destroyers and a cruiser as it passed by the Cliffs of Dover and plowed through the English Channel. On Sunday, July 15, the *Augusta* docked in Antwerp, Belgium. General Eisenhower was there to greet Truman.

The delegation drove south to an airfield in Brussels in a forty-seven-car caravan along a highway secured by the 35th Division, Truman's old outfit from World War I, dressed in full battle regalia. At the airfield, the presidential plane, *The Sacred Cow*, plus two other C-54 transports, waited to take the president and his party on the last leg of his journey, a three-and-a-half hour flight to Berlin.[12] As the planes entered German airspace, Truman, Byrnes, and Leahy got their first glimpses of the awful destruction wrought, much of it from the air, on Hitler's shattered Reich. Hardly a single urban center or a building within escaped; it was beyond comprehension. As the three planes passed Frankfurt, they picked up an escort of twenty P-47 Thunderbolts.

JULY 11, 1945
26 DAYS TO HIROSHIMA

Japan's Foreign Minister continued his exchanges with Ambassador Satō in Moscow. Tōgō's July 11 message, marked "extremely urgent," read:

> We are now secretly giving consideration to the termination of the war because of the pressing situation which confronts Japan both at home and abroad. Therefore, when you have your interview with Molotov you should not confine yourself to the objective of a rapprochement between Russia and Japan but should also sound him out on the extent to which it is possible to make use of Russia in ending the war.
>
> As for our proposal that we pledge mutual support in the maintenance of peace…that should be put forward in conjunction with sounding out Russia's attitude toward Japan…While we naturally hope to obtain a treaty through the negotiations between Hirota and Malik, those talks are also intended to find out the extent to which it is possible to make use of Russia in ending the war.
>
> We would like to know the views of the Russian Government on this subject with all haste. Furthermore, the Imperial Court is tremendously interested in this matter…

Later in the day, Tōgō sent a second "extremely urgent" message to Satō:

> …Therefore, please tell them that: We consider the maintenance of peace in East Asia to be one aspect of the maintenance of world peace. Accordingly, Japan—as a proposal for ending the war and because of her concern for the establishment and maintenance of lasting peace—has absolutely no idea of annexing or holding the territories which she has occupied during the war.
>
> We should like you to have the interview with Molotov in a day or two. Please reply at once as to his answer.[13]

Tōgō's choice of the word rapprochement to describe Japan's relationship with Russia was noteworthy, because it recognized just how poor that relationship had been in advance of the present circumstances. Yet this was the only political track the Big Six and the Emperor chose to use, one that had yielded absolutely nothing since being initiated two months earlier in mid-May by Tōgō through Hirota to Malik. As for Tōgō's comments about maintaining the peace in East Asia and that Japan had no intention of holding territories it had occupied during the war, Satō had already told Tōgō that the world viewed Japan as the lone obstacle to peace. His offer, if it could be called that, was empty and self-serving, as if the peace it implied was a continuation of the peace between Russia and Japan and nothing more. Regarding the territories still occupied by Japan, the only reason she was now willing to broach giving up control over them was the rapid erosion of Japan's military power.

JULY 12, 1945
25 DAYS TO HIROSHIMA

The following day, with no reply from Satō, Tōgō sent another message, this one marked "very urgent."

> I have not yet received a wire about your interview with Molotov…We should…like you to present the matter to Molotov in the following terms:
>
> His Majesty the Emperor, mindful of the fact that the present war daily brings greater evil and sacrifice upon the peoples of all belligerent powers, desires from his heart that it may be quickly terminated. But so long as England and the United States insist upon unconditional surrender the Japanese Empire has no alternative but to fight on with all its strength for the honor and the existence of the Motherland. His Majesty is deeply reluctant to have any further blood lost among the people on both sides, and it is his desire for the welfare of humanity to restore peace with all possible speed.
>
> …It is the Emperor's private intention to send Prince Konoye to Moscow as a Special Envoy with a letter from him containing the statements given above.
>
> …Although it will be impossible for this delegation to get there before the big men in Moscow leave for the Three Power Conference, we must arrange for a meeting immediately after their return.[14]

With regard to the Emperor's desire to put an end to the bloodshed, as of June 22, the end of the Battle of Okinawa, there were no land battles being fought between the Japanese and the Allies other than the American mop-up operations of Japanese troops in the Philippines. America's blockade and bombardment of the Japanese home islands continued, but the casualties were overwhelmingly Japanese. The only other real losses were to the civilians in territories still occupied by the Japanese military and to Allied POWs. Tōgō had sent another meaningless offer, as its primary beneficiary was the Japanese. The final sentence in Tōgō's message, as it turned out, carried huge consequences—because it threw away the time from July 13 through August 2, the final day of the Potsdam Conference, and in actuality, most of the following week. Molotov didn't finally meet with Satō until August 8, when the former gave Satō Russia's declaration of war.

Three and a half weeks before the atomic attack on Hiroshima, Japan stood at the precipice. In the four months of the strategic bombing campaign, Japan's major and even middle-sized cities had or were being systematically razed to the ground—approximately two hundred thousand Japanese had died in those bombings, and millions more had lost their homes and their possessions. Production of both military hardware and civilian goods was in a precipitous decline and included a dire forecast for one of worst rice crops in decades. Iwo Jima and Okinawa had fallen, as well as most of the Philippines. The Americans had an almost complete naval blockade around the Japanese home islands and routinely shelled Japanese facilities with its surface ships while regularly sending hundreds of planes in tactical fighter sweeps over most of the length and breadth of Japan.

The Japanese had begun a half-hearted peace initiative in mid-May with the Soviet Union, a nation the Emperor himself labeled in 1940 as "untrustworthy" and one that would "betray us and take advantage of our exhaustion fighting the United States." A year earlier, Stalin had branded Japan an "aggressor state" and in early April, the Soviet government informed the Japanese they would not be renewing their Neutrality Pact. Japanese intelligence in Manchuria showed massive numbers of Soviet troops and equipment moving east since March. Nevertheless, Japan's leadership still thought they were in a position to negotiate an armistice to end the war rather than accepting the Allied demand for unconditional surrender.

On July 12, Satō responded to Tōgō. He told the Foreign Minister he would attempt to meet with Molotov on July 13. But he believed Japan's chances for peace were very poor unless the government was willing to accept "virtually the equivalent of unconditional surrender." In an effort to hammer home his beliefs about the state of the Soviet position, Satō replied to Tōgō with extreme bluntness:

> I received your [two] messages of 11 July and immediately after I had reported to you on my 12 July interview with Molotov. I realize that the gist of your idea is a basic sounding out of the Russians on the possibility of using them in ending the war.
>
> In my frank opinion, it is no exaggeration to say that the Russians are not attracted by the proposals which former Premier Hirota made to Ambassador Malik [for a nonaggression and mutual assistance pact in return for various concessions by Japan]…and that there is no hope that they will meet our terms. [Such proposals] run completely counter to the Russia's foreign policy, as I have explained in detail on numerous occasions…
>
> …Furthermore, the reasoning in your messages of 11 July consists of nothing more than academic fine phrases.
>
> …Assuming…the course of the war has brought us to a real extremity, the Government should make the great decision. Once that resolve has been taken, there may perhaps be some hopes of getting the Russian Government into motion and obtaining its good offices [influence or mediation] in terminating the war. There can be no doubt, however, that the situation we would face in that event would be virtually equivalent to unconditional surrender.
>
> I have expressed my views frankly, and I fear that I must apologize for the unceremoniousness of my words. I am filled with thoughts of fear and heartbreak…I send this message in the belief that it is my first responsibility to prevent the harboring of illusions which are at variance with reality.
>
> …If they [the Russians] should agree to this [our Special Envoy] it is entirely out of the question to limit the functions… to sounding out the extent to which we might make use of the Russians in ending the war or to presenting abstract exposition—as suggested in your messages of 11 July.

...If the proposal...brought by the Special Envoy at the Emperor's particular desire, goes no further than we have gone in the past, if it is to be a proposal that contains only abstract words and lacks concreteness—we shall uselessly disappoint the expectations of the authorities in this country...[15]

Meanwhile, in a suburb of Berlin, the last wartime meeting of the Chiefs of Government of the three great powers was about to begin. Code named "Terminal," the meeting would be the longest of any of the gatherings, from July 16 to August 2, 1945, and would encompass the largest assortment of topics of any of the Big Three summits. To the Anglo-Americans, the conference would also become the most frustrating due to the Russians' incessant haggling on almost every issue, which would cause endless redrafting of the proposals.[16]

Cecilienhof Palace had been chosen as the site for the Potsdam Conference. Nearly untouched by the war, the palace, located in the wooded resort town of Babelsberg thirteen miles southwest of Berlin, had been the playground for Germany's movie industry and the former residence of the Crown Prince Wilhelm of Prussia. The neo-Tudor-style home featured two-story stone and yellow stucco walls covered with ivy, picturesque gardens extending from the back of the home to the banks of the beautiful Griebnitz Lake, and a courtyard where the Russians had planted a giant star of red geraniums in front of the three stately arches leading to palace entrance.

Inside, the spacious forty-by-sixty-foot reception hall would function as the main conference room. Dimly lit except for its wrought-iron chandeliers and a very large window looking out on the gardens and lake, the walls of the room were covered with dark oak panels and accented in red, black, and gold. In the center of the room sat a large round table covered in a burgundy tablecloth, surrounded by fifteen chairs—five each for Russia, the United States, and England. Three of the chairs, noticeably larger, had a pair of gilded cupids perched on the back, and were designated for Stalin, Truman, and Churchill. Each of the three leaders also had a separate entrance, heavily guarded by Russian soldiers, who quickly disappeared after each of the heads of state entered.[17]

A short distance from the conference center, Truman was quartered in a yellowish-brown, three-story stucco rococo mansion, once the home of a German movie producer. The home, nicknamed the

"Little White House," showcased a second-story balcony overlooking Griebnitz Lake and the numerous weeping willows and spruces encircling the property. The interior featured a lavish ballroom and the den serving as Truman's remote Oval Office. Its walls were covered with rectangular, sable-colored wood panels about twelve by eighteen inches. Atop the nine-foot-high paneled walls rested a lavish modeling cap, affirming the status of its owner. The fireplace—bordered with decorative ceramic tiles and floor-to-ceiling bookshelves on each side—and a baroque desk in the center of the room provided its focal points.

The home would serve the president, Leahy, and Byrnes well, the men becoming very relaxed and at ease within its confines. Emilio Collado, a State Department official, would observe:

> There was a big ballroom and it was like ballrooms, empty. Little glitz chairs around the edge; it was quite a handsome big room looking out on this lake, with a raised platform and a grand piano on it. Seated at the grand piano was an alert small man in shirtsleeves with a drink on the corner of the piano. Standing alongside him was a naval gentleman with no coat on, just the uniform pants. The third gentleman was the Secretary of State. He said, "What have you got there?"
>
> I said, "Well this is the letter to the Prime Minister."
>
> He said, "Have you got it cleared by everybody?"
>
> I said, "We finished clearing it with the Admiral just before lunch" and the Admiral looked up and said, "Yeah, I agreed to it." The President looked up from the piano and asked for a fountain pen. I produced one and he signed the memorandum. I then turned around (when you're ahead you leave) and he started to play the piano and they were singing as I left. I thought it was nice, these three people sitting there playing...They weren't drunk or anything like that; they each had a drink. I have often thought of that picture: the five-star admiral, the Secretary of State, and the President together on a Saturday afternoon, having a little music.[18]

JULY 16, 1945
21 DAYS TO HIROSHIMA

On the day the Potsdam Conference was meant to begin, a cable arrived for the president providing early news of the successful test of the first explosion of an atomic bomb in the New Mexico desert. The Washington cable read:

July 16 7:30 P.M.

Operated on this morning. Diagnosis not yet complete but results seem satisfactory and already exceed expectations. Local press release necessary as interest extends great distance. Dr. Groves pleased. He returns tomorrow. I will keep you posted.

Byrnes also had an urgent cable awaiting him when he arrived. Prior to his departure for Europe, he had decided to confer with former Secretary of State Cordell Hull to get his take on the wording of Stimson's July 2 memorandum to the president, defining or eliminating the demand for unconditional surrender. Hull told Byrnes that it sounded "…too much like appeasement. The Emperor of the ruling classes must be stripped of all extraordinary privileges and placed on a level before the law of everybody else." Thus, Hull was tying the two issues—unconditional surrender and the preservation of the Emperor—together.

Later, by memorandum, Hull warned that even with the elimination of unconditional surrender there would be no guarantee of acceptance by Japan, and that its failure would serve to embolden its militarists at the cost of "terrible political repercussions" at home.[19] And public opinion validated this perspective. "In a recent Gallup Poll one third [of the Americans polled] had favored executing Hirohito, and thirty-seven percent wanted him put on trial, imprisoned for life or executed. Only seven percent believed he should be left alone or used as a puppet."[20]

With Stalin's arrival delayed by a day, Truman decided to take a two-hour tour of Berlin. Leahy and Byrnes accompanied the president in the back seat of an olive drab, four-door convertible sedan with a single white star painted on each side. Truman, bedecked in a tan Stetson, wore a dark suit; Byrnes donned a tan suit and hat; Leahy wore his dark blue naval uniform and matching hat. The driver, dressed in civilian clothes and sunglasses, sat alone in the front seat.

As the presidential motorcade entered the main road after leaving No. 2 Kaiser Strasse, an impressive sight greeted it. On each side of the road as far as one could see was the 2nd Armored Division, commanded by Brigadier General John H. Collier. Truman stood to take the review. Later, the president told Leahy what an inspiring sight the men and equipment had been and how he wished he had been permitted to serve in uniform during the war.[21]

With the caravan's arrival in Berlin, the scene changed radically. Only the endless skeletal ruins of buildings, in the once expansive metropolis, remained standing; virtually none had escaped unscathed. The streets had been cleared of the rubble, pushed to the sides, creating a wall of debris.[22] Among the shambles, old men, women, and children wandered aimlessly, pushing or pulling what was left of their belongings, "headed nowhere in particular, with nothing but blank expression on their faces, no anger, no grief, [and] no fear…Truman found [this] extremely disturbing."[23] The three men were awe struck by the sheer magnitude of the devastation. As the procession turned down Wilhelmstrasse and passed by the remains of the Reich Chancellery, Truman said, "That's what happens when a man overreaches himself."[24]

That evening, the three men discussed the scenes they had observed earlier. Leahy said in his memoir, "It was noticeable to me, as the President's own personal party at dinner that evening discussed scenes we had witnessed, that there was no mood of vindictiveness or revenge, but rather a realization brought home to those of us who fought the war from Washington of the horrible destructiveness of modern conflict."[25]

JULY 17, 1945
20 DAYS TO HIROSHIMA

Tōgō replied to Satō's July 12 communication, conceding the strained relationship between the two countries, the slim prospects for gaining Soviet assistance, and the unwillingness of the Japanese to accept unconditional surrender.

> We have been fully aware from the outset that it would be difficult under existing circumstances either to strengthen the ties of friendship between Japan and Russia or to make effective use of Russia in ending the war.
> …If today, when we are still maintaining our strength, the Anglo-Americans were to have regard for Japan's honor and existence, they could save humanity by bringing the war to an end. If, however, they insist unrelentingly upon unconditional

surrender the Japanese are unanimous in their resolve to wage a thoroughgoing war.

...Please bear particularly in mind...that we are not asking [for] the Russians' mediation in anything like unconditional surrender.[26]

Once again Tōgō's words seem puzzling and misdirected. Japan's position deteriorated every day as more death and destruction visited its people and economy, and what reason would cause the Anglo-Americans to have any regard for Japan's honor, considering its ruthless and unprovoked commencement of the war and her brutal and barbaric behavior throughout it? Twice more in his message Tōgō returned to the issue of unconditional surrender and declared the Japanese Government and its people would fight to the bitter end if the Anglo-Americans refused to yield on the subject. The only actionable part of the message for Satō was the clear instruction that if he ever gained an audience with Molotov, he was to unequivocally reject unconditional surrender as a non-starter for ending the war.

Around noon on July 17, Stalin finally arrived in Babelsberg and almost immediately visited Truman at the Little White House. Eschewing strict political protocol, Truman casually invited Stalin to stay for lunch. During their visit, unsolicited, Stalin informed Truman that the Soviets would be ready to enter the war against Japan in early August. He also told Truman of the recent Japanese peace overtures. Regarding the latter, Molotov told Truman and Byrnes "that the Japanese could scarcely mistake the Soviets' intention, as the massing armored divisions of the Red Army had been visible at the Manchurian border for weeks."[27] In April, the Soviets had begun "a flow of 136,000 railcars to move 403,335 men and 2,119 tanks and self-propelled guns over the fragile 10,000-kilometer rail link connecting Europe to Manchuria. The great influx doubled Soviet forces in the far east from forty to more than eighty divisions."[28]

The first plenary session of the conference was held later that afternoon, and at Churchill's and Stalin's urging Truman was made chairman of the meetings. At their conclusion, Charles McMoran Wilson, Churchill's personal physician, asked Churchill if he thought Truman had any real ability. Churchill responded, "I should think he has. At any rate, he is a man of immense determination. He takes no notice of delicate ground; he just plants his foot firmly on it."[29] Leahy also said afterward, "I thought Truman handled himself very well at the first session. He was positive in his manner, clear and direct in his statements. He seemed to know exactly what he wanted to say and do."[30]

JULY 18, 1945
19 DAYS TO HIROSHIMA

In a short letter to Bess, written before sessions began on July 18, Truman provided a short glimpse into the previous day:

> The boys say I gave them an earful. I hope so. Admiral Leahy said he'd never seen an abler job and Byrnes and my fellows seem to be walking on air...Anyway, a start has been made and I've gotten what I came for—Stalin goes to war August 15 with no strings on it...I'll say that will end the war a year sooner now, and think of the kids who won't be killed! That is the important thing...
>
> Wish you and Margie were here. But it is a forlorn place and would only make you sad.[31]

It had been one of Truman's major goals at Potsdam to reconfirm the pledge Stalin made at Yalta to enter the war against Japan ninety days after the defeat of the Germany; one day into the conference he already had it in hand.

Stimson arrived, uninvited, on July 18, bringing with him further details of the nuclear test in Alamogordo, New Mexico, as later recalled by Truman:

> I received him at once and called on Secretary of State Byrnes, Admiral Leahy, General Marshall, General Arnold, and Admiral King to join us at my office at the *Little White House*. We reviewed our military strategy in light of the revolutionary development. We were not ready to make use of this weapon against the Japanese, although we did not know as yet what affect any new weapon might have, physically or psychologically, when used against the enemy. For that reason the military advised that we go ahead with the existing military plans for the invasion of the Japanese home islands.[32]

Truman also wrote in his diary, "Believe Japs will fold up before Russia comes in. I am sure they will when Manhattan [the atomic bomb,

S-1] appears over their homeland. I shall inform Stalin about it at an opportune time."

Just before the plenary session began, Stalin said he wished to make an announcement. He stated that the Russian delegation had received a proposal from Japan. The date of the latest communication was July 13; the purpose centered around the Japanese request to allow Prince Konoye to come to Russia to discuss ending the war through Soviet assistance. Stalin's interpreter then read the communication, which Truman later recalled:

> The mission of Konoye was to ask the Soviet Government to take part in mediation to end the present war and to transmit the complete Japanese case in this respect. He would also be empowered to negotiate with respect to Soviet Japanese relations during the war and after the war. Simultaneously, he wished to repeat that Konoye was especially charged by His Majesty, the Emperor, to convey to the Soviet Government that it was exclusively the desire of His Majesty to avoid more bloodshed by the parties engaged in the war. In view of the foregoing, he hoped that the Soviet Government would give favorable attention to his request and would give its consent to the arrival of the mission.[33]

The Soviets had previously rejected Japan's requests, using as an excuse their non-specific nature. Stalin said they would likewise refuse this one.[34]

Over lunch that Wednesday, the president spoke with Churchill and broached the subject of telling Stalin about the bomb. The Prime Minister said if Truman had "resolved to tell" him, then he should tell Stalin he was not advised sooner because Truman was waiting for a successful test.

Churchill then switched the topic of conversation to the demand for unconditional surrender and suggested a possible change. The Prime Minister confessed the term bothered him. Couldn't it be communicated such that the Allies got "all the essentials for future peace and security, and yet left the Japanese some show of saving their military honor and some assurance of their national existence, after they had complied with all safeguards necessary for the conqueror"?

"I don't think the Japanese have any honor after Pearl Harbor," Truman countered.

"At any rate they have something for which they are ready to face certain death in very large numbers, and this may not be so important to us as to them," Churchill said.

Truman then turned quite sympathetic, according to Churchill, and spoke of "the terrible responsibilities upon him in regard to unlimited effusion of American blood. He invited personal friendship and comradeship." "He seems a man of exceptional character," Churchill wrote.[35]

Also, that day, Satō dispatched the following message, marked "very urgent" to Tokyo.

> It is extremely regrettable that the Russian Government has expressed its disapproval of the plan for dispatching a Special Envoy on the ground that the Envoy's mission has not been made concrete.

Satō then made two important points. In the first he clarified his definition of the "unconditional surrender" he believed the Japanese should accept; specifically, that it excluded the elimination of the national structure. His second point warned that no other conditions should be sought.

> It goes without saying that in my earlier messages calling for unconditional surrender or closely equivalent terms, I made an exception of the question of preserving our national structure [the imperial system].
>
> ...Except for the matter of maintenance of our national structure, I think that we must absolutely not propose any conditions. The situation has already reached the point where we have no alternative but unconditional surrender or its equivalent.[36]

In Tokyo, Tōgō met with the Emperor:

> I was received in audience on the 18th, and reported to the Emperor in detail the views of the government concerning this tripartite conference in our measures vis-à-vis the U.S.S.R. In response to the Emperor's inquiry whether our communication had reached the Soviet leaders, I told him that since his wishes for peace had been known by Ambassador Satō at 5 P.M. on the 13th, while Stalin and Molotov had left Moscow only in the afternoon of the 14th, it seemed certain that our requests had reached them. The

Emperor said simply that the fate of our proposal was now beyond our control; it depended on the response of the other party not only, but on the destiny itself of Japan; and he expressed himself as satisfied that we had been able to get it delivered to the Soviet leaders in time.[37]

JULY 20, 1945
17 DAYS TO HIROSHIMA

A few days into the Potsdam Conference, President Truman invited Eisenhower and Bradley to lunch. A day earlier, at the Combined Chiefs session, the target date for forcing the unconditional surrender of Japan had been set for November 15, 1946.[38] And now, according to Bradley, the conversation focused on the strategy in the Pacific and the use of the atomic bomb. Bradley, a fellow Missourian, said of Truman, "He was direct, unpretentious, clear-thinking and forceful." Bradley believed Truman had already made the decision to use the bomb. In fact, the president did not specifically ask either Bradley or Eisenhower for their opinion on the bomb's use.

Bradley and Eisenhower were the most senior American military commanders in the European Theater, but neither was familiar with the details of the Pacific War. As such, their opinions were personal rather than professional, and Eisenhower later admitted as much when he confessed that he had done no analysis of the subject. Eisenhower also expressed an opinion on the topic of Soviet entry into the war against Japan. Disagreeing with Marshall, he counseled against begging the Russians to join the fight against Japan, but acknowledged "no power on earth could keep the Red Army out of the war unless victory came before they could get in."[39]

After lunch, Bradley and Eisenhower accompanied Truman on a second trip into Berlin, this time to the American sector to speak at a ceremony to raise the flag that had flown over the Capitol in Washington the day Pearl Harbor was attacked. The observance took place in a modest cobblestone square in brilliant sunshine. Stimson and Patton also attended, the latter magnificently attired.

"Truman spoke without notes and with obvious emotion," historian David McCullough writes, "choosing his words carefully, as he stood shoulders braced, thumbs hooked in the side pockets of his double-breasted suit, his eyes shadowed by his very unmilitary western-style Stetson"[40]:

We are here today to raise the flag of victory over the capital of our greatest adversary...we must remember that...we are raising it in the name of the people of the United States, who are looking forward to a better world, a peaceful world, a world in which all the people will have an opportunity to enjoy the good things of life, and not just a few at the top.

Let us not forget that we are fighting for peace, and for the welfare of mankind. We are not fighting for conquest. There is not one piece of territory or one thing of a monetary nature that we want out of this war.

We want peace and prosperity for the world as a whole. We want to see the time, when we can do things in peace that we have been able to do in war.

If we can put this tremendous machine of ours, which has made victory possible, to work for peace, we can look forward to the greatest age in the history of mankind. That is what we propose to do.[41]

JULY 21, 1945
16 DAYS TO HIROSHIMA

Tōgō responded to Satō's July 19 clarification, making the national structure an exception under unconditional surrender. His message read:

Special Envoy Konoye's mission will be in obedience to the Imperial Will. He will request assistance in bringing about an end to the war through the good offices of the Soviet Government.

Please understand especially my next wire.

Sent the same day the wire read:

With regard to unconditional surrender, (I have been informed of your 18 July message) [which included as an exception to unconditional surrender the preservation of the imperial system] we are unable to consent to it under any circumstances whatever. Even if the war drags on and it becomes clear that it will take much more than bloodshed, the whole country as one man will pit itself against the enemy in accordance with the Imperial Will so long as the enemy demands unconditional surrender. It is in order to avoid such a state of affairs that we are seeking a peace, which is not so-called unconditional surrender, through the good offices of Russia...[42]

Tōgō concluded:

Therefore, it is not only impossible for us to request the Russians to lend their good offices in obtaining a peace without conditions, but it would also be both disadvantageous and impossible, from the standpoint of foreign and domestic considerations, to make an immediate declaration of specific terms.[43]

Tōgō's response made Japan's position crystal clear to Satō and to the Americans listening in through MAGIC. Japan would not accept unconditional surrender with just the inclusion of the imperial system—that too was a non-starter; she wanted additional conditions. But even at this late date, Japan's leaders had not agreed on what the "specific terms" needed to be. Why? Because the Big Six had made no progress in defining them over the previous two months while they waited for the Soviet Union to agree to assist Japan in bringing the war to an end. Those discussions had gone nowhere, at least partly due to Japan's inability or unwillingness to provide any concrete statements about its requirements for peace.

Perhaps a better explanation is that Japan's leaders weren't actually serious about ending the war. After all, Suzuki had publicly stated on multiple occasions that the nation remained determined to fight to the bitter end. And there was still a widely held belief by the senior members of Japan's military that in the decisive battle for the homeland, the Americans could be made to suffer horrific losses. If they could be convinced of this, whether through perceived or actual casualties, the Japanese could yet achieve a peace on terms acceptable to them. This explanation also syncs with the complete lack of urgency shown by the Japanese government, since the military believed invasion was still months away.

At the Little White House, Stimson read aloud to Truman and Byrnes a detailed report from eyewitnesses describing the awesome atomic spectacle at Alamogordo. General Groves and his deputy Brigadier General Thomas Ferrell had witnessed the explosion from a distance of 10,000 yards. Overwhelmed by the sight, Ferrell shouted, "The war is over." Groves said, "as soon as we drop one or two on Japan!" It took Stimson nearly an hour to read the entire report to the president and Byrnes, and by the time he finished, both men looked enormously pleased. The president in particular was "tremendously pepped up," wrote Stimson. "He said it gave him an entirely new confidence and he thanked me for having come to the conference and being present to help [him] this way."[44]

The president had come to Potsdam anxious to reconfirm Stalin's pledge to enter the war against Japan, and had received it on July 17. Now, after just a few days, he was seeing firsthand the "pigheadedness" he had been reading and hearing about for months. Almost immediately after the Yalta agreements had been reached in February, the Soviets had begun reneging on commitments. Truman had first confronted Molotov about it in April, just a few days into his presidency. At Potsdam, no amount of negotiating with Stalin could change the Soviets' position if Stalin was unwilling to compromise; Eastern Europe was already a *fait accompli* that would last forty years.

In the Pacific, as far as Churchill and Truman were concerned, the decision had been made; if the Japanese failed to surrender after being given one last chance, then the bomb would be used. But three members of the American military continued to debate the issue. Beyond his moral reservations, Admiral Leahy suspected that the scientists and others in the program wanted to use the bomb "because of the vast sums that had been spent on the project." General Arnold believed conventional bombing alone could end the war. Marshall believed it was either the bomb or a costly invasion, possibly both.[45]

As always, the issue of casualties weighed heavily on Truman. On July 21, William B. Shockley wrote a memorandum on the topic. After World War II broke out, Shockley, a PhD from MIT and future Nobel Prize Winner in Physics in 1956, began working on defense-related projects, including radar, counter-submarine tactics, depth charge patterns, and training for B-29 pilots to use radar-guided bomb sights. In the course of his work he made frequent trips to the Pentagon and Washington where he met many high-ranking officers and government officials. A little more than a year after the war ended, Shockley would receive the Medal of Merit on October 17, 1946, at the time the highest civilian award given to a citizen in service to the United States.

In the summer of 1945, Dr. Edward L. Bowles, Consultant to the Secretary of War (Stimson) from 1942–1947, asked Shockley to prepare a report on the question of probable casualties, Japanese and American, from an invasion of the Japanese mainland (Downfall, both Olympic and Coronet). Shockley's report read:

July 21, 1945
MEMORANDUM FOR DR. EDWARD L. BOWLES
Proposal for Increasing the Scope of Casualties Studies:

If the study shows that the behavior of nations in all historical cases comparable to Japan's has in fact been invariably consistent with the behavior of the troops in battle, then it means that the Japanese dead and ineffectives at the time of the defeat will exceed the corresponding number for the Germans. In other words, we shall probably have to kill at least 5 to 10 million Japanese. This might cost us between 1.7 and 4 million casualties including 400,000 to 800,000 killed.

—W.B. Shockley, Expert Consultant[46]

Since the information in the report was at the request of Bowles, Assistant to the Secretary of War, it's possible Stinson may have been made aware of its content. Shockley's estimates for American dead were quite similar to Hoover's estimates in late May (500,000 to 1,000,000), and a second study validating the first certainly would have made Truman, if he knew, very uneasy. But the total casualties, both for Americans and the Japanese, may have come as a complete shock.

JULY 23, 1945
14 DAYS TO HIROSHIMA

Stimson visited the president at his office early Monday morning, and once again argued for removing the demand for unconditional surrender from the proclamation that would be made during the conference. This time, he offered as alternative wording that the Allies would "prosecute the war against Japan until she ceases to resist." His justification for the change was that the Japanese interpreted the phrase "unconditional surrender" to mean it would be the end of their Emperor.

Byrnes strongly disagreed and stated that unconditional surrender had been a long-established goal of the Allies, frequently reaffirmed, most recently by Truman in his first speech to Congress after assuming the presidency. The Nazis had been forced to accept it, and at this late date, after so much bloodshed, acceptance of anything less seemed like appeasement. Byrnes once again voiced his fear of the political repercussions to the president.[47]

That evening, Churchill hosted a banquet. During what had basically become a daily ritual at these dinners, Stalin toasted Truman, saying, "Honesty adorns the man." He then praised Truman at length. Admiral King, also in attendance, leaned over to McMoran and whispered, "Watch the president. This is all new to him, but he can take it. He is a more typical American than Roosevelt, and he will do a good job, not only for the United States but for the whole world."[48]

7

THE FINAL
COUNTDOWN BEGINS

JULY 24, 1945
13 DAYS TO HIROSHIMA

The president's day began with more news about the atomic bomb. Truman was told it should be ready by August 4–5, no later than August 10. Truman also received the *Combined Chiefs of Staff Report to the President and Prime Minister.* The report still recommended, despite the successful test of the bomb, that Russia be brought into the war as soon as possible to affect the quickest Japanese surrender. The recommendation likely exposed the Chiefs' skepticism about a weapon never before used in combat. Churchill and Byrnes had no such misgivings about the bomb's potential and saw it as a means to end the war without Soviet involvement. And during the course of the conference, Truman later wrote, a consensus to use the bomb developed among Stimson, Generals Marshall and Arnold, and Admirals King and Leahy, to use the bomb. Truman reached his own conclusion "after long and careful thought," adding, "I did not like the weapon."[1]

Truman later stated:

> The final decision of where and when to use the atomic bomb was up to me. Let there be no mistake about it. I regarded the bomb as a military weapon and never had any doubt that it should be used. The top military advisers to the president recommended its use, and when I talked to Churchill, he unhesitatingly told me that he favored the use of the atomic bomb if it might aid to end the war.

"Truman made no decision because there was no decision to be made," recalled George Elsey, remembering the atmosphere of the moment. "He could no more have stopped it than a train moving down the track...It's all well and good to come along later and say the bomb was a horrible thing. The whole goddamn war was a horrible thing."[2]

General Spaatz, who commanded the strategic air forces which would deliver the bombs on the targets, was given some latitude as to when and on which of the four targets the bombs would be dropped, primarily because weather conditions over Japan in August could often be poor, making it impossible to do visual bombing of the target—a requirement for its use. To get preparations underway, the War Department gave orders to General Spaatz stating that the first bomb was to be dropped as soon after August 3 as possible, weather permitting.[3] The order read:

July 24, 1945

To: General Spaatz
    Commanding General
    United States Army Strategic Air Forces

The 509 Composite Group, 20th Air Force will deliver its first special bomb as soon as weather will permit visual bombing after about 3 August 1945 on one of the targets: Hiroshima, Kokura, Niigata, and Nagasaki. To carry military and civilian scientific personnel from the War Department to observe and record the effects of the explosion of the bomb, additional aircraft will accompany the airplane carrying the bomb. The observing planes will stay several miles distant from the point of impact of the bomb.

Additional bombs will be delivered on the above targets as soon as made ready by the project staff. Further instructions will be issued concerning targets other than those listed above.

Discussion of any and all information concerning the use of the weapon against Japan is reserved to the Secretary of War and the President of the United States. No communiqués on the subject or releases of information will be issued by commanders in the field without specific prior authority. Any news stories will be sent to the War Department for specific clearance.

The foregoing directive is issued to you by direction and with the approval of the Secretary of War and the Chief of Staff, USA. It is desired that you personally deliver one copy of this directive to General MacArthur and one copy to Admiral Nimitz for their information.

/s/ Thos. T. Handy
General, GSC
Acting Chief of Staff

Copy for General Groves

TOP SECRET[4]

It is noteworthy that the order authorizes use of the bomb after August 3, which was calculated to be after the Potsdam Conference ended. If Truman had really wanted to use the bomb for explicit intimidation of the Soviets to secure advantages, why not authorize use of the bomb while negotiations were still going on at Potsdam? With the order, Truman believed he had made the decision and that the wheels were in motion for the first use of atomic weapons in combat. The president further instructed Stimson that the order stood unless Truman notified him that he deemed Japan's reply to our ultimatum (yet to be issued) acceptable.[5] The earliest use of the bomb was also such that Japan's leaders would have at least a week to respond before the first bomb fell on Japan.

A measure of just how difficult it would be to finally gain Japan's surrender is reflected in General Marshall's view of this indomitable enemy. He believed even after the bomb was used that the Japanese would continue to fight. He saw the bomb as a way of hopefully reducing American casualties in the invasion, but to believe it could actually prompt Japan's surrender was overreaching. "We knew the Japanese were determined and fanatical," Marshall said, "and we would have to exterminate them man by man. So, we thought the bomb would be a wonderful weapon as a protection and a preparation for the landings."

Marshall's belief that the Japanese would have to be exterminated "man by man" had been revealed in his endorsement to use poisonous gas at Okinawa, during the JCS meeting in May to approve the plans for Downfall, and in his suggestion to do so during the president's June 18 briefing on the invasion.[6] At no time in the Pacific War had there ever been the organized surrender by any Japanese military unit. Marshall believed any slackening of American resolve to obtain unconditional surrender would be viewed by the Japanese as an indication of weakening resolve: "We had 100,000 people killed in Tokyo [March 10] in one night and it had seemingly no effect whatsoever."

After lunch, America's top military leaders met for the first time with the Soviet Military Chiefs. The meeting's purpose was to brief each other on their respective plans for ending the war with Japan. Leahy presided. After giving the Russians an overview of the American invasion plans, General A. E. Antonov of the Red Army presented the Soviet plans to enter the war against Japan. They expected to invade Manchuria in late August, he explained, with the objective of destroying Japan's armies and occupying the Liaotung Peninsula, which contained Port Arthur and Darien. The Russians estimated enemy strength in Manchuria at thirty Japanese divisions and twenty divisions of "Manchu puppet troops." Antonov made no mention of an invasion of the southern half of Sakhalin Island (lost to the Japanese in the Russo-Japanese War), something the Russians had spoken of at Yalta. When asked about it, Antonov said that there would be a second offensive, but provided no date.[7] And there were never any Soviet plans for an invasion of Hokkaido during the war—even the administrative landing after the surrender was ultimately cancelled.

After adjournment of the plenary session, Truman asked Stalin if he could have a word with him. After a short exchange between the interpreters, Truman gestured with his arm, and the group moved to an area where they could have a private conversation.

Truman, without using the words "nuclear" or "atomic," told Stalin that America had recently completed work on "a new weapon of unusual destructive force." Stalin replied casually that he was glad to hear such news and hoped the Americans would make "good use of it against the Japanese."[8] Churchill, perhaps fifteen feet away, watched closely.[9] Stalin appeared delighted at the news, but did not betray his true feelings. Even through translation, it's likely that he understood the true meaning of Truman's words. The Soviets had infiltrated the Manhattan Project and knew of the bombs' existence.

JULY 25, 1945
12 DAYS TO HIROSHIMA
President Truman wrote in his diary on July 25, 1945, that he had ordered the bomb used. According to his memory, he had ordered its use on a military target and not women and children.

We have discovered the most terrible bomb in the history of the world. It may be the fire and destruction prophesied in the Euphrates Valley Era, after Noah and his fabulous Ark.

Anyway we "think" we have found the way to cause a disintegration of the atom. An experiment in the New Mexico desert was startling—to put it mildly. Thirteen pounds of the explosive caused the complete disintegration of a steel tower 60 feet high, created a crater 6 feet deep and 1,200 feet in diameter, knocked over a steel tower ½ a mile away and knocked men down 10,000 yards away. The explosion was visible for more than 200 miles and audible for 40 miles or more.

This weapon is to be used against Japan between now and August 10th. I have told the Secretary of War, Mr. Stimson, to use it so that military objectives and soldiers and sailors are the target and not women and children. Even if the Japs are savages, ruthless, merciless and fanatic, we as the leader of the world for the common welfare cannot drop that terrible bomb on the old capital or the new.

He and I are in accord. The target will be a purely military one and we will issue a warning statement asking the Japs to surrender and save lives. I'm sure they will not do that, but we will have given them the chance. It is certainly a good thing for the world that Hitler's crowd or Stalin's did not discover this atomic bomb. It seems to be the most terrible thing ever discovered, but it can be made the most useful.[10]

It should be mentioned that Truman stating that the bomb would be used "so that military objectives and soldiers and sailors are the target and not women and children" was engaging in self-deception. However, given the breaching of almost all prewar taboos about bombing cities and citizens, this is not really surprising in the context of the time.

Sometime during the evening of July 25, General Marshall and the president had a conversation, revisiting the subject of invasion casualties projected from both phases of Downfall. In response to Truman's question this time, Marshall offered up a much larger number than the one he gave the president at the June 18 meeting in the Oval Office. He told the president, if Americans were forced to invade, Olympic and the follow-on Operation Coronet to take Tokyo could cost a minimum of a quarter-million and possibly as many as a million American casualties.[11]

There may be a few explanations for Marshall's latest casualty count. He, like Truman, knew of the incredible buildup of Japanese forces in Kyūshū since the plans had been drawn up in May. The development would have serious consequences for the American invaders. Marshall also believed, even with the atomic bomb, that the invasion would be necessary in order to compel Japan's unconditional surrender—so Truman, and likely the American public, had to be warned of the potential cost.

If the most recent battles of Iwo Jima and Okinawa were good indications, one in four—or 62,500–250,000 men—in Marshall's casualty range would be KIA. The latter figure, if it came to pass, amounted to more than sixty percent of the American war dead for the entire conflict in all theaters, and Marshall's numbers were still only one fourth of Hoover's and Shockley's estimates.

Whatever the number, Truman rightfully envisioned appalling casualties if the American invasion of Japan went ahead. That American soldiers and Marines would be engaging by far the greatest number of Japanese troops and civilians they had ever fought was beyond dispute. Truman said, "It occurred to me that a quarter of a million of the flower of our young manhood were worth a couple of Japanese cities, and I still think they were and are."[12]

But beyond the thoroughly depressing casualty estimates, the Japanese were a despised enemy, perpetrators of the sneak attack on Pearl Harbor and the Bataan Death March, the details of which had just become known in early 1944. In Manila, close to twenty thousand Japanese sailors and soldiers held out for weeks. "They blew up square miles of the city," historian Gavan Daws writes. "And they massacred [100,000] Filipinos, raping, bayoneting, machine-gunning, burning."[13] Manila became one of the most decimated cities in the entire war. The Japanese had massacred 150 American POWs at the Palawan Prisoner of War Camp in December of 1944 by herding them into air raid shelters, dousing them with gasoline, setting them afire, and then clubbing, bayoneting, or machine gunning any who attempted to escape. A few days after the German surrender in May, US newspapers showed a photograph of an Australian POW, blindfolded and kneeling with his hands tied behind his back. Behind him stood a Japanese officer wielding a Samurai sword about to behead him. At Potsdam, as American interpreter Chip Bohlen wrote, "The spirit of mercy [was] not throbbing in the breast of any Allied official," either for the Germans or the Japanese.[14]

Late on July 25, Stimson visited the president with news regarding the primary target for the first atomic attack; it would be Hiroshima. The city was the major port of embarkation used by the Imperial Army and Navy for decades, and also housed the headquarters of Field Marshal Hata's Second General Army. Counting Hata's headquarters, there were about 43,000 soldiers in the city among as many as 280,000 civilians.[15]

The same day, General Spaatz began his four-day flight to Guam with the momentous July 24, 1945, presidential order authorizing the first atomic attack, any time after August 3.

JULY 26, 1945
11 DAYS TO HIROSHIMA

After completing her high-speed voyage from San Francisco to Tinian in the Marianas, the cruiser *USS Indianapolis* dropped anchor the morning of July 26 about a half-mile off shore with its Top-Secret cargo. Several small vessels swarmed around the warship, as did numerous high-ranking officers from all the services over her deck, all there to watch her unloading. Inside the ship's holds were Uranium-235 charges encased in lead along with the fifteen-foot wooden crate containing the firing gun for the *"Little Boy"* atomic bomb. The ship's new captain, Charles Butler McVay, had been given strict orders to guard the precious cargo day and night until his arrival. With the materials successfully unloaded onto a Landing Ship, Tank (LST), and the first part of his mission over, McVay set sail for Leyte in the Philippines, and the *Indianapolis*'s next assignment, the invasion of Japan. But the *Indy* never arrived. On July 30, she and three quarters of her 1,195-man crew were lost first to a torpedo attack by Japanese submarine I-58 and second due to the negligence of the American Navy who failed to notice the ship had not arrived and begin a search for her. Four days later, a patrol aircraft accidentally spotted the surviving 316 crewmen, spread out over miles, and rescued them.[16] The sinking of *Indianapolis* resulted in the greatest single loss of life at sea, from a single ship, in the history of the US Navy.

As the Potsdam Conference moved into its final week, the U.S. Third Fleet, Task Force 37 and Task Force 38, commanded by Admiral Halsey, ranged at will along the Japanese coast and launched a series of massive air strikes on cities, harbors, and any Japanese warships still afloat. On July 24, carrier-born aircraft had attacked the Kure Naval Base where, according to Halsey, "Jap warships went to die." By the end of July 28, Halsey reported with great satisfaction that the Imperial Navy had "ceased to exist."[17]

In Potsdam, the United States, Great Britain, and China (the Soviet Union was not a party since it had not yet entered the war against Japan) issued the Potsdam Declaration to Japan. Much of the content in Stimson's July 2 memorandum to the president, specifically articles 5 and 6, formed the basis for terms 1, 2, 3, 6, 8, 10, 11, and 12 of the declaration. And while Stimson wasn't completely successful in eliminating the phrase "unconditional surrender" from the document, it now defined what the Allies meant by it. Their final appeal for Japan's surrender would not be the blanket unconditional surrender forced on Germany. To some, both within the Allied ranks and certainly within Japan, the fact that terms were now on the table indicated a weakening in Allied determination to pay the ultimate price to defeat Japan by invading the country.

Regarding the preservation of Japan's National Structure—the other major topic of the July 2 meeting between Stimson, Truman, and Byrnes—Byrnes convinced the president not to include an explicit assurance in the wording of the Potsdam Declaration, but neither did it specifically exclude it. It was a subtle distinction, according to Naval Intelligence Officer Lieutenant George Elsey, intended to signal its possibility to the Japanese. Elsey, a trusted member of FDR's staff and now Truman's, had been the duty officer in the White House Map Room since 1941. In that role, he regularly provided information to Roosevelt and Truman on war events, decoded and encoded classified messages for the presidents, and accompanied Truman to Potsdam. The first five Articles of the declaration described the circumstances Japan now faced; Articles 6 through 13 specified the real terms contained in the document. The declaration read:

PROCLAMATION DEFINING TERMS FOR JAPANESE SURRENDER

Issued at Potsdam, July 26, 1945
1. We, the President of the United States, the President of the National Government of the Republic of China, and the Prime Minister of Great Britain, representing the hundreds of millions

of our countrymen, have conferred and agree that Japan shall be given an opportunity to end this war.

2. The prodigious land, sea and air forces of the United States, the British Empire and of China, many times reinforced by their armies and air fleets from the west, are poised to strike the final blows upon Japan. This military power is sustained and inspired by the determination of all the Allied Nations to prosecute the war against Japan until she ceases to resist.

3. The result of the futile and senseless German resistance to the might of the aroused free peoples of the world stands forth in awful clarity as an example to the people of Japan. The might that now converges on Japan is immeasurably greater than that which, when applied to the resisting Nazis, necessarily laid waste to the lands, the industry and the method of life of the whole German people. The full application of our military power, backed by our resolve, will mean the inevitable and complete destruction of the Japanese armed forces and just as inevitably the utter devastation of the Japanese homeland.

4. The time has come for Japan to decide whether she will continue to be controlled by those self-willed militaristic advisers whose unintelligent calculations have brought the Empire of Japan to the threshold of annihilation, or whether she will follow the path of reason.

5. Following are our terms. We will not deviate from them. There are no alternatives. We shall brook no delay.

6. There must be eliminated for all time the authority and influence of those who have deceived and misled the people of Japan into embarking on world conquest, for we insist that a new order of peace, security and justice will be impossible until irresponsible militarism is driven from the world.

7. Until such a new order is established and until there is convincing proof that Japan's war-making power is destroyed, points in Japanese territory to be designated by the Allies shall be occupied to secure the achievement of the basic objectives we are here setting forth.

8. The terms of the Cairo Declaration shall be carried out and Japanese sovereignty shall be limited to the islands of Honshu, Hokkaido, Kyushu, Shikoku and such minor islands as we determine.

9. The Japanese military forces, after being completely disarmed, shall be permitted to return to their homes with the opportunity to lead peaceful and productive lives.

10. We do not intend that the Japanese shall be enslaved as a race or destroyed as a nation, but stern justice shall be meted out to all war criminals, including those who have visited cruelties upon our prisoners. The Japanese Government shall remove all obstacles to the revival and strengthening of democratic tendencies among the Japanese people. Freedom of speech, of religion, and of thought, as well as respect for the fundamental human rights shall be established.

11. Japan shall be permitted to maintain such industries as will sustain her economy and permit the exaction of just reparations in kind, but not those which would enable her to re-arm for war. To this end, access to, as distinguished from control of, raw materials shall be permitted. Eventual Japanese participation in world trade relations shall be permitted.

12. The occupying forces of the Allies shall be withdrawn from Japan as soon as these objectives have been accomplished and there has been established in accordance with the freely expressed will of the Japanese people a peacefully inclined and responsible government.

13. We call upon the government of Japan to proclaim now the unconditional surrender of all Japanese armed forces, and to provide proper and adequate assurances of their good faith in such action. The alternative for Japan is prompt and utter destruction.

After naming the issuing parties in Article 1, Articles 2 and 3 warned the Japanese of what they were about to face militarily. Articles 4, 5, and 6 took aim at the Japanese leadership responsible for the war and its continuation. Grew and Stimson had long thought there was a "submerged" element in Japan who wanted to end the war and make peace. The text made one last attempt to get them to act, if they could. At the end of Article 5, the document included an ominous warning, "We shall brook no delay." The clock was ticking toward the August 3 deadline for the first deployment of the bomb.

Article 7 broached the issue of occupation, the single most important element in the declaration; because only through occupation could the Allies "secure the achievement" of the terms of the agreement and put a permanent end to "Japan's war-making power."

Article 8 restricted Japanese sovereignty to the home islands of Honshu, Hokkaido, Kyūshū, and Shikoku and stripped her of: South Sakhalin, Hong Kong, Vietnam, Cambodia, Laos, Thailand, Malaysia, Indonesia, Singapore, Korea, all of the islands in the Pacific which she seized or occupied since the beginning of World War I, and all the territories Japan had stolen from the Chinese, including Manchuria, Formosa, and the Pescadores.

Article 9 struck a conciliatory tone, telling the Japanese, after being completely disarmed by the Allies, Japan's military forces would be allowed to return home and resume "peaceful and productive lives."

Article 10 contained three major components: 1) "we do not intend to enslave or destroy Japan as nation and people"; 2) "but stern justice shall be meted out to war criminals, including those who have visited cruelties upon our prisoners"; and 3) the new "Japanese Government shall remove all obstacles to the revival and strengthening of democratic tendencies among the Japanese people." As it had in discussions among Allied political and military leaders, the issue of POWs was raised, explicitly putting the Japanese on notice that at the conclusion of the war those people responsible would be quickly sought out and dealt with harshly.

Articles 11 and 12 dealt with the resumption of a peaceful economy in Japan, its participation in world trade, and the eventual withdrawal of occupation forces.

The final Article, 13, contained two important statements. The first included the only use of the term unconditional surrender, applying it to "all Japanese armed forces." The second, again, warned the Japanese that time was critical to what happened next. They were told to accept the terms, or "The alternative for Japan is prompt and utter destruction."

Japan's rejection of the Potsdam Declaration meant atomic weapons would be employed against her.[18] Her leaders wrongly assumed prompt and utter destruction simply meant the Allies would attack with greater conventional weapons and forces to subdue her now that they could concentrate their entire war effort on defeating Japan. And the Soviets were not a signatory to the declaration, as they had not yet entered the war against Japan.

Stimson, Grew, and Churchill had been largely successful in getting the language they wanted in the Potsdam Declaration, which now specified what unconditional surrender meant in "terms" to the Japanese.

Only their categorical statement guaranteeing the Japanese they could keep the imperial system was missing, and as seen in the MAGIC DIPLOMATIC SUMMARY NO. 1214, dated July 22, Tōgō told Ambassador Satō on July 21, that sole condition would not have been enough to elicit Japan's surrender.

Stimson and Grew must have been greatly disappointed at what transpired next. Their belief in a submerged peace faction within Japan failed to act, or more likely did not have the power to act, as the military members of the Big Six held firm their control of the government.

As noted, Truman included the topic of prisoner of war treatment in Article 10 of the Potsdam Declaration and would do so again in his August 9 speech announcing the second atomic attack on Nagasaki, the Allied reply to Japan's first surrender offer, and finally in the Instrument of Surrender.

In fact, securing their safety and determining their locations so food and medical supplies could be air dropped was a top priority immediately after Japan surrendered on August 15. There can be no doubt it was a matter of great importance to the president, and for good reason. From the very early stages of the war, after the fall of the Philippines, Guam, and Wake Island to the Japanese, stories began to surface about the mistreatment of American POWs.

Hirohito had received instruction in international law from Sakutarō Tachi, an expert in the subject. Sakutarō had studied law in Europe for four years and became a professor of law at Tokyo Imperial University. In 1919, he had served on the *Commission of Responsibilities*, which dealt with the matter of World War I war crimes. Hirohito knew that Japan had signed (but not ratified) the 1929 Geneva Convention, which contained provisions dealing with the Treatment of Prisoners of War. He knew from Imperial rescripts that his grandfather and father believed international law needed to be respected. Yet Hirohito never issued orders to his military that required them to provide humane treatment of prisoners that would have prevented mass slaughter or abuse of Chinese POWs. The act of omission reflected broad opinion in Japan during the 1930s that viewed international law as purely a Western invention intended to protect the interests of the Americans and British.[19]

In World War II, Japanese malfeasance directed at Allied POWs reached its pinnacle on August 1, 1944, when policy became government-sanctioned murder in the form of a *Japanese Kill Order*, which stated, "It is the aim not to allow the escape of a single one [POW], to annihilate them all, and not to leave any traces." In the city of Taihoku, on Formosa (modern day Taiwan), an entry in a Japanese headquarters journal recorded "extreme measures to be taken against POWs in urgent situations: Whether they are destroyed individually or in groups, or however, it is done, with mass bombing, poisonous smoke, poisons, drowning, decapitation, or what, dispose of the prisoners as the situation dictates."[20] Historian Gavan Daws proffered this description of Japanese during the war:

> Asia under the Japanese was a carnal house of atrocities. As soon as the war ended, evidence of war crimes began piling up, in mountains. POWs, civilian internees, and Asian natives starved, beaten, tortured, shot, beheaded. The water cure. Electrical shock. Vivisection. Cannibalism. Men strung up over open flames or coiled in barbed wire and rolled along the ground, nails torn out, balls burned with cigarettes, dicks cut off and stuffed in mouths. Women dragged naked behind motorcycles, raped and ripped open, babies skewered on bayonets. Cities in China and providences in the Philippines laid waste, mass murderers in the Indies, towns and villages wiped out, all the way to the remotest of small places in the Pacific, the island of Naura, where the 34 sufferers in the leprosy hospital were taken out to sea and drowned, and Ocean Island, where days after the war ended all the native laborers were pushed over a cliff.[21]

From the end of the Battle of Okinawa until the end of the war has often been depicted as a time when, apart from America's ongoing blockade and bombardment and the atomic attacks, most of the killing had ceased. For Allied military and civilian POWs and Asians still under Japan's brutal occupation, this was not the case.[22]

In the course of the war the Japanese took more than 140,000 Caucasian prisoners of war (mostly American, British, and Dutch), the overwhelming majority in the first six months of the war. Nearly one third died in captivity.[23] Of the 24,992 Americans captured, 8,634 died—or thirty-five percent of the total. By contrast, of the 93,653 US Army personnel taken prisoner by the Germans, only 833 died—or slightly less than one percent.[24]

In addition to the military POWs who died in camps, more than a third of the Allied POWs slated for use as slave laborers in Japan died during transport when their ships were sunk by American submarines and aircraft. None of the ships carrying these men had markings identifying them that would have warned off attackers. The Japanese estimated 10,800 POWs died in these crossings.[25]

A relatively small subset of American POWs were airmen, but they were often singled out for some of the worst treatment. As early as April of 1942, the Japanese executed three of the eight captured Doolittle Raiders. But the most despised were the crewmen of B-29s, who were shot, bayoneted, decapitated, burned alive, and had boiling water poured over them.[26] However, the ghastliest treatment occurred on May 17, 23, and 29, and June 3, 1945, when Japanese doctors used captured B-29 airmen in vivisection experiments at Kyūshū Imperial University. Under orders from the Western Japan Military Command and Professor Ishiyama Fukujirō, director of external medicine, the experiments involved removing the prisoner's lungs, liver, and stomach; stopping the blood flow near the heart by pinching off a major artery to see how long death took; and drilling holes into the skull of the victim and inserting a knife to see what would happen.[27]

The Japanese also imprisoned 130,895 Allied civilians, again captured mostly during the early days of the war. While the percentage who died was one third of the military prisoners, nevertheless, 14,650 perished—a sickening eleven percent.

Far surpassing the number of Allied military and civilian personnel taken by the Japanese were the 600,000, mostly Asian peoples, called *romusha*, taken as slave laborers from the conquered and occupied territories of the Empire. Of those, it is believed nearly half, 290,000, perished.[28]

JULY 27, 1945
10 DAYS TO HIROSHIMA

Now in receipt of the Potsdam Declaration, Japan's leaders began their deliberation of the document. Tōgō's first reaction, which he recounted years later in his book *The Cause of Japan*, was:

> In view of the language, 'Following are our terms,' it was evidently not a dictate of unconditional surrender. I got the impression that

the Emperor's wishes had reached the United States and Great Britain, and had had the result of this moderation of attitude. It appeared also that a measure of consideration had been given to Japan's economic position;…I felt special relief upon seeing the economic provisions of the declaration—the gist of them being that the function of Japan as a processing nation,…would be recognized, and that to this end severe reparations would not be imposed.

The territorial provisions of declaration I did not deem in the light of the Atlantic Charter to be fitting, for—putting aside the question of the independence of Korea—Formosa and our other territories would have to be surrendered in conformity with the edict of the Cairo Declaration, and our sovereignty would in effect be limited to the four main islands of Japan. As to the occupation, also, there were some doubts. The occupation seemed, it is true, to have applicability to designated points in our country, and it apparently was to be—unlike the treatment of Germany after her surrender—a guarantee occupation not involving extensive administration; there was a question, however, whether Tokyo and the other large cities would be included among the points designated. I considered, further, that there were some ambiguities concerning the eventual form of the Japanese government, and also that complications might result from the language relating to disarmament and war criminals.

…I thought it desirable to enter into negotiation with the Allied Powers to obtain some clarification, and revision—even if it should be slight—of disadvantageous points in the declaration.[29]

Clearly, Tōgō immediately saw the distinction between the Potsdam Declaration's terms and unconditional surrender and, as a result, the opportunity to negotiate. However, his reaction to the "territorial provisions" seems out of character with his previous stance. Tōgō had earlier conceded in his second communiqué to Satō on July 11 that Japan would not attempt to hold on to territories outside Japan as a concession to end the war. In that message he stated:

Please tell [the Soviet Government] that: We consider the maintenance of peace in East Asia to be one aspect of the maintenance of world peace. Accordingly, Japan—as a proposal for

ending the war and because of her concern for the establishment
and maintenance of lasting peace—has absolutely no idea of
annexing or holding the territories which she has occupied during
the war.

So why now did he believe the Japanese held a better position? Perhaps it was just the nature of being a diplomat—as soon as the other
side makes an offer, everything is up for discussion. Because nothing
had occurred in the intervening two weeks to improve Japan's bargaining power, and Tōgō had already acknowledged Japan's weakness in his
first July 11 message to Satō, stating:

> We are now secretly giving consideration to the termination of the
> war because of the pressing situation which confronts Japan both
> at home and abroad.

Only in an invasion would the plans for Ketsu-Gō have a chance
of inflicting the desired horrific casualties that would convince the
Americans that the price for unconditional surrender would be too
high, thus creating an opportunity for the Japanese to negotiate more
favorable terms. But if the United States decided instead to continue
the blockade and bombardment of the Japanese homeland in a prolonged siege, they might literally strangle the life out of the nation.
The biggest downside to the Allies' slow-death strategy was the indefi-
nite timeline to ultimately secure Japan's surrender.

Perhaps as Marshall and Hull had feared, any sign of a flagging
resolve by the Allies would automatically trigger a belief by even the
most moderate Japanese to overestimate their position.

That Tōgō and his peers simultaneously ignored the time-critical
warnings in the declaration, specifically "we shall brook no delay" and
"the alternative is prompt and utter destruction," would turn out to be
a ruinous and lasting mistake. Throughout the war Japan had consistently underestimated American resolve. Perhaps now, all evidence to
the contrary, they thought the Americans were bluffing.

The morning of July 27, the Emperor met with Tōgō, who reported
on Soviet engagement, the British election, and the Potsdam Declaration. Regarding the latter, Tōgō stressed that "the declaration must be
treated with the utmost circumspection, both domestically and inter-
nationally. In particular, he feared the consequences if Japan should

manifest an intention to reject it." Regarding the Soviets, Tōgō told the Emperor that nothing had come to date from their efforts and their "attitude toward the declaration should be decided in accordance with [the] outcome."[30]

Tōgō reiterated his position on the Potsdam Declaration at a 10:30 a.m. meeting of the Big Six, and then later in the afternoon with the full Cabinet. After discussing some concern that the public would get wind of the Allied offer and force the government to take a stance, Tōgō thought he had secured an agreement that nothing would be said until a clarification of Soviet intentions had been determined.

In Washington, War Department analysts distributed a Naval Intelligence assessment to all top policymakers in the MAGIC Diplomatic Summary, detailing the Japanese political situation that had been woven together from the Ultra and MAGIC evidence.[31] It stated:

> An analysis of Japan's situation, as revealed through Ultra sources, suggests her unwillingness to surrender stems primarily from the failure of her otherwise capable and all-powerful Army leaders to perceive that the defenses they are so assiduously fashioning actually are utterly inadequate. There is nothing in the Japanese mind to prevent capitulation per se, as demonstrated by the advocacy of virtual unconditional surrender by an increasing number of highly placed Japanese abroad. However, until the Japanese leaders realize that an invasion cannot be repelled, there is little likelihood that they will accept any peace terms satisfactory to the Allies.[32]

This accurately depicted what confronted America's political leaders. While there were a growing number of overseas Japanese diplomats willing to countenance "virtual unconditional surrender," the military leaders in control of the government would not, and they were the ones who mattered.

JULY 28, 1945
9 DAYS TO HIROSHIMA

On the morning of July 28, to Tōgō's anger and amazement, Japanese newspapers reported that the government had decided to ignore the Potsdam Declaration.

The *Ashai Shimbun*, one of Japan's largest newspapers, ran the headline:

July 28, 1945

LAUGHABLE MATTER

Imperial Prime Minister Suzuki characterizes the Allies' Potsdam Declaration as "a thing of no great value."[33]

Secretary of War Stimson later wrote that once the Japanese rejected the proclamation as "unworthy of public notice," the United States was bound to demonstrate what the threat of "prompt and utter destruction" meant.

Sometime after the July 27 meeting of the Big Six had adjourned, one of the military members, probably Anami, persuaded Suzuki to openly reject the Allied peace offer and the agreement Tōgō thought he had achieved.

Throwing salt into Tōgō's open wounds, beginning at 3:00 p.m. Suzuki held an hour-long press conference in the Grand Drawing Room of the Prime Minister's residence. During the session, a member of the press asked Suzuki, "What is the Premier's view regarding the Joint Proclamation by the three countries?" to which he replied, "I believe the Joint Proclamation by the three countries is nothing but a rehash of the Cairo Declaration. As for the Government, it does not find any important value in it, and there is no other recourse but to ignore it entirely and resolutely fight for the successful conclusion of this war." [34]

The actual word Suzuki used to describe Japan's position was *mokusatsu*, interpreted as "to ignore it entirely." *Mokusatsu* is a Japanese word meaning "ignore," "take no notice of," or "treat with silent contempt." It is composed of two kanji characters: moku ("silence") and satsu ("killing"). If there was any ambiguity over the meaning of the word *mokusatsu*, Suzuki should not have used it in the first place. Undoubtedly, he did not consult with Tōgō. He and his government owned the obligation to make clear Japan's position. And contrary to Tōgō's belief that once the words had been spoken nothing could be done to retract them, the Japanese had nine days until Hiroshima to elucidate what they meant.

They chose to do nothing.

Also surprised by his government's dismissal of the Allied surrender offer was Rear Admiral Sōkichi Takagi, a confidant of the allegedly moderate Yonai and longtime opponent of the war. He asked Yonai why Suzuki had been allowed to reject the Potsdam Declaration, to which Yonai replied:

> If one is the first to issue a statement, he is always at a disadvantage. Churchill has fallen, America is beginning to be isolated. The government therefore will ignore it. There is no need to rush.[35]

The Potsdam Declaration had been continuously broadcast and also sent "through the customary neutral diplomatic channels; that is, through the intermediaries of Switzerland and Sweden since July 26 but no formal reply had come." [On July 28], "radio monitors reported that…Tokyo had reaffirmed the Japanese government's determination to fight. Our proclamation had been referred to as 'unworthy of consideration,' 'absurd,' and 'presumptuous,'" said Truman.[36]

What was the Emperor's reaction to the Potsdam Declaration? First it should be remembered that until early June, he fully embraced the "decisive battle doctrine," as attested to in the *Showa Tenno Dokuhakuroku*, Hirohito's memoir. Sometime shortly after Suzuki's June 9 speech, when the Prime Minister repeated that the country would "fight to the last," Hirohito, convinced by Kido to do so, began advocating a démarche through the Soviets to mediate an end of the war. With no meaningful response or movement in their attempted discussions more than five weeks later, the Emperor and his government had nothing to react to other than the Allied joint declaration.

The *Showa Tenno Dokuhakuroku* also contained disparagements of the failures of the Emperor's advisors during the war, but conspicuously absent was any mention of Suzuki's use of the word *mokusatsu* regarding his government's response to the Potsdam Declaration. Nor was there a contrary response by Hirohito, publicly or privately at the time. A man known to read the newspapers daily and in nearly constant contact with his government, he certainly knew of the rejection. Had he been displeased or concerned, Kido would likely have mentioned it in his detailed diary of his conversations with the Emperor. But he did not.[37] Also absent in the *Showa Tenno Dokuhakuroku* were any claims by the Emperor that he intended for Konoye to immediately terminate the war or that terms for an end to the war had been formulated.[38]

The Emperor's failure matches that of his government. Satō had repeatedly told Tōgō he needed concrete terms to present to the Soviets and Tōgō had been unable to provide them; in fact, he acknowledged the leadership had not reached agreement on the terms to secure Soviet mediation in his August 2 message to Satō, let alone terms to end the war.[39]

Two events overlapped in this period of time and revealed the Emperor's highest priorities. First on July 25 and again on July 31, Hirohito instructed Kido to safeguard the Imperial Regalia of Japan—a mirror, a sword, and a curved jewel—all passed down from his ancestors over a thousand years and all symbols of the Imperial line and his right to rule. Securing these objects was more important than the fate of millions of his subjects.[40]

As for Hirohito's government, its attempts to seek Soviet assistance in navigating an end to the war were bland. There was no finite decision to end the war with "concrete" positions that would have taken into consideration its political, economic, and military circumstances. There is no record of the Big Six or the rest of Suzuki's Cabinet ever attempting to discuss specific conditions under which the Japanese government would accept an end to the war to present to the Soviets, let alone gain the unanimous agreement of those terms, as demanded by its government. If any such meetings took place, they were an abject failure. It is most likely that Anami, Umezu, and Toyoda, the power clique inside the Big Six, were not interested in bringing the war to end; Suzuki was a weak leader, and even Yonai, a moderate, was still unmoved by the plight of his countrymen.

From July 11 until August 3, Tōgō and Satō exchanged a series of messages, the former interminably asking Satō to seek the "good offices" of the Russians and begin discussions on the termination of the war, as long as it was clear that it did not mean unconditional surrender. Repeatedly, Satō responded that the Japanese offer was too vague because the Soviets were insisting on "a concrete plan." But Tōgō refused to listen and continued to press Satō, only to be rebuffed in unusually brusque language by Satō and the inaction of the Soviets.

This pattern of impasse within the Japanese government and the inability to recognize consequences to it would be repeated by the members of the Big Six in the days to come.

JULY 30, 1945
7 DAYS TO HIROSHIMA

Part II of Satō's message to Tōgō regarding the "Three Power

Proclamation"—a message intercepted and interpreted by MAGIC—read:

> The important point in connection with the Joint Proclamation is that America and England have demanded Japan's immediate unconditional surrender and have stated clearly that they have no intention of softening the terms set forth in the Proclamation. If it is to be understood that Stalin was completely unable to influence the intentions of America and England on this point, it follows that he will be unable to accept our proposal to send a Special Envoy. ...There is no alternative but immediate unconditional surrender if we are to try to make America and England moderate and to prevent [Russia's] participation in the war.
>
> Moreover, immediately after Japan's surrender, Stalin will bring full and heavy pressure on America, England, and China with regard to Manchukuo, China, and Korea, and will proceed in the hope of achieving his own demands. Since he actually possesses the real power [to do this] there is no reason why he should now want to make a treaty with Japan...
>
> Furthermore, it is worthy of note that [Herbert Vere] Evatt, the Austrian Foreign Minister, has stated that he is opposed to the tendency of the Joint Proclamation to show greater leniency toward Japan than the United Nations showed Germany...[41]

Once again Satō shows a clear understanding of the circumstances when he says, "If it is to be understood that Stalin was completely unable to influence the intentions of America and England...it follows that he will be unable to accept our proposal to send a Special Envoy." In fact, he states the situation has disintegrated to the point where the Japanese need to forget about relying on the Soviets to mitigate with the Anglo-Americans and instead use "America and England...to prevent [Russia's] participation in the war". against Japan.

Late in the evening, another urgent Top-Secret cable for President Truman arrived. But due to the lateness of the hour, the message was held for delivery until 7:48 a.m. the following morning. The message, concerning the development of the atomic bomb, came from George Harrison, Stimson's special assistant in Washington:

The time schedule on Groves project is progressing so rapidly that is now essential that a statement for release by you be available no later than Wednesday, 1 August...

It was time for Truman to give a final greenlight for the use of the bomb, a decision only the president could make. Writing in large, distinct letters with a lead pencil, Truman penned:

Suggestion approved. Release when ready but no sooner than August 2.[42]

And then he handed the message to Elsey for transmission.

AUGUST 1, 1945
5 DAYS TO HIROSHIMA

On Tinian, in an air-conditioned bomb hut, *Little Boy*'s firing mechanism was being fitted into the ten foot by twenty-eight-inch bomb casing for the 9,700-pound device. The blunt-nosed bomb, with four tail fins, looked like any other conventional bomb, except for its enormous size. "It was an ugly monster," said the pilot who would deliver it, Colonel Paul W. Tibbets, aka the "Old Bull."[43] Two (U-235) slugs were all that remained to complete the assembly. One arrived with the *Indy*; the second had been loaded aboard a B-29 at Hamilton Air Force Base in California the same day the cruiser delivered its momentous cargo.[44] Both slugs would remain under constant guard in the ordnance area until the bomb's loading, the day of the mission.

The components for more bombs were in route.

AUGUST 2, 1945
4 DAYS TO HIROSHIMA

Throughout the Potsdam Conference, according to Leahy, Truman had stood up to Stalin. He had rejected a war reparations agreement that would've repeated a mistake made after World War I that saw Americans paying for German reparations.[45] Leahy said, "Our new President, in my opinion... handled himself extremely well at Potsdam. He had been firm where firmness was dictated by our national interest. Like myself, he was disappointed that Soviet objection prevented acceptance of many proposals that he considered highly important to the future peace of Europe."[46]

The endless Soviet objections to proposals related to the peace of Europe left Leahy with "serious doubts that any peace treaties acceptable to our government could be negotiated." Byrnes echoed Truman and Leahy's sentiments, since all of the concessions won still relied on the Russians carrying out their obligations, and by now Byrnes too had "little confidence in their pledges."[47]

At the conclusion of the conference, British Prime Minister Clement Attlee, Stalin, and Truman all expressed their satisfaction in the agreements reached, but it belied a sense, at least by the Anglo-Americans, of discontent and foreboding that they had traded one tyrant for another. And Truman privately decided not to allow the Soviets "any part in the control of Japan."[48]

How would Roosevelt have done had he been at Potsdam instead of Truman? Bohlen, for one, believed worse. Roosevelt had a vested interest in previous agreements with Stalin, and given his obstinacy on virtually every issue, FDR would likely have reacted angrily. For Bohlen, Harriman, and others knowledgeable in dealing with the Russians, Truman showed himself a capable leader. "He was never defeated or made to look foolish or uninformed in debate," Bohlen wrote.[49]

Tōgō responded to Part II of Satō's July 30 message, an answer also captured by the MAGIC codebreakers:

> I have been fully apprised of Your Excellency's views by your successive wires…However, it should not be difficult for you realize that, although with the urgency of the war situation our time to proceed with arrangements for ending the war before the enemy lands on the Japanese mainland is limited, on the other hand it is difficult to decide on concrete peace conditions here at home all at once. At present, in accordance with the Imperial Will, there is a unanimous determination to seek the good offices of the Russians in ending the war, to make concrete terms a matter between Japan and Russia, and to send Prince Konoye, who has the deep trust of the Emperor, to carry on discussions with the Russians. It has been decided at any rate to send a Special Envoy in accordance with the views of the highest leaders of [this] Government and…we are exerting ourselves to collect the views of all quarters on the matter of concrete terms.
>
> (Under the circumstances there is a disposition to make the Potsdam

Three Power Proclamation the basis of our study concerning terms.)[50]

Thus, nearly three months after the May 11 secret meeting when the Big Six had first broached the topic of peace, they could only agree on the same three things Tōgō had been communicating to Satō since July 11—"There is a unanimous determination to seek the good offices of the Russians in ending the war, to make concrete terms a matter between Japan and Russia, and to send Prince Konoye." Tōgō then confessed, "We are exerting ourselves to collect the views of all quarters on the matter of concrete terms."

The last statement indicated that in the same three-month period, the Japanese hadn't even reached out to everyone whose opinion needed to be heard on the subject of terms. Worse still, when the entire issue of Japanese terms should have been put aside in favor of using the Potsdam Declaration as the starting point for any future discussions, outside of Tōgō and perhaps the Emperor, there was no agreement to do so. In fact, every other member of the Big Six believed Japan was in a position to negotiate something even better.

AUGUST 3, 1945
3 DAYS TO HIROSHIMA

Several days after his public rejections of the Potsdam Declaration to the Japanese press, Suzuki met in the afternoon with the members of his Cabinet Advisory Council. The council included the president of Asano Cement, the founder of the Nissan consortium, the vice president of the Bank of Japan, as well as other representatives of the nation's leading businesses, who had profited greatly from the war. The group recommended acceptance of the Potsdam terms on the basis that they allowed Japan to retain its nonmilitary industries and participate in world trade. In a response that likely surprised the men, Suzuki said:

> For the enemy to say something like that means circumstances have arisen that force them also to end the war. That is why they are talking about unconditional surrender. Precisely at a time like this, if we hold firm, then they will yield before we do. Just because they broadcast their declaration, it is not necessary to stop fighting. You advisors may ask me to reconsider, but I don't think there is any need to stop [the war].[51]

Had the Allies mistakenly inferred Japan's rejection of the Potsdam Declaration? Absolutely not. For the third time, twice publicly and now privately among the nation's most important businessmen, Suzuki refused to accept it.

The second half of Tōgō's August 2 message to Satō contained a statement that for the first time expressly indicated the Japanese Army supported the effort to end the war with Soviet assistance. The message, intercepted and translated by MAGIC codebreakers, read as follows:

> The most urgent task which now confronts us is to persuade the Soviet government to accept the mission of our Special Envoy. His Majesty, the Emperor, is most profoundly concerned about the matter and has been following developments with the keenest interest. The Premier and the leaders of the Army are now concentrating all their attention on this one point...
>
> Whatever happens, if we should let one day slip by, that might have [word uncertain, probably 'results'] lasting for thousands of years. Consequently, if the Soviet government should reply in the negative [to Japan's 25 July request that a Special Envoy be sent for the purpose of obtaining Russia's 'good offices'] I urge you to do everything possible to arrange another interview with Molotov at once...and do your best to induce the Soviet government to reconsider the matter and furnish us with an immediate reply.[52]

Only two parts of this message from Tōgō differed from all the previous ones. The Army now supported sending the Special Envoy, and finally, Tōgō himself recognized the importance of moving quickly or risking potentially disastrous consequences. Everything else was rehash and gave Satō nothing of substance to present to the Russians.

AUGUST 4, 1945
2 DAYS TO HIROSHIMA

Not surprisingly, the always candid Satō sent Tōgō a cold reply:

> Regardless of whether we are able to obtain the good offices of the Russian Government for the termination of the war, the fact is undeniable that the Three Power Proclamation of 26 July by America, England, and China already provides a basis for ending the

Greater East Asia War...I feel that the statement in your [message of 2 August] indicating that you are disposed at least to make the Three Power Proclamation the basis for study of our conditions is extremely auspicious...

As for the peace terms which would [ultimately] be worked out...if one looks at the terms for the handling of Germany decided upon at Potsdam, it is not far-fetched to surmise that a certain amelioration [of conditions for Japan] would be possible... However, if the Government and the Military dilly-dally in bringing this resolution to fruition, then all Japan will be reduced to ashes and we will not be able [to avoid] following the road to ruin...[53]

8

HIROSHIMA

AUGUST 5, 1945
1 DAY TO HIROSHIMA

Although radar had been used to identify and bomb cities in Japan for many months, the atomic attacks were to be conducted visually—this meant weather would play an important role in the selection of potential targets for each mission and on the day of the mission against the final target. Rather than relying entirely on weather forecasts, Colonel Paul W. Tibbets came up with a simple solution. If the weather looked generally favorable for an attack, three B-29s would leave about an hour in advance of the plane carrying the atomic bomb. Their purpose was to scout each of the three potential targets and radio their respective weather conditions back to bombing formation. For the first atomic attack, *Full House*, *Jabit III*, and *Straight Flush* were charged with performing weather reconnaissance. On the morning of August 5, the heavy cloud cover that had hung over the Japanese islands for several days finally began breaking up, and the forecast was favorable for takeoff after midnight.

In addition to the weather scout planes and the *Enola Gay*, the plane named for Tibbets's red-haired mother and which carried the atomic bomb, three other B-29s participated in the first atomic mission: *The Great Artiste*, carrying scientific instruments to measure the intensity of the blast; *Necessary Evil*, with photographic equipment to make a pictorial record of the event; and *Top Secret*, as a backup plane in case the *Enola Gay* developed mechanical trouble.[1]

The previous night, Captain "Deak" William Parsons, the Navy ordnance expert responsible for arming the bomb, witnessed two overloaded B-29s crash in fiery, thunderous explosions when they failed to become airborne. Parsons told Major General Thomas Farrell if the plane carrying the atomic bomb crashed on takeoff the bomb might explode, devastating the island and its occupants.[2] As a result, Deak managed to secure Farrell's permission to attempt to learn how to arm the bomb in flight to avoid such a disaster.

In Moscow, Ambassador Naotake Satō learned of Soviet Foreign Minister Vyacheslav Molotov's return from Germany on August 5 and requested a meeting. He secured an appointment two days hence on August 8.

On Tinian, preparations for August 6's unprecedented mission began late in the afternoon. An ordnance crew rolled *Little Boy*, covered with vulgar messages to the Emperor, out of its air-conditioned sanctuary into the blazing sun to Atomic Bomb Pit 1. The concrete underground pit, which had two twin sisters for backup—a second on Tinian and a third, for emergencies, on Iwo Jima—contained a hydraulic lift, much like those used to lift an automobile. The pits were necessary to load the massive bombs into the aircraft; because the weapons were so large, they could not be loaded conventionally; due to the lack of clearance under the bomber and the weight of the bomb. The bomber had to be towed backwards over the pit with its bomb bay doors open. Then, the hydraulic lift hoisted the bomb inside the belly of the B-29.

At dusk, Parsons climbed into the stifling fuselage. He squatted beside the bomb, where he practiced the final assembly hour after hour, until his hands were covered in blood. But his effort ultimately proved successful.[3]

After evening mess at the *Dogpatch Inn*, the seven flight crews taking part in the mission met in the assembly hut for a routine briefing—routine with a couple exceptions. First, Tibbets changed the radio call sign from *Victor* to *Dimples* to confuse any Japanese listening posts that might be monitoring their communications. Second, because the bomb bay was an unpressurized part of the plane, the first leg of the flight would be flown at no greater than 5,000 feet while Parsons armed the bomb. Tibbets also took the opportunity to describe the air rescue capabilities that had been arranged for the mission. Submarines and surface ships would be spaced along the entire 1,700-mile corridor from Tinian to the south coast of Japan.[4]

A few hours later, at 11:00 p.m., Tibbets gave his final briefing of the night to the three crews that would fly with him on the thirteen-hour mission to drop the first atomic bomb on Japan. Joining Tibbets at the front of the room were Parsons and Norman F. Ramsey Jr.—a physicist and leader of Group E-7 of the Ordnance Division, created at Los Alamos, and the man responsible for integrating the bomb's design with its delivery system, the B-29. By now, the tension among the crewmen had become palpable; all recognized the magnitude of what they were about to do and its potential impact on the war. Tibbets began by issuing welder's goggles to everyone, explaining they were to protect their eyes against the bright flash, far brighter than the sun, when the bomb exploded.

Tibbets didn't prepare a written statement, but William Laurence, Science Editor of the *New York Times*, the only newspaper covering the story and who took notes, quoted Tibbets as saying:

> Tonight is the night we have all been waiting for. Our long months of training are to be put to the test. We will soon know if we have been successful or failed. Upon our efforts tonight it is possible that history will be made. We are going on a mission to drop a bomb different from any you have ever seen or heard about. This bomb contains the destructive force equivalent to 20,000 tons of TNT.[5]

The number left the men in shocked disbelief; none could imagine a single bomb with such destructive force. "Frankly, neither could I," Tibbets later recalled.[6]

The briefing closed with a prayer by Chaplain William Downey, a husky twenty-seven-year-old pastor from Hope Lutheran Church in Minneapolis:

> We pray Thee that the end of the war may come soon, and that once more we may know peace on earth. May the men who fly this night be kept safe in Thy care, and may they be returned safely to us.
>
> We shall go forward trusting in Thee, knowing that we are in Thy Care now and forever. In the name of Jesus Christ. Amen.

After the prayer the men returned to the *Dogpatch Inn* for a preflight meal. As they were about to leave, flight surgeon Don Young came to Tibbets's table and handed him a cardboard pillbox containing twelve cyanide capsules, one for each member of the crew. Young told Tibbets, "I hope you don't have to use these," to which Tibbets replied, "Don't worry. The odds are in our favor," and then he slipped them into a pocket of his coveralls. Except for Deak Parsons, none of the flight crew knew of the suicide preparations.[7]

AUGUST 6, 1945
ZERO DAY

Shortly after 1:00 a.m. the men left the mess hall to pick up their flight gear. In Tibbets's case, it included a lengthy list of smoking equipment, consisting of cigars, cigarettes, pipe tobacco, and pipes for the long journey.

Finally ready, the men headed for the flight line in jeeps. To their surprise, they found *Enola Gay*, bathed in floodlights like the star of a Hollywood movie surrounded by motion picture and still cameras and a throng of photographers and well-wishers. Apart from its memorable name, the plane carried two identifying markers, the number 82 on its nose and fuselage and a large capital R encircled in black on its tail.

Besides Tibbets, twelve men climbed aboard *Enola Gay* in the wee morning hours of August 6. They included: Captain Robert A. Lewis, the copilot; Major Thomas W. Ferebee, bombardier; Captain Theodore J. Van Kirk, navigator; Lieutenant Jacob Beser, radar countermeasures officer; Navy Captain William S. Parsons, weaponeer and ordnance officer; Second Lieutenant Morris Jeppson, assistant weaponeer; Sergeant Joe Stiborik, radar operator; Staff Sergeant George R. Caron, tail gunner; Sergeant Robert H. Shumard, assistant flight engineer; Private Richard H. Nelson, radio operator, and Tech Sergeant Wyatt E. Duzenbury, flight engineer.[8]

After nearly thirty minutes of preflight checking and warmup of the plane's four R-3350 Wright Duplex Cyclone engines, Tibbets waved to the crowd and began his taxi of over a mile to the southwest end of Runway Able. Behind Tibbets were his two escorts and the backup plane, the three weather reconnaissance planes having left a little more than an hour earlier at 1:37 a.m.

With a quick glance over his shoulder to make sure everyone was ready and at their posts, Tibbets called to the tower, "Dimples Eight Two to North Tinian Tower. Ready for takeoff on Runway Able." The tower replied promptly, "Dimples Eight Two. Dimples Eight Two, cleared for takeoff."

From the control tower, Laurence watched intently at General Farrell's side as *Enola Gay* released her brakes and slowly rumbled down the runway to begin Special Bombing Mission No. 13, code name

"Centerboard." Accelerating to 155 miles an hour but burdened by a nearly five-ton bomb and 7,000 gallons of fuel, she seemed earthbound. The onlookers remembered the two Superfortresses that had crashed the night before, their black skeletal remains still visible, and strained as if to help lift the plane into the air.

As *Enola Gay* neared the end of the runway, Tibbets continued to hold the aircraft's nose down to build up more speed; his copilot Lewis thought it was "gobbling a little too much runway" and began to pull back on the yoke, but Tibbets held firm. At last, with only a hundred feet of the nearly two-mile-long oiled coral left, *Enola Gay* soared up into the darkness. Farrell looked over to a Navy officer and said, "I never saw a plane use that much runway. I thought Tibbets was never going to pull it off." It was exactly 2:45 a.m., August 6. *The Great Artiste, Necessary Evil,* and *Top Secret* followed quickly after.[9]

The rendezvous point for the quartet of planes, before heading onto the final leg of the mission, was Iwo Jima. Van Kirk noted in the official log for the flight their arrival at 5:55 a.m., as *Enola Gay* circled the island waiting for *The Great Artiste, Necessary Evil,* and *Top Secret* to catch up. With *Enola Gay* functioning perfectly, *Top Secret* dropped down and landed on Iwo Jima and awaited the outcome of the mission.

At 6:07 a.m., a flaming red sun, the symbol of Japan's rising sun war flag, beckoned the new day on the eastern horizon, as the three planes headed for the Japanese mainland and their still unknown target. The fate of one of three cities—Hiroshima, Kokura, and Nagasaki—depended entirely on the cloud cover over it three hours in the future.

As the three-plane formation departed Iwo Jima, Tibbets changed course fourteen degrees to a compass heading of 322-325 degrees northwest, on a path toward Shikoku and Hiroshima on the southern tip of Honshu. Over the next hour the planes steadily climbed to reach the bombing altitude of 30,700 feet and waited for word from the weather planes.

In Hiroshima, an air raid warning sounded at 7:09 a.m. and twenty-two minutes later at 7:31 a.m. ended with the "all-clear." At 7:30 a.m., a coded dispatch from *Straight Flush*, high over Hiroshima, came in. Dick Nelson, Tibbets's radio operator, wrote down the cryptic missive, "Y-3, Q-3, B-2, C-1." Leaning over Nelson, Tibbets "translated the message to mean that the cloud cover was less than three-tenths at all altitudes. 'C-1' was advice, quite unnecessary under the circumstances, to bomb the primary target."[10] Over the intercom, Tibbets informed his crew: their target was Hiroshima.

Within a few minutes, the shores of Shikoku, the smallest of Japan's four home islands, came into view. The men hurriedly strapped on their flak jackets. After crossing it, only a narrow body of water called the Iyo Sea stood between *Enola Gay* and Hiroshima. Tibbets thought they might be greeted by anti-aircraft fire or Japanese fighters, but recent flights by other small groups of B-29s had made the Japanese complacent to high flying B-29s, so they paid no attention to the approach of only three aircraft.

At about eight minutes before the scheduled bomb release, Hiroshima became visible and Tibbets made his next-to-last course change, a leftward sixty-degree turn to 264 degrees, almost due west. As the planes neared the Initial Point (IP), where the bombing run began, *Necessary Evil* dropped back. Parsons and Van Kirk came forward and looked over Tibbets's shoulder. Van Kirk compared notes with Ferebee on the ground speed, 285 knots (330 mph), and the fact that their drift to the right required an eight-degree correction. Ferebee quickly made the necessary adjustments to the Norden bombsight, which was now engaged with the autopilot for the bomb run.[11]

Things were happening fast, and suddenly Ferebee said, "Okay, I've got the bridge," pointing straight ahead. Van Kirk agreed, "No doubt about it," comparing what he was seeing to a reconnaissance photo. The Aiming Point (AP) for the bomb, the T-shaped Aioi Bridge over the Ota River in the heart of the city, was easily recognizable. No other bridge in the sprawling city even slightly resembled it.[12] The plane was only ninety seconds from bomb release.

"It's all yours," Tibbets told Ferebee, as he removed his hands from the controls and sat back in his seat.[13]

Ferebee, pressing his left eye to the viewfinder as the T-shaped bridge crept into the cross hairs of his bomb sight said, "We're on target." At 8:14:17, a minute before bomb release, he flicked a switch activating a high-pitched radio tone that sounded in the headphones of all the men in the three planes flying over Hiroshima, alerting them to the impending drop.[14] Bob Lewis leaned over and made a short notation in his informal log for Laurence: "There will be a short intermission while we bomb our target."

In the months leading up to the atomic attack, 140,000 civilians had left the city from its wartime peak of 380,000. They had fled for the safety of the countryside, leaving behind nearly a quarter of a million residents.[15] Two days prior to the bombing, the Americans had dropped 720,000 leaflets "warning [the residents] that their city among others would be obliterated unless Japan surrendered at once," but few paid them any mind.[16] Those who stayed had become accustomed to the frequent visits of the *B-san* or *Mr. B*, as the residents referred to the B-29s, and like the people of Dresden before them, thought they would be spared.

Dresden has almost universally been represented, for the past sixty years, as having no military value—but there are similarities between the two cities. Frederick Taylor's book, *Dresden*, published in 2005, revealed that the city was the center for high-tech manufacturing of very high-end optical equipment, mechanical fire control, and other very important war material production. Hiroshima was a major embarkation port for the Imperial Army during its advance across the Pacific, and home to 90,000 military personnel at the time of the atomic bombing.[17] The Second General Army was headquartered there and included some 43,000 troops. According to a Twentieth Air Force Tactical Mission Report produced that summer:

> The entire northeast and eastern sides of the city are military zones. Prominent in the north central part of the city are the Army Division headquarters marked by the Hiroshima Castle, numerous barracks, administrative building and ordnance storage houses. In addition, there are the following military targets: Army Reception Center, large Military Airport, Army Ordnance Depot, Army Clothing Depot, Army Food Depot, large port and dock area, several shipyards and ship building companies, the Japan Steel Company, railroad marshalling yards and numerous aircraft component parts factories.[18]

The city also served as a port through which supplies and communications passed from Honshu to Kyūshū. In short, Hiroshima was a beehive of Japan's war industry.[19]

The radio tone ceased exactly one minute after it began, replaced by the pneumatic sound of the front bomb bay doors automatically opening. Tibbets ordered the crew to put on their protective goggles. The immense, gun-metal gray *Little Boy* atomic bomb tumbled, tail first, out of the belly of the silver bomber. As it descended, it tipped over and hurtled nose down toward the metropolis below. By Tibbets's watch, the time was 9:15 a.m. plus seventeen seconds. In Hiroshima, it was 8:15 a.m.; *Enola Gay* had crossed a time zone in its flight from Tinian.[20]

With the abrupt loss of weight, the plane lunged upward. Tibbets turned 155 degrees violently to the right, pushed the aircraft down in a sixty-degree bank, and accelerated away from the bomb as fast as the plane's four 2200 horsepower radial engines could propel it. At the same time, *The Great Artiste* swung open its bomb bay doors and dropped, by parachute, its three scientific packages; it then banked at the same steep angle to the left. *Necessary Evil*, there to record the event on film, circled from a safe distance.

Below, the fan-shaped city of Hiroshima, lying mostly on the six islands formed by the seven estuarial rivers that branch out from the Ota River, was serene, an azure blue sky above it.[21] People engaged in their daily routine, adults going to work, children to school; it was morning rush hour. The residents paid no attention to such a small group of American planes.

The bomb dropped for forty-three seconds, exploding 1,890 feet above the ground at 8:16 a.m. in a pinkish burst that cut across the sky. A fireball, a football field in diameter, erupted from the flash without a sound. An iridescent bolt of light struck the ground. The heat from the blast melted the surface of granite within a thousand yards of the hypocenter. Roof tiles softened and changed color from black to olive or brown and were ripped off. A huge mushroom cloud, filled with every color in the rainbow, ascended five miles above the ground.[22]

In the center of the city, eerie human silhouettes were burned onto walls and the streets where people once stood before being instantly vaporized. A mile from the epicenter, thousands of Japanese soldiers doing morning calisthenics on the military base drill grounds burned to death.

A supersonic blast of wind tore across Hiroshima in a concentric ring, demolishing all but a few earthquake-proof buildings for two miles. It picked up people, blowing them through the air and smashing them against anything still upright. Some were transformed into grotesque carbon statues that littered the ground like leaves fallen from a huge tree.

The city became pitch black, silent, and then gradually the blackness dissipated like fog and gave way to gray. Zombie-like figures slogged slowly through the ruined city; their shredded and burned skin hung from them. A woman carried a baby with no head. Fires burned every-where. Dead bodies glutted the river and cluttered the ground; many were nothing but skeletal bones. Children cried for their mothers. Black rain fell.

Nine miles from the explosion, the supersonic blast wave rocked *Enola Gay*. Tibbets and Lewis held the yoke firmly to maintain control; finally, Parsons yelled, "We're in the clear now." Tibbets brushed aside his goggles, glanced over at the control panel, and turned the aircraft back toward Hiroshima to witness the devastation. He then ordered Nelson "to send a message in the clear that the primary target had been bombed visually with good results."

Parsons sent another, this one in code:

> Results clear-cut, successful in all respects. Visible effects greater than Trinity. Conditions normal in airplane following delivery, proceeding to Papacy [Tinian].[23]

Inside *Enola Gay*, Tibbets described what he saw: "The giant purple mushroom, which the tail-gunner [Caron] had described, had already risen to a height of 45,000 feet. 3 miles above our own altitude and was still boiling upward like something terribly alive. It was a frightening sight, and even though we were several miles away, it gave the appear-ance of something that was about to engulf us."[24]

President Truman was eating lunch in the mess hall with the ship's crew aboard the *USS Augusta*, on his way back to Washington from the Potsdam Conference. Captain Frank Graham, the White House Map Room Watch Officer, entered and greeted Truman, "Mr. President, I have an urgent cable for you." The message originated from the Navy Department and bore the highest priority marks.

The cable read:

> Following info regarding Manhattan received. "Hiroshima bombed visually with only one 10th cover at 052315A. There was no fighter opposition and no flak. Parsons reports 15 minutes after drop as follows: 'Results clear-cut successful in all respects. Visible effects greater than in any test. Conditions normal in airplane following delivery.'"

Truman, excited by the news, shook hands with Graham and called

Byrnes to give him the news. Truman then told the group of sailors near him, "This is the greatest thing in history. It's time for us to get home."

A few minutes later a second message was handed to the president. It read:

To the President

From the Secretary of War

Big bomb dropped on Hiroshima August 5 at 7:15 P.M. Washington time. First reports indicate complete success which was even more conspicuous than earlier test.[25]

At approximately 1:00 p.m., Truman, wearing a light-colored suit and a dark tie, sat at a desk, a microphone in front of him, and delivered a radio address to the world announcing the atomic attack on Hiroshima. Truman read from a prepared statement:

Sixteen hours ago, an American airplane dropped one bomb on Hiroshima, an important Japanese Army base. That bomb had more power than 20,000 tons of T.N.T. It had more than two thousand times the blast power of the British "Grand Slam," which is the largest bomb ever yet used in the history of warfare.

The Japanese began the war from the air at Pearl Harbor. They have been repaid many fold. And the end is not yet. With this bomb we have now added a new and revolutionary increase in destruction to supplement the growing power of our armed forces. In their present form these bombs are now in production and even more powerful forms are in development.

It is an atomic bomb. It is a harnessing of the basic power of the universe. The force from which the sun draws its power has been loosed against those who brought war to the Far East.

Before 1939, it was the accepted belief of scientists that it was theoretically possible to release atomic energy. But no one knew any practical method of doing it. By 1942, however, we knew that the Germans were working feverishly to find a way to add atomic energy to the other engines of war with which they hoped to enslave the world. But they failed. We may be grateful to Providence that the Germans got the V-1s and V-2s late and in limited quantities and even more grateful that they did not get the atomic bomb at all.

The battle of the laboratories held fateful risks for us as well as the battles of the air, land and sea, and we have now won the battle of the laboratories as we have won the other battles.

…We have spent two billion dollars on the greatest scientific gamble in history—and won.

But the greatest marvel is not the size of the enterprise, its secrecy, nor its cost, but the achievement of scientific brains in putting together infinitely complex pieces of knowledge held by many men in different fields of science into a workable plan. And hardly less marvelous has been the capacity of industry to design, and of labor to operate, the machines and methods to do things never done before so that the brain child of many minds came forth in physical shape and performed as it was supposed to do. Both science and industry worked under the direction of the United States Army, which achieved a unique success in managing so diverse a problem in the advancement of knowledge in an amazingly short time. It is doubtful if such another combination could be got together in the world. What has been done is the greatest achievement of organized science in history. It was done under high pressure and without failure.

We are now prepared to obliterate more rapidly and completely every productive enterprise the Japanese have above ground in any city. We shall destroy their docks, their factories, and their communications. Let there be no mistake; we shall completely destroy Japan's power to make war.

It was to spare the Japanese people from utter destruction that the ultimatum of July 26 was issued at Potsdam. Their leaders promptly rejected that ultimatum. If they do not now accept our terms, they may expect a rain of ruin from the air, the like of which has never been seen on this earth. Behind this air attack will follow sea and land forces in such numbers and power as they have not yet seen and with the fighting skill of which they are already well aware…

In contrast to Truman's exuberance, Leahy's mood became sullen. A few days later he wrote in his diary:

The press this morning reports that the atomic bomb, dropped on Hiroshima the day before yesterday, destroyed more than half the city and brought from the Japanese Government charges against us of cruelty and barbarism in that the attack was effective principally against noncombatants, women and children. Although Hiroshima was a naval base it is probable that the destruction of civilian life was terrific.

Some of our scientists today say that the area attacked will be uninhabitable for many years because the bomb explosion has made the ground radioactive and destructive of animal life.

The lethal possibilities of such atomic action in the future is frightening, and while we are the first to have it in our possession, there is a certainty that it will in the future be developed by potential enemies and that it will probably be used against us.[26]

Even though details remained sketchy, Japanese intelligence in Tokyo had picked up the radio broadcasts of Truman's speech about the use of an atomic bomb against Hiroshima.[27] And fifteen minutes after the bomb's detonation, the Kure Navy Depot sent a message to Tokyo stating a massively destructive bomb had hit Hiroshima of an unknown type. Just after 10:00 a.m., another message from Hiroshima reached the Army Ministry in Tokyo, referring to a new bomb the United States had been working on, "this must be it."[28] At about noon, a Domei News Agency transmission arrived in Tokyo, but details of the extent of the catastrophe did not become available until late afternoon in the form of a report from Second Army Headquarters—and even then they were imprecise.[29]

As the Japanese struggled to understand exactly what had happened in Hiroshima, the latest Ultra information provided horrifying evidence of a massive Japanese buildup on Kyūshū opposing Olympic. The same day the first atomic bomb destroyed Hiroshima, the Joint War Plans Committee of the JCS sent a report entitled, "Alternatives to Olympic," to the Joint Staff Planners. Stressing their great concern over the newest information, the committee tersely stated:

The possible effect upon OLYMPIC operations of this build-up and concentration is such that it is considered commanders in the field should review their estimates of the situation, re-examine objectives in Japan as possible alternatives to OLYMPIC, and prepare plans for operations against such alternate objectives.

The authors sent messages to MacArthur and Nimitz stating that while the rapid build-up had not yet forced a decision to change the directive, it had reached a point where it necessitated commanders to consider "alternate plans and submit timely recommendations." It further instructed that "operations against extreme northern Honshu, against the Sendai area, and directly against the Kanto Plain are now under intense study [in Washington]."[30] Although carefully worded, there was no mistaking the import of the message: the scale of enemy forces now on Kyūshū mandated a re-examination of US invasion plans.

AUGUST 7, 1945
1 DAY AFTER HIROSHIMA

At dawn, General Kawabe received a dispatch informing him that all of Hiroshima had been wiped out by a solitary bomb. Kawabe's diary entry details his reaction.

> As soon as I arrived at the office, I looked through the reports on the air attack by [the] new bomb on Hiroshima performed on the morning of the 6th. I was shocked tremendously. I once saw the studies being made by B Ken [its title is unclear, but this was the main Japanese research Institute]. The study made by [unclear words] was regarded by us as hopeless. However, the enemy has turned it into reality and it seems that they have used this against us with great success…It is too late to have regrets or to cry over this. If we expended time crying, the war situation will deteriorate further and become more difficult. We must be tenacious and active.[31]

Truman's radio broadcast, transmitted from Washington, announcing the use of an atomic bomb against Japan, confirmed Kawabe's suspicions.

But rather than accept the reality that a single bomb, likely atomic, had just destroyed Hiroshima, the Army downplayed the significance of the event. They also dismissed Tōgō's recommendation that Japan accept the Potsdam Declaration, based on his belief that the bomb "drastically alters the whole military situation and offers the military ample grounds for ending the war." Instead Anami countered, "Such a move is uncalled for, furthermore, we do not yet know if the bomb was atomic." After all, they only had Truman's word for it. It might be a trick. Anami wanted Dr. Yoshio Nishina, the nation's leading nuclear scientist, sent at once to Hiroshima to investigate.[32]

Anami's comments deserve analysis. First, regardless of whether the bomb was atomic, an entire city had just been obliterated by a single bomb, the first such occurrence in human history. To Anami, this was apparently irrelevant. Second, the Japanese, including Anami, were more than casually familiar with the concept of an atomic bomb; Anami's appointment of Dr. Nishina to go to Hiroshima to investigate makes this clear. Nishina had led the Army's atomic bomb program and had consulted with the Navy's.

The possibility of creating a Japanese atomic bomb was first explored by the Lieutenant General Takeo Yasuda, Director of Aviation Technology for the Army, who quickly concluded that Japan did not want to be caught napping on this issue. In April of 1940, he tasked Lieutenant Colonel Tatsusaburō Suzuki, at the Army Aviation Headquarters, with determining Japan's potential to create an atomic bomb. Six months later, Suzuki reported to Yasuda that Japan possessed or had access to sufficient uranium ore deposits to produce an atomic bomb. General Yasuda next contacted Professor Masatoshi Okōchi, Director of Japan's Physical and Chemical Research Institute, to further research the possibility of creating an explosive using nuclear fission. Professor Okōchi turned the problem over to Yoshio Nishina, at the same institute, who was already overseeing the activity of a hundred and ten of Japan's brightest young physicists.[33]

Shortly after Japan's attack on Pearl Harbor, Nishina said of the war, "What an insane war Japan has launched! Any fool knows the power and might of the United States. The consequences to Japan can only be disastrous. We are all aboard a sinking ship; a ship called Japan. We must do what we can to save it."[34]

By the spring of 1942, after the staggering losses at Midway, the Navy began a separate effort to produce an atomic bomb, headed by Lieutenant Commander Kiyoyasu Saski of the Electrical Research Division of the Naval Technological Research Institute. Under the name "B-research," the project was described in the following manner:

> The study of nuclear physics is a national project. Research in this field is continuing on a broad scale in the United States, which has recently obtained the services of a number of Jewish scientists, and considerable progress has been made. The objective is the creation

of tremendous amounts of energy through nuclear fission. Should this research prove successful, it would provide a stupendous and dependable source of power which could be used to activate ships and other large pieces of machinery. Although it is not expected that nuclear energy will be realized in the near future, the possibility of it must not be ignored. The Imperial Navy, accordingly, hereby affirms its determination to foster and assist studies in this field.

Behind the contrived fluff disguising its intentions, the real purpose of the project was the creation of an atomic bomb.[35]

In an effort to accelerate progress on B-research, the Naval Technological Research Institute formed a committee that included top representatives from Japan's chief universities and private industries. Professor Nishina became chairman of the team.[36]

The Navy's effort lasted two years until March 6, 1943, when the committee dissolved the project, on the rationale that an atomic bomb could not be produced, by anyone, in time to make a difference in the present war.

On May 5, 1943, the staff working on the Army project reported that in their opinion an atomic bomb was technically feasible. Upon receiving such news, the Army Aviation Headquarters initiated the top-secret "N-research" project ("N" for Nishina).[37] However, by the end of 1943, Nishina and his staff were already coming to the same conclusions as the Navy—an atomic bomb could not be created in time to affect the war. The Army's project finally came to an end on April 13, 1945, when an American bombing raid destroyed the laboratory, just four months before the atomic attacks on Hiroshima and Nagasaki.[38]

At 1:30 p.m. the day after the bombing of Hiroshima, Lord Keeper of the Privy Seal Marquis Kōichi Kido had an audience with the Emperor and found him unsettled and asking a lot of questions. Hirohito had already learned of the nuclear attack from court circles the previous day.[39]

Kido remembered the Emperor as saying, "I don't care what happens to me personally. We should lose no time in ending the war so as not to have another such tragedy."[40]

The Army's only action on August 7 was to issue a communiqué at 3:30 p.m. to quell the growing fear among Japanese civilians. The message stated that an attack on Hiroshima by "a small number of B-29s" caused considerable damage and that a new type of bomb had been used. "Details," said the Army, "are now under investigation."[41]

In the afternoon, the Big Six held a short meeting. The War and Home Ministers gave reports on the Hiroshima bombing. Of the meeting, Tōgō later wrote, "The Army, plead [for] the necessity of awaiting the results of the investigation which had been ordered, obviously intended not to admit the nature of the atomic attack, but to minimize the effect of the bombing."[42]

The Army's fanatical opposition remained as strident as ever. Kawabe, a close confidant of Anami and Umezu, both in his diary and later, under interrogation by the U.S. Strategic Bombing Survey November 2, 1945, stated the army leaders had "made up our minds to fight to the last man and thought we still had a chance." He added that if "the war had continued to a finish fight, I would've crashed my plane into the enemy and I feel that everyone in the Air Force feels the same way."[43]

Still unwilling to give up Japan's diplomatic overtures to the Soviet Union, Tōgō cabled to Ambassador Satō in Moscow:

> The situation is becoming so acute that we must have clarification of the Soviet attitude as soon as possible. Please make further efforts to obtain a reply immediately.

The Japanese reaction defies Western logic. A possible explanation, at the heart of the impasse between the Allies and Japan, may be found in another portion of Kawabe's November 2 testimony given to the USSBS. Asked whether the damage being done by B-29s had ever caused the Japanese to believe the war was lost, Kawabe said:

> We believed probably we would lose the war and we knew we could never win the war; but we never gave up the idea of continuing the fight, using whatever special attack planes we could manufacture and we intended to continue the fight until the very end and make a showdown fight of it, involving transports at landing; that is, we intended to wait until we could attack the transports at landing although it was very clear to us that you could eventually destroy our industries to the point where we could no longer wage war.
>
> ...I want to explain something to you; this is a very difficult thing which you may not be able to understand. The Japanese to the very end believed that by spiritual means they could fight on

equal terms with you, yet by any other comparison it would not appear equal. We believed our spiritual conviction in victory would balance any scientific advantage and we had no intention of giving up the fight. It seemed to be especially Japanese.

By August of 1945, the spiritual superiority Kawabe spoke about had experienced nothing but defeat for more than three years. And on August 6, its enemy had proven beyond anyone's doubt to be vastly superior scientifically.

How is an enemy with a belief system so different ever persuaded to surrender? Such was the dilemma faced by the Allies' leadership in the summer of 1945, and it is a problem that remains very real more than three quarters of a century later with regard to radical Islam.

In Washington, reacting to the incredible buildup of Japanese forces on Kyūshū, nearly 900,000 men versus the 350,000 Olympic had planned on, General Marshall sent the following dispatch to MacArthur, as well as Admiral Leahy:

Intelligence reports on Jap dispositions which have been presented to me and which I understand have been sent to your Staff are that the Japanese have undertaken a large buildup both of divisions and of air forces in Kyushu and Southern Honshu. The air buildup is reported as including a large component of suicide planes which the intelligence estimate here considers are readily available for employment only in the vicinity of their present bases. Concurrently with the reported reinforcement of Kyushu, the Japanese are reported to have reduced forces north of the Tokyo plain to the point where the defensive capabilities in Northern Honshu and Hokkaido appear to be extraordinarily weak viewed from the standpoint of the Japanese General Staff. The question has arisen in my mind as to whether the Japanese may not be including some deception in the sources from which our intelligence is being drawn.

In order to assist in discussions likely to arise here on the meaning of the reported dispositions in Japan proper and the possible alternate objectives to OLYMPIC, such as Tokyo, Sendai [Northern Honshu], Ominato [extreme Northern Honshu], I would appreciate your personal estimate of the Japanese intentions and capabilities as related to our current directive and available resources.[44]

172 • DAVID DEAN BARRETT

Meanwhile, Marshall, who had for some time believed use of the atomic bomb on Japanese cities would be insufficient to achieve her surrender, considered the unthinkable—the use of as many as nine atomic bombs. To make Olympic viable again, he pondered, should the US use atomic bombs as tactical weapons, three for each of the major landing areas over which American troops and Marines would then attack? The bombs would be used to soften up the Japanese forces. Lest anyone believe Marshall was not seriously contemplating this possibility, it should be noted that he had been reviewing the scientific data coming out of Alamogordo after the Trinity test, and he believed American forces would be better off facing the risks of radiation than the vast numbers of Japanese defenders.

However, in no way did that mean Marshall or anyone else in the US, including the Manhattan Project scientists, clearly understood what those risks entailed. In fact, six years after the atomic attacks on Japan, the United States government was still using American soldiers and Marines essentially as human guinea pigs, placing them a mere two miles from the epicenter of nuclear explosions and then minutes later, after the blast wave had passed, marching them to the detonation point.

On Guam, the decision to drop the second atomic bomb, the plutonium-based *Fat Man*, was made. Initially scheduled for August 10, the date was moved to the August 9, to avoid bad weather.

AUGUST 8, 1945
2 DAYS AFTER HIROSHIMA

With only silence from Japan's leaders two days after the atomic attack on Hiroshima and favorable weather over Yawata on northern Kyūshū, a major steel-producing city of over a quarter million people, the Twentieth Air Force sent 245 B-29s armed with incendiary bombs to strike the city. The attack scorched twenty-two percent of the metropolitan area.[45]

In Tokyo, Tōgō met with the Emperor, advising him to accept the terms of the Potsdam Declaration. Hirohito agreed and told the foreign minister to inform Suzuki that in light of the new weapon, Japan was now powerless to respond. As such, he wanted the war terminated as quickly as possible. Suzuki reacted by calling an emergency session of the Big Six, but the meeting had to be delayed until August 9 because, as unbelievable as it may sound, a member of the council decided he had "more pressing business" elsewhere.[46] No explanation of what the "more pressing business" entailed exists in the historical record.

At the same time, the Army began its damage control in an effort to avoid panic over the news of the atomic bomb. It did so by attempting to both blanket the American broadcasts about the bomb from Manila and Okinawa and nullify the effect of leaflets dropped over Tokyo conveying the Allies' desire to end the war without completely destroying Japan. And in an act of supreme hypocrisy by the Japanese government, both because it was denying its existence to its own people and had attempted during the war to develop its own atomic bomb, filed a formal protest through Switzerland against the government of the United States for using such a weapon on the Japanese.[47]

In Moscow, in the afternoon, after a nearly a month's delay, Satō met Molotov in his study. Satō tried to set a friendly tone for the meeting, but Molotov cut Japan's ambassador short and read him a brief note ending with the words: "The Soviet government declares that from tomorrow, that is from August 9, the Soviet Union will consider herself in a state of war against Japan."

The Japanese government denounced the Russian declaration of war as being inexcusable and illegal, since the neutrality pact between the two nations did not expire until April 1946. But at last, Japan's feeble attempt to obtain Soviet assistance or intervention on their behalf was over, and the reply they knew all along was coming had landed.

9

A SHIFT OF POWER, THE FIRST IMPERIAL INTERVENTION

AUGUST 9, 1945
3 DAYS AFTER HIROSHIMA

The Soviet Union was now officially at war with Japan, and the culmination of the greatest conflict of the twentieth century was now clearly in the hands of a select group of men in Japan's halls of power. These would be the critical final days and hours that diarists and historians would doggedly recount and research, so intensely that dialogue between Japan's leaders can rather faithfully be reconstructed and readers of accounts like this one can be placed squarely in the middle of these crucial events. In addition to the diaries and memoirs of key figures, four crucial works and their primary sources provide a fly-on-the-wall perspective in the days that follow.

The first, *Japan's Longest Day*, was penned by the fourteen members of The Pacific War Research Society, a group of Japanese historians who devoted years of their lives to interviewing eyewitnesses of the drama that unfolded during those historic days. Over one year alone, the Society interviewed and crosschecked the accounts of seventy-nine of the men who took part in the decision to surrender.

The second volume, told from the Japanese perspective, is John Tolland's Pulitzer Prize-winning book *The Rising Sun: The Decline and Fall of the Japanese Empire*.

Japan's Decision to Surrender, written by Robert J.C. Butow, a preeminent historian of US-Japan relations from 1941 to the end of the war in 1945, is another invaluable source. His book is still universally regarded as "the classic work" on the end of the Asia-Pacific War.

The fourth book was authored by Lester Brooks. Brooks served in the US Army in the Pacific during World War II and was stationed at Supreme Commander for the Allied Powers (SCAP) General Headquarters (GHQ), General Douglas MacArthur's headquarters for the occupation. Brooks' research for *Behind Japan's Surrender: The Secret Struggle That Ended an Empire* included personal interviews he conducted in 1965 with thirty eyewitnesses. He also pulled from transcripts of 1965 interviews of other witnesses provided by the National Broadcasting Company (NBC); General MacArthur's Military History Section, two volumes of unpublished "Statements of Japanese Officials on World War II"; "Interrogations of Japanese Officials" by USSBS immediately after Japan's surrender; and the Tokyo Trials—the International Military Tribunal for the Far East, which lasted more than two years, from April 29, 1946, through November 12, 1948, and included testimony from nearly every significant figure in Japanese political and military life.

And so, with this cache of resources available, this author echoes the words of Lester Brooks, who wrote: "From these invaluable sources have come the actual words of the men who led Imperial Japan in its final days."

IN THE JAPANESE CAPITAL, AT 8:00 a.m., an angry Tōgō arrived at the Prime Minister's home in Koishikawa in north-central Tokyo to brief him on the Soviet declaration of war and the Red Army's invasion of Manchuria. Tōgō demanded a meeting of the Supreme War Council, which had been postponed from the previous day, and exhorted Suzuki to stop the war at once.[1]

Suzuki agreed.

General Kawabe's detailed diary entries on August 9, and later matching testimony to the United States Strategic Bombing Survey (USSBS), made clear, even after the now-confirmed atomic attack on Hiroshima and the Soviet Union's entry into the war against Japan, the Army's zealous determination to fight on. Kawabe's diary entry stated:

1. Soviets finally started this morning [literally, the Soviets finally have risen]. My estimate was wrong. However, now that things have come to this end, we can give no thought to peace. We should have expected at least partly such an event during the war. There is nothing to reflect on now. We simply have to rely on the honor of the Japanese people and continue fighting. I was very cautious and almost cowardly in approaching [war with the Soviets], once however this is come to pass, I can never think of peace or surrender. Whatever the end, we

have no choice but to try. I confirmed my decision and came to the office.

2. The Vice Minister [of Foreign Affairs, Sunichi] Matsumoto also visited me and he did not oppose my decision.

3. After I came to the office, I prepared a memo as follows about what came to my mind:

Decision: No change with regard to continuing the war (with United States as the main enemy).

ACTIONS TO TAKE:

1. Within the whole nation we should declare martial law. I will push for this, and if necessary, we will change the government and the Army and Navy will take control.

2. As for operations, all the overseas armies and air general army understand their missions and will conduct strong resistance along the Manchurian border line. When the time comes to abandon Manchuria, the main formations will withdraw to southern Korea. China will be left generally in the present status. Those in Mongolia should gradually retreat to North China.

3. About the Manchurian Emperor, he should be moved to Japan...

4. Measures to stop unrest among the military units. One means is a statement from the Minister of the Army.

I waited for the Chief of the Army General Staff [Umezu] to come to the office and explained my proposals to him. As usual he did not show a clear indication of his views. However, he did not express any disagreement. I do not wish to "make waves" at this time and decided to wait and see as the situation develops and also to await further information.

I heard that there would be a meeting of the Supreme War Direction Counsel at 1030 and visited General Anami at the office of the Army Minister. He was cheerful as usual, he told me: "Good, I'll take your opinion as representative of the entire army general staff." I said, "I hope you do well in today's conference, the meeting should be very stormy." Then the minister answered: "It will be rough, but I will risk my life," and after saying this he stood up. He said to himself, "If what I insist cannot be accepted,

I will resign and have myself conscripted into a unit in China so I can fight there." And then he laughed and showed his high-spirit. Some people might say that he lacks ability and he is too optimistic or he is possessed by something, but I thought that he was really dependable in such a difficult situation, keeping up his spirit and charging ahead.[2]

After conferring with Matsumoto and Generals Umezu and Anami, all agreed (or in Umezu's case did not disagree) Japan should "give no thought to peace," and make "No change with regard to continuing the war (with United States as the main enemy)." Further, the group agreed to "declare martial law...change the government [with] the Army and Navy tak[ing] control," a military coup d'état. Anami began the process, instructing War Ministry officers to begin work on a plan to implement martial law. Kawabe also reiterated the May decision to have the Kwantung Army conduct a fighting withdrawal of Japanese forces from Manchuria, China, and Mongolia. Thus, despite the nuclear attack on Hiroshima, and a new enemy, the Soviet Union, Japan's Army leaders were as determined as ever to fight to the bitter end.

From his headquarters in the Philippines, MacArthur responded to Marshall's August 7 message regarding the continued practicality of Olympic, writing, "I am certain personal estimate that the Japanese air potential reported to you as accumulating to counter our Olympic operation is greatly exaggerated." MacArthur then cited as evidence the almost non-existent reaction by Japan's military to the ongoing attacks by the American Third Fleet against the Japanese mainland, and backed that up by citing similar exaggerated reports prior to landing on Luzon that subsequently proved incorrect. (Actually, MacArthur had this backward. His G-2, military intelligence, had grossly underestimated Japanese strength on Luzon. The reports placing those numbers much higher were proved correct.) The general disavowed any belief in Japan's ability to move and support significant new troops in Kyūshū:

The Japanese are reported as trying to concentrate in the few areas in which landings can be affected from Tokyo southward, and it is possible that some strength may have been drawn from the areas of northern Honshu. I do not credit, however, the heavy strengths reported to you in southern Kyushu. The limited capacity railroads and the shipping losses discourage belief that large forces can be concentrated or supported effectively in southern Kyushu.[3]

MacArthur unequivocally believed that Allied air power, both tactical and strategic, would "quickly seek out and destroy" Japanese air potential and "practically immobilize" and "greatly weaken" Japanese troops in southern Kyūshū.[4]

MacArthur continued with an endorsement of Olympic, stating: "In my opinion there should not be the slightest thought of changing the Olympic operation." The plan was "sound and will be successful." MacArthur concluded with an intentionally misleading interpretation of his experience in the Pacific that played upon Marshall's own fears that Japan had somehow managed to fool Ultra:

> Throughout the Southwest Pacific Area campaigns, as we have neared an operation, intelligence has invariably pointed to greatly increased enemy forces without exception. This buildup has been found to be erroneous. In this particular case, the destruction that is going on in Japan would seem to indicate that it is very probable that the enemy is resorting to deception.[5]

MacArthur's carefully crafted response had more to do with his desire to lead the greatest amphibious assault in history than it did with giving Marshall an honest evaluation of the rapidly degrading situation relative to Olympic.

After receiving MacArthur's assessment, Admiral King, who had long harbored misgivings over the potential human cost of Olympic, acted to bring the entire invasion back into debate. Months before, King had warned the members of the JCS that the decision would have to be revisited in August or September. The increasingly disturbing information being derived from Ultra now demanded it. King put together a package of Marshall's original message along with MacArthur's reply in a for your "Eyes Only" communiqué and had it sent to Nimitz for his comments.[6]

President Truman took time to respond to a telegram he had just received from Georgia Senator Richard Russell two days prior. The message had implored him to discontinue efforts to gain Japan's surrender and instead continue dropping atomic bombs on them until "they are brought groveling on their knees." The president wrote:

August 9, 1945

Dear Dick:
I read your telegram of August seventh with a lot of interest.

I know that Japan is a terribly cruel and uncivilized nation in warfare but I can't bring myself to believe that, because they are beasts, we should ourselves act in the same manner.

For myself, I certainly regret the necessity of wiping out whole populations because of the "pigheadedness" of the leaders of a nation and, for your information, I am not going to do it unless it is absolutely necessary. It is my opinion that after the Russians enter the war the Japanese will very shortly fold up.

My object is to save as many American lives as possible but I also have a humane feeling for the women and children in Japan.

Sincerely yours,
Harry S. Truman

Truman's letter to Senator Russell on August 9 once again shows the President's willingness to accept Soviet involvement; because it meant saving American lives.

At 10:10 a.m., on a hot, sultry Thursday morning in Tokyo, Suzuki met with Kido, who informed him that the Emperor wanted the war terminated "immediately taking advantage of the Potsdam Declaration."[7]

Twenty minutes later, at 10:30 a.m., the Big Six finally came together in the Prime Minister's bomb shelter outside the Imperial Palace in Tokyo. By the time the men met, all were aware of the Soviet declaration of war and attack by the Red Army against Kwantung Army in Manchuria.

Moments before Suzuki walked into his emergency meeting with the Big Six, the Prime Minister is said to have accosted Lieutenant General Sumihisa Ikeda, a man who had just transferred to Japan from Manchuria. As someone very familiar with the operational status of Japan's forces there, Suzuki asked, "Is the Kwantung Army capable of repulsing the Soviet Army?" Ikeda responded, "The Kwantung Army is hopeless." Despondent, Suzuki reportedly said, "If the Kwantung Army is that weak then the game is up."[8]

Assuming the exchange took place, Suzuki's reaction should be seen as indicative of his own ignorance or poor memory of the situation; because Kawabe, Umezu, and Anami were certainly aware, as already noted, of the severely weakened fighting condition of the Kwantung Army, a fact reflected in Japan's final defensive plans.

As recently as March, as part of Ketsu-Gō, six divisions had been transferred out of the Kwantung Army—three to Japan for the defense of the home islands and three to Korea. The drain only stopped when Russia announced it would not be renewing the Soviet–Japanese Neutrality Pact in April. And the most recent moves were in addition to the twelve divisions that had already been extracted from it to halt the American advance through the Pacific.[9] Once a formidable force, by now it had been thoroughly gutted of its best divisions and equipment.

Suzuki should have known as much, and he should have known that three months earlier, in May of 1945, the mission of the Kwantung Army had been contracted from its once offensive operations to be a holding force along the border of Manchuria and Russia, and now the abandonment of Manchuria "while conducting a fighting withdrawal to the mountains astride the border with Northern Korea."[10] What Suzuki and the leaders of the Army did not know that morning and well into the afternoon was the scale of the Soviet assaults, described initially as "not large," by the Kwantung Army who erroneously underestimated the Red Army forces opposing it.[11] Nevertheless, the Russian entry into the war against Japan had failed to impress Umezu, Toyoda, and Anami, who calmly told an aide, "The inevitable has come."

The reaction of these three men, Anami and Umezu in particular, provides an important insight into their true thoughts—relative to the use of the Soviet Union to aid the Japanese in brokering a peace with the Allies—all along. It was never any more than an appeasement of the "peace faction."

As Suzuki stepped into the room to begin the meeting, what should have been clear to everyone was that their only alternatives to unconditional surrender were to continue the war and risk an internal revolt by a desperate Japanese population that would topple the whole imperial structure, or total annihilation by the Allies, which now included the Soviet Union and atomic bombs. Instead, in the stifling heat of the underground chamber, Suzuki encountered an unsettled, grim, and contentious mood—an attitude exaggerated by rumors that Tokyo would be the target of the next atomic attack. Nevertheless, Anami, Toyoda, and Umezu all remained determined to resist the urgency of the situation.[12]

Suzuki began by saying, "In view of Hiroshima and the Soviet invasion of Manchuria, it is virtually impossible for Japan to continue the war. I believe that we have no alternative but to accept the Potsdam Declaration, and I would now like to hear your opinions."[13]

But Suzuki's suggestion was too abrupt, too "un-Japanese," in its directness, and the men recoiled from action; only silence ensued. Suzuki's frankness had caught the men off guard, though no one understood the importance of the situation and the necessity for urgent action better than the members of the Big Six.[14]

As the quiet continued, the tension in the room became unnerving. Finally, Yonai's booming voice broke through: "This silence will lead us nowhere." He offered two suggestions to begin the discussion: should they accept the Potsdam Declaration, or should they attach conditions; and if they believed conditions should be added, what should they be? With the silence broken, the men began stating their positions and it quickly became apparent there was only agreement on one condition—the preservation of the Imperial structure.

Tōgō opened the discussion stating, "The war had become more and more hopeless, and now that it had no future, it was necessary to make peace without the slightest delay. Therefore... the Potsdam Declaration must be complied with, and the conditions for its acceptance should be limited to those only which were absolutely essential to Japan," in his opinion, only the preservation of the Imperial polity.[15]

Anami, Umezu, and Toyoda (the hardliners) countered first with an argument over whether the devastation in Hiroshima had been caused by an atomic bomb. When the group had met briefly on August 7, they had only been able to verify the complete destruction of the city. Later Umezu received a message that said the whole city of Hiroshima had been destroyed instantly by a single bomb. Both the Army and Navy had sent teams to investigate the cause; but due to their delay in reaching the city, their work had not yet resolved that the attack had been atomic. To date, the teams had only confirmed that the damage was immense and only one or two planes had done it.

As the Big Six began its deliberations in Tokyo to possibly decide the fate of the nation, high above Nagasaki, a second nuclear attack was about to befall another Japanese city. *Bockscar*, piloted by Major

Charles W. Sweeney, the man who three days earlier had flown *The Great Artiste*'s scientific mission during the first atomic attack on Hiroshima, had taken off a little more than seven hours earlier from Tinian's North Field at 3:49 a.m. Inside *Bockscar*'s bomb bay was the *Fat Man* plutonium bomb. Manhattan Project scientists expected it to be even more powerful than the uranium bomb dropped on Hiroshima.

But Sweeney's mission had not been running nearly as smoothly as Tibbets's had. *Bockscar*'s takeoff was delayed by an hour due to mechanical issues with one of its fuel tanks, and the weather forecast over the primary, secondary, and tertiary targets was not good as *Bockscar* thundered down the runway early on August 9. Its primary target was Kokura and its huge army arsenal. There were also technical problems getting the *Fat Man* armed, but as the mission progressed, the weather planes ahead of Sweeney's bomber reported acceptable bombing parameters for both Kokura and Nagasaki. Unfortunately, by the time *Bockscar* made it to Kokura, seventy percent of the city was blanketed by clouds and smoke, including the Aiming Point, from fires started the day before during a fire-bombing mission by 224 B-29s on nearby Yahata. Over the next fifty minutes, Sweeney's crew made three bombing passes over the city, each time receiving greater anti-aircraft fire. With fuel now becoming an issue, Sweeney diverted to his secondary target, determined to use an alternative dropping zone over Nagasaki. With his reserve fuel tanks not functioning by the time he arrived over Nagasaki shortly before 11:00 a.m., Sweeney decided to ignore orders and bomb by radar, as Nagasaki too had significant cloud cover. Then, in the final seconds of the bomb run, his bombardier, Captain Kermit K. Beahan, found a hole in the overcast, allowing him to attempt to bomb the target visually. The detonation of *Fat Man* produced an estimated twenty-one kiloton blast, instantly taking the lives of 35,000 people and flattening the northern stretches of the city. Auspiciously for the residents, the bomb's damage was limited because of the shielding effect of the surrounding hills.[16]

Inside the Prime Minister's bunker, Toyoda spurned President Truman's threat of more atomic attacks, boldly stating that not even the United States had enough fissile material to mount the attacks Truman threatened. And world opinion, he predicted, would not stand for the use of such an inhumane weapon.[17] Neither Umezu nor Anami disagreed.

Regardless of whether Toyoda believed, based on Japan's own

attempts to create an atomic weapon and difficulty in synthesizing enough fissile material for a bomb, let alone many bombs, his remark is a shocking indictment of all three men. Because it still implied that Hiroshima could simply be written off as a casualty of war, since there was no or little need to fear any more nuclear attacks by the Americans. And once again, it also showed a willingness to rely on other means, in this case "world opinion," to resolve problems Japan's leaders were still unwilling to deal with.

The Army also rejected the notion that Japanese forces in Manchuria were already defeated, since they did not have precise information about the Russian advances.[18] Their banal reaction was, as mentioned previously, likely because the mission of the Kwantung Army in the event of a Soviet invasion had been reduced three months earlier to a fighting retreat to the northern border of Korea.

In the end, the hardliners demanded one of two options. To end the war, the Allies would have to agree to four conditions: the continuation of the Imperial polity; Japanese control over war crimes trials; minimal or no occupation; and Japanese control over the demobilization and disarmament of its military. If the Allies refused to accept those terms, it was time to lure the Americans ashore, where General Anami called for one last great battle on Japanese soil—as demanded by the national honor, saying, "Would it not be wondrous for this whole nation to be destroyed like a beautiful flower?"[19]

Tōgō utterly disagreed, stating "that in view of the recent attitude of Britain, America, Russia, and China" Japan risked having the Allies break off negotiations. So, unless the military could guarantee victory in the decisive battle, there was only one condition the Japanese government should entreat. Anami defiantly countered that while they could not guarantee victory, most assuredly they could inflict severe damage on the invading Americans. Umezu added that if all went well, the Army might even be able to drive the enemy into the sea, although he admitted some percentage might successfully form a beachhead. Tōgō responded that it would be useless, as the Americans would most certainly send a second assault wave, and by then Japan would have spent itself and be incapable of reinforcing its troops or air forces. That being the case, Japan had no option but to accept the position he had already stated.

The two sides were at an impasse and according to Tōgō the ensuing discussion became "rather impassioned."[20]

Moments later, an aide burst into the room, hands shaking as he passed his message to Suzuki. Suzuki read the chilling communication: "Nagasaki City was struck this morning by severe attack of Hiroshima type. Damage is extensive."

The mood of the meeting shifted from grim to grave.

The second nuclear strike, coming only three days after the first on Hiroshima, should have prompted all of the members of the Big Six to contemplate a new and devastating reality. The United States had just demonstrated itself capable of multiple atomic attacks; maybe Truman wasn't bluffing after all. And if Truman continued to use his nuclear option rather than invading, the US could complete the destruction of Japan without risking the horrific casualties of an invasion. In doing so, he would simultaneously deprive Japan's military of any ability to inflict significant casualties on American forces and remove Japan's last bargaining chip to achieve something better than unconditional surrender. Ketsu-Gō would be rendered impotent.

Suzuki said, "This, added to the previous barbaric attack on Hiroshima, compounds the impact of the Russian attack on Japan."[21]

After the war, Suzuki explained the effect of the second bomb:

> The Supreme War Council was making every possible preparation to meet a landing. They proceeded with that plan until the atomic bomb was dropped, after which they believed the United States would no longer attempt to land when it had such a superior weapon—that the United States need not land when it had such a weapon, so at that point they decided that it would be best to sue for peace.[22]

Prior to Nagasaki, Japan's military leaders believed rightly that Ketsu-Gō could deliver devasting losses to their Americans invaders and win a settlement to the war well short of unconditional surrender.

But amazingly, the "grave mood" triggered by the second atomic attack passed as quickly as it had come. The second atomic strike—and proof that there could be more—had no effect on gaining compliance from Anami, Umezu, and Toyoda, all of whom stubbornly reverted to the two options they had already promulgated.

For purposes of postwar rationalizations, both the Japanese Army and Navy wanted to be seen as voluntarily disarming in order to save the world from further death and destruction. By doing so, they could sell the notion after the war that Japan's military had not really suffered defeat.[23] Essentially, it amounted to a repeat of the tale the Nazis had spun about the German Army at the end of World War I. But to accomplish this, they needed to avoid occupation and war crimes trials being controlled by the Allies.

Finally, Yonai broke in: "It is past the time to take this stand. We have to accept the terms. We have to follow the Foreign Minister's recommendation."

Yonai's comments were directed at the hardliners in general and Toyoda in particular, a man he had intentionally brought into the council as an ally. But Toyoda simply ignored Yonai, turning his head away, glaring off into space.[24]

Seemingly detached from the details of the discussion, Suzuki had been sitting quietly for some time, sipping tea and smoking his cigar. But as the argument intensified, he had grown noticeably uncomfortable. After Yonai's comment he finally added his voice to the argument, shouting at the hardliners, "You are putting in too many conditions. You are deliberately opposing my opinion in order to break up the peace negotiations!"[25]

When Suzuki called for a vote around 1:00 p.m., there was little doubt what the outcome would be. Anami, Umezu, and Toyoda all favored four conditions or the continuation of war, whereas Tōgō, Yonai, and Suzuki voted to require just one, the preservation of the Imperial House, the *kokutai.*

Still visibly upset, the Prime Minister informed the group the Potsdam Declaration would have to be considered by the full Cabinet anyway, and announced that the Cabinet meeting would be convened at 2:00 p.m. The men emerged from the insulated, artificial safety of the bomb shelter into the reassuring blaze of the midday sun.

As the men went their separate ways, Tōgō sought out Suzuki, telling him the standoff was unlikely to change when the full Cabinet met. If that happened, their only recourse would be to request an Imperial Conference, at which time the Emperor could deliver his *seidan* (sacred Imperial Decision). But before that could ever happen, Suzuki must take care, lest his Cabinet be forced to resign.[26]

Anami returned to his office at the War Ministry brimming with confidence. None who saw him, an entourage of high-ranking officers in tow, doubted he was the master of his nation's fate.[27]

The Cabinet assembled in Suzuki's residence at 2:00 p.m., where the Prime Minister calmly called the meeting to order by asking the Foreign Minister to outline the situation. Tōgō began by reminding the group that his office, at the behest of the Supreme War Council, had begun a diplomatic course with the Soviets in May. At that time, his office expressed its concern that such a political track, given Japan's current military state, would not likely meet with success. Unfortunately, that concern had been proven true. The Soviets formally declared war on Japan earlier that day and had attacked Japanese forces in Manchuria. Further, the United States had introduced atomic weapons to the war, doing catastrophic damage to both Hiroshima and Nagasaki, despite statements by members of Japanese military that no nation possessed the materials to produce more than one of these devices.

Toyoda, likely incensed by the not so subtle jab, interrupted Tōgō, stating that Japan still had the means to win the decisive battle against its enemies, and in doing so gain better peace terms. Yonai chimed in, reiterating an argument Tōgō had made earlier in the day: "We might win the first battle for Japan, but we won't win the second. The war is lost to us. Therefore, we must forget about 'face,' we must surrender as quickly as we can, and we must begin to consider at once how best to preserve our country."[28]

Anami snapped back, "We cannot pretend to claim that victory is certain, but it is far too early to say that the war is lost. That we will inflict severe losses on the enemy when he invades Japan is certain, and it is by no means impossible that we may be able to reverse the situation in our favor, pulling victory out of defeat. Furthermore, our Army will not submit to demobilization. Our men simply will not lay down their arms. And since they know they are not permitted to surrender, there is really no alternative for us but to continue the war."[29]

The Ministers of Agriculture, Commerce, Transportation, and Munitions all disagreed that the war could be continued. They pointed to the fact that the Americans had already begun using Okinawa as a base of operations for their forthcoming invasion of Kyūshū and that the population was exhausted. Worse still, the forecast for the fall rice crop looked to be the poorest in fifteen years, perhaps fifty, and day by day Allied air and sea attacks became ever more powerful and destructive. In short, Japan no longer had the means to carry on the war.[30] The Minister of Agriculture also offered a face-saving excuse for Japan's defeat in the war. It was not because the Army had lost the war; it was because, "We have lost a scientific war. The people may be dissatisfied with the military for the defeat. But if we say we lost a scientific war, the people will understand."[31]

Unmoved, Anami cried impatiently. "Yes, yes! Everyone understands the situation…but we must fight the war through to the end no matter how great the odds against us!"[32]

Lending support to Anami, Home Minister Genki Abe said he feared civil disobedience in the event the Cabinet agreed to end the war by surrendering, recalling the *February 26 Incident* in 1936. Therefore, he recommended against accepting the Potsdam Declaration.[33]

Education Minister Saburō Ota then issued a chilling statement to Suzuki—one they all feared to contemplate. "I will not express my opinion on this problem, for this is a serious matter. I insist the Cabinet should tender its resignation because it has failed in its responsibility."[34]

Ota was absolutely correct. Under normal circumstances, the stalemate within Suzuki's government would have necessitated its resignation, but these were anything but normal times. Angered and afraid that Ota's words would force the removal of his government and replace it with a purely military Cabinet, Suzuki fired back, "I'm fully aware of our responsibility, but this is no time for the Cabinet to argue about responsibility. Instead we must take steps to remedy the matter."[35]

For a perilous instant the lives of millions rested in the hands of one man, General Anami. He could have used the opportunity to end the discussion of peace then and there and destroyed Suzuki's government, something he had taken steps toward doing when he met with Kawabe earlier in the day. Forcing the collapse of the Suzuki government would have given Anami what he was seeking—the bitter fight to the death against the Americans on Japan's sacred soil (if the Americans obliged). But astonishingly, the moment passed as Anami brushed Ota's suggestion aside. Suzuki wiped the sweat from his forehead and again polled the members of the group. To no one's surprise, the men were hopelessly divided. [36]

Meanwhile, at Imperial General Headquarters, while the supreme military commanders were in session discussing what action they should take in response to the Soviet declaration of war, a group of middle-grade officers had reached their flashpoint over their perceived belief that the peace faction might be successful in its efforts to bring the war to an end. They were determined to eliminate these men and help the Emperor regain his senses, if necessary, by a coup d'état.[37]

During a welcome break of the Cabinet meeting at 5:30 p.m., Suzuki began the process, discussed earlier with Tōgō, to call an Imperial Conference. He turned to his forty-three-year-old Chief Cabinet Secretary Sakomizu, a politically savvy man and a skilled manipulator. Sakomizu told Suzuki he would need Umezu's, Toyoda's, and Suzuki's signatures on the required petition to make it valid. Suzuki shuddered at the thought, knowing neither of his colleagues was likely to sign it. Both had been incessant barriers to any discussion of peace, and they appeared intent on blocking a decision and continuing the war. Suzuki had no choice but to sign the petition and hope for the best. He handed it to Sakomizu, who promptly set off to canvass the Chiefs of Staff.[38]

He found Toyoda at the Navy Ministry building and Umezu at Imperial General Headquarters. Sakomizu offered a credible justification to both men. Suzuki had asked him to get the signatures of the Chiefs of Staff on a petition for an Imperial Conference now to save time later:

> After all, it is certain that an Imperial Conference must be held sooner or later to take care of crucial issues such as a declaration of war against the Soviets. And with conditions now so unpredictable, the meeting might be called on very short notice—even in the middle of the night. When that time comes, I will have to start looking for you to sign the petition and it will only mean additional trouble for you and for me and the loss of precious time. Of course, I will be sure to call on you beforehand to let you know if and when the petition will have to be used. In order to be ready for such an emergency please sign these papers.[39]

The soundness of Sakomizu's request struck home with both Chiefs. It had been nearly a day and the Japanese had provided no formal response to the Soviet declaration of war. A reciprocal declaration required an Imperial Rescript, and to accomplish that an Imperial Conference had to be convened. It was a perfect pretext to disguise the true purpose of the meeting, to allow the Emperor to render his *seidan* and break the deadlock.

After all, Imperial Conferences were used to inform the Emperor of the Cabinet's decisions, not for him to actively participate in debate. The practice was developed to keep the Emperor free of responsibility in case a decision backfired. But Umezu and Toyoda each wanted to hear Sakomizu's affirmation one more time before they would endorse the document: "You will let us know in advance if the petition is to be used?" With Sakomizu's assurance that he would, Umezu and Toyoda took out their brushes and signed.[40] With the executed document now in hand, Sakomizu rushed to give it to Suzuki.

The Prime Minister was now ready to complete the process, later that day if need be, that he Tōgō and Kido agreed upon weeks earlier, should the Cabinet fail to reach a unanimous decision on how to end the war. Suzuki had already been told by Tōgō of the Emperor's desire to accept the Potsdam Declaration with the single proviso guaranteeing the continuation of the Imperial System, and he had been reassured by Kido that the Emperor would state his will, affirming this at the "full-dress" Imperial Conference.

For Tōgō this must have seemed like the climactic event of a narrative he'd been struggling to write since he accepted his second appointment as Foreign Minister months before. In November 1937, at the request of the Emperor, the responsibility for his military briefings moved to the Imperial General Headquarters Government Liaison Conference. The objective of the move was to bring the Chiefs of the Army and Navy General Staff into closer consultation with Japan's government and to present its final decisions for approval by the Emperor.

During Tōgō's first service as Foreign Minister, in Prime Minister Hideki Tōjō's Cabinet, Tōjō discussed all the decisions made at the Liaison Conference with the Emperor. As such, Tōgō believed the Emperor was getting a purely military briefing and perspective. At Tōgō's insistence and with the approval of Prime Minister Suzuki and the Lord Keeper of the Privy Seal Kido, from the onset of his second appointment to the Foreign Ministry, Tōgō conferred with the Emperor about the final decisions and held discussions directly with him on state affairs.[41]

With that access Tōgō had briefed the Emperor about Hiroshima the previous day. He had told the Emperor, "This should be used as an opportunity to decide for the earliest possible termination of the war." The Emperor agreed and responded:

> Now that this sort of weapon has been used, it is becoming increasingly impossible to continue the war. I do not think it is a good idea to miss an opportunity to end the war by attempting to

secure advantageous conditions. Besides, even if we try to discuss terms, I am afraid we won't be able to come to an agreement. Therefore, I hope you will take measures that will conclude the war as soon as possible. [42]

The Emperor then asked Tōgō to convey his opinion to the Prime Minister.

Coming on August 8, prior to the Soviet Union's entry into the war against Japan, the statement offers powerful evidence that Hiroshima moved the Emperor to end the war.

After an hour break, round two of the tireless debate began anew with the Cabinet. Hour after hour the men droned on unceasingly in their efforts to persuade the opposing side, accomplishing nothing. Shortly before 10:00 p.m., Suzuki once again called for a vote, and still found the group in gridlock. With the lateness of the hour and still no unanimity of opinion, the meeting ended. The ministers bowed themselves out of the chamber and into the darkness, the fate of their country as doubtful as ever.

Suzuki and Tōgō drove straight to the *Gobunko* in the Fukiage Gardens to meet with His Majesty. The Prime Minister asked Tōgō to outline the disagreement among the Cabinet.[43] Tōgō told the Emperor it was hopeless to expect a consensus in either the Big Six or among the full Cabinet, as the hardliners refused to relinquish their demand for four conditions. Suzuki then urged Hirohito to convene the Imperial Conference that night in His presence. The Emperor immediately agreed. All three understood this could be their last opportunity to bring the war to an end. It had to succeed, despite the fact that it was an abuse of the Meiji Constitution. It was their last hope.[44]

Ever efficient, Sakomizu had been hard at work preparing the notices for the Imperial Conference, which were now ready to send. After looking one over, Suzuki directed Sakomizu to send them out. All but the Prime Minister and the Foreign Minister where shocked upon receipt and the revelation of the meeting's true purpose. The rest of the men did not expect the conference to be called until the SCDW had attained an agreement, and that clearly had not happened.[45] What bothered Umezu, Toyoda, and Anami most was the fact that the Prime Minister had seized the initiative. By asking for the involvement of the Emperor, while the Big Six and Cabinet remained divided, Suzuki had not only broken with all precedent but was assuming he knew the mind of His Majesty, and he had taken a significant step in emasculating their positions. But faced with a request to attend an Imperial Conference, the men had no choice but to attend.[46]

By the time the conferees began stepping out of their cars into the gleaming moonlight at 11:30 p.m., the mood of Anami, Umezu, and Toyoda bordered on anger. Umezu and Toyoda felt tricked at not receiving the early notice promised by Sakomizu.[47]

In addition to the members of the Supreme War Council, six other members of the Japanese government gathered near the hill-side entrance to the *Gobunko* annex: Director of the Overall Planning Bureau, General Ikeda; Director of the Bureau of Naval Affairs, Admiral Zenshiro Hoshina; President of the Privy Council, Baron Hiranuma; Chief aide-de-camp to the Emperor, General Shigeru Hasunuma; Director of the Bureau of Military Affairs at the War Ministry, Lieutenant General Masao Yoshizumi; and Chief Cabinet Minister Sakomizu. No one was certain of the outcome of the meeting. Those in attendance had the legal right to reject the Emperor's wishes. But would they defy Him?[48]

As the meeting neared, a chamberlain escorted the men one by one through a small door that descended fifty feet down mat-covered steps to a tunnel that led to the bunker. The complex, surrounded by up to twenty-one feet of reinforced concrete on all sides and buried in a hill by an additional forty-five feet of earth, was impervious to enemy bombing. The shelter had been built as an underground attachment of the *Gobunko*, where the Emperor had been living since the Imperial Palace had been bombed during a B-29 air raid on May 25.

As the men waited for the Emperor in the anteroom, Toyoda and Umezu, their swords at their side, crowded in on Sakomizu, accusing him of obtaining their approval for the meeting under false pretenses.[49] Lying, Sakomizu said, "We are not going to make any decision at this conference."

The door to the *Gobunko* opened at 11:50 p.m., quietly signaling the Emperor had arrived. Only eighteen by thirty feet, poorly ventilated and infernally hot, the bunker had a musty smell and buzzed with the sound of mosquitos. The ceiling of the bunker was supported by steel beams, the walls paneled in dark wood. The men, dressed in formal clothes or uniforms, used white handkerchiefs to dab their perspiration from their somber faces. They sat at long, cloth-covered tables, six on one side and five on the other, a walkway in between. The twelfth man took his seat in a plain, straight-backed chair at the head of the space. Behind him, at the highest part of the room, stood a simple screen, which, at exactly 11:55 p.m., against tradition, the Emperor, wearing the uniform of Marshall Commander of the armed forces, pulled back to reveal himself. The men all bowed, avoiding looking at the Emperor, and sat down.

For only the second time in his reign as Emperor—the first time being the *February 26 Incident* of 1936, when members of Japan's military attempted a coup to overthrow the government—Hirohito was about to take an active role in a political decision and declare his opinion on an unresolved issue.[50]

Prime Minister Suzuki, standing at the Emperor's left, asked Sakomizu to read the Potsdam Declaration aloud. Afterward, Suzuki, addressing the Emperor, stated that after considerable time and discussion, the Supreme War Council remained at an impasse in their deliberations on how or whether to end the war. He offered his apology to His Majesty for requesting His presence at a time when His ministers were still not in agreement.[51]

Suzuki then turned to Tōgō and asked him to state his position. The Foreign Minister maintained that Japan had to limit its demand to only those conditions that it absolutely could not do without. Since the military situation had swung decidedly in favor of the United States and Britain, and because the Soviet Union had joined the war against Japan, Tōgō said, it was unrealistic to think Japan could require that the Allies change the terms of their ultimatum further. From their standpoint, there seemed no reason or room for further compromise. Therefore, Japan's demands needed to focus upon the single most important issue, the preservation of the Imperial House, since it was the fundamental basis for the future development of the nation.[52] The Prime Minister next asked Yonai the same question. Yonai rose to his feet and responded, "I agree with the Foreign Minister," and then sat back down.

Yonai had no sooner sat down than an enraged Anami leapt to his feet to express his unflagging dissent; he remained unflinching in his resolve that the nation should continue the war. The outcome of the decisive Battle for Japan, he declared, could only be known after it had been fought. But if Japan chose peace, there could be no wavering on the demand that the Allies accept four conditions—not only the guarantee of the Imperial polity, but also control over disarmament and war crimes trials, and a limited occupation.[53] Anami continued, saying he could not agree to a plan with an immoral nation, such as the USSR, even if it meant the sacrifice of a hundred million people. The war must go on whatever the price in order to satisfy the devotion and patriotism of the nation. Anami was confident of victory in its fight against the US and in the impending decisive battle in the homeland. And he opined that Japanese troops overseas would never accept unconditional surrender, nor would those at home who were determined to fight to the death. If Japan surrendered now, anarchy would result.[54]

General Umezu stood next to address the assembly. He expanded on Anami's argument regarding Japan's potential in a decisive battle for the homeland, adding that the country's forces were more than a match for the enemy. He continued that while Soviet entry into the war was unfavorable, it had no effect on Ketsu-Gō.[55] He believed to surrender now dishonored all those who had already died. But if Japan decided to surrender, then he too demanded the four conditions.

It was now Toyoda's turn, but instead Suzuki called on Baron Hiranuma, representing the Privy Council in the proceedings, because that body would be expected to ratify any and all foreign treaties. Hiranuma launched into an exhaustive series of questions about the Soviets, the men likely to be tried as war criminals, the ability of the nation to protect itself against air raids and invasion, and the probability of civil disobedience. But in the end, he sided with Tōgō and Yonai, saying the additional three conditions were doomed to failure.[56]

Admiral Toyoda, finally given his chance to speak, announced his support of Anami and Umezu. The admiral emphasized that unless the Japanese controlled the disarmament of troops, he could not guarantee their compliance. He also concurred with Umezu's comments if the war went on, saying, "We cannot say that final victory is certain but at the same time we do not believe that we will be positively defeated."[57]

The Emperor and his leaders were all determined, in the words of historian Herbert Bix, "...to lose without losing—a way to assuage domestic criticism after surrender and allow their power structure to survive."[58]

Anami's comment describing the USSR as an "immoral nation" bears further mention, because it was the same nation he and the rest of the Big Six had been seeking assistance from to help negotiate an end of the war—or perhaps even entice into an alliance against the

Anglo-Americans—since early May. Anami's statement during the Imperial Conference exemplifies not only the true feelings of the hard-liners toward the Soviet Union throughout the period of the Suzuki government, but also the same feelings expressed several years earlier by the Emperor. Japan's so-called peace overtures using the "good offices" of the Russian government were, in fact, never anything more than a sham. The military leaders wanted the effort to be unsuccessful because they were all determined to continue the war.

All eyes returned to Suzuki. He arose and calmly restated his original premise about the incontrovertible divide among the Big Six. Given the urgency of the situation, the Prime Minister said there was only one thing left to do. Turning to the front of the room to directly address Emperor Hirohito, he said, "Your Imperial Majesty's decision is requested as to which proposal should be adopted, the Foreign Minister's or the one with four conditions."[59] Suzuki concluded, "We would ask for a *seidan* and accept His Majesty's opinion as the final decision of the council."[60] Suzuki then stepped toward Hirohito. There were audible gasps. Anami exclaimed, "Mr. Prime Minister!" Suzuki, ignoring Anami's plea, approached the foot of the small podium next to the Emperor, then bowed very low. His Majesty bid Suzuki to sit down, but the old man did not hear the words well enough to understand them and cupped his hand next to his left ear. The Emperor gestured for him to return to his seat.[61] The silence in the stifling little room was absolute.

AUGUST 10, 1945
4 DAYS AFTER HIROSHIMA

At 2:00 a.m., Friday, August 10, 1945, after two hours of discussion, it was now Hirohito's turn to speak. The Emperor leaned forward, gripping the arms of his simple wooden chair and rose to his feet. Instantly, everyone else in the room snapped to attention and bowed toward Him. Slowly, with anguish in His voice but conviction in His words, He said:

"I will state my opinion. I agree with the Foreign Minister."

Anami shuddered as if he had just received a body blow.

My reasons are as follows:

> After serious consideration of [the] conditions facing Japan both at home and abroad I have concluded that to continue the war can mean only destruction for the homeland and more bloodshed and cruelty in the world. I cannot bear to have my innocent people suffer further. Ending the war is the only way to restore world peace and to relieve the nation from the terrible suffering it is undergoing.

Heavy sighs became audible and rippled across the chamber. The Emperor struggled to maintain His composure; His words came in an agonizing flow.

He also knew from experience He must provide some indictment of the military, especially the Army, if He expected to gain their acquiescence.

> I was told by the army chief of staff that in June the coastline defenses at Kujukuri-hama would be complete, with new divisions installed in fortifications ready to repel the invaders' landing operations. But the report of my aide-de-camp, who made an on-the-spot inspection of the area, is completely contrary. It is now August and the fortifications still have not been completed.

The words of the usually soft-spoken monarch grew in intensity.

> It was officially reported to me that equipping of a newly created division had been completed. But I know that in reality these soldiers have not yet been supplied even with bayonets! I understand it will be after mid-September before the required equipment is delivered.
>
> Furthermore, the scheduled increase in aircraft production has not materialized as promised. Air raids are becoming more intense day by day.
>
> Some advocate a decisive battle in the homeland as a way to survival. In past experience, however, there has always been a discrepancy between the fighting services' plans and the results. If, in conditions such as these, Japan should be rushed into a decisive battle in the homeland, how could an enemy be repulsed? What would become of Japan? I do not want to see our people continue to

suffer any longer. Also, I do not desire any further destruction of our culture, nor any additional misfortune for the peoples of the world.

The Emperor paused again to regain His self-control.

I am afraid that faced with a situation such as this the Japanese people are doomed, one and all. But in order to hand the country of Japan to posterity, I want as many of our people to survive as possible and rise again in the future.

Again, Hirohito was forced to stop. Gazing up at the ceiling to collect His thoughts, He wiped His glasses and cheeks with His white-gloved hand, brushing away His tears. The deep sobs of Japan's most powerful leaders hung like a pall over the room. Regaining His poise, but with a voice still thick with emotion, the Emperor continued:

I feel great pain when I think of those who have served me so faithfully—the soldiers and sailors who have been killed or wounded in distant battles, destitute families who have lost all their possessions—and often their lives as well—in air raids in the homeland. Indeed, disarmament of my brave and loyal military is excruciating to me. It is equally unbearable that those who have rendered me devoted service should be considered war criminals. However, for the sake of the country it cannot be helped. To relieve the people and to maintain the nation we must bear the unbearable. When I recall the fortitude of my Imperial Grandsire the Emperor Meiji at the time of the Triple Intervention, I swallow my own tears.

All of you, I think, will worry about me in the situation. But it does not matter what will become of me. Determined, as I have stated, I have decided to bring the war to an end immediately. For this reason, I agree with the Foreign Minister's proposal.[62]

Hirohito wiped the tears from His eyes one last time and walked slowly from the room.

As many of the men used their white handkerchiefs to dry away their tears and sweat, Suzuki said, "His Majesty's decision ought to be made the decision of this conference as well."

Continued silence gave consent.[63]

However, the constitutional authority to affect the surrender still resided with the Cabinet. The ministers left the bunker in favor of Suzuki's residence and a meeting with the full Cabinet. Discussion centered around whether to accept the *seidan*. After nearly two more hours haranguing, at 4:00 a.m. the Cabinet at last agreed to follow the Emperor's wishes; by 7:00 a.m., dispatches had been sent to Switzerland and Sweden, for transmission to the Allied powers. The communiqué stated:

> The Japanese Government today addressed the following communication to the Swiss and Swedish Governments respectively for transmission to the United States, Great Britain, China and the Soviet Union:
>
> In obedience to the gracious command of His Majesty the Emperor, who, ever anxious to enhance the cause of world peace, desires earnestly to bring about an early termination of hostilities with a view to saving mankind from the calamities to be imposed on them by further continuation of the war, the Japanese Government several weeks ago asked the Soviet Government, with which neutral relations then prevailed, to render good offices in restoring peace vis-à-vis the enemy powers.
>
> Unfortunately, these efforts in the interest of peace having failed, the Japanese Government, in conformity with the august wish of His Majesty to restore the general peace and desiring to put an end to the untold sufferings engendered by the war, have decided on the following:
>
> The Japanese Government are ready to accept the terms enumerated in the joint declaration which was issued at Potsdam on July 26th, 1945, by the heads of the Governments of the United States, Great Britain, and China, and later subscribed to by the Soviet Government, with the understanding that the said declaration does not compromise any demand which prejudices the prerogatives of His Majesty as a Sovereign Ruler.
>
> The Japanese Government hopes sincerely that this understanding is warranted and desires keenly that an explicit indication to this effect will be speedily forthcoming.[64]

The final phrase in the penultimate paragraph, added at Baron Hiranuma's insistence, really amounted to two conditions: the preservation of the Imperial system, and "with the understanding that the said declaration does not compromise any demand which prejudices the prerogatives of His Majesty as a Sovereign Ruler." In other words, Hirohito would remain the unfettered leader of Japan. Hiranuma's inclusion in the meeting and his doggedness on the wording was to make certain the expression of the Shintoist, right-wing view of the *kokutai*—the theocratic view of a divine Emperor, rather than the secular or cultural view proposed by Tōgō. Hirohito supported this view because He believed Himself to be a monarch by divine right.[65]

Hiranuma's inclusion was not a benign statement carrying no weight. It amounted to an affirmation of the Emperor's rite to supreme command and real political, military, and diplomatic authority. In the face of all that had happened during the war, the Suzuki government "was asking the Allies to guarantee the Emperor's power to rule on the theocratic premises of the state Shinto."[66] This was not a constitutional monarchy, but one based on oracular sovereignty with the ongoing subjecthood or *shimmin* status of the Japanese people and a continuing role for the military after the surrender.[67]

The statement very nearly took the lives of untold more because Anami had extracted a final concession from both Suzuki and Yonai during the night's long deliberations. "Suppose, the enemy refuses to give you any assurance that the Imperial House will be preserved—will you go on fighting?" Both men said, "Yes, we will continue the war."[68] Within a few hours, the phrase sparked controversy among Truman and his top advisors, leading to a counteroffer by the Allies.

The Japanese proposal was not what the signors of the Potsdam Declaration had in mind, or what Roosevelt was thinking when he first framed the demand for unconditional surrender. FDR wanted to do away with, permanently, the governments and men who had brought such incredible destruction and loss of life to the world.

With the thirteen-hour time difference between Tokyo and Washington, Japanese intelligence picked up a second speech given by Truman on August 9 at 4:00 a.m. Delivered during a nationwide radio broadcast, the president's speech gave full expression to the vengeful mood of most Americans.

> The British, Chinese, and United States governments have given the Japanese people adequate warning of what is in store for them. We have laid down the general terms on which they can surrender. Our warning went unheeded. Our terms were rejected.

Since then, the Japanese have seen what our atomic bomb can do. They can foresee what it will do in the future.

The world will note that the first atomic bomb was dropped on Hiroshima, a military base. That was because we wished in the first attack to avoid insofar as possible, the killing of civilians. But that attack is only a warning of things to come. If Japan does not surrender, bombs will have to be dropped on her war industries and unfortunately thousands of civilian lives will be lost. I urge Japanese civilians to leave industrial cities immediately and save themselves from destruction.

I realize the tragic significance of the atomic bomb. Its production and its use were not lightly undertaken by this government. But we knew that our enemies were on the search for it. We know now how close they were to finding it. And we knew the disaster which would come to this nation and to all peace-loving nations, to all civilization, if they had found it first. That is why we felt compelled to undertake the long and uncertain and costly labor of discovery and production. We won the race of discovery against the Germans.

Having found the bomb, we have used it. We have used it against those who attacked us without warning at Pearl Harbor, against those who have starved and beaten and executed American prisoners of war, against those who have abandoned all pretense of obeying international laws of warfare. We have used it in order to shorten the agony of war; in order to save the lives of thousands and thousands of young Americans. We shall continue to use it until we completely destroy Japan's power to make war. Only a Japanese surrender will stop us...

It is difficult to imagine a more clearly stated threat.

At 9:30 a.m. on the 10th, in the War Ministry's underground bomb shelter, Anami ordered all personnel above the chief-of-section rank to gather.[69] Anami informed his staff of the momentous event that had taken place earlier in the morning and of the Emperor's pronouncement:

I do not know what excuse I can offer but since it is the decision of His Majesty that we accept the Potsdam Proclamation there is nothing that can be done. The really important consideration is that the Army act in an organized manner. Your individual feelings and those of the men under you must be disregarded.

Since the imperial decision is predicated upon the assumption that the Allies will guarantee the preservation of our national polity, it is too soon to say that the war has already ended. The Army must therefore be prepared either for war or for peace.

If there is anyone here who is dissatisfied and who wishes to act contrary to His Majesty's decision, he will have to do so over my dead body.[70]

The men were stunned by the development and Anami's apparent submission. For so long the Army had been the most powerful force in Japan; now it might completely cease to exist. The Emperor's decision revealed His Majesty's loss of faith in the Army.

As the meeting concluded, Lieutenant Colonel Masao Inaba of the Military Affairs Bureau approached Anami with a plan to keep order until the surrender had been finalized. He said, "Regardless of whether we end the war or not, we must send out instruction to keep fighting, particularly with the Soviet troops advancing in Manchuria." Anami responded, "Write it out."[71] Inaba immediately left to draft the statement.

Meanwhile, the Cabinet had yet to reach an agreement on what the public should be told. The military did not want the Emperor's decision to be known for fear that it would lead to chaos. Since the public had been kept in the dark throughout the war, word of surrender would come as a complete shock. In the compromise, the men agreed to release only a vague statement to help prepare the people for surrender. In truth, it did nothing of the kind.

The statement, finished too late to appear in all of Japan's morning newspapers the morning of August 10, had to wait until the following day for public dissemination. It included the typical bromides about the spirit of the country's fighting forces and Japan's defeat of enemy forces everywhere—though it did warn the people the Allies were about to invade the Empire and derided its "diabolical enemies" for their use of a "new-type bomb" that was ravaging the innocent on a scale "unprecedented, in the history of the human race, in ruthlessness and barbarity." Only the concluding paragraph gave the slightest hint of what was to come.

In truth, we cannot but recognize that we are now beset with the worst possible situation. Just as the government is exerting its utmost efforts to defend the homeland, safeguard the polity, and preserve the honor of the nation so too must the people rise to the occasion and overcome all manner of difficulties in order to protect the polity of their Empire.[72]

All that the Cabinet's statement managed to accomplish was to convince the populace that they should ready themselves for a fight to the death from one end of the country to another.

At about 2:00 p.m., having obtained general approval for his idea from Anami, Inaba showed a draft of his proposed announcement to the Vice Minister of War Lieutenant General Tadaichi Wakamatsu, the Chief of the Military Affairs Bureau, and the Military Affairs Section. Each of the men who read the draft suggested several revisions and then approved the document. At that moment, Anami could not be located so Inaba asked Colonel Okikatsu Arao, who was to see Anami that evening, to obtain the general's endorsement.

Later that afternoon, two officers sympathetic to Inaba's views arrived and asked for a copy of the announcement to be broadcast that evening, but by then Arao had left with the original, bound for Anami's signature. Inaba and the two officers proceeded to dig out of the trash can the original crumpled draft, and after rewriting a clean copy, Inaba revised it in line with the suggestions he had gotten earlier from his superiors. Without ever getting Anami's approval, he gave the document to the officers for broadcast that evening and publication in the newspaper the morning of August 11.[73] No attempt was ever made by anyone, including Anami, to clarify any of the content. In fact, when Takeshita ultimately came to Anami to apologize for his role in the unauthorized publication of the statement, Anami brushed it aside, telling his brother-in-law, "It's all right. Don't worry about it. I was asked by [Information Bureau President Dr. Hiroshi] Shimomura at the cabinet meeting about the statement, and I explained that I had given my approval to the purport of the message." By reassuring Takeshita, Anami condoned yet another breach in discipline, of *Gekokujō*.[74]

At 7:00 p.m. the message, entitled INSTRUCTION TO THE TROOPS, which also became known as the Anami Proclamation, was broadcast on the radio. It stated:

My fellow members of the armed forces, the Soviets have finally invaded this Imperial Nation. Despite their efforts to embellish their motives, their real aim to invade and occupy the Greater East Asia is apparent. Since events have reached this point, there is nothing further to be said. The only thing we have to do is to fight the sacred war to defend this Land of the Gods. Even though we may have to eat grass and chew dirt and lay in the field we must fight on to the bitter end, ever firm in our belief that we shall find life in death. This is the spirit to serve your country by using your seven lives which is the spirit of Masashige Kusunoki [a 14th-century samurai who fought for Emperor Go-Daigo in the Genkō War] when he aimed to save the country saying please have peace in your mind if you hear that I alone am alive. And again [recall] the words by Tokimune Hojo upon the time of the Mongol Invasion: [With no thought except to] surge forward to destroy the invading enemy, the soldiers in the whole country without any exception will show his own spirit of Masashige Kusunoki and fighting spirit of Tokimune Hojo to charge straight ahead to destroy the arrogant enemy.

—August 10, 1945, Minister of the Army [75]

The content directly contradicted the decision made by the Emperor and full Cabinet, as well as Anami's own comments to his men on the morning of August 10. The cause of the faux pas was yet another example of the fanatical attitudes within the Army that refused to countenance surrender. Inaba seized on the second part of Anami's statement to his staff earlier that morning and decided until the war was officially over, that Japan's troops should be encouraged to fight with unshakeable resolve, to prevent the rise and spread of unrest once word got out of the surrender.

On August 11, the printed version of the Anami Proclamation appeared side by side with the Cabinet's dispatch. Knowing the broadcast could send the wrong message to the Allies about Japan's intention to surrender (with the single condition) and given the slow movement of the official communication sent earlier in the day, Vice-Minister of Foreign Affairs Shunichi Matsumoto and other members of the Foreign Office devised a means they thought would go unnoticed by the prying eyes of the military's sensors—they would send their message out by simple Morse code. The evening of August 10, the message was repeated several times without observation by the Army until the following morning, but by then it was too late to do anything about it.[76]

With the time zone differences, it was 7:33 a.m. on August 10 in the American capital when Truman and Leahy first heard the radio broadcast announcing Japan's conditional acceptance of the Potsdam

Declaration. Truman immediately asked Admiral Leahy to summon Secretaries Byrnes, Stimson, and Forrestal, to the Oval Office for a meeting at 9:00 a.m. to discuss the Japanese offer. Stimson was surprised to get the call that the Japanese had responded so quickly. He was about to depart on a vacation, an indication that he, like Marshall, did not believe the atomic bomb would be enough to gain the capitulation of the Japanese—at least not so soon.

In keeping with Truman's order to continue conventional attacks on Japan, earlier that morning the Navy sortied hundreds of carrier planes against the Japanese capital, while seventy B-29s struck the Tokyo Arsenal. From Okinawa, five hundred fighters bombed the city of Kumamoto and attacked Japanese shipping. The raids were considered by the Japanese to be "the most impressive and nerve-wracking demonstration of the whole war."[77]

Upon their arrival at the White House, Stimson, Leahy, Byrnes, and Forrestal received the message from the Japanese government originating from the chargé d'affaires of the Swiss delegation in Washington. The Japanese had agreed to accept the terms of the Potsdam Declaration on one condition—that the Imperial System be allowed to continue and "with the understanding that the said declaration does not compromise any demand that prejudices the prerogatives of His Majesty as Sovereign Ruler" of Japan.

Truman in turn asked the men for their opinions on three questions: "Were we to treat this message from Tokyo as an acceptance of the Potsdam Declaration? There had been many in this country who felt that the Emperor was an integral part of that Japanese system which we were pledged to destroy. Could we continue the Emperor and yet expect to eliminate the warlike spirit in Japan? Could we even consider a message with so large a 'but' as the kind of unconditional surrender we had fought for?"[78]

General Marshall did not attend the meeting, but he did send a memorandum dealing with the possibility of an abrupt surrender that focused on Allied prisoners of war. As of mid-June, the Japanese still held 168,500, of whom 15,000 were American. Marshall composed a statement saying, "precedent to a discussion of the proposal of the Japanese government," all POWs had to be transported "immediately forth with and without delay" to designated locations for release. To accomplish this would have taken several days, an indication that Marshall believed finalizing the surrender was not going to happen fast.[79]

Truman echoed Marshall's concern. The president had repeatedly mentioned the treatment of Allied POWs in the months since assuming office, most recently in his August 9th radio address. Marshall's proposal was transformed into a "solemn warning," issued by all the Allied governments putting Japan "individually and collectively" on notice not to harm prisoners of war.[80]

In response to the president's questions, Stimson promptly reverted to his now consistent refrain, that the Japanese should be allowed to keep the Emperor, if for no other reason, because he served American interests. His status among the Japanese people would greatly aid in getting the country's military to lay down their arms and thus avoid "a score of bloodied Iwo Jimas and Okinawas all over China and the New Netherlands [Indonesia]." The former would have translated into over 600,000 total casualties with more than 170,000 KIA or MIA—the latter, nearly a million total casualties, of which a quarter of million would have been killed or missing. And Stimson's horrific forecast did not include the casualties from Downfall, the two-phased invasions of the Japanese homeland.[81]

Forrestal and Admiral Leahy were also in favor of accepting the Japanese offer, Leahy having already drafted a proposal to accept it. He justified his endorsement later by saying:

> I recommended accepting the Japanese proposal. This did not mean that I favored the Emperor's retaining all his prerogatives. I had no feelings about little Hirohito, but was convinced that it would be necessary to use him in affecting the surrender.
>
> Some of those around the President wanted to demand the Emperor's execution. If they had prevailed, we might still be a war with Japan. His subjects would probably have fought on until every loyal Japanese was dead, and at that moment there were more than five million Japanese soldiers in the field.[82]

Byrnes stood alone in opposition, angrily dissenting. In his view, Japan's requirement to include the phrasing "with the understanding that the said declaration does not comprise any demand which prejudices the prerogatives of His Majesty as a Sovereign Ruler" amounted to a refusal by Japan's government to accept the unconditional surrender stipulated in the Potsdam Declaration. He reminded Truman of the Allies' agreement of the terms at Potsdam, that they would "not deviate from them. There are no alternatives." Byrnes said, "I cannot understand why now we should go further [in accepting a conditional peace] than we were willing to go at Potsdam when we had no atomic bomb, and Russia was not in the war."[83]

Forrestal suggested that with some changes to the wording, perhaps the offer could be made acceptable—an idea that appealed to Truman.

Byrnes's "diary-keeping" assistant was quoted as saying that afternoon, at "bullbat time" Byrnes said if Truman had accepted Leahy's original draft to accept the Japanese surrender, it "would have led to the crucifixion of the President." It was an opinion hardened for years by politicians in Washington who had bluntly and publicly reviled the Emperor. If the American government suddenly reversed itself, "too many people were likely to cry shame," and the repercussions for the man in the Oval Office could be very serious.

Whether or not Byrnes's remark overstated the potential effect on the president, after listening to the opinions of his top advisors, Byrnes's argument persuaded Truman not to accept the Japanese offer as written. He asked Byrnes to come up with a counteroffer that the Allies could accept.[84]

Byrnes's remarks also may have resonated with Truman because the president had always believed in listening to the American public. Henry Wallace, FDR's former vice president and Truman's Secretary of Commerce, wrote, concerning the hard and soft terms for Japan, "Truman referred to one hundred and seventy telegrams precipitated by the peace rumor of August 9. One hundred fifty-three of the one hundred and seventy were for hard terms—unconditional surrender. They were free-will telegrams—not inspired—and were mostly from parents of servicemen."

Byrnes's task required careful thought. What justification could there be in accepting outright the demand of a vanquished foe? On the other hand, rejection could mean the continuation of a long, bloody conflict with no end in sight. Too weak or too harsh a reaction could carry political consequences for the presidency. The language also had to be acceptable to America's Allies, avoiding anything that could come across as a revision of the Potsdam Declaration.

Byrnes wasted no time in getting to work on the language for the Allied response. Around 2:00 p.m., Leahy and Truman joined Byrnes in the effort to complete a final draft.[85] Copies were then sent off to Britain, China, and the Soviet Union. The original Allied counterproposal to the Japanese stated:

August 11, 1945

Mr. Max Grassli
Chargé d'Affaires ad interim of Switzerland

I have the honor to acknowledge receipt of your note of August 10, and in reply to inform you that the President of the United States has directed me to send to you for transmission by your government to the Japanese government the following message on behalf of the governments of the United States, United Kingdom, the Union of Soviet Socialist Republics, and China:

With regard to the Japanese Government's message accepting the terms of the Potsdam proclamation but containing the statement "with the understanding that the said declaration does not compromise any demand which prejudices the prerogatives of his Majesty as the sovereign ruler"—our position is as follows:

From the moment of surrender the authority of the Emperor and the Japanese Government to rule the state shall be subject to the Supreme Commander of the Allied Powers who will take such steps as he deems proper to effectuate the surrender terms.

The Emperor and the Japanese High Command will be required to sign the surrender terms necessary to carry out the provisions of the Potsdam Declaration, to issue orders to all the armed forces of Japan to cease hostilities and to surrender their arms, and to issue such other orders as the Supreme Commander may require to give effect to the surrender terms.

Immediately upon the surrender the Japanese Government shall transport prisoners of war and civilian internees to places of safety, as directed, where they can be quickly placed aboard Allied transports.

The ultimate form of government of Japan shall, in accordance with the Potsdam Declaration, be established by the freely expressed will of the Japanese people.

The Armed Forces of the Allied Powers will remain in Japan until the purposes set forth in the Potsdam Declaration are achieved.

James Byrnes
Secretary of State[86]

British Prime Minister Attlee and Secretary of State for Foreign Affairs Ernest Bevin recommended a few changes to the third paragraph, offering as an alternative:

> The Emperor shall authorize and ensure the signature of the Government of Japan and the Japanese General Headquarters of the surrender terms necessary to carry out the provisions of the Potsdam Declaration, and shall issue his commands to all Japanese military, naval, and air authorities and to all the forces under their control wherever located to cease active operations and to surrender their arms, and to issue such other orders as the Supreme Commander may require to give effect to the surrender terms.[87]

Truman and Byrnes agreed with their British Ally's suggested changes. After making the revisions and receiving approval from the Chinese, and belatedly from the Russians by the evening of the 10th, the Allies transmitted their reply to Hirohito's government through the same communication channel used by the Japanese a little more than a day earlier.

Taken in its entirety, the counterproposal did not explicitly guarantee the Imperial institution or that Hirohito would remain Emperor.[88]

Attached to diplomatic exchanges taking place between Japan and the Allies was the question of what, if any, military action the Americans should continue. According to the diary of Henry Wallace, the president said, "the thought of wiping out another 100,000 people was too horrible. He didn't like the idea of killing 'all those kids.'" Truman's reference to 100,000 casualties was not a randomly chosen figure by the president. It corresponded exactly with a casualty estimate for Hiroshima contained in an Imperial Navy message reported in an Ultra summary the day before.[89]

Truman knew another bomb would not be available until August 21. Nevertheless, American commanders in the Pacific had created a list of recommendations for the third bomb. Generals Farrell, Twining, and Spaatz, along with Admiral Nimitz and Captain Parsons, had already met to discuss the situation, and by the afternoon of August 9 had sent their list of targets to Washington. By August 14, Twining's new list of targets, in priority order, included: Sapporo, Hakodate, Oyabu, Yokosuka, Osaka, and Nagoya.[90]

Conventional weapons were another matter. Despite being urged by

Forrestal and Stimson to cease all naval and air operation as a humane gesture, Truman wanted the pressure on Japan's leaders maintained to discourage any thoughts of further concessions.[91]

Truman wrote in his memoir, "I was determined that the Japanese occupation should not follow in the footsteps of our German experience. I did not want divided control or separate zones. I did not want to give the Russians any opportunity to behave as they had in Germany and Austria. I wanted the country administered in such a manner that it could be restored to its place in the society of nations."[92] He hoped the sustained pressure of American conventional attacks would more quickly gain Japan's final capitulation and thus avoid Soviet involvement.

In Tokyo, Tōgō, Matsumoto, and Sakomizu anxiously awaited the Allied response.

AUGUST 11, 1945
5 DAYS AFTER HIROSHIMA

Saturday morning, with air raid sirens howling in the background, the general population had an opportunity to read in the newspaper, side by side, the statements from the Cabinet and the War Ministry—the "Anami Proclamation." They were still blithely unaware that their government had conditionally agreed to accept the Potsdam Declaration.[93]

As Tōgō, Matsumoto, and Sakomizu impatiently waited for the Allied response, the Emperor received Anami and reprimanded him for his "proclamation." Anami offered as an excuse to the Emperor, and later to the Cabinet who also took him to task, that the Army would naturally have to go on fighting until the surrender became a fact.[94]

On the night of the 11th, in the War Office bomb shelter in Ichigaya (the eastern part of the Shinjuku ward in Tokyo), Lieutenant Colonel Mahahiko Takeshita, the senior officer present, presided over a group of extremist middle-grade officers. Among those present were: Major Kenji Hatanaka, Lieutenant Colonel Masataka Ida, Lieutenant Colonel Jiro Shiizaki, Lieutenant Colonel Kiyoshi Minami, Major Hidemasa Koga, and Lieutenant Colonel Masao Inaba (author of the Anami Proclamation), some fifteen men in all. Takeshita told the group they must act quickly to stop the peace process that had just been announced. He said the first thing they needed to do was isolate the Emperor from the traitorous members of the "peace-faction," who had perpetrated this dishonorable action. Suzuki, Tōgō, and Kido must be assassinated, and if Lieutenant General Takeshi Mori, commander of the Imperial Guards and charged with the protection of the Emperor, refused to join their conspiracy, he would also have to go. Their plan called for using troops stationed in Tokyo to encircle the Palace grounds, followed by cutting off the lines of communication by occupying radio stations, newspapers, and key government buildings. Takeshita's very participation in the plot, with his direct family connection and personal relationship to Anami, inferred the war minister's knowledge and tacit approval. Takeshita assured the men they could count on the support of his brother-in-law General Anami, and "Once the biggest fish was in the net, the smaller fish would follow"—but he also warned them their treasonous coup was punishable by death.[95]

Nevertheless, the group remained optimistic their plan would succeed, and once it did it would no longer be treason. Like their eventual leader, Anami, they believed a hard-fought, decisive battle on the mainland could exact massive casualties on the Americans and win an honorable peace for Japan. If it did not, they would retreat to the mountains and carry on a guerrilla war.[96] In either case, Japan and its Imperial Army would remain unstained by surrender. Only more death could assuage defeat and pacify the souls killed in battle. The suffering of the Japanese populace would have to continue until a righteous peace could be realized.

10

THE SECOND
IMPERIAL INTERVENTION

AUGUST 12, 1945
6 DAYS AFTER HIROSHIMA

Secretary of State James Byrnes's message, like the Japanese surrender offer, initially reached the Foreign Office in Tokyo in Morse code. It was 12:45 a.m. on Sunday, the August 12. The early delivery gave the Japanese government the information it needed a full eighteen hours before the official reply arrived.

But the Allies' somewhat ambiguous response, because it did not explicitly guarantee the Imperial Polity or the Emperor's unconstrained right to rule, disheartened those initially reading Byrnes's reply. Over the course of the day, word of what it said touched off a flurry of activity along the now familiar battle lines. Each side passionately attempted to convince anyone still on the fence, as well as the opposition, that their position would save the nation.

To make Byrnes's counteroffer more acceptable to Hirohito, the Imperial Army, and Baron Hiranuma, Matsumoto and Sakomizu in the Foreign Ministry decided to intentionally mistranslate a few key words from the English text. In the sentence *"From the moment of surrender, the authority of the Emperor and the Japanese government to rule the state shall be subject to the Supreme Commander of the Allied powers,"* Matsumoto changed *"shall be subject to"* [*reizoku subeki*] to read *"shall be circumscribed by"* [*seigen no shita ni okareru*].[1] There was also concern over how broadly to view the word *"government,"* which had been transcribed incorrectly. Byrnes had written *"The ultimate form of government of Japan,"* but the translation read, *"The ultimate form of the Government of Japan."* The issue was whether the capital *"G"* referred exclusively to the civilian government or if it included the Emperor. If it included the Emperor, they were obligated to reject Byrnes's reply. The two men agreed it did not.[2] Lastly, Byrnes's note contained the statement, *"the ultimate form of government shall be established by the freely expressed will of the Japanese people."* The declaration contradicted the established form of government and the position of the Emperor in it, and it did not explicitly guarantee the continuation of the Imperial Throne.

However, taking into consideration the risks of delay, which included further Allied attacks, the potential dissolution of the Suzuki government, and the potential of a military coup, the staff of the Foreign Ministry decided the wording had to be "swallowed without chewing." "Let's push it through in its present form," urged the Vice-Minister.[3]

After hearing the argument for accepting the Byrnes note provided by Matsumoto and Sakomizu at 5:30 a.m., Tōgō agreed on the soundness of their conclusion. Their strategy would be to take an aggressive stance that the Allied reply was satisfactory, and they would move full speed ahead toward surrender before the opposition within their government coalesced sufficiently to block it.[4] Tōgō left for home to prepare. He had two meetings to attend, one with Suzuki to inform him of the Allies' reply, and then a conference with Emperor at 11:00 a.m.

At around 8:00 a.m., word of the Byrnes counteroffer reached some of the officers in the Army and Navy considering a coup to overthrow the government. They instantly reacted by storming into the offices of General Umezu and Admiral Toyoda, demanding a public rejection of the offer. Their tenor was so vehement, Toyoda and Umezu immediately rushed to the Imperial Palace where the Emperor received both at 8:30 a.m. After listening to their rather confusing and disjointed arguments, the Emperor could tell the men had been pressured by their subordinates. He informed them that no decision had yet been made.

From 9:15 to 9:35 a.m., the Emperor granted Kido an audience. Top among their topics of discussion, Kido explained the potential problems for the Emperor in the Byrnes reply, chiefly the choosing of Japan's ultimate form of government. "That's all beside the point," said Hirohito. "It would be useless if the people didn't want an Emperor. I think it's perfectly all right to leave the matter up to the people."[5] If Hirohito held this opinion at the time of the Potsdam Declaration, why had he not made it known to his government? Had he done so, he might have saved Japan from the atomic bombs and the Soviet entry into the war as an enemy of Japan.

At 10:00 a.m., a dozen excited officers charged into Anami's office. Their leader, Takeshita, brazenly threatened Anami, exclaiming, "The proposed surrender must not take place. If it does, the War Minister ought to commit suicide with his own sword." Anami gritted his teeth but did not speak.[6]

Earlier that morning, around 8:30 a.m., War Minister Anami and Baron Hiranuma had already come to the same conclusion—they believed the Prime Minister was failing in his duties to protect the Throne. About mid-morning, both men drove to the Prime Minister's residence to express their opinions. Hiranuma was the first to speak. He stated flatly that the Byrnes counterproposal must be turned down because it patently eliminated the Imperial structure. Since the Emperor was divine, He could not be subject to a foreign power, which he translated as slavery, nor could His authority to rule over Japan be subjugated to the will of the Japanese people. Both created an unacceptable change in the national polity.

Anami then reminded Suzuki of their conversation in the early hours of August 10, after the Imperial Conference. When the Prime Minister could not recall the exchange, Anami became annoyed and said that they had all agreed that if the Allies failed to accept their condition regarding the sovereignty and right to rule of the Emperor, then the war would continue. His memory jogged, Suzuki agreed to stand firm with Anami and Hiranuma.[7]

Anami next sought out Prince Takahito Mikasa, Hirohito's youngest brother, who was known as unconventional in his thinking. Anami believed he could elicit the Prince's support. To the War Minister's surprise, however, Takahito rebuked him.

"Since the Manchurian Incident the Army has at times acted not quite in accordance with the Imperial wish," Prince Mikasa said. "It is most improper that you should still want to continue the war when things have reached this stage."

Seeing no opportunity to change the Prince's mind, Anami departed—but the Prince was left wondering how such a responsible officer could still hold views in opposition to the Emperor, and how widespread those beliefs were at the War Ministry.[8]

Prince Mikasa's reference to the entire period of Japanese aggression in Southeast Asia and the Pacific significantly overstated the breadth of the differences between the military and the Emperor, but the Prince's comments gave voice to a clear rift that now existed between Hirohito and the Army, as the Emperor had expressed two days earlier during the Imperial Conference.

Around ten in the morning, Tōgō left to see Suzuki at the Prime Minister's Official Residence. On the ride over, in the back seat of his Buick limo, he mused over what lay ahead:

> My task is to win over the military leaders...my strategy must be to gain my point by persuading a majority of the Cabinet, including the premier, to agree with me. If the PM changes his mind, I will be checkmated, and to insist on my point in the face of growing support for continuing the war will result in forced resignation of the Cabinet. This, in turn, may well mean not only loss of the present opportunity, but increased agitation against ending the war...and an end to all hope of peace.
>
> But today could be the day to end the whole bloody war.[9]

He found Suzuki "pacing the quarter deck" in a fog of cigar smoke, and quickly got the impression the Prime Minister had already been intimidated by his earlier visit from the War Minister.[10] Over some green tea, the Foreign Minister sat down with Suzuki and went over the Byrnes note line by line. Believing he had convinced Suzuki of the merits of accepting it, Tōgō left.

His next stop was the Imperial Palace, where he first had a brief meeting with Kido. Tōgō reviewed the salient issues about the Allied response and his belief that the reply was not demanding sweeping changes to the national polity. As such, and unless Japan was ready to break off negotiations and resume the war, it had no alternative but to accept the offer without asking for further conditions.[11]

At 11:00 a.m., a chamberlain ushered the Foreign Minister to his meeting with His Majesty where he found the Emperor's appearance to be a bit disheveled. Tōgō scrutinized the Byrnes note in detail for Hirohito. He explained that the terms meant relying on the Allies' word for the Emperor's safety and continuation of the Imperial line. At the same time, he said the Allies understood the value of the Emperor in creating an orderly and peaceful occupation of Japan and would not do anything to jeopardize it.[12]

The Emperor told Tōgō, "I think the [US] reply is all right. You had better proceed to accept the note as it is." The meeting strengthened the Emperor's belief that accepting Byrnes's counteroffer was only way to save Japan, and it provided Tōgō with the renewed conviction he needed in his battle with the diehards.[13] The Emperor asked Tōgō to please convey his decision to the Prime Minister.

Tōgō climbed into the back seat of his limo and returned to the Prime Minister's residence to relay the message that His Majesty had endorsed the acceptance of the Byrnes note. After doing so, he was about to leave when he unexpectedly encountered Hiranuma. The Baron reiterated the same arguments he had given to Suzuki earlier that morning, over two of paragraphs in the Byrnes reply, specifically, *"the authority of the Emperor and the Japanese Government to rule the state shall be subject to the Supreme Commander…and that the ultimate form of government of Japan shall, in accordance with the Potsdam Declaration, be established by the freely expressed will of the Japanese people."* Tōgō, needing to prepare for the Cabinet meeting that afternoon, told Hiranuma briefly about the statement he intended to give to the assembly and took his leave.

Between 3:00 p.m. and 5:20 p.m., Hirohito met with all of the senior members of the Imperial House in the Palace's basement shelter. The Emperor explained to the thirteen men his reasons for accepting both the Potsdam Declaration and the new Byrnes note, and asked the Imperial Court for its united support for his decision. Hirohito told the men he believed the nation's resources had been exhausted, its military had experienced nothing but defeat for some time, and the prospect for winning the decisive battle in the homeland appeared bleak. Prince Nashimoto Morimasa, speaking on behalf of the entire court, pledged their unanimous support.[14]

At 3:00 p.m., the Prime Minister called the Cabinet into special session. Tōgō began the discussion with a lengthy statement:

> The United States' response to our inquiry could not be said to be entirely reassuring. We had raised the question of sovereignty of the Emperor, and the answer was that Japan's sovereignty would not be unlimited during occupation, but that the authority of the Supreme Commander for the Allied powers would be paramount, in order that the provisions of the Potsdam Declaration might be effectuated. This was not unforeseen; it is inevitable that under a guarantee occupation the sovereignty of the state will be limited to the extent requisite to implement the surrender terms. The position of the Emperor nevertheless remained, in principle, unimpaired; Paragraph 2 of the reply was accordingly not unacceptable.

Paragraph 3 provided that the Emperor was under obligation to carry out the terms of surrender, which was natural. Paragraphs 4 and 6, on the delivery of prisoners of war and the duration of the occupation, respectively, were self-explanatory and offered no difficulty. The problem was paragraph 5.

The idea of establishing the form of government by the freely expressed will of the people appeared in the Atlantic charter, which the Potsdam Declaration in this particular echoed; but this very provision, that the national polity of Japan was to be determined by the Japanese themselves, negated any suggestion that there should be interference from without. At all events, even if the Allies had any intention of submitting the question to a referendum, it was impossible to conceive that the overwhelming loyal majority of [the Japanese] people would not wish to preserve [the] traditional system. On the other hand, there were reasons to believe that much antagonism existed among the Allies to the Imperial system of Japan, but that the Anglo-American leaders had managed to restrain it to the extent that Byrnes' reply evidenced. If [they] should now demand revisions in its phraseology, it was most probable that [they] should fail...and if [they] persisted in debating the point, it was quite likely that the harsher opinions among the Allies would then be given free reign, and demand for abolition of the Imperial House would be the upshot. In such an event, [they] should have to be resigned to complete breaking off of the negotiations.

Inasmuch as the Imperial conference decision of the 9th constituted a recognition that continuation of the war was intolerable even if not impossible, the negotiations for surrender should at all hazards be consummated at their very present stage.[15]

Anami once again reminded Suzuki and Yonai that they had agreed, when they sent the peace offer to the Allies on August 10, that the war would continue if the Allies did not accept Japan's single condition. In his mind they had not done so by requiring the Emperor to be subject to the Supreme Allied Commander and the ultimate form of government in Japan to be determined by the free will of the people.[16] Since the Allies had not agreed with Japan's single condition to terminate the war, Anami now believed Japan should reopen the negotiations and include the items that had been taken out of their August 10 proposal—or continue the war. Tōgō leapt angrily to his feet, stating, "Any

further request by this government will lead to a breaking off of negotiations, which is contrary to the Imperial decision given to me this
morning, and it will only ensure the continuance of the war. This is
senseless behavior."[17]

As had been the case during the meetings on August 9, the two sides
again drew their now very familiar political battle lines, and after more
than an hour of debate, the two camps showed no signs of bridging the
chasm between them. Sensing things were turning against him, Tōgō
left the room and telephoned Matsumoto, who urged him to get the
meeting adjourned before a vote could be taken.[18]

Suzuki had been silent throughout the discussion. Tōgō returned
in time to hear the Prime Minister say, "If disarmament is forced upon
us, we have no alternative but to continue the war." Tōgō was livid at
Suzuki's remark, but managed to maintain his composure before stating, "Inasmuch as the official reply of the Allies has not yet arrived,
we had better continue our discussion after receipt of it." Finding no
objection, the group adjourned.

But Tōgō couldn't wait to get to Suzuki, and he followed him into
his private office and exploded.

> What are you thinking of? I completely disagree with you. This
> is no time to bring up the question of disarmament. Incessant
> bandying of words over the ultimatum from the enemy is profitless.
> Unless we are prepared for a breakdown of negotiations, there is
> no alternative but to accept their reply as it stands. As the premier
> is well aware, the Emperor wants to end the war. It goes without
> saying that his opinion, as Commander-in-Chief, should prevail.
> But the question now at issue involves the very existence of the
> Imperial house. I warn you, if you and the Cabinet insist on
> continuing the war, I will be forced to report my opposing view
> directly to the Emperor!

With his warning delivered, Tōgō stormed out of Suzuki's office.[19]

Still reeling from Tōgō's verbal assault, Suzuki was next greeted by
Matsumoto who brought news from Japan's embassy in Sweden. The
dispatch stated that the Allies would harden their stance, not soften it, if
Japan rejected the Byrnes note.[20] Under the circumstances Matsumoto
said, "please give full play to your great statesmanship at this time."
Suzuki gave Matsumoto a blank stare and shrugged his shoulders, then

said, "I have the same idea, but as the War Minister and Mr. Hiranuma are making strong representation to the Emperor, it's a very hard problem." Masumoto left with a deep feeling of foreboding.[21]

By the time Tōgō returned to his office, his mood had shifted from anger to depression. He told Matsumoto he might have to resign. The Vice Minister beseeched him not to do so. Then he suggested, "Although a formal reply from the Allies is expected at any moment why don't we pretend it didn't arrive until tomorrow morning. Tonight, please go home and rest." Tōgō consented and headed for his car, but he had one last task to perform before he could momentarily relax. He had to let Kido know of Suzuki's betrayal.[22]

Acting on Tōgō's portrayal of Suzuki's comments in the Cabinet meeting, Kido telephoned the Prime Minister's office and requested his presence. Finally, at 9:30 p.m., the Prime Minister arrived at the Imperial Household Ministry, grumbling about the "Hiranuma crowd," the self-appointed protectors of the *kokutai*. Kido said, "I don't intend belittling the argument of those who are anxious to jealously guard the national existence, but on the basis of careful study, the Foreign Minister assures us that there is nothing objectionable in the paragraph in question...Should we turn down the Potsdam Proclamation at this stage and should the war be continued, one million innocent Japanese would die from bombings and starvation. If we bring about peace now, four or five of us may be assassinated but it would be worth it. Without wavering or hesitation, let us carry out the policy to accept the Potsdam Proclamation!"

"Let us do it!" shouted Suzuki.[23]

While Suzuki maintained a fear that the agreed-upon form of surrender could eliminate the Throne, Yonai harbored concern over a different risk:

> I think the term is inappropriate, but the atomic bombs and the Soviet entry into the war are, in a sense, gifts from the gods [*tenyu*, also "heaven–sent blessings"]. This way we don't have to say that we have quit the war because of domestic circumstances. Why I have long been advocating control of the crisis of the country is neither from fear of an enemy attack nor because of the atomic bombs and the Soviet entry into the war. The main reason is my anxiety over the domestic situation. So, it is rather fortunate that we now can control matters without revealing the domestic situation.

Yonai's concern, one also shared by both Kido and Hirohito, referred to the danger of the Throne being toppled by a revolt by the Japanese people, putting a permanent end to the Imperial institution.[24] The possibility ran counter to Tōgō's contention that he could not conceive of the Japanese people not voting with their "free will" to keep the national polity.

But Yonai, Kido, and the Emperor weren't the only men sharing this concern for the Imperial system. The first priority of the *jushin* (senior advisors composed of all former living prime ministers) was to uphold the national polity. The *jushin* believed if the war was not terminated, civilian discontent might sweep away the throne and everything else with it. This was their justification for accepting the Allies' offer to end the war—not to spare the Japanese people from the ongoing blockade and bombardment, starvation, more atomic bombs, or an Allied invasion of Japan. The "national polity" took precedence over the people.[25]

AUGUST 13, 1945
7 DAYS AFTER HIROSHIMA

All through August 12 and 13, Truman waited for a reply from the Japanese—but none came. The Washington rumor mill ran at full tilt. To reporters, Truman's composure was extraordinary. None of "the drama and tenseness, the waiting and watching of the war's end" fazed the president. Byrnes, by contrast, seemed "a little frantic." Crowds gathered outside, the media packed the press room, all waiting for news. Truman ordered Marshall to resume conventional B-29 bombing attacks on Japan.[26]

Long after midnight, Anami could not sleep. In the early morning hours, he awakened his secretary, Colonel Saburo Hayashi, tasking him with calling his staunchest ally, General Umezu. Anami wanted Umezu to ask Field Marshall Shunroku Hata to reach out to the Emperor on behalf of the Army's senior officers. Umezu remained silent, as he paced back and forth. Finally Umezu responded, "You must forgive me, but I now favor acceptance of the Potsdam Proclamation." Anami was so surprised he had difficulty taking in Umezu's words. Another prolonged silence ensued. Anami dejectedly responded, "Thank you, General," and hung up the phone and retired to his bedroom to lie down.[27]

While startled by Umezu's change of heart, Anami persisted, and at 7:30 a.m. he nearly accosted Kido, abruptly interrupting him over breakfast. No sooner had he arrived than words began streaming out of the War Minister. He said that the Allied counterproposal would destroy the essence of Japan. He believed a passionate defense of the homeland would lead to more acceptable Allied terms. As such, he favored a continued state of belligerence. "Couldn't you just once more request the Emperor to reconsider acceptance of the note?"

Kido responded that he could not. He disputed Anami's claim that allowing the people of Japan to choose their government would lead to the termination of the national polity. Next, he turned Anami's appeal for a decisive battle back onto the War Ministry, saying, "Supposing the Emperor does change his mind, resend the peace proposal of August 10, and issue a proclamation for the final decisive battle? The Allied powers would undoubtedly regard His Majesty as a fool or lunatic. It would be unbearable to subject Him to such insults."

Regaining his composure, Anami said, "I understand how you feel. In your opinion, you must protect the Emperor."

Empathetically, Kido replied, "The Army is very powerful, and you will have a difficult job to keep it under control."

Forcing a smile, Anami countered, "You have no idea what it's like in the War Ministry."[28]

Shortly before 8:00 a.m., Sakomizu was already hard at work at his desk preparing for the Cabinet meeting when an Army lieutenant walked into his office and dropped a mountain of Top-Secret papers, dealing with fighting the war to the bitter end, on his desk. After creating a mess that spilled not only the delivered papers, but much of the content on Sakomizu's desk onto the floor, the young officer did an abrupt about-face and left the room.

No sooner had he left than Sakomizu found himself staring into the face of Lieutenant General Sanji Okido, commander of the *Kempeitai*. But Okido was not there for Sakomizu—he wanted to see Suzuki.

After informing the general that Suzuki had not yet arrived, Okido, growing increasingly obstinate, told Sakomizu, "If Japan surrenders, the Army will rise. This is certain. Has the PM confidence that he can suppress the revolt? The *Kempei* is receiving reports almost hourly from regiments all over the country. They all point to an insurrection. We cannot take the responsibility for what happens," he snapped. "The *Kempeitai* urges that the war be continued. Tens of millions of lives may be sacrificed, but we will not surrender!" roared Okido. Sakomizu promised to relay the general's message to Suzuki. Okido turned and haughtily departed, stopping for a few moments in the doorway to look back with a final scowl, as if to say, "I know where to find you, Sakomizu."[29]

At 8:45 a.m., in the bomb shelter of the Prime Minister's Official Residence, sitting around a green-felt-covered table, the Big Six resumed the debate the Cabinet had been impotent to resolve the previous day. On one side sat Anami, Umezu, and Toyoda, on the other side, Tōgō, Yonai, and Suzuki. Moments into the meeting, word reached the group that the Emperor wanted to see Umezu and Toyoda immediately.

Arriving at the *Gobunko* a few minutes later, Umezu and Toyoda met with His Majesty, who was dressed in His Grand Marshal of the Army uniform and accompanied by His aide-de-camp General Hasunuma. Concerned over potential military actions that could jeopardize the peace discussions, the Emperor wanted assurances from His senior military leaders. He asked, "What is your plan as to the air operations we will conduct while the negotiation is in progress?" Speaking for himself and Toyoda, Umezu responded, "We shall refrain from making aggressive attacks. Only when we are attacked and when there is need for defensive measures, we shall return fire."

Hirohito nodded, the conference ended, and the two men returned to the SCDW meeting.[30]

Upon their return to the meeting of the Big Six, Anami and the Chiefs of Staff argued for four changes to the Byrnes note. First, the Allies had to drop their requirement subjugating the Emperor to the Supreme Allied commander; second, the phrase "the ultimate form of government in Japan to be determined by the free will of the people" had to be struck; third, they renewed their demand that Japan be permitted to disarm its military; and fourth, the Allies should not be allowed to occupy the home islands. Tōgō disputed the notion of the new or renewed demands as absurd, as it risked the termination of negotiations, and then he reminded the group that the Emperor had already signified his desire to drop these demands.[31]

Yonai, who had been listening quietly, snapped, "These are problems which have already been settled by the Imperial Decision [August 10]. Therefore, anyone who revives these arguments is a rebel against His Majesty." An audible gasp could be heard, then silence. Anami seethed, Toyoda shook his head. Suzuki finally broke his silence, testily asking, "Do the military leaders intend to upset our efforts to end the war by deliberately grumbling about Byrnes's reply? Isn't it all right if we interpret it as we see fit?"[32]

But the Prime Minister's comment did little to halt the opposition of the hardliners or to reassure Tōgō about the direction of the discussion, other than establishing that Suzuki was now on the "peace side."

Adding to the Foreign Minister's concerns was a cable received overnight, dispatched by Suemasa Okamoto, Japan's Minister in Stockholm. The cable described the Byrnes note as a diplomatic victory for the United States and by corollary the Japanese, since America's Allies had not been prone to support the American position on the Emperor and the Imperial institution.[33] America's Allies wanted the system dismantled.

Anami and Umezu continued their harangue about the impracticalities of disarmament and occupation by the Allies. Toyoda discounted the notion that the Allies would break off negotiations and return to all-out war against Japan, when Japan had clearly signaled it wanted to end hostilities.[34] The fruitless debate ended at 2:00 p.m. when, out of cigars and patience, Suzuki brought it to a close.

Once again, the military hardliners had accomplished exactly what they had wanted—a halt to the peace process and a return, despite Toyoda's comment, to continued war. Before the men departed, the Prime Minister told the Cabinet that they would convene again at 3:00 p.m.

But the increasingly heated talks were not yet over. As the meeting ended, Anami moved quickly to confront the Prime Minister, getting so close as to invade Suzuki's personal space. Anami, still angered by being outmaneuvered by the old man three nights hence, barked, "The Imperial Decision should not have been asked for before we had reached agreement. That mistake must not be repeated."

Nearby, and overhearing Anami's threat, Tōgō entered the conversation and fired back, "The high command is trying to upset the negotiations. We have to let the Allies know our intentions quickly. Therefore, we must decide the matter promptly."

The Foreign Minister's implication was clear. Whether Anami liked it or not, he would not hesitate to reengage the Emperor if the military persisted in its defiance.[35]

While the maddeningly futile debate among Japan's leaders stiffened belowground, millions living aboveground were without a home, and forced to sift through the rubble in rags for anything that would help sustain their meager existence.

Meanwhile, Kido again raised the two issues in the Byrnes message with Hirohito. The Emperor responded, "If the Japanese people no longer want the Imperial House, even if the United States allows it to continue, there will be no use trying to save it. If the Japanese people still continue to trust the Imperial House, I would like them to make that decision through their freely expressed will."[36] Thus, the Emperor was far more willing to accept the decision of the people than were any of leaders in his government.

At 3:00 p.m., the Cabinet reconvened with Sakomizu reading the official Byrnes reply. After he finished, the Prime Minister asked for a vote and found twelve favoring an immediate acceptance of the Allied response and three opposed.

Shortly after the meeting had begun, Anami pushed himself away from the table and motioned to Sakomizu to accompany him in the next room, where Anami telephoned the chief of the Military Affairs Bureau, the short-tempered General Masao Yoshizumi. Anami said, "The Cabinet meeting has just started, and the ministers are moving toward the direction that is receptive to your cause. So, I want you to take no action and wait for me calmly until I return there. I have the Cabinet Chief Secretary here with me." Sakomizu couldn't believe his ears; Anami's words utterly contradicted the majority attitude of the meeting. Anami winked. "I am right here with the Cabinet Secretary, and if you want you can speak to him directly about how things are going in the meeting." Suddenly, Sakomizu understood. Anami was playing *haragei* (the art of the hidden psychological technique) to quell his rebellious subordinates at Army Headquarters.[37]

Unfortunately, Anami's ploy came too late to cool off his hot-tempered subordinates, because some among them had already taken matters into their own hands. At 3:45 p.m., a messenger interrupted the Cabinet meeting with news of an Army communiqué, scheduled to be released by newspapers and radio stations in fifteen minutes. It read: "The Army, upon receipt of a newly issued Imperial command, has renewed offensive action against the United States, United Kingdom, the Soviet Union and China."[38]

"I don't know anything about this!" Anami exclaimed. Exasperated, Anami phoned Umezu, who had returned earlier to Army Headquarters. Umezu was outraged, too, and he immediately issued an order to quash the communiqué, which had originated in the press section of IGHQ and had been issued without approval by Vice Minister of War General Tadaichi Wakamatsu and Vice Chief of Staff Kawabe. Umezu managed to get the message stopped by his staff minutes before it was to be broadcast.[39]

With the near catastrophe averted, the Cabinet meeting resumed. Tōgō insisted, "The Byrnes reply unquestionably represents the least common denominator of the terms of the several allies, and it is imperative that we accept them as they now stand, if we are to bring about peace for the sake of the reconstruction of Japan and the welfare of the human race."

With no progress, finally, at 7:00 p.m., a weary Suzuki had had enough. The old man put down his cigar and said:

> I have made up my mind to end the war at this critical moment in compliance with the wishes of the Emperor. On examining the Allied reply, I found some points that seemed unacceptable but when I carefully perused them, I discovered that the United States had no ill will toward us in laying out these conditions, and I feel they have no intention of changing the status of the Emperor. I believe I must end the war as desired by His Majesty, so I will fully report to the Throne what we have discussed here and ask for his final decision.[40]

With Suzuki's notice, the military knew if a coup was going to take place it would have to happen before the second Imperial Conference.

At the end of the meeting, Anami once again approached Suzuki, imploring him, "Won't you please give me two more days before calling another Imperial Conference?"

"I'm sorry," replied Suzuki. "This is our golden opportunity and we must seize it at once."[41]

Even at this late stage, Anami remained conflicted. On one hand, he was personally responsible for the outcome of the war. Surrendering to the enemy without their forces so much as setting foot on Japan—a country steeped in the warrior tradition, that most Japanese believed had never surrendered to a foreign power in a history stretching back some 2,600 years—was simply incomprehensible. Anami had never lost his desire to fight the decisive battle against the Americans. On the other hand, His Majesty the Emperor had already expressed His desire to end the war without delay three days earlier, and there was every reason, based on Suzuki's admonition, that He would again. To which entity—the Army or the Emperor—did he owe the greatest loyalty?

Anami's actions throughout these critical days demonstrated profound internal conflict, including deep anxiety over the threat from his subordinates who might rise up and attempt to overthrow the government. Time after time the general revealed that had it not been for the obligation he felt to the Emperor, he would have sided with the do-or-die fanatics under his command and opted to support the coup and continue the war, regardless of the consequences to the Japanese people or his country.

The man emerging as the leader of that coup was not the War Minister's brother-in-law, Takeshita, but someone he out-ranked, Major Kenji Hatanaka. His unwavering defense of the *kokutai* and refusal to settle imbued him with uncontested influence among the officers considering the revolt. Nevertheless, he still needed Anami's recognition, position, and widespread trust among the Army to make it work. Twice before Hatanaka had pursued Anami's complicity, but the War Minister had remained elusive.

At 8:00 p.m., ten young officers, among them, Ida, Hatanaka, Arao, Koga, and Takeshita, received another chance to convince Anami, at the general's modest one-story wooden residence. Hatanaka began by telling Anami that the peace faction intended to assassinate him, something the War Minister quickly laughed off. The plan itself called for imprisoning Kido, Tōgō, Suzuki, and Yonai, declaring martial law, and isolating the palace from outside communication. To accomplish this, Hatanaka believed the conspiracy needed not only Anami's participation, but that of Generals Umezu and Mori, as well as General Shizuichi Tanaka, in command of the Eastern District Army.[42] Ignoring the treasonous nature of the plot, Anami took issue with the details—for example, how would communications be handled? His reaction left the plotters uncertain of his intentions. To avoid exciting them, he promised to use his influence with the Cabinet in the morning and agreed to see one of their number, Colonel Arao, again at midnight. Still, he never said he disapproved of their idea.

As Anami accompanied the men to his porch, he called out solicitously, "Be careful! You may be under surveillance. You had better return in separate groups instead of all altogether."[43]

Anami was not the only member of the Big Six to receive visitors that night. Unable to suppress their misgivings about accepting Byrnes's counteroffer, Toyoda and Umezu visited Tōgō at a private dinner party he was attending in the underground conference room of the Prime

Minister's Official Residence. Their mission was to get him to join their side and reject the counteroffer. But the same arguments he had already heard many times failed to convince him.

As their conversation was ending, a commotion in a nearby room could be heard, and moments later, Admiral Takijirō Onishi, the "father of the kamikaze," suddenly broke into their room. Pleading first with the Chiefs of Staff and then the Foreign Minister, Onishi offered as a means to reverse the Emperor's loss of faith in the military that "it is necessary to submit to the Emperor a plan to gain the victory, and to ask his reconsideration. If we sacrifice twenty million Japanese in kamikaze attacks there would be no doubt of our ultimate victory." Neither Toyoda nor Umezu responded; Onishi then turned to Tōgō, "What is the Foreign Minister's opinion?" Tōgō replied, "If only we had a any real hope of victory, no one would for a moment think of accepting the Potsdam Declaration; but winning one battle will not win the war for us." After the brief exchange, Tōgō left for home.[44]

In Washington, there was growing doubt that Japan was about to surrender. A MAGIC intercept of a communiqué from Tōgō to Japan's allied governments in Asia stated that the Japanese Army and Navy had not yet agreed to the Allies' counteroffer to lay down arms. Tōgō's message amplified a dispatch from IGHQ the same day instructing all commands to continue to prosecute the war and not be distracted "by the numerous reports on the progress of the war."[45]

General Marshall, now believing that further nuclear attacks on cities would not push the Japanese to surrender, wanted to conserve all additional production of atomic bombs for possible use as tactical weapons to support the November 1 invasion of Kyūshū, Operation Olympic.

Acting on orders from Marshall, Major General John E. Hull, the Assistant Chief of Staff for Operations at the War Department, called Colonel L. E. Seeman of the Manhattan Project to get his assessment of the availability of bombs and their use as tactical weapons. Seeman informed Hull he had given "a good deal" of thought to the possibility and said at least seven bombs would be ready by October 31. He also stated that the greatest hazard to troops would come from an unexploded bomb, and therefore he recommended waiting a minimum of forty-eight hours after a bombing before American ground forces moved into the area of the drop. Seeman predicted the ground would be safe within one hour of the atomic explosion, and at no time warned Hull (and thus Marshall) of the risks of radiation to soldiers and Marines fighting over an atomic battlefield.[46]

But Marshall wasn't the only senior official in Washington concerned over the time Japan was taking to respond. The president also had growing misgivings over whether the Japanese planned to surrender. As a result, Army air commanders and the Navy received orders stating, "the President directs that we go ahead with everything we've got."[47]

AUGUST 14, 1945
8 DAYS AFTER HIROSHIMA

As sunlight pierced the eastern horizon, seven B-29s arrived over Osaka, Nagoya, Kobe, Kyoto, and Tokyo. To the east of the capital, a lone B-29 headed for the center of the city. This time the American planes did not drop an atomic bomb or payloads of napalm. Instead, they released canisters that exploded in midair, spreading five million 4" x 5" blue leaflets printed in the Japanese language over the five cities.

To the Japanese people

These American planes are not dropping bombs on you today. They are dropping leaflets instead because the Japanese Government has offered to surrender, and every Japanese has a right to know the terms of that offer and the reply made to it by the United States government on behalf of itself, the British, the Chinese, and the Russians. Your government now has a chance to end the war immediately.

Byrnes had ordered the missions because the Japanese government still had not responded to Allies' reply to their offer to surrender. Believing the Japanese government had been withholding that information from its people, Byrnes hoped by leaking the Japanese offer and the American reply to the people of Japan, popular pressure to end the war would force the government's hand.[48]

As the notes came fluttering down, some landed on the Imperial Palace grounds. Kido picked up one in the courtyard and after reading it immediately requested a special audience with the Emperor. He knew that it was no longer possible to keep their surrender overture a secret.[49] At 8:30 a.m., Kido told the Emperor he believed there was risk of an uprising if the military en masse, who knew nothing of the negotiations to end the war, came in possession of the leaflets. Kido implored Hirohito to convoke an Imperial Conference without delay so that he could once again inform the Cabinet and the SCDW of his desire to bring the war to an immediate end.[50]

The Emperor instructed Kido to find Suzuki. Fortunately, the Prime Minister was already in the anteroom waiting to see the Emperor. Under the circumstances, Suzuki said, it would take too much time to obtain the seals of the two Chiefs of Staff; instead, he would ask the Emperor to take the unprecedented step of mustering the Imperial Conference on His own authority. Kido agreed. Hirohito not only agreed to call the meeting at 10:30 a.m., but He went even further; if there were a deadlock, He would "command" the Cabinet to accept the terms of the Byrnes note.[51]

Suzuki drove back to his office and called for Sakomizu at once, ordering him to notify the Cabinet members and the SCDW to an Imperial Conference at the palace air-raid shelter at 10:00 a.m., just fifteen minutes hence.

At the same time the leaflets were descending across Tokyo, the conspirators prepared to take control of the government. At 7:00 a.m., Colonel Arao and Anami were scheduled to meet with Umezu in an effort to change his mind and secure his participation. The plotters had also placed calls to the commanders of Imperial Guards Division, the Eastern District Army, and the *Kempeitai*, asking them to meet at Anami's office later that morning. At that meeting, assuming Umezu now supported the coup, the War Minister would order the Guards, the Eastern District Army, and the *Kempei* to cooperate in the rebellion when the clock struck ten that morning.[52]

At about the same time, Anami was having breakfast with Marshal Hata, who had just returned from visiting Hiroshima with Lieutenant Colonel Michinori Shiraishi. Hata told Anami that sweet potato roots, just an inch or two below the surface, had not been affected by the atomic bomb and that white clothing reflected the blast. Enlivened by such news, Anami urged Hata to tell the Emperor and encourage him to reject the surrender.[53]

After breakfast, Anami left for the War Ministry to speak with Colonel Arao, who planned to accompany him to see General Umezu. Arao took the lead and presented the strategy for instituting martial law, forming a military government, and "neutralizing" the peace faction. But Umezu surprised both men by remaining firm, and rejected the plan, saying, the "employment of armed forces in the sanctuary of the Palace would be a sacrilege."[54]

With the failure to gain Umezu's participation in the coup, Anami felt compelled by the plotters to give them a clear answer on where he stood: "After discussing the matter with the Chief of Staff, I've decided not to support your action."[55] But this would not be the last time the subject would be broached with the War Minister.

At 9:00 a.m., Anami called the War Ministry's senior section members together and informed them, "The Army should act in unison, because Japan is now facing the critical situation. Strengthen your unity. Beware of any undisciplined acts. Those who consider any arbitrary actions will have to carry them out over my dead body." He then slapped his knee with his swagger stick to add emphasis.[56]

Minutes before the Cabinet meeting began, Anami and Hata had a short conference with the Emperor. Anami had expected Hata to minimize the effects of the atomic bombing of Nagasaki and to convince the Emperor to fight on. Instead, with tears in his eyes, Hata told Hirohito he had no confidence in Japan's ability to repulse an enemy invasion of the homeland and did not dispute the Emperor's decision to accept the Potsdam Declaration. The Emperor responded that the Soviet entry into the war against Japan and the enemy's "scientific power" could not be effectively countered, and He requested the support of His field marshals and fleet admirals in bringing the war to an end.[57]

The Cabinet meeting had barely begun when the men were directed to the *Gobunko* annex for an emergency Imperial Conference, the meeting with the Emperor and the full Cabinet the first since December 1, 1941. Because the meeting had been called on such short notice, many of the men were caught in state of dress they deemed inappropriate to be seen by the Emperor. Even though they had been informed that "Informal clothing is permissible," many felt compelled to upgrade their appearance by buttoning up shirts and borrowing jackets and even pants from their aides to look more presentable. And for the second time in five days, the military found themselves unprepared and outwitted by their Prime Minister.[58]

As the men filed into the hot and humid underground conference room, water dripped from the walls. The tables from a few days earlier had been replaced with two long rows of chairs, necessary to handle the larger group. By the time the Emperor arrived, twenty-five minutes later, the room was like a steam bath.[59] At 10:55 a.m., the Emperor, dressed in His Army uniform and white gloves, entered the claustrophobic chamber with Hasunuma.

"The Emperor walked directly to the front of the room and sat down on a plain straight-backed chair at a small table covered in gold brocade." "Behind him stood a gilded screen."[60] The twenty-four men already in the room rose to their feet and bowed low; their eyes cast toward the floor.

Suzuki opened the meeting by informing the group His Majesty had called the conference so the Allied reply could be considered in His presence, and so the dissenters from the majority view, Anami, Umezu, and Toyoda, could be heard by Him.[61] The Prime Minister then apologized to the Emperor that his Cabinet had not been able to come to a unanimous agreement. Suzuki then clearly and succinctly outlined the opposing positions and identified Umezu, Toyoda, and Amani as the three individuals who disagreed with acceptance of the Allies' offer. The Prime Minister concluded by asking each of those men to state their arguments against acceptance.

Perhaps out of a sense of allegiance to his War Minister, Umezu retreated from the answer he had given Anami early on the 13th and called for the continuation of the war, saying he believed acceptance would mean the end of the national essence. As such, the entire nation should sacrifice itself in the final battle rather than accept the Allies' terms. Toyoda spoke eloquently, but his contentions were depressingly and thoroughly familiar. Anami, his words crowded with emotion, wanted to fight on unless the Allies guaranteed the Emperor's safety. As he had stated many times before, Anami believed the Japanese had a chance of winning the decisive battle, or at a minimum, inflicting so much harm on the Americans that they would agree to end the war on terms more advantageous to Japan.[62]

The Prime Minister rose to address the Emperor, who was seated alone on one end of the room and above everyone else. "I apologize to His Majesty for presenting Him with a divided Cabinet and for soliciting once again an Imperial decision." The silence in the crowded, sweltering room was absolute.[63] Emperor Hirohito said:

> If there are no more opinions, I will state mine. I want you all to agree with my conclusions.

I have listened carefully to all of the arguments opposing Japan's acceptance of the Allied reply as it stands. My own opinion, however, has not changed. I shall now restate it. I have examined the conditions prevailing in Japan and in the rest of the world, and I believe that a continuation of the war offers nothing but continued destruction. I have studied the terms of the Allied reply, and I have come to the conclusion that they represent a virtually complete acknowledgement of our position as we outlined it in the note dispatched a few days ago.

The Emperor paused for a moment.

In short, I consider the reply to be acceptable.

He wiped the tears from His eyes, then continued.

Although some of you are apprehensive about the preservation of the national structure, I believe that the Allied reply is evidence of the good intentions of the enemy. The conviction and resolution of the Japanese people are, therefore, the most important consideration. That is why I favor acceptance of the reply.

I fully understand how difficult it will be for the officers and men of the Army and the Navy to submit to being disarmed and to see their country occupied. I am aware also of the willingness of the people to sacrifice themselves for their nation and their Emperor. But I am not concerned with what may happen to me. I want to preserve the lives of my people. I do not want them subjected to further destruction. It is indeed hard for me to see my loyal soldiers disarmed and my faithful ministers punished as war criminals.

The Emperor paused again. As He went on, it was apparent that He was speaking with great effort.

If we continue the war, Japan will be altogether destroyed. Although some of you are of the opinion that we cannot completely trust the Allies, I believe that an immediate and peaceful end to the war is preferable to seeing Japan annihilated. As things stand now, the nation still has a chance to recover.

I am reminded of the anguish Emperor Meiji felt at the time of the Triple Intervention. Like him, I must bear the unbearable now and hope for the rehabilitation of the country in the future. But this is indeed a complex and difficult problem that cannot be immediately solved. However, I believe that it can be done if the people will join together in a common effort. I will do everything I can to help.

I cannot express the sorrow I feel as I think of all who were killed on the battlefield or in the homeland and of their bereaved families. I am filled with anxiety about the future of those who have been injured or who have lost all their property or their means of livelihood. I repeat, I will do everything in my power to help.

As the people of Japan are unaware of the present situation, I know they will be deeply shocked when they hear of our decision. If it is thought appropriate that I explain the matter to them personally, I am willing to go before the microphone. The troops, particularly, will be dismayed at our decision. The War Minister and the Navy Minister may not find it easy to persuade them to accept the decision. I am willing to go wherever necessary to explain our action.

I desire the Cabinet to prepare as soon as possible an Imperial Rescript announcing the termination of the war.[64]

Suzuki strained to stand, then asked His Majesty for forgiveness before bowing to Him. The Emperor rose and left the room.

With the Emperor's departure came audible cries of sorrow. Some of the twenty-four men present lost control and slunk to the floor where they knelt weeping. More disturbing than the surrender itself was their concern over the fate of the small, mild-mannered, bespectacled man who had just left them. He was the embodiment of their sacred homeland, a man they had sworn with their lives to protect, the symbol of Japan's immortality.[65]

After the war Sakomizu described the amazing scene thus:

> Because Japan had no recollection of a previous military defeat, all the cabinet members listening to the Emperor cried like children. They [now] all remember the moment just like a dream. The Emperor was wearing snow white gloves and he put his hand to his eyes to brush away the tears. To see that, everyone felt that the Emperor had come back to his people from his capture by the military.
>
> Everyone was impressed with the feeling that the curtain that had hereto for hung between the Emperor and the people was drawn aside, and that for the first time since the [1889] Restoration,

the Emperor actually stepped from behind his curtain and came directly and personally before the people and on the side of the people.[66]

Shockingly, moments after the conference, Anami corned Umezu and asked, "Do you believe that the war should be continued even at the risk of launching a coup d'état?" Umezu unflinchingly responded:

> No, it is impossible, because the decision of His Majesty the Emperor has already been given. Launching a coup d'état in complete defiance of the Emperor's decision will, first of all, invite a split within military circles. Moreover, the nation will not follow us. There is nothing we can do now but to comply with the Emperor's decision.[67]

The Cabinet sat down for lunch, although few but Suzuki had the appetite to eat the whale meat and black bread being served. Afterward, Anami headed for the men's room along with his secretary, Colonel Hayashi, and for a second time, Anami contemplated action in disobedience of the Imperial decision given just minutes earlier. Anami, strangely animated, exclaimed to Hayashi, "that the United States Fleet is outside Tokyo Bay! What do you think about attacking them with everything we have?" Hayashi could hardly believe his ears. It was as though the Emperor's words had had no effect on Anami. "It won't do," Hayashi said, "In the first place it's only a rumor that the U.S. fleet is outside Tokyo Bay. Secondly, the Emperor has just demanded an end to the war."[68]

Before leaving for the Cabinet meeting that morning, two of the conspirators had burst into Umezu's office and berated him for allowing Japan's surrender. In attempt to placate them, Umezu had told them he didn't "absolutely" oppose the coup. When Anami returned to the War Ministry during the lunch break, before the Cabinet reconvened, he ran into Takeshita. "General Umezu has changed his mind." For a moment, Anami's mood brightened. "Is that so? But everything has already been decided." Takeshita pleaded, "At least resign from the Cabinet," to dissolve the Suzuki government and halt the termination of the war. "Get me some ink, I will write my resignation," said Anami. But just as quickly, his vacillation flipped again. "And if I resign, I will never see the Emperor."[69]

Returning to his office, Anami found it occupied by fifteen members of the conspiracy. The time for mollifying their impassioned fervor to continue the war had passed. Anami told them,

> A council in the Imperial presence has just been held, and the Emperor has finally decided to end the war. The entire Army must act in complete accord with this decision. Japan will face difficult times, but no matter how arduous life becomes, I ask you to do your utmost to preserve the national essence.[70]

The officers were confused but remained silent. Four days earlier, the Anami Proclamation had stated, "We must fight on, even if we have to chew grass and eat earth and live in fields—for in our death there is a chance of our country's survival." Now they were being told the Army was about to make a complete about-face and accept a humiliating defeat.[71]

Hatanaka burst out crying, "For what reasons did you change your resolve, Minister?" Anami closed his eyes for a few moments, then said,

> I could not resist the Emperor's own desires any longer. Especially when he asked me in tears to forbear the pain, however severe it might be, I could not but forget everything and accept it. Moreover, His Majesty said he was confident that the national polity would be guaranteed. Now, if you try to rise in revolt, kill Anami first![72]

Tears flowed down Hatanaka's cheeks as the men silently left Anami's office.

A few minutes after 1:00 p.m., three directors of NHK (Japanese Broadcasting Corporation) were asked to gather at the Information Bureau. Hachiro Ohashi, the chairman of the company, Kenjiro Yabe, director of the Domestic Bureau, and Daitaro Arakawa, director of the Technical Bureau, were met by a Cabinet secretary.

"An Imperial Rescript ending the war, will soon be announced," said the Cabinet secretary quietly. "Shimomura says the Emperor himself will speak! He will read the Rescript over the radio…The Cabinet is now considering the question whether the Emperor should broadcast directly or whether a recording should be made. You will be informed as soon as the final decision is reached. Meanwhile, will you make all preparations for either eventuality?"

Director Ohashi took responsibility on behalf of NHK to make the necessary preparations.[73]

At the same time, the Cabinet resumed its meeting. Nineteen men took their places at a large, round table in Suzuki's official residence. Aside from the Prime Minister, who had been sleeping well and eating heartily, the other men looked exhausted, their eyes bloodshot. Outwardly, they appeared as though they were delivering the last rites to someone they loved.[74]

Suzuki began by admonishing his Cabinet for troubling the August Mind of their Emperor twice because two the factions could not reach agreement. "It should not have happened, it was an afront to the Throne. It happened only because we did not try hard enough," he said.

With his rebuke delivered, Suzuki shrank into his more typical expressionless state, and the Cabinet unanimously approved the Emperor's decision and signed the document accepting the Potsdam Declaration. Recognizing there was no more he could do to stop the surrender, Anami sat back in his chair and finally relaxed.[75]

Only one crucial issue remained—how to tell the nation of the surrender. The idea of an Imperial Rescript had been in the works for a few days by then. As distasteful as that was to be believed, the people needed to hear of the country's capitulation from Hirohito Himself. But it was too much to ask the Emperor to do so in a live broadcast—it needed to be done using a recording.[76]

By 2:40 p.m., word of the rumored American fleet circulated all through Army Headquarters. Panicked officers seized classified documents and began burning them in the courtyard. Discipline began breaking down. *Kempei* non-coms assigned to the building had deserted, taking food and supplies with them. Junior officers became even more obstinate toward their superiors. Senior officers locked themselves in their offices and drank *sake* and whiskey.

At the suggestion of Major General Suichi Miyazaki, Kawabe brought together the senior-most members of the Army—Wakamatsu, Umezu, Hata, Inspector of Training Kenji Doihara, and General Hajime Sugiyama—believing the men needed to reach accord on how to proceed to keep the Army from revolting. Hata agreed, declaring, "this is of the utmost importance." Kawabe responded, "Under the present circumstances, I do not think that the situation calls for any discussion or consideration. I think the only thing for the entire Army to do is to loyally obey the Imperial decision." With verbal or visual gestures of agreement from all, Kawabe proposed they put it in writing. Their simple written accord stated:

August 14th, 2:40 p.m.

Imperial Ministry of War

The Imperial Forces will act strictly in accordance with the decision of His Imperial Majesty the Emperor.[77]

Just as the leaders finished affixing their seals to the accord, Anami entered and he, too, without objection, added his seal, approving the document. General Umezu said he believed it was essential to control the activities of the Air Force as well, and so he suggested they secure the signature of its commander, General Masakazu Kawabe (elder brother of General Torashirō Kawabe).[78]

At 2:49 p.m., an American radio operator on Okinawa hurriedly scribbled down a message from the Domei News Agency in Tokyo.

Flash flash Tokyo August 14—it is learned that an Imperial message accepting the POTSDAM proclamation is forthcoming soon

Meanwhile, in the War Ministry, all section chiefs were told to report to conference room one, where the War Minister would address them.

At 3:30 p.m., Anami, standing on a platform, said:

The Emperor has decided to end the war. It is therefore proper that we abide by the Imperial wish. His Majesty is confident that the kokutai will be maintained and has expressed that conviction to the Field Marshals. Difficulties lie ahead for all of us, but you officers must face the fact that death does not absolve you from your duty. You must stay alive, even if it means eating grass and sleeping on thorns and rocks.[79]

Anami's speech ended any senior officers' notions of joining the coup, but Hatanaka and several other die-hards remained determined to act. There remained a good chance to seize the Palace grounds, since two majors in General Mori's division, Major Sadakichi Ishihara and Major Hidemasa Koga (Tōjō's son-in-law), remained loyal to the coup. There was also a new high-priority objective, the Imperial Rescript recording, which was to be played the following day from the NHK Building.[80]

With Takeshita, Arao, and Inaba believing there was no longer any hope for a successful coup, Hatanaka seized the reins and moved forward with the plan. After the meeting, hoping to gain Ida's support, Hatanaka said:

> The government and the highest military leaders have decided to terminate the war—a decision which I cannot accept as things stand now. My idea is that we should establish ourselves within the palace, sever communications with the outside, and give assistance to the Emperor in a final effort to retrieve the situation. I have already got in touch with the Imperial guards division and have made the necessary arrangements. I'd like you to take part in the plan.

Unconvinced, Ida responded:

> Since the situation has come to such a pass, I feel the entire army should, without question, comply with his Majesty's wishes and that the Army's leaders should also commit suicide. I do not mean to ignore your idea of making a final effort to save a lost cause, but the merit of your idea is beyond my power to judge. If the underlying spirit of your coup d'état plan is founded upon your firm conviction, the success or failure of the plan will depend upon the destiny ordained by the gods and therefore need not be considered. At any rate, I will not dare to restrain you.

Hatanaka nodded and said:

> Well, I understand you...but as for myself I'll do my best and leave the rest to Providence.[81]

High on the list of objectives for a successful coup was the support of the Eastern District Army. Hatanaka went to the district's HQ to meet with General Tanaka. Entering the orderly's room outside the commanding general's office; Hatanaka demanded a meeting with the general. When the orderly asked the purpose of the meeting, Hatanaka refused to provide one, and an argument broke out. The conversation became so noisy that it attracted the attention of General Tanaka, who came out to investigate the disturbance. At full voice, he bellowed, "What's going on here?" The orderly said that Major Hatanaka wanted to see the general but had refused to state why. Tanaka, hands on hips, thundered at Hatanaka, "You fool! Why have you come here? I know what you are after...you don't even have to open your mouth...get out!"

Hatanaka could say nothing. He bowed and left quietly.[82]

Undeterred, Hatanaka returned to the War Ministry to meet with Lieutenant Colonel Jirō Shiizaki and two staff officers of the Imperial Guards Division, Major Ishihara and Major Koga. The four men agreed the coup still had a chance to unite the Army and avoid the surrender if they could prevent the Imperial Rescript from being aired to the Japanese people the following day, and if they cut off communication to the Emperor from the outside.

Not long after the Cabinet began its deliberations on the wording to the Imperial Rescript, disagreement erupted. Once again the source of dispute originated with Anami, who refused to accept the sentence, "the war situation is growing more unfavorable for us every day." Endorsing such a statement, in his opinion, branded all communiqués from Imperial Headquarters a lie. Besides, Japan still hadn't lost the war.[83] As the Cabinet was writing the Emperor's surrender speech, Anami still could not accept that Japan had been defeated and the war would end in less than twenty-four hours.

Yonai countered Anami's statement by noting the catastrophic Japanese losses that had recently occurred in Burma and on Okinawa. As a compromise, Sakomizu came up with an alternative that avoided yet another lengthy squabble. It stated, "the war situation has developed not necessarily to Japan's advantage."[84]

Late in the afternoon, Umezu and Anami dispatched a message to all Army operational commanders, a message that said in part:

> Negotiations have taken place with the enemy on the basis of our conditions that the national polity be preserved and the Imperial domain maintained. The stipulations laid down by the enemy, however, rendered the realization of these conditions extremely

difficult, and for that reason we vigorously and consistently maintained that the stipulations were absolutely unacceptable. Although we reported to the Throne to this effect on various occasions, His Imperial Majesty nevertheless as decided to accept the terms of the Potsdam Declaration...

The Imperial decision has been handed down. Therefore, in accordance with the Imperial will, it is imperative that all forces act to the end in such a way that no dishonor shall be brought to their glorious traditions and splendid record of meritorious service and that future generations of our race shall be deeply impressed. It is earnestly desired that every soldier, without exception, refrain absolutely from rash behavior and demonstrate at home and abroad the everlasting fame and glory of the Imperial Army.[85]

Yonai undertook similar precautions at naval GHQ.

At 8:30 p.m., Hirohito, accompanied by the Prime Minister, signed the completed eight-hundred-character Imperial Rescript and affixed His seal. But before the formal surrender could be transmitted to the Allied Governments, all of the Cabinet members had to sign the document. The last, the Transportation Minister, did so at 11:00 p.m. Finally, the surrender was official. The Foreign Ministry sent identical cables in English to its legations in Switzerland and Sweden with instructions to transmit them to United States, Great Britain, the Soviet Union, and China. The message read:

With reference to the Japanese Government's note of August 10 regarding their acceptance of the provisions of the Potsdam Declaration and the reply of the Governments of the United States, Great Britain, the Soviet Union, and China sent by American Secretary of State Byrnes under the date of August 11, the Japanese Government have the honor to communicate to the Governments of the four powers as follows:

His Majesty the Emperor has issued an Imperial Rescript regarding Japan's acceptance of the provisions of the Potsdam Declaration.

His Majesty the Emperor is prepared to authorize and ensure the signature of his government and the Imperial General Headquarters of the necessary terms for carrying out the provisions of the Potsdam Declaration. His Majesty is also prepared to issue his commands to all the military, naval, and air authorities of Japan and all the forces under their control wherever located to cease active operations, to surrender arms and to issue such other orders as may be required by the Supreme Commander of the Allied Forces for the execution of the above-mentioned terms.[86]

The only task that remained was the en masse resignation of the Suzuki Cabinet. The ministers sat numb around the table. Anami rose and walked over to his old nemesis, Tōgō. Squaring his shoulders, Anami said, "I have seen the Foreign Minister's draft of the communication to the Allied powers regarding the occupation and disarmament, and I am grateful beyond description. Had I known that the matter would be dealt with in this way, I would not have felt it necessary to speak so zealously at the Imperial conference."[87]

The communication that had engendered Anami's comments, transmitted to the Allies on August 16, read:

The Swiss Chargé to the Secretary of State

WASHINGTON, AUGUST 16, 1945

The Japanese Government would like to be permitted to state to the Governments of America, Britain, China and the Soviet Union what they most earnestly desire with reference to the execution of certain provisions of the Potsdam Proclamation. This may be done possibly at the time of the signature. But fearing that they may not be able to find an appropriate opportunity, they take the liberty of addressing the Governments of the Four Powers through the good offices of the Government of Switzerland.

In view of the fact that the purpose of occupation as mentioned in the Potsdam Proclamation is solely to secure the achievement of the basic objectives set forth in the said Proclamation, the Japanese Government sincerely desire that the Four Powers, relying upon the good faith of the Japanese Government, will facilitate discharge by the Japanese Government of their obligations [so] as to forestall any unnecessary complications.

It is earnestly solicited that:

In case of the entry of the Allied fleets or troops in Japan Proper, the Japanese Government be notified in advance, so that arrangements can be made for reception.

The number of the points in Japanese territory to be designated by the Allies for occupation be limited to minimum number, selection of the points to be made in such a manner as to leave such a city as Tokyo unoccupied and the forces to be stationed at each point be made as small as possible.

Disarming of the Japanese forces, being a most delicate task as it involves over 3 millions of officers and men overseas and having direct bearing on their honor, the Japanese Government will, of course, take utmost pains. But it is suggested that the best and most effective method would be that under the command of His Majesty the Emperor, the Japanese forces are allowed to disarm themselves and surrender arms of their own accord.

Disarming of the Japanese forces on the Continent be carried out beginning on the front line and in successive stages.

In connection with the disarming it is hoped that Article 35 of the Hague convention will be applied, and the honor of the soldier will be respected, permitting them, for instance, to wear swords. Further, [that] the Japanese Government be given to understand the Allies have no intention to employ disarmed Japanese soldiers for compulsory labor. It is sincerely hoped that shipment and transportation facilities necessary for the evacuation of the soldiers to their homeland will be speedily provided.

Since some forces are located in remote places, difficult to communicate the Imperial Order, it is desired that reasonable time be allowed before the cessation of hostilities.

It is hoped that the Allies will be good enough quickly to take necessary steps to extend us facilities for the shipment of indispensable foodstuffs and medical supplies to Japanese forces in distant islands, and for the transport of wounded soldiers from those islands.[88]

Several of Tōgō's appeals warrant comment. First, that the Allies could "rely...upon the good faith of the Japanese Government," to carry out the provisions of the Potsdam Declaration. What actions by the Japanese government during the war, in compliance with international law, would have given the Allies any cause to believe Japan could be counted on to do so? The Japanese had been the aggressor in starting the war and ruthlessly applying its military power until the Allies destroyed it. Regarding the request to severely limit the areas of Japan occupied and the number of forces used in the occupation, this was clearly intended to reduce the visual appearance of Japan's defeat to its citizens, and potentially degrade the Allies' ability to implement the terms of the Potsdam Declaration.

Probably the most objectionable elements of the message dealt with invoking the Hague Convention regarding the "honorable" disarming of Japanese troops, the avoidance of using the same disarmed Japanese troops as "compulsory labor," providing her wounded aid, and finally implying that Japanese military personnel should be given priority in their re-patriotization to Japan over the needs of the Allies. That Tōgō, a highly experienced diplomat, chose to invoke the Hague Convention agreements when his country had consistently violated its provisions all through the war in its treatment of both military and civilian POWs, as well as in its development and use of biological and chemical weapons created by its infamous UNIT 731 (also in violation of the 1925 Geneva Convention), smacks of incredible hypocrisy and a double standard the Japanese lived by during the entirety of the war.

Thus, while the content of Tōgō's message may have appeased Anami, to the Allies, in particular the Americans, the audacity of Tōgō's plea was difficult to comprehend. Japan had perpetrated all kinds of cruelties on Allied POWS, including execution, vivisections, torture, slave labor (often working them to death), starvation, and refusing them any sort of medical treatment. Regarding execution, which had been routine during the war, by August 1, 1944, as noted earlier, the Japanese had turned it into an official Kill Order: "It is the aim not to allow the escape of a single one [POW], to annihilate them all, and not to leave any traces," if POWs were at risk of being re-patriated by Allied forces. As a direct result of the inhuman treatment they received, around thirty percent of Allied military POWs died in Japanese captivity, eleven percent of Allied civilian POWs.

Tōgō may not have been fully aware of the handling of Allied POWs outside of Japan, but it's difficult to imagine, with his position, that he wasn't cognizant of how Allied POWs were being executed, used as slave laborers for the war industry, and even subjected to vivisection inside Japan.

The request highlights the incredible disconnect between what the Allies perceived as that reality of Japan's conduct in the war and the

242 • DAVID DEAN BARRETT

"reality" held by the Japanese, who apparently thought the Allies were either blind to the atrocities they had committed, or had forgotten them by the end of the war. MacArthur had not, and he advised Marshall to ignore Tōgō's message.

As for Tōgō's reaction to Anami's comments, he saw them as disingenuous, and he awkwardly replied that he had always been sympathetic toward the conditions Anami had been proposing.

With that brief exchange over, Anami buckled on his sword and strode into Suzuki's private office. He saluted his Prime Minister, then said, "Ever since the peace talks started, I have given you a great deal of trouble, and I'm here to express my regrets. What I did was only so that the *kokutai* could be maintained—that was all. I hope you understand this and I deeply apologize."

Empathetically, Suzuki replied, "I am fully aware of that." Walking up to Anami, the general's eyes blinking away the tears, Suzuki grasped the War Minister's hand. "But Anami-san, please rest assured that the Imperial household will always be blessed by peace, for His Majesty always prayed for peace at the spring and autumn festivals of his Imperial ancestors."[89]

Even now, Anami refused to admit the truth behind his actions. His stance, three times that very day after the second Imperial *seidan*, had not been limited to the preservation of *kokutai*. Extremely frustrated by the Imperial Army's inability to defeat the Americans in combat, Anami wanted desperately to fight the decisive battle in the Japanese homeland, regardless of the casualties to his own people and destruction to the country. Absent that opportunity, he clung to his previously stated objectives of maintaining control over disarmament and Japanese war crimes, and avoiding an occupation—because it preserved the status quo and the military's power to control the government, using the Emperor's status with the people as the armed force's basis for authority.

With his apologies and responsibilities complete, Anami returned to his office long enough to gather up a few belongings, among them a short ceremonial sword sheathed in a cherrywood scabbard. Then he left for home.

In the Household Ministry, the now four-man crew from NHK had been waiting to record the Emperor's rescript since midafternoon. Daitaro Arakawa had set up the recording equipment in adjoining rooms on the second floor.

At 10:00 p.m., Ida was awakened by Hatanaka and Shiizaki. Hatanaka quickly outlined their plan then said, "We have roughly completed our preparations but we need one thing: your support to help persuade General Mori, commander of the Imperial Guards Division. You must come with us and induce him to join us." Inspired, Ida replied:

> Well, I'll go with you. But in this critical time, we must judge quickly and accurately whether our attempt will succeed, because it is not our true intention to cause public disorder by going to extremes. Therefore, if we feel we have failed, we should resign ourselves and [commit hara-kiri].

All agreed. The three men left for Guards Division HQ, where they met Koga and Ishihara, who had prepared a divisional order that required the signature of General Mori. With the general's signature, the coup would be set in motion.[90]

Sometime after 11:00 p.m., the Emperor prepared to make His way to the Imperial Household Ministry to record the Imperial Rescript when an air-raid warning sounded.[91] Chamberlain Irie recommended that the Emperor wait until the targets for the air raid were known. The sirens ended within a few minutes, and the Emperor decided to proceed to the Household Ministry, arriving at 11:30 p.m.

Inside the room on the second floor where the recording was to be conducted, the lights seemed intolerably bright after the darkness outside. After being escorted to the microphone, which stood in front of two gold foiled screens, the engineers asked Chamberlain Yasuhide Toda, whose voice somewhat resembled the Emperor's, to speak into the microphone so they could judge how to adjust the volume for His Majesty. After Hirohito asked, "How loudly shall I speak?" Shimomura responded that the Emperor's ordinary voice would be fine.[92] The Imperial Rescript read:

> To Our Good and loyal subjects:
>
> After pondering deeply the general trends of the world and the actual conditions obtaining in Our Empire today, We have decided to effect a settlement of the present situation by resorting to an extraordinary measure.

We have ordered Our Government to communicate to the Governments of the United States, Great Britain, China and the Soviet Union that Our Empire accepts the provisions of their Joint Declaration.

To strive for the common prosperity and happiness of all nations as well as the security and well-being of Our subjects is the solemn obligation which has been handed down by Our Imperial Ancestors, and which We lay close to heart. Indeed, We declared war on America and Britain out of Our sincere desire to secure Japan's self-preservation and the stabilization of East Asia, it being far from Our thought either to infringe upon the sovereignty of other nations or to embark upon territorial aggrandizement. But now the war has lasted for nearly four years. Despite the best that has been done by everyone—the gallant fighting of military and naval forces, the diligence and assiduity of Our servants of the State and the devoted service of Our one hundred million people, the war situation has developed not necessarily to Japan's advantage, while the general trends of the world have all turned against her interest. Moreover, the enemy has begun to employ a new and most cruel bomb, the power of which to do damage is indeed incalculable, taking the toll of many innocent lives. Should we continue to fight, it would not only result in an ultimate collapse and obliteration of the Japanese nation, but also it would lead to the total extinction of human civilization. Such being the case, how are We to save the millions of Our subjects; or to atone Ourselves before the hallowed spirits of Our Imperial Ancestors? This is the reason why We have ordered the acceptance of the provisions of the Joint Declaration of the Powers.

We cannot but express the deepest sense of regret to Our Allied nations of East Asia, who have consistently cooperated with the Empire towards the emancipation of East Asia. The thought of those officers and men as well as others who have fallen in the fields of battle, those who died at their posts of duty, or those who met with untimely death and all their bereaved families, pains Our heart night and day. The welfare of the wounded and the war-sufferers, and of those who have lost their home and livelihood, are the objects of Our profound solicitude. The hardships and sufferings to which Our nation is to be subjected hereafter will be certainly great. We are keenly aware of the inmost feelings of all ye, Our subjects. However, it is according to the dictate of time and fate that We have resolved to pave the way for grand peace for all the generations to come by enduring the unendurable and suffering what is insufferable.

Having been able to safeguard and maintain the structure of the Imperial State, We are always with ye, Our good and loyal subjects, relying upon your sincerity and integrity. Beware most strictly of any outbursts of emotion which may endanger needless complications, or any fraternal contention and strife which may create confusion, lead ye astray and cause ye to lose the confidence of the world. Let the entire nation continue as one family from generation to generation, ever firm in its faith of the imperishableness of its divine land and mindful of its heavy burden of responsibilities, and the long road before it. Unite your total strength to be devoted to the construction for the future. Cultivate the ways of rectitudes; foster nobility of spirit; and work with resolution so as ye may enhance the innate glory of the Imperial State and keep place with the progress of the world.[93]

When He finished the Emperor turned to the crew and asked, "Was that all right?" An engineer in the other room said that he was sorry, but a few words were unclear. The Emperor, showing concern over the importance of the recording, readily agreed to a second take. While not perfect either, the crew decided not to subject the Emperor to a third recording. The second would be the primary, the first would only be used in an emergency. The two ten-inch discs were carefully placed in separate cardboard containers and then each wrapped in a khaki-colored cotton bag.[94]

A brief discussion ensued in the booth about what to do with the recordings until the broadcast the next day. Aware of the rumors about a conspiracy to stop the surrender, Chamberlain Yoshihiro Tokugawa agreed to take the recordings. A technician handed the two copies of the recordings to Tokugawa, and he took them into an adjacent office used by the Empress's retinue, where he opened a small safe in the wall and placed the recordings.[95] He locked it, then piled enough papers in front of it to hide the safe from sight.

The Imperial Rescript deserves some scrutiny, starting with "We declared war on America and Britain out of Our sincere desire to secure Japan's self-preservation and the stabilization of East Asia, it being far from Our thought either to infringe upon the sovereignty of other nations or to embark upon territorial aggrandizement." Just as modern-day Japan must trade with other nations in the world because it lacks great natural resources of its own, Imperial Japan could have chosen that path. Instead, it started a fourteen-year war of conquest to take whatever resources it wanted by force, natural and human, from Manchuria, China, Southeast Asia, and the Southwest Pacific—primarily from the nations of Japan's so-called "Greater East Asia Co-prosperity Sphere." In the process, they enslaved those peoples and killed millions of them, all for the benefit of only one country—Imperial Japan.

Closely tied to the previously referenced statement was the following declaration: "We cannot but express the deepest sense of regret to Our Allied nations of East Asia, who have consistently cooperated with the Empire towards the emancipation of East Asia." While those nations initially collaborated with Japan, under the genuine experience of occupation, the source of massive loss of life, they overwhelmingly turned against the Japanese, with the exception of Subhas Chandra Bose in India.

To mollify Anami, the final draft included Sakomizu's compromised change, "the war situation has developed not necessarily to Japan's advantage, while the general trends of the world have all turned against her interest." It was a monumental understatement. Japan had seen nothing but defeat after the first six months of the war (save in China and a few transient successes, notably in Burma); its naval and merchant fleets were at the bottom of the Pacific Ocean; the majority of its major and even medium sized cities lay in ashen ruin, and its primary ally—Nazi Germany—had been utterly devasted by the Allies, and had been forced to surrender unconditionally with absolutely no *predefined terms.*

The only reference to a specific cause for ending the war were the statements that "the enemy has begun to employ a new and most cruel bomb, the power of which to do damage is indeed incalculable, taking the toll of many innocent lives. Should we continue to fight, it would not only result in an ultimate collapse and obliteration of the Japanese nation, but also it would lead to the total extinction of human civilization." The Soviet Union's recent entry into the war was not acknowledged as a reason for surrender. And it should be noted, since a secondary message from the Emperor was sent to Japan's military personnel, there were millions of Japanese troops within the homeland who heard the

Emperor's August 15 broadcast. Finally, the allusion to an atomic bomb that "also…would lead to the total extinction of human civilization" was a lie designed to elicit sympathy for the benevolent action of Japan as the nation that had sacrificed on behalf of the entire world.

11

A FAILED COUP D'ÉTAT AND SURRENDER

AUGUST 15, 1945
9 DAYS AFTER HIROSHIMA

Around 12:30 a.m., Colonel Ida, Captain Shigetarō Uehara, Major Hatanaka, and Colonel Shiizaki—all of whom had been camped out in an outer office waiting to see the commander of the Imperial Guards, Lieutenant General Takeshi Mori—barged into the general's office. Mori rose and snapped, "What are you doing here at this time?" After a momentary pause, Hatanaka piped back, "General, we have come to ask you to lead the Guards Division against the surrender. If the Guards rise, we are sure the whole army will follow suit." Mori responded, "You are asking me to use my men in an unauthorized scheme? How can I do such a thing without an order from the Eastern District Army?"[1]

Hatanaka looked at his watch. He pulled Ida aside and said, "I just remembered something I've got to do," and then hurriedly left, taking Shiizaki with him. As it happened, Colonel Shiraishi, Mori's brother-in-law, who had flown in with Marshal Hata from Hiroshima earlier in the day, was with Mori when the conspirators charged in.

Mori, recognizing what Ida and Uehara were up to, attempted to stall the conspirators' efforts by not allowing them to speak. Instead, slowly and calmly, he began to tell them his philosophy of life, as though no war had just been fought and no threat of a conspiracy existed. Each time Ida attempted to interrupt, Mori said, "Hold on a minute," and then launched into another of his views on life. All Ida and Uehara could do was listen as Mori droned on.[2] The small room, only nine by nine and containing four men, was hot, and Ida grew more frustrated by the minute.

In the meantime, Hatanaka had made his way to Takeshita's quarters. After four long days and restless nights Takeshita was drained and attempting to get some rest. At 1:00 a.m., without warning, Hatanaka burst into the colonel's room. Hatanaka told Takeshita the plan was proceeding well, "The Second Regiment of the Imperial Guards is already inside the Palace. They will secure the grounds at two o'clock," glancing at his watch again, "in just over an hour. General Mori is the only one not with us so far—and I'm sure he will be by two. But we need Lieutenant Colonel Takeshita too."[3]

Takeshita had earlier withdrawn his support of the coup, since he had been unable to bring Anami into the plot. "Isn't it better to take the point of view that everything has ended? We've failed to win over the four most important officers in the Army," said Takeshita.

"Because they're bewildered," interrupted Hatanaka. "Just like their men. They don't know what to do. If we show them the right path to take, they'll follow. Once there's a state of real emergency, they'll all be with us."

"Not General Anami," Takeshita replied.

"Whatever happens he'll stick by his word."

Resolutely, Hatanaka replied, "He won't once we take power. You're the only man who can explain the situation to him. No one but the Lieutenant Colonel can convince the War Minister."[4]

"Well," said Hatanaka, "I must get back to the Guards. There isn't much time."

He rose, "Maybe after our plan is already working the Lieutenant Colonel will join us."

As he started for the door, Takeshita exclaimed, "Wait a minute, I'm coming too." Hatanaka asked, "Where?"

"You know where I'm going. To the Minister of War."[5]

IN HATANAKA'S ABSENCE, IDA FINALLY managed to seize an opportunity to express the purpose of his meeting with Mori. He said that the relationship between the Emperor, a living god, and His people, was represented not only in the national polity but as Japan's national faith. To surrender without absolute protection of the Imperial House risked the obliteration of the country, and only a treasonous coward would do so.

"Whatever truth there may be in your words," Mori said, "the fact remains that the Emperor has spoken his decision. As Commander of the Imperial Guards, I must obey that decision, and I must insist that my men obey it."[6]

Ida persisted, "General, I do not believe that any honest officer can subscribe in his heart to such baseness. This is the moment for a regeneration of the Japanese spirit—and the Imperial guards are the ones to lead us."

"I sympathize with you; I appreciate your objectives and confidentially—I respect them. I might even say that under other circumstances I would share them. But that is no longer possible: I am sworn to abide by the Emperor's decision…However, and I speak now as a plain, ordinary Japanese, my present intention is to go to the Meiji Shrine. Prayer may give me the answer to my problem."

Ida bowed his head, satisfied with Mori's reply and that he had done all that he could.[7]

Hatanaka and Uehara returned to Mori's office at 1:30 a.m. Under time pressure to get things moving quickly or abandon the effort, Hatanaka said to Mori:

Your Excellency, have you reconciled yourself to the humiliation of surrender, which Japan now faces? The Emperor, who is all-wise, would surely continue the war if it was not for the advice of a few treacherous counselors around him. The orders you will issue to the division will save our country. They have already been drafted by Major Koga…[8]

Mori replied that he wanted to visit the Meiji shrine to help him decide. He also asked Colonel Mizutani, Chief of Staff of the Division, for his opinion. The colonel said he didn't know enough to make a decision, at which point Mori pointed at Ida and told him to go next door with Mizutani and explain their plan.

In Mori's office, the discussion grew more impassioned. Mori, defending the Imperial decision, said, "The Emperor thought out and made a decision to save the Yamato race and our country. I am commander of his personal bodyguards, the Imperial Guards Division, and I can only respect and follow his will. Though you men are in a hurry, I cannot decide such an important question on such short notice. I will have to meditate at the Meiji Shrine and consult the commander of the Eastern District Army."

Hatanaka replied, "We have already seen the *Tobugun* (Tanaka). He doesn't seem to understand our intentions."

Mori responded, "If that is so, all the more reason why I cannot consent."

Hatanaka was nearing the end of his patience. "We are asking you for your own decision, sir," he said. "If you issue the orders, we are certain the *Tobugun* commander will sanction them!"

"No," Mori roared, "Since the Imperial decision has already been given, I will not act against His Majesty's will."

"You mean in any case?" Hatanaka asked.

"No, never!"[9]

Moments later, several pistol shots rang out from Mori's office. Ida and Mizutani rushed to investigate. As they reached the door to the general's office, an ashen-faced Hatanaka emerged, smoking pistol in hand.

"There was just no time," Hatanaka said, "There was not time to argue, so I killed him. What else could I do?"

As the major stepped aside, Mizutani and Ida peered into Mori's office. Uehara stood silently, wiping his bloody sword. A dazed Shiizaki sat in a chair. The hacked and bleeding bodies of Mori and the completely decapitated Shiraishi lay on the floor. His blood, grotesquely splattered across the walls and ceiling, began to pool on the floor as more blood spouted from his neck and detached head.[10] Astonishingly, Hatanaka and Uehara came to attention and saluted the two dead men.

IDA KNEW THE CONSPIRACY HAD already failed before it really began with Mori's death, but there only seemed one thing to do: carry on. He told Hatanaka that he and Mizutani needed to go to the Eastern District Headquarters, and the duo got in a car and drove off.

Hatanaka had intended to get General Mori to sign "Imperial Guards Division Strategic Order No. 584," drafted by Major Koga, which read:

1. The Division will defeat the enemy's scheme; it will protect the Emperor and preserve the national polity.

2. The commander of the First Infantry Regiment will occupy the East Second in the East Third garrison grounds (including the surroundings of the Eastern District Army strategy room) and the environs of Honmaru Baba, thus guarding the Imperial Family from this sector. The commander will also order a company to occupy Tokyo Broadcasting Station and prohibit all broadcasts.

3. The commander of the Second Infantry Regiment will use his main force to guard the Imperial Family at the Fukiage district of the Imperial Palace.

4. The commander of Sixth Infantry Regiment will continue present duties.

5. The commander of the Seventh Infantry Regiment will occupy the area of Nijubashi Gate and prevent any contact with the Imperial Palace.

6. The commander of the Cavalry Regiment will order a tank force to Daikan Avenue to await further orders. The commander of the First Artillery Regiment will await further orders.

7. The commander of the First Engineers will await further orders.

8. The commander of the Mechanized Battalion will guard the Imperial Palace at its present strength.

9. The commander of the Signal Unit will sever all communication with the Imperial Palace except through division headquarters.

10. I shall be at Division Headquarters.[11]

To create the appearance that Mori had approved the order, Hatanaka took Mori's private seal from the desk and affixed it to multiple copies of the order.

Sometime around 1:00 a.m. Takeshita arrived at Anami's official residence in Miyakezaka. He had wanted to see his brother-in-law, perhaps one last time, regardless of his role in the insurrection. But before he could see Anami, he was greeted by guards and the War Minister's maid. As he had feared, Anami planned to commit suicide.

Takeshita requested permission to enter, and after questioning why he wanted to do so,

Anami said, "All right. Welcome! Come in."

He found the general writing something that looked like a will. Anami rolled up the paper and put it in a nearby cupboard. Gesturing to Takeshita he said, "Sit down, sit down."

Anami then asked the maid to bring larger glasses and, after she did, to calmly pour some *sake* for Takeshita and said, "As you probably know, I decided some time ago to commit *seppuku*. I intend to do so tonight."

"Yes," said Takeshita, "I knew this afternoon that you had decided. Under the circumstances, I will not attempt to dissuade you."

"I am glad to hear it," said Anami. "When I heard that you had come so unexpectedly, I was afraid you might try to stop me. I am glad I was mistaken. I bid you welcome—you have come at an opportune moment."

Anami laughed. "You know, I had my vitamin injection tonight the same as I always do. When the maid asked me, I could hardly say I didn't want it because I was going to die. Could I now?"[12]

At the Eastern District Headquarters, Ida and Mizutani knocked on the door of Chief of Staff, Major General Takashima. Before he could respond, the door flew open and Ida and Mizutani practically fell into the room.

"Mori's been murdered!" exclaimed Mizutani, "The Guards are occupying the Palace. I've come to the Eastern Army for instructions and..." And with that, he fainted.

But Ida, like his compatriot Hatanaka, attempted to continue the ruse. "The Eastern Army must act at once; it will be too late after the noon broadcast. If the Eastern Army takes a stand now, the national polity will be preserved, the natural relationship between the Emperor and the people will be restored, the old Japan—"

Takashima interrupted, "What precisely, are you asking the Eastern Army to do?"

"To approve the action the Guards have taken," said Ida, "And to send some men to join the division forces."

"I can do nothing," said Takeshima, "without an order from General Tanaka. I suggest you discuss the matter with Lieutenant Colonel [Tōru] Itagaki, while I report to the Commander."[13]

ALTHOUGH HATANAKA KNEW THE SUCCESS of his plan depended on the outcome of two conversations, between Ida and General Tanaka and Takeshita and Anami, he knew he couldn't delay taking further action. He ordered a group of the men accompanying him to set up machine guns at every entrance to the Palace and take prisoner anyone attempting to pass. His thoughts then shifted to the interrogation of the men taken into custody with the objective of locating the recording of the Imperial Rescript. But all he could determine was that a recording had been made; no one would admit to knowing its whereabouts.[14]

> Between 3:00 and 4:00 a.m., Ida returned to Hatanaka's command post. Exiting the car, he headed toward Hatanaka, who could tell by Ida's expression the news was not good.
>
> Ida said bluntly, "It's all over. There isn't any chance. The Eastern Army is absolutely opposed to us. If you occupy the Palace any longer, you'll find yourself fighting a battle against the entire Eastern Army."
>
> Irascible as ever, Hatanaka replied, "I'm not afraid of a battle. I've occupied the Palace, and the Emperor's behind me—what's there to be afraid of? I even have some prisoners." He laughed. "Including Shimomura."
>
> "Don't be a fool," cried Ida. "How can you fight the Eastern Army? You don't even have agreement with the Guards! And when they hear about Mori's death, they'll all be against you. Can't you understand that? Listen to me, Hatanaka. Withdraw the soldiers before dawn. Let's take the consequences together. They won't be serious—people will say it was all a midsummer night's dream. They'll be too busy with the surrender, anyway, to worry about a coup that didn't come off. Do you understand Hatanaka?"
>
> Hatanaka replied, "Yes, yes, I understand."[15]

HOWEVER, HATANAKA STILL HAD NOT resigned himself to the failure of his plan. He decided to continue the search for the Imperial Rescript in the Household Ministry. Unfortunately for him and his men, its labyrinth design of small narrow rooms that all looked alike, coupled with the fact the building remained in total darkness because Tokyo was still blacked out due to the continuing air-raid warnings, rendered the search a nearly impossible task.

At Eastern Army Headquarters, Tanaka, attempting to regain control and put down the rebellion, issued new orders to his commanders. The orders stated:

1. The Commander of the First Imperial Guards Division has been killed by insubordinate officers.

2. First Imperial Guards Division will until further order be under the direct command of the Commander of the Eastern District Army.

3. The First Imperial Guards Division orders as of today's date are false. They are herewith canceled.

4. All troops surrounding the Imperial Palace are ordered to disperse.[16]

Inside the War Minister's residence, Anami began to prepare for his suicide.

"I'd like to ask one favor of you," said Anami to Takeshita.

Takeshita nodded.

"If I don't succeed in killing myself, will you give me the coup de grace? I doubt rather it will be necessary, however—I think I am capable of taking my own life."

Takeshita remained silent. Anami removed from a nearby cabinet two ancient daggers, family heirlooms. He pulled one from its sheath and ran a finger along the blade.

"This is the one I shall use, for a soldier, having respect to a soldier's honor, he would not use his sword."

He picked up the second dagger and handed it to Takeshita. "Keep this," as he refilled their *sake* glasses, "in memory of me."[17]

At that moment, Takeshita was called away to another room where Uehara waited for him.

"Major Hatanaka has sent me to inform the Lieutenant Colonel that the plan is proceeding as scheduled," Uehara said.

"Is it indeed?" asked Takeshita. "Then did General Mori agree?"

"Actually no," said Uehara, "he didn't. That's why we had to kill him. The Colonel had to be killed also. Everything is going beautifully!"

Takeshita thought otherwise but decided not to respond.

"We don't know definitely yet, what attitude the Eastern District Army is going to take, but no doubt they'll join us very soon," said Uehara.

Takeshita believed they would not. Anami was right, the Eastern Army would not rebel.

"Have you any messages?" Uehara asked.

Takeshita smiled, "Not yet."[18]

THE TIME WAS NEARING FOR the final act in Anami's life. He had wrapped a band of white cotton around his abdomen.

"Have you any message that you want me to take to your family?" asked Takeshita.

Anami nodded. "Tell my wife that I am very grateful to her and that I have absolute confidence in her. She has done well. Yes, Ayako has done well. I have three sons; I can die in peace. Tell Koretaka to do nothing rash. I don't mind dying for I shall be going where Koreakira already is."

Takeshita filled their glasses with more *sake*.

Anami continued: "Remember me to Umezu and Suzuki."

He paused and named other friends as Takeshita wrote them down.

"What about Yonai?" Takeshita asked.

The War Minister's face went flush and turned angry.

"Kill him!" cried Anami, "Kill Yonai!"[19]

OUTSIDE, IDA'S CAR PULLED UP and the colonel jumped out. But a guard stopped him from entering, saying the War Minister was preparing to commit suicide. Hearing the car and conversation, Takeshita left Anami to see who had arrived, intercepting Ida just as he was about to leave. The sun had peered over the horizon as Takeshita led Ida into the War Minister's home. Pausing at the end of a corridor, Ida could see Anami, naked from the waist up, kneeling on a mat.

"Welcome Ida," called Anami, "Come in, come in."

Ida entered the room and dropped to his knees.

"Come nearer!"

Ida inched forward until his knees nearly touched Anami's.

"I have decided to commit seppuku," said Anami. "What do you think?"

"I think it is a glorious thing," replied Ida.

"I'm glad you approve," answered Anami.

Ida could not speak. Finally he muttered, "I'll follow you—"

Ida had hardly finished before Anami barked, "Don't be a

fool!" Anami slapped Ida in the face twice. When Ida reopened his eyes, he saw Anami smiling. "Don't let me hear you say that again. There's no need for you to die. My death alone is sufficient. Do you understand?" Anami hugged Ida close. "You must not die—do you understand?"

"Yes," Ida said, "I understand."

"Good, good, you must do your best to help rebuild Japan—that takes more courage than dying! Now, come on," said Anami, "pull yourself together, and let's drink our *sake*. I don't know how long it will be before our next *sake* party together—in some other place."[20]

AT THE EASTERN DISTRICT HEADQUARTERS, General Takashima finally managed to reach the Imperial Guard's command post through a telephone line Hatanaka had accidentally left open.

Colonel Toyojirō Haga, Commander of the 2nd Regiment, Imperial Guard Division, answered the phone. Over a very poor connection Takashima repeated multiple times that the order signed and sealed by Mori was an invention of Koga. As such, the troops around the Palace should be dispersed immediately, and troops should be sent to the Eastern District Headquarters for new orders.

Then Takashima said, "You're not alone there, are you?"

Haga replied that Hatanaka was there.

"Let me talk to him," said Takashima.

Hatanaka came to the phone. "This is Major Hatanaka. I beg the Chief of Staff to try to understand our position. Our men are zealous and eager to—"

Takashima cut him off, saying:" I understand! But it makes no difference. Your situation is hopeless, you are alone, the Eastern Army will not join you. You may think you are succeeding because you hold the palace temporarily, but you are defeated, you are like soldiers trying to defend a hopeless position in a cave with no way out. Listen to me carefully! Don't do anything rash—you will only sacrifice more lives uselessly. I respect your feelings as a private individual Hatanaka, but as an officer in the Army you must obey the Emperor. Japan's supreme virtue is in obedience! Are you listening to me, Major?"

Hatanaka replied, "I am, General! but—let me think! General!"

"Yes" said Takeshima.

"I have one request to make of the General," responded the now fanatical Hatanaka, "Before the Emperor's recording is broadcast, may we have ten minutes on the air to explain our position? The reasons for what we have done and the goals we still hope to win… Ten minutes, that's all, only ten minutes to talk to the people. With the permission of the Eastern District Army!"

"You are still trying to hold an untenable position," replied Takashima. "Can't you understand that? There is no hope whatsoever. The only thing you can do now is to make sure there are no more unnecessary deaths. Have you got that, Major?"

Hatanaka could not find his voice to reply and simply put down the receiver.[21]

STILL UNDAUNTED, JUST BEFORE 5:00 a.m. Major Hatanaka arrived at the offices of the NHK building and went straight to Studio 2. Wielding a pistol, he demanded to be put on the air. Mario Tateno, an announcer, refused. Risking his life, he used the excuse that the air-raid warning still in effect prevented him from doing so.

In Washington, it was still August 14. At 4:05 p.m., Truman received word that the Japanese had accepted the Byrnes counteroffer. The official word, from the Swiss chargé d'affaires in Washington, reached Byrnes at the State Department two hours later at 6:10 p.m.[22]

At 5:10 a.m. in Tokyo, General Tanaka's car arrived at the Guards Headquarters. Colonel Watanabe and his fully armed men were about to leave for the Imperial Palace to execute Division Order No. 584.

Lieutenant Colonel Hiroshi Fuha leapt from Tanaka's car announcing, "His Excellency the Commander!"

Watanabe hurried to meet Tanaka and then escorted him into his personal office, where Tanaka informed him that Mori had been murdered and that the order he had been acting on was false. Watanabe told Tanaka the order had originated with Major Sadakichi Ishihara, who was in the next office. Tanaka ordered Ishihara in.

"How dare you? You are an officer of the Japanese Army," Tanaka shouted. "How dare you disobey the Emperor's command? What you have done today is high treason! Put him under guard!"[23]

At Anami's home, the time had come for the general's final act—committing *seppuku*.

> Anami stood and put on a white shirt, saying to Takeshita, "This was given to me by the Emperor when I was his aide-de-camp. He had worn it himself. I can think of nothing I prize more highly—and so I intend to die wearing it."
>
> The War Minister then pinned all of his decorations on his dress uniform, folded it with the sleeves in the back and laid it in front of the *tokonoma*; then he placed a photo of his dead son between the sleeves.
>
> "When I'm dead, will you drape this over me?"[24]
>
> Takeshita nodded and left the room.
>
> Around 5:30 a.m., Anami knelt in an outer hallway of his home. With his torso erect and shoulders back, he removed the dagger from its scabbard. When Takeshita retuned to the corridor moments later, he found Anami kneeling. The War Minister had already drawn the dagger horizontally across his belly with his right hand; now, moving the blade to his left hand, he slashed at the right side of his neck to sever his carotid artery. Anami began to sway as a torrent of blood gushed forth.
>
> "Shall I help you?" asked Takeshita.
>
> "No, leave me," said Anami.[25]
>
> In the garden outside Anami's home, Takeshita and Ida spoke quietly. Whispering, Takeshita said, "Listen, I have Anami's seal. I could issue an order that would make the whole Army rebel. Shall we do it? Why should we surrender like schoolboys?"
>
> Ida replied, "False orders would soon be exposed. And do you think Anami's spirit would be content?"
>
> "No, no, I was only joking after all," said Takeshita.[26]

AT NHK, HATANAKA STILL HADN'T convinced the station's personnel to put him on air when he received a phone call from an officer in the Eastern District Army. Hatanaka pleaded his case and then halved his demand to just five minutes of airtime, but the officer was unremitting. Finally, Hatanaka responded, "Very well, it can't be helped." He put down the receiver, turned to his fellow collaborators and said, "We've done everything we could. Let's go."[27]

At 7:21 a.m., NHK radio broadcasted a special announcement. "His

Imperial Majesty the Emperor has issued a rescript. It will be broadcast at noon today. Let us all respectfully listen to the voice of the Emperor." Tateno paused, then repeated, "Let us all respectfully listen to the voice of the Emperor at noon today."[28]

Sometime after 11:00 a.m., Major Hatanaka, on a motorcycle, and Colonel Shiizaki, on horseback, attempted to distribute leaflets outside the Imperial Palace to anyone who would take one. The note read:

> We, officers of the Imperial Japanese Army, who, this morning of August 15th, 1945, have risen up in arms, declare to all officers and soldiers of the Armed Forces and to the Japanese people:
>
> That our intention is to protect the Emperor and to preserve the national polity despite the designs of the enemy;
>
> That our prime concern is neither victory nor defeat; nor are we motivated by selfish interest;
>
> That we are ready to live, or die, for the sole just and righteous cause of national loyalty; and
>
> That we devoutly pray that the Japanese people and the members of the Armed Forces will appreciate the significance of our action and join with us to fight for the preservation of our country and the elimination of the traitors around the Emperor, thus confounding the schemes of the enemy.[29]

Finally, shortly before the broadcast of the Imperial Rescript, between the Double Bridge and the Sakashita Gate of the Imperial Palace, Major Hatanaka drew his pistol and put a bullet through the center of his forehead; Colonel Shiizaki cut open his abdomen with his sword and then fired a bullet into his head.[30] At Imperial Headquarters, beside the coffin containing the body of General Mori, Major Koga ripped open his stomach with two cuts, one vertical and one horizontal.[31]

In Washington, a little before 7:00 p.m. on August 14, with the sun still brightly shining outside, a crowd of 10,000 in Lafayette Square waited excitedly for the impending announcement by the president.

The official communiqué from Japan read:

> Communication of the Imperial government of August 14, 1945.
>
> With reference to the Japanese government's note of August 10 regarding the acceptance of the provisions of the Potsdam

The Japanese military called their plan for the defense of home islands Ketsu-Gō. In addition to the millions of men in the armed services, the plan also conscripted civilian males from fifteen to sixty and females from seventeen to forty. *(Alamy Stock Photo)*

Kamikazes (special-attack units) have very often been portrayed by the Japanese as supreme examples of the devotion of the Japanese people to their Emperor. And while some willingly flew to their death, many others were coerced and subjected to extreme psychological pressure by both superiors and subordinates. *(World War II Today)*

Japan began flying kamikaze missions against Allied warships in October of 1944, reaching their peak during the Battle of Okinawa, when during the eighty-two-day battle approximately 2,000 attacked the fleet supporting the invasion. Ten thousand awaited the American invasion of Japan. *(US Navy)*

The principle targets of the kamikazes, until the end of the Battle of Okinawa, were Allied aircraft carriers. For Ketsu-Gō, it would be troop ships and landing craft, in an effort to inflict as many casualties as possible on the invaders in the hopes of gaining better terms than unconditional surrender to end the war. *(US Navy)*

For Ketsu-Gō, special-attack forces of every type, air, land, and sea, became official policy of the government and would be used on a scale beyond anything yet seen in the war. Pictured, is a Kaiten suicide manned torpedo. *(World War Photos)*

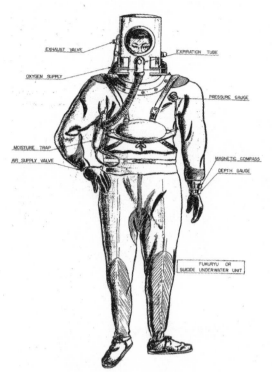

EXHAUST VALVE

OXYGEN SUPPLY

EXPIRATION TUBE

PRESSURE GAUGE

MOISTURE TRAP

AIR SUPPLY VALVE

MAGNETIC COMPASS

DEPTH GAUGE

FUKURYU OR
SUICIDE UNDERWATER UNIT

Waiting in the shallows in front of the invasion beaches would be thousands of Japanese Fukuryu suicide divers. Their objective: to ram and explode their ten-kilogram mine into the approaching landing craft. *(Wikimedia Commons)*

With almost no conventional warships other than submarines, the Japanese developed variants, the Koryu and Kairyu Midget Submarines, to be used in suicide missions. Most were based at Yokosuka to defend the entrance to Tokyo Bay. *(US Navy)*

Named for Colonel Paul W. Tibbet's mother, the B-29 Enola Gay
dropped the first atomic bomb used in combat on Hiroshima, Japan,
the morning of August 6, 1945. *(US Air Force)*

In order to load the enormous bombs into the bomb bay of a B-29, the
plane had to be backed over the top of a specially designed atomic bomb
pit. A hydraulic lift in the pit raised the bomb into the plane. Pictured is
the Little Boy atomic bomb, dropped on Hiroshima, inside one of the
two atomic bomb pits on Tinian. *(National Archives and Records Administration)*

In the immediate aftermath of the atomic explosion a huge mushroom cloud rose over Hiroshima tens of thousands of feet into the air. *(World War II Database)*

The uranium Little Boy atomic bomb exploded over the city of Hiroshima at 8:16 a.m. local time on August 6, 1945, devastating the city with the force of fifteen kilo tons of TNT.

(National Archives and Records Administration)

Three days after the Hiroshima attack, weather permitted a second atomic strike on the city of Nagasaki. Once again, a huge mushroom cloud ascended after the atomic explosion.

(Truman Library Institute)

The plutonium Fat Man bomb, dropped on Nagasaki, unleashed a force of twenty-one kilotons of TNT, but because of the marginal visibility available to the bombardier at the time of the drop, the bomb missed its aiming point and thus caused less damage to Nagasaki than it could have.

(World War II Database)

In the moments after the broadcast of Emperor Hirohito's speech announcing Japan's termination of the war (not surrender), on August 15, 1945, Japanese civilians reacted in shock. They had been told until the very end that Japan was winning the war. *(Wikimedia Commons)*

The Emperor also sent a message to the men of Japan's armed services telling them to cease hostilities and lay down their arms. *(IWM)*

The official ceremony ending World War II occurred September 2, 1945 aboard the USS Missouri in Tokyo Bay. Pictured is the small Japanese surrender delegation on the deck of the mighty American battleship. Among the men, the only member of the Big Six, front row right, is Army Chief of Staff General Yoshijirō Umezu. *(Naval History and Heritage Command)*

In reaction to the news of the Japanese surrender, the evening of August 14, 1945, a huge celebration erupts in Times Square, New York.
(National Archives and Records Administration)

Also, the evening of August 14th, a large crowd gathers to celebrate outside the White House. *(Harry S. Truman Library & Museum)*

Declaration and the reply of the governments of the United States, Great Britain, the Soviet Union, and China sent by American Secretary of State Byrnes under the date August 11, the Japanese government have the honor to communicate to the governments of the four powers as follows:

His Majesty the Emperor has issued an Imperial rescript regarding Japan's acceptance of the provisions of the Potsdam Declaration.

His Majesty the Emperor is prepared to authorize and ensure the signature by his Government and the Imperial General Headquarters of the necessary terms for carrying out the provisions of the Potsdam Declaration. His Majesty is also prepared to issue his commands to all the military, naval, and air authorities of Japan and all the forces under their control wherever located to cease active operations, to surrender arms, and to issue such other orders as may be required by the Supreme Commander of the Allied forces for the execution of the above-mentioned terms.[32]

Truman called the Cabinet to his office to join him in the announcement of Japan's unconditional surrender. When Truman arrived, he found many members of his Cabinet and Former Secretary of State Cordell Hull, as well as a great gathering of news correspondents. Standing behind his desk, the president, looking sharp in a double-breasted, navy-blue suit, read from a single sheet of paper. Hull, in a light summer suit, sat in a chair to Truman's left, Byrnes—also in a navy-blue suit—on his immediate right, and next to him Admiral Leahy in his khaki naval uniform.

Along with Truman, Hull, Leahy, and Byrnes were: Secretary of the Interior Julius Krug, Lend Lease Administrator Leo Crowley, Federal Works Administrator Philip B. Fleming, William Davis of the National War Labor Board, Director John Snyder of the Office of War Mobilization, Secretary of the Navy James Forrestal, Attorney General Tom Clark, Secretary of Labor Lewis Schwellenbach, Housing Administrator John Blandford, and Postmaster General Robert Hannegan.

The doors were locked. Truman glanced at a clock on the wall, and at exactly one minute before seven with the newsreels running, the president stood and read slowly from the paper he held in his right hand:

I have received this afternoon a message from the Japanese Government, in reply to the message forwarded to that Government, by the Secretary of State on August 11th. I deem this reply a full acceptance of the Potsdam Declaration, which specifies the unconditional surrender of Japan. In the reply there is no qualification. Arrangements are now being made for the formal signing of the surrender terms at the earliest possible moment. General Douglas MacArthur has been appointed as the Supreme Allied Commander to receive the Japanese surrender. Great Britain, Russia, and China will be represented by high ranking officers. Meantime, the Allied armed forces have been ordered to suspend offensive actions. The proclamation of V-J Day must wait upon the formal signing of the surrender terms by Japan.

The room erupted in cheers.

Truman announced that August 15 and 16 were designated as days of national celebration. The doors were unlocked, and the press made a mad dash to leave so they could send their reports of the surrender to the world.

Leahy returned to his office to send messages to America's armed forces, directing them to suspend offensive operations against Japan.

Leahy said of the experience that day:

To me the occasion seemed appropriate for thoughtful appreciation of our good fortune and having gained the victory over fanatical enemies. But the people considered noise appropriate—and the greatest number in democracies must have their way.

What the people of the United States, and the entire world, were celebrating was the definite end of the war which started in 1914, had a temporary adjournment for further preparations from 1918 to 1939, and which had been fought to this successful conclusion for the past six years.[33]

David McCullough, Truman's biographer, wrote of the president's extraordinary first ninety days as chief executive:

In just three months in office Harry Truman had been faced with a greater surge of history, with larger, more difficult, more far-reaching decisions than any President before him. Neither Lincoln after first taking office, nor Franklin Roosevelt in the tumultuous first hundred days, had had to contend with issues of such magnitude and coming all at once, [and]…if ever a man had been caught in a whirlwind not of his own making, it was he.[34]

On the night of August 14, crowds celebrated V-J Day in Times Square in New York, as well as in Washington, DC. Byrnes joined in the celebration in Washington, wrote historian David Robertson, "But neither then nor later did he exult over what he considered the necessary use of incendiary bombs and the atomic blasts over Japanese cities in order to spare Americans future combat."[35]

At noon in Japan, "A broadcast of the highest importance," said announcer Wada, "is about to be made."

"All listeners will please rise."

The people of Japan all stood and listened to the broadcast of the Imperial Rescript.[36]

The broadcast was followed by an announcement stating that the advent of the atomic bomb had been the greatest reason for Japan's decision to surrender. In Hiroshima hospital, now teeming with victims of the first attack, Dr. Hachiya couldn't believe his ears.

> "Like others in the room, I had come to attention at the mention of the Emperor's voice, and for a while we all remained silent and at attention. Darkness clouded my eyes, my teeth chattered, and I felt cold sweat running down my back…By degrees people began to whisper and then to talk in low voices until, out of the blue sky, someone shouted: "How can we lose the war!"
>
> Following this outburst, expressions of anger were unleashed.
>
> "Only a coward would back out now!"
>
> "There is a limit to deceiving us!"
>
> "I would rather die than be defeated!"
>
> "What have we been suffering for?"
>
> "Those who died can't go to heaven in peace now!"
>
> The hospital suddenly turned into an uproar, and there was nothing one could do. Many who had been strong advocates of peace and others who had lost their taste for war following the *pika* [to glitter, sparkle, or shine] were now shouting for the war to continue…

The one word—surrender—had produced a greater shock than the bombing of our city."[37]

OBVIOUSLY, FANATICISM WAS NOT THE exclusive domain of the military. Civilians had been told up to the very end that Japan was winning the war.

Two days later, a second Imperial Rescript was issued to Japan's armed forces. It read:

IMPERIAL RESCRIPT OF AUGUST 17, 1945

More than three years and eight months have elapsed since we declared war on the United States of America and Great Britain. During this period our beloved officers and men of the armed forces have devoted themselves gallantly in fighting on barren fields and on the raging ocean, and we deeply appreciate it. The Soviet Union has now entered the war, and in view of the state of affairs both here and abroad, we feel that prolongation of the struggle will merely serve to further the evil and may eventually result in the loss of the very foundation on which the Empire exists. Therefore, in spite of the fact that the fighting spirit of the Imperial Army and Navy is still high, we hereupon intend to negotiate a peace with the United States of America, Great Britain, the Soviet Union and the Chunking Government for the sake of maintaining our glorious national polity.

We deeply mourn the loss of numerous loyal and courageous soldiers who have perished in action and from disease, and believe that the devoted and distinguished services rendered by ye officers and men of the armed forces will long be remembered by the people. We expect ye officers and men of the armed forces to comply faithfully with our desire, unite firmly, exercise complete prudence, endure hardships and privatizations with undying patients and thus lay the permanent foundation for the nation.[38]

Some historians have suggested that the second Imperial Rescript, issued on August 17, actually revealed the true nature of why Japan surrendered on August 15—specifically the Soviet Union's entry into the war against Japan. This reasoning ignores the reference to the atomic bomb in the first Imperial Rescript and the subsequent broadcast immediately afterward stating that the advent of the atomic bomb had been the greatest reason for Japan's decision to surrender. The fact that millions of Japanese military personnel were stationed in Japan as part of Ketsu-Gō, and had been ordered to listen to these broadcasts, was also apparently immaterial, and those members of Japan's armed forces were in no way threatened by the Soviet Army.

Nevertheless, by the reckoning of these historians, the Japanese government was afraid of one of two things. First, the Red Army's attack by over a million men on the gutted Kwantung Army in Manchuria on August 9. The Kwantung Army was in headlong retreat to the border of Northern Korea—per orders established by the Japanese Army May of 1945—specifically in the event of a Soviet invasion. Second, because they were afraid of a Soviet invasion of Japan itself.

A Russian invasion of Japan would have required an amphibious capability akin to what the United States could accomplish. While the Americans had spent over three years perfecting amphibious warfare, the Red Army was a land army; and while it could cross a river, open seas or the ocean were a different matter entirely.

To get to Japan, the Soviets would have had to either cross from mainland Russia to Sakhalin Island (6.2 miles over water), then from southern Sakhalin, attempt to cross to Hokkaido, Japan (approximately 24 miles over water); or they could have attempted to cross the Sea of Japan from Vladivostok (Russia's eastern most port) to somewhere else in Japan, at least several hundred miles away. With the resources available to the Red Army at the time, it would have been impossible to have attempted anything more than a very modest landing on the west side of Hokkaido.

Apart from the logistics issue, if Japan's leaders were so concerned, why did Anami, Umezu, and Kawabe consider the Soviet attack on the Kwantung Army to be only a matter of time? The Soviet entry had absolutely no impact whatsoever on their thinking and their positions during any of the meetings of the Big Six, the full Cabinet, or in the two Imperial Conferences held between August 9 and 14. Anami, Umezu, and Toyoda never changed their positions all the way through the second Imperial Conference on August 14, staunchly recommending that Japan fight on. In none of these meetings did the hardliners even bring up the Soviets as a threat demanding an immediate cessation to hostilities.

Absent an agreement to continue the war, Anami, Umezu, and Toyoda were more than willing to prolong the negotiations, with essentially just the United States (not Russia), for however long it took to get the expanded terms that they had been advocating for since August 9, and in the process risk the consequences of continuing the war with the Red Army. At no time from August 9 to 14 did the Japanese attempt to engage the Soviet Union in any diplomatic dialog to halt the Russian attack. The Japanese's biggest concern, relative to the Soviet Union's joining the war against Japan, was in drafting a reciprocal declaration of war against the Russian government.

The second Imperial Rescript fulfilled an obligation included among the requirements of the Byrnes note and Potsdam Declaration, ordering the Japanese military to surrender and lay down its arms. In that regard, the second Rescript did gain the compliance and peaceful surrender of Japanese troops in China and the Southern Area of the Pacific Theater, an issue that had been in doubt. And it's reasonable to say the Red Army's presence played an important role in gaining the acquiescence of those Japanese commanders.

Also, on August 17, General MacArthur wrote to General Marshall regarding Tōgō's aforementioned request to amend the terms of the Potsdam Declaration.

General of the Army Douglas MacArthur to Chief of Staff (Marshall)

[Manila,] 17 August, 1945

The Secret terms proposed by the Japanese are fundamentally violative of the provisions of the Potsdam Declaration and would completely traverse the previous attitude not only of the Allied nations but of Japan herself in her successes and conquests of this war. The incidents of Bataan and Singapore are still fresh in the minds of the World. The enemy's suggestion goes even to the point of preferential repatriation treatment of Japanese soldiers. The suggested ameliorations would relieve Japan of much of the physical and psychological burdens of defeat. I believe that public opinion throughout the Allied world would not support favorable consideration of the stipulations. In my opinion the Potsdam provisions should be put into effect as drawn and the suggestions made by the Japanese Government should be rejected. In China I believe the stipulations made by the Generalissimo as to the details of the surrender should be supported by the Allies.[39]

Fifteen days after the Japanese surrender, on August 29, 1945, Byrnes held a news conference in Washington and spoke of the final days of the war. He acknowledged the United States knew of the Japanese peace overtures rejected by the Russians.

Then Byrnes turned to his advocacy for using the atomic bomb, saying, "Whenever we think of the effects of the bomb, we ought to recall that if it only facilitated the surrender, and it certainly did that, it saved the lives of hundreds of thousands of American boys." He then called attention to the fact that it also saved "the lives of hundreds [of thousands] of Japanese boys and millions more of its people who would've perished," if the war continued and the Americans invaded. Then, as put by historian David Robertson, Byrnes "summed up as honestly and simply as he ever would the multiplicity of fears, ambitions, patriotism, and good intentions paving the way to the use of the atomic bomb. 'It was not a one-way street,' he said."[40]

On September 1, 1945, three weeks after the second atomic bomb dropped on Nagasaki, the Japanese had already begun to switch the tables on the Allies, turning themselves from perpetrator into the victim of the war, by using negative publicity associated with the atomic attacks. The strategy was first concocted by Minister Okamoto in Stockholm, who had been analyzing public opinion in the US and Great Britain. He informed his superiors in Tokyo that there was widespread distrust of the Japanese by Anglo-Americans, but,

> ...the people of England and America were deeply shocked at the use of the atomic bomb, of which on the whole they disapprove... In my opinion, we should judge [and make use of] the condition of enemy public opinion on the subject of the atomic bomb. Since it is difficult to justify the heavy damage inflicted in the massacre of hundreds of thousands of innocent people, there is the opportunity—by making use of the Diet, the radio, and various other means—to play on enemy weakness by skillfully emphasizing the extreme inhumanity of the bomb. I also think that we should expose the bad faith of Russia, with who we had neutral relations, and ignoring Japan's request to mediate for peace and in entering the war.[41]

Four days after Japan's official September 2 surrender, Hirohito wrote a short note to his twelve-year-old son and his eventual successor on the Throne, Crown Prince Akihito, about why Japan had been defeated.

> Let me say a few words about the reasons for our defeat. Our people placed too much confidence in the Empire and held England and America in contempt. Our military placed too much emphasis on spirit and forgot science. During the time of Emperor Meiji, there were renown commanders in the Army and the Navy, such as Yamagata, Oyama, and Yamamoto. But this time, as in the case of Germany in the First World War, the military ran rampant and failed to take a broad view of the situation; they knew how to advance but did not know how to retreat. If we had continued the war, I would not have been able to protect the Three Sacred Treasures of the Imperial House, and [more Japanese] people would have been killed. I swallowed my tears and tried to save the Japanese race from extinction.[42]

Nowhere in this short letter to his son was there any expression of contrition for starting and waging a war of aggression, causing the death of an estimated seventeen million civilians and another six million combatants, all in the name of Shōwa Emperor. Hirohito's sole regret was that Japan's military had relied on the wrong things in the war, and it proved their downfall. And importantly, out of all proportion to their importance, to the lives lost and the incredible destruction wrought, Hirohito was grateful he had managed to protect Japan's Three Sacred Treasures.

Also absent in this letter is any reference to the Russian entry into the war as the cause of Japan's surrender—only to Japan's lack of emphasis on "science," which was a direct reference to the United States' successful development of the atomic bomb. The Emperor mentions the atomic bomb three times as the reason for Japan's defeat and surrender: in the Imperial Rescript on August 15, in his follow-up broadcast on August 15, citing the atomic bomb as the primary reason, and on September 6, 1945, in his private letter to his son. And on September 7, Hirohito told General MacArthur about the moment when the opposition to peace collapsed. Hirohito said, "The peace party did not prevail until the bombing of Hiroshima created a situation which could be dramatized."[43]

By September 13, Minister Okamoto's recommendation had already begun to codify. American MAGIC codebreakers, still monitoring Japanese diplomatic traffic, sent Marshall a message stating that, "the Japanese leaders intended to play up the atomic bombings not only to explain Japan's surrender [to an army that did not believe it was defeated in combat], but to offset publicity on Japan's treatment of Allied prisoners [of war] and internees [plus countless other atrocities]." Japan's new Foreign Minister, Mamoru Shigemitsu, had just sent a message to the Japanese legations in Sweden, Switzerland, and Portugal, saying:

> The newspapers have given wide publicity to the Government's recent memorandum concerning the atomic bomb damage in Hiroshima and Nagasaki, the sending of an Imperial messenger, the daily rising count of the dead, and the like. Also an American investigating party went to Hiroshima on the eighth, part of the group having gone previously to Nagasaki, and the head of the group, Brigadier General [Thomas F.] Farrell, is reported to have said "We knew from aerial photographs that the damage it Hiroshima was tremendous, but, having visited the scene, we know now that the damage was beyond description. So horrible a weapon must never be used again."

The statement attributed to Farrell attracted a great deal of attention. Farrell was not just any American general; he was Deputy Commanding General and Chief of Field Operations for the Manhattan Project. General Groves reported to Farrell. The codebreakers highlight in a footnote that "American press dispatches on the findings of the preliminary survey of Hiroshima contained no such statement by General Farrell."[44] Shigemitsu continues:

> All these reports have been sent abroad by Domei [the Japanese news service] in full detail. To what extent have they been carried by the newspapers and other media at your place? Since the Americans have recently been raising an uproar about the question of our mistreatment of prisoners, I think we should make every effort to exploit the atomic bomb question in our propaganda. If necessary, we shall telegraph further details. Please let me know by wire whether that would be desirable.[45]

As a result of Shigemitsu's use of Domei to promulgate Japan's propaganda, MacArthur restricted the papers' distribution to within the country. To get around that, Okamoto recommended having "The Anglo-American news agencies carry these announcements. [Also] have Anglo-American newspapermen write stories on the bomb damage and thus create a powerful impression abroad."[46]

American monitoring of these secret Japanese communications ended November 3, 1945, when, during an investigation of Pearl Harbor by Congress, the fact was disclosed over the objections of President Truman and General Marshall. But the Japanese cover story, begun just days after the end of the war, has continued to this day.

EPILOGUE

TRADITIONALISTS AND REVISIONISTS

For the past seventy-five years, there has been a debate among historians, mostly American, over President Truman's decision to use the atomic bomb against Japan at the end of World War II.

Traditionalists believe the bomb helped bring the war to a much quicker conclusion than alternative military plans, avoiding either extremely costly American casualties in an invasion of Japan or a blockade and bombardment—essentially a siege that would have killed untold millions of Japanese by actual attacks, starvation, disease, and exposure. Ending the war brutally, but within days of its use, the atomic bomb may have saved the lives of tens of thousands of Allied military and civilian POWs still in Japanese captivity, and perhaps millions of Asians and Western Pacific Natives, living in Japan's Greater East Asia Co-Prosperity Sphere, who were dying at a rate of 100,000 to 250,000 per month, perhaps as high as 400,000 according to a postwar estimate by the United Nations.

Revisionists, on the other hand, claim the high American casualty estimates for the invasion were a postwar fabrication by President Truman and Secretary of War Stimson to justify the use of the atomic bomb, and that those numbers grossly overstated the expectations of the American military planners.

Other revisionists assert that it was really the Russian entry into the war on August 9 that compelled the Japanese to surrender when they did, out of fear over the rapid advance by the Red Army against Japan's Kwantung Army in Manchuria and a potential invasion by the Soviets of Hokkaido, the northernmost of Japan's home islands.

Another theory involving the Soviets suggests the atomic bomb was used as a form of "atomic diplomacy" by the Americans to get the Russians to a more tractable position in the postwar era in Eastern Europe (already a fait accompli by then). The same historians likewise claim the employment of the atomic bomb led to the subsequent Cold War between the US and Russia. Frequently tied to the Soviet rhetoric is the contention that Secretary of State Byrnes manipulated a new and weak President Truman into using the atomic bomb to keep the Soviets out of the postwar administration of Japan.

Finally, there is a theory stating that the Japanese were about to surrender without the bomb, or that they likely would have no later than November 1, the time of the American invasion of Kyūshū, but certainly no later than December 31, 1945, if the Americans had simply guaranteed the preservation of the national polity.

WHAT DOES THE EVIDENCE SHOW?

Regarding the issue of casualties, Truman and Stimson knew the following by the spring/summer of 1945: the draft call in the United States had been increased to 140,000 men per month in March, in anticipation of the needs of a soon-to-be one-front war (unmistakable evidence that American military planners expected very high casualties from an invasion of Japan); the content of the Hoover memo, dated May 30, citing 500,000 to 1,000,000 Americans killed in an invasion of Japan; the findings (known at least by Stimson) in the William Shockley memo dated July 21, projecting a cost of between 1,700,000 to 4,000,000 casualties to invade Japan, including 400,000 to 800,000 killed; and lastly, that Marshall had revised his estimate of the casualties, in a private conversation with Truman at Potsdam on July 25, to a minimum of 250,000 upward to as many as 1,000,000 American casualties.

On August 10, Stimson told Truman, during the discussions over Japan's initial peace offer, that the Emperor would play a vital role in securing the surrender of Japan's armed forces. Without that service by the Emperor, Stimson stated that the US could be facing a score of "Iwo Jimas and Okinawas all over China and the New Netherlands [now Indonesia]." That analogy would work out to between 634,160 US casualties (171,720 killed) and 982,660 casualties including 250,400 killed and missing. And those figures did not include potential losses in the invasion of the Japanese home islands.[1]

All of these estimates—figures we *know* were staring Truman and Stimson in the face—vastly exceed the modest numbers offered up by revisionists. And, in fact, they closely match the postwar numbers given by Truman and Stimson.

Independently of what Truman and Stimson knew, Marshall took into consideration the incredible buildup of Japanese troops on Kyūshū. By August, the Japanese garrisoned there had reached 900,000 men. So, looking at massive potential casualties, he ordered all atomic bomb production to be held for potential use as a tactical weapon to support the invasion.

In addition to Marshall, Army Corps of Engineers General Sam Sturgis—awarded two Distinguished Service Medals, two Silver Stars, and a Legion of Merit—"inspected Japanese shoreline fortifications immediately after the war and found them so imposing that he thought an invasion might cost as many as one million American lives."[2]

In May, King and Nimitz had both expressed their concerns over the casualties associated with an invasion, and in all probability would have forced a reopening of the discussion with Truman long before the scheduled D-Day for Olympic.

In terms of enemy casualties, civilian and military, resulting from the American invasions of Japan—something revisionists callously dodge in their narratives—US planners forecasted between 5,000,000 and 10,000,000 million Japanese dead.

The supposition that it was the Soviet entry into the war that compelled the Japanese to surrender doesn't sync with the reactions and actions of Anami, Umezu, and Kawabe, all of whom anticipated the Soviet declaration of war—none were surprised or overwhelmed when it happened. Nor were they aghast over the rapid advance of the Red Army in Manchuria, since they were well aware of the Kwantung Army's severely depleted condition and change in its mission in May to a fighting withdrawal to Northern Korea. Even accepting that none of these men were immediately aware of the scale of the Soviet invasion in Manchuria, they all still opposed ending the war, or wanted to do so with four conditions five days later on August 14, when they clearly had to know considerably more.

Lastly, while the Red Army was a highly formidable land army, the idea that it had the ability to mount a major amphibious invasion of northern Japan has been aptly put by Dennis Giangreco as *The Hokkaido Myth*. In the summer of 1945, Soviet Prime Minister Joseph Stalin had begun pressuring President Truman for an occupation zone in Hokkaido, even though the Soviets had not yet joined the war against Japan. As the request had not been part of the agreements struck at the Yalta Conference of the Big Three a few months earlier, Truman flatly rejected Stalin's appeal.[3] Undeterred, a month prior to the meeting at

Potsdam, Stalin held a high-level meeting of his military and political leaders at the Kremlin, on June 26–27, 1945, to express his interest in a full-scale invasion of the island of Hokkaido.

In the course of the meeting, Stalin asked General Georgy Zhukov, the man who had led the Red Army all the way to Berlin, what kind of force would be required to accomplish the task. Zhukov replied that they would need four field armies, each possessing an average of six combat divisions. The number was so large it would have threatened the already highly planned invasion of Manchuria.[4]

Then there was the issue of how to transport and support so many troops along with their required equipment and provisions. *Project Hula*, a program in which the US began transferring naval vessels to the Soviet Union in anticipation of Russia joining the war against Japan, had only just begun that spring. As such, the naval support for an operation of the scale required would not be possible for at least a year, if at all. Marshal Aleksandr Vasilevsky, chief of the general staff for the Red Army, further dismissed the plan, stating that the invasion of mainland Japan would be exceedingly risky and outright unworkable, and that "the Soviet Army should not 'expose' itself to the strong Japanese defenses on the main islands."[5]

The next day, Stalin took the full-scale invasion of Hokkaido off the table. However, after Japan announced its surrender on August 15, and soon after the Imperial forces in Manchuria, in compliance with the Emperor's second rescript, began surrendering en masse and laying down their arms, the Soviets saw an opportunity to exploit the political situation by landing a largely administrative force on Hokkaido.

On the evening of August 18, three days after Japan's surrender, the Red Army issued orders to attempt a landing of its 87th Rifle Corps' 342nd and 345th Rifle Divisions on August 23. The location chosen for the landing was the small remote port of Rumoi on northwest coast of Hokkaido, as far away from the heavily defended cities in the south as possible.[6] At this point, the Russians had no idea if the Japanese would put up a fight. They found out during their small amphibious attack on the Japanese base on the Kuril island of Shumshu on August 18–21. The engagement saw the Imperial Army inflict nearly 1,600 casualties on the Russians, and Japanese artillery destroy five of the sixteen LSIs (Landing Ship, Infantry) the US had given the Soviets as part of Project Hula.[7] On August 22, Stalin wisely pulled the plug on any further attempt to land troops in Japan.

With regard to the atomic diplomacy theory, Truman had good reason, based on his recent experiences with Stalin at Potsdam, to attempt to avoid similar Russian influence in Japan. The Soviets had played their hand to the greatest extent possible during the last conference of the Big Three, and the people of Eastern Europe and Germany would live with the consequences for the next forty years. Truman held by far the better hand in the Pacific, where the Americans, after nearly four years of fighting, were primarily responsible for Japan's looming defeat. But Truman's overriding objective was to end the war as soon as possible to preserve American lives, even if that meant accepting Soviet involvement. That's why one of his primary objectives at Potsdam was the reaffirmation of the pledge Stalin had made to FDR at Yalta five months earlier—to enter the Pacific War against Japan, approximately ninety days after the end of the war with Germany. Twice during the final weeks of the war, the President expressed the importance of this accomplishment. First, when Truman wrote his wife Bess on July 18, stating, "I've gotten what I came for—Stalin goes to war August 15 with no strings on it…I'll say that will end the war a year sooner now, and think of the [American] kids who won't be killed! That is the important thing." Truman's letter came two days after he had already been made aware of the successful test of the first atomic bomb on July 16. The second instance occurred on August 9 when Truman reiterated essentially the same in a letter to Senator Russell.

Byrnes, the supposed manipulator of Truman, who successfully convinced the president to counter the Japanese surrender offer with two changes (subjugating the authority of the Emperor to rule to the Supreme Commander of the Allied Powers and establishing a new government according to the freely expressed will of the Japanese people) against the advice of Stimson, Leahy, and Forrestal, delayed the end of the war by four days. But Byrnes actually risked—as we know from what happened in Tokyo from August 12 to 15—extending the war indefinitely when he insisted on these changes. By doing so, for every day the war continued, the Russians' position potentially improved in terms of its influence over the postwar peace and the spoils they could exact. If Byrnes's primary objectives in advocating the use of the atomic bomb had been to intimidate the Russians and end the war before they could have a major say in the postwar peace, then he had possibly made a grievous blunder by forcing the continuation of the negotiations.

The atomic bomb potentially initiating the Cold War between the

US and Russia after the war is irrelevant. There is no evidence that Truman ever weighed the impact on US–Soviet relations in his decision-making about the atomic bomb.

The claim that the Japanese would have surrendered perhaps as early as the spring of 1945, but likely before the scheduled invasion, and certainly no later than the end of 1945, is the most outrageous of all. First, there is the July 21 MAGIC decrypt between Tōgō and Satō, where, after being told by Satō that the best the Japanese could hope for was unconditional surrender and the preservation of the Imperial system, Tōgō rejects, without explicitly doing so, Satō's recommendation. Neither does he acknowledge as a viable option just the continuation of the *kokutai*. Rather he responds that the Japanese government will never accept unconditional surrender.

We also have Anami, Umezu, and Toyoda demanding three additional conditions to the preservation of the national polity—specifically, control over disarmament, control over war crimes trials, and no occupation of Japan by the Allies—during the Imperial Conference in the early morning hours of August 10. Absent getting the Allies' agreement on those four conditions, all three men were determined to fight the decisive battle against the Americans on Japanese soil. The three only relented after the Emperor was allowed to give His opinion, favoring an end to the war with the single condition of protecting the national polity.

But four days later, on August 14, Anami, Umezu, and Toyoda were at it again, contending that the Byrnes note did not guarantee the Imperial System. They again demanded the continuation of the war. And finally, in defiance of the Emperor, who once again restated His desire to end the war and accept the Potsdam Declaration and the Allies' counteroffer, Anami, in its immediate aftermath, three times contemplated ways to stop the peace and continue the war.

Related to this theory, but also conspicuously absent from revisionists' accounts, is the complete lack of acknowledgment of what would have happened if there had been no atomic bomb and the war simply continued. Because for every month the war went on, the Japanese would have been subjected to the effects of the ongoing blockade and bombardment—starvation, disease, and exposure. Kido, on August 12, and Tōgō in his memoir, noted the potential scale of those losses, placing them in the millions.

Regarding the conventional bombardment of Japan, the Eighth Air

Force was already in the process of redeploying from Europe to Okinawa and converting from its B-17s and B-24s to B-29s. With them, the Twentieth and Eighth Air Forces would have mustered 1,648 B-29s and over 1,000 long-range fighters.

At the same time, early analysis of the strategic bombing of Germany indicated attacks on the Third Reich's oil industry and rail infrastructure had had the most crippling impact on the Nazi war economy. As a result, on August 11, new operational directives for the Twentieth and Eighth Air Forces reflected those conclusions. Army Air Forces staff officers believed that had the war continued, from mid-August to the start of Olympic on November 1, they could have dropped 50,000 tons a month in conventional munitions on Japan—or in two and half months the equivalent of what they had dropped from November of 1944 to early August 1945.[8] With the shift to railroads, further disrupting an already failing transportation system and preventing the movement of food from places of production to areas of consumption, everyone in Tokyo and southwest Honshu would have faced starvation.[9]

Additionally, Japan faced the worst rice crop since 1905. Even with Japan's surrender on August 14, almost immediately after the occupation began, US officials recognized an estimated 10,000,000 Japanese were at risk of starvation. It would have been only a matter of time before this disaster unfolded, without the atomic bomb.[10] And undoubtedly, the loss of basic services, like sanitation and clean water, would have also led to the onset of diseases taking many lives. With winter only a few months away, and millions homeless, exposure to the elements would have killed untold more.

Revisionists also point to members of Truman's administration who didn't want the atomic bomb used, in particular William Leahy, perhaps Truman's closest advisor. Leahy represents a paradox whose other side rarely gets mentioned—Leahy had also described Japan as "our Carthage" to Vice President Henry Wallace in September of 1942. Leahy said of Japan, "we should go ahead and destroy her utterly."[11] So, Leahy apparently felt it was ok to completely destroy Japan, just not by using atomic bombs. Revisionists also conspicuously avoid the fact that Leahy fully supported the US Navy's preferred strategy to gain Japan's capitulation, by continued blockade and bombardment.

Had the US opted for this plan instead of using the atomic bomb, Japanese losses could certainly have exceeded those at Hiroshima and Nagasaki, and may well have reached into the millions due to the effects of conventional bombing, starvation, exposure, and disease. Nor does this revisionist approach recall the hundreds of thousands more, POWs and the Asians still under Japanese occupation, who would have been lost every month as long as the war went on.

There is an associated point to be made here. Too often American scientists and the military have been portrayed as fully understanding the qualitative differences associated with the use of a nuclear weapon. The issue lies at the heart of the debate, because the United States could do equal destruction by August of 1945 with conventional and atomic weapons—one just required far more planes. The qualitative difference was radiation.

The Los Alamos scientists, monitoring the Trinity Test on July 16, stood 10,000 yards—or about 5.7 miles—from the epicenter of the explosion. Truman noted in his diary on July 25 that some were knocked down by the blast wave. Marshall—following the radiological data coming out of Los Alamos after the Trinity Test, coupled with information he received from Colonel L.E. Seeman of the Manhattan Project, who had given considerable thought to the use of the bomb for tactic purposes in an invasion—came to the conclusion he could send American soldiers and Marines over an irradiated battlefield.

Over the succeeding seventeen years after the bombs were dropped on Hiroshima and Nagasaki, all the way until 1962, the United States subjected its own servicemen to nuclear weapons testing. For example, in 1951, at the Nevada Test Site sixty-five miles north of Las Vegas, American soldiers and Marines were placed in trenches only two miles away from the center of a nuclear explosion. After the blast wave passed over them, they walked to ground zero. The federal government finally began compensating veterans subjected to the effects of nuclear testing with up to $75,000 in 1990. The "Atomic Veterans," as they became known, contracted, as a result of their radiation exposure, one or more of the twenty-one different cancers. Eventually, the US government paid out $800,000,000 in claims. That would equate to a minimum of 10,666 claims if every man received the maximum payout of $75,000, which seems unlikely. What seems clear from the length of the testing, seventeen years after Hiroshima and Nagasaki, is how little they apparently knew.

UNCONDITIONAL SURRENDER

Was the Allies' demand for unconditional surrender the right decision? Roosevelt's vision sought to preserve the relationship with the Allies by avoiding disagreement over specific terms. It worked, and the Allies won the war. Unconditional surrender also succeeded in the permanent removal of the governments and leaders in Germany and Japan who fought a war of aggression against the world, essentially imposing a revolution on each nation. The occupation allowed the Allies to enforce those changes to the governments of Germany and Japan, including the removal of leaders, disarmament, and war crimes trials.

Without the forced change in government, there is no reason to assume either or both countries would not have reemerged as a threat to peace a later time. Without forced disarmament, both Germany and Japan could have restarted their nuclear weapons programs. Without the war crimes trials, regardless of how flawed they may have been, the atrocities perpetrated by Germany and Japan may never have come to light, most certainly not to the degree they have.

THE ATOMIC BOMB

The atomic bombing of Hiroshima and Nagasaki did not convince the hardliners, Anami, Umezu, and Toyoda, or the Army as a whole, to surrender. All wanted to continue fighting even after the dropping of both bombs and the Soviets' declaration of war. If the bombs did not change their minds, they did do fatal damage to Japan's strategic argument for continuing the war. That argument rested on the premise that the US would ultimately stage a massive invasion giving Japanese arms the opportunity to inflict enormous casualties and break American will to pursue the war to unconditional surrender. But the bombs signaled that the US might not attempt an invasion and instead employ a strategy of blockade and bombardment (that would likely include more atomic bombs). Japan was powerless to respond to that threat, as the Japanese no longer had any ability to project their military beyond the home islands.

But the bomb did convince the Emperor (he refers to it four times in the immediate aftermath of the surrender). And with Suzuki, Sakomizu, and Tōgō's skillful political moves, the peace faction in the government outmaneuvered the hardliners to set the first Imperial Conference and obtain the Imperial *seidan*. When Anami, Umezu, and Toyoda again attempted to block the surrender four days later, using the Byrnes note as their latest justification, the Emperor called the second Imperial

Conference of His own accord and in the second *seidan* ordered the acceptance of the Potsdam Declaration and the Byrnes note.

JAPAN'S DYSFUNCTIONAL GOVERNMENT AND MILITARY

At least part of the reason for the delay in the Japanese surrender can be attributed to its dysfunctional government, which required a unanimous vote to make a decision. Each of its leaders had the power of veto—or worse, through resignation, the power to terminate an entire administration. And by the last year of the war, decisions rested almost entirely in the hands of the Supreme War Council, just six men, all of whom were members of the military, excepting the foreign minister. This almost completely slanted the views of the government toward militarism.

The government was also hampered by a practice the military had allowed and condoned, known as *Gekokujō*. This behavior, by middle grade officers, had frequently resulted in the assassination of leaders in the decades leading up to the onset of the Pacific War. In the final days, it also influenced the behavior of Anami, Umezu, and Toyoda during the deliberations of the Big Six and Cabinet, and finally the attempted coup to stop the surrender.

To the very end, Japan's senior military leaders never took a sufficiently hard line against this behavior to permanently put an end the problem.

SOEMU TOYODA

Despite being a member of the Big Six, Toyoda, owing to the Navy's almost complete destruction and resulting loss in stature relative to the Army, had minimal impact during the final months of the war. His primary distinction was his unwavering support for the continuation of the war, along with fellow hardliners Generals Umezu and Anami. In that sense, his votes garnered a degree of influence because they prevented a unanimous vote in favor of accepting the terms of the Potsdam Declaration and ultimately the Byrnes counteroffer.

The surprising aspect to Toyoda's tenure in the Suzuki Cabinet was the fact that Yonai had brought him, thinking he would be an ally in the peace faction.

In 1948, the Supreme Commander for the Allied Powers (SCAP) arrested Toyoda and jailed him in Sugamo Prison in Tokyo. Charged with violating "the laws and customs of war" by the International

Tribunal for the Far East (aka the Tokyo War Crimes Tribunal), Toyoda was acquitted and released in 1949.

He published his memoir in 1950 and died of a heart attack in 1957, at the age of 72.

MITSUMASA YONAI

Although Yonai was a holdover from the Konoye Cabinet, a former Prime Minister, and one of the most important members of the Navy, he too had very limited power within the Big Six. While he sided with Foreign Minister Tōgō's effort to end the war, Yonai failed to take strong a stand until the very end, after the Emperor's first *seidan*. It is also notable that Yonai, like Suzuki, interpreted the Potsdam Declaration as a signal that American resolve was weakening, and thus awaiting the Decisive Battle was the proper Japanese strategy—rather than attempting to immediately end the war.

Admiral Yonai was not indicted as a war criminal after the war, but he did participate in the Tokyo War Crimes Tribunal, largely in an effort to keep Hirohito from being prosecuted. He died of pneumonia on April 20, 1948; he was 68.

MARQUIS KŌICHI KIDO

For a time after the war, Hirohito's closest advisor represented the Japanese to the Allied occupation forces. He also advised General MacArthur on many logistical issues. But eventually SCAP caught up with Kido, accusing him of being a Class A war criminal. Convicted on five counts, Kido was sentenced to life in prison. During his trial, he voluntarily turned over his diary, kept since 1930, to the prosecution. It proved to be an excellent insight into the inner workings of the Japanese government.

In 1951, as the Allied occupation of Japan neared its end, Kido sent a message to Hirohito advising him to accept responsibility for the war and resign; Hirohito did not. With the end of the occupation in April of 1952, and with his growing health problems, Kido was released by the now autonomous Japanese government in 1953. Kido lived another twenty-four years until April 6, 1977, dying at the age of 87 from cirrhosis of the liver.

YOSHIJIRŌ UMEZU

Umezu had been one of the most powerful men in the Army for

decades and held its highest posts. He had supported Tōjō's rise to Prime Minister, even though he favored war with Russia and believed war with the United States to be a mistake. He had aided Anami's career and his rise within the Army on multiple occasions. But in the end, Umezu followed Anami's lead.

Umezu was a member of the Japanese delegation who signed the official instrument of surrender on September 2, 1945, aboard the *USS Missouri*.

SCAP arrested Umezu and charged him with five counts of being a war criminal. The court found him guilty and sentenced him to life in prison on November 12, 1948. Umezu converted to Christianity while in prison, and died of rectal cancer on January 8, 1949, at the age of 67.

KANTARŌ SUZUKI

Suzuki persuaded Tōgō to join his administration by promising support for Tōgō's objective of ending the war efficiently. But his actions were far more consistent with the posture of Anami, Umezu, and Toyoda, until the final days before surrender, when the Emperor, Kido, and Tōgō forced him to switch his allegiance.

Suzuki often appeared divorced from the discussions taking place in his Cabinet and Big Six meetings, and he clearly hadn't paid attention to the status of the Kwantung Army in military briefings, or he would not have reacted to the Soviet invasion the way he did the morning of August 9.

His most important accomplishment as Prime Minister occurred when he, along with Sakomizu and Tōgō, outwitted Toyoda, Umezu, and Amani to convoke the first Imperial Conference. It was that conference where Hirohito expressed his desire to end the war under the terms of the Potsdam Declaration, with the single condition that the national polity be protected.

But even after hearing the Emperor's wishes in the first *seidan*, the hardliners managed to pull Suzuki back into their camp temporarily when the Byrnes note was received. Suzuki only acceded to end the war when Tōgō threatened to go over Suzuki's head and have the Emperor command him to accept the Potsdam Declaration and the Byrnes note, coupled with Kido's prompting.

Sixteen months after his government resigned en masse, the Privy Council chose Suzuki as its Chairman, where he served for just seven months, until June 13, 1946. Suzuki died of natural causes on April 17, 1948, at the age of 80.

SHIGENORI TŌGŌ

No one in the Japanese government worked harder than Tōgō to bring the war to end. He alone understood international diplomacy, Japan's predicament, and the folly of seeking the "good offices" of Soviets, even though he continued those overtures on behalf of his government to the very end. Throughout it all, he confronted the opinions and dangerous beliefs of his peers in the Big Six. Unfortunately for the Japanese, his arguments fell on deaf ears, as the United States methodically razed Japan. That his frustration in dealing with such men never caused him to resign was fortunate for the Japanese; because without him, the war may have lasted for many more months, perhaps years.

Tōgō retired briefly to his home in Karuizawa after his resignation from the Suzuki Cabinet—but once again SCAP interceded, arraigning Tōgō as a Class A war criminal for his participation in the Tōjō government that had started the war. On November 4, 1948, the Tokyo War Crimes Tribunal convicted Tōgō and sentenced him to twenty years imprisonment at Sugamo Prison. During his time in prison Tōgō wrote his memoir, *The Cause of Japan*, which was published posthumously in 1956.

The final words in Tōgō's memoir were:

> Vividly before my eyes is the scene of the Imperial Conference at which the Emperor decided for surrender, and my feeling of then returns to me: that while the future of Japan is eternal, it is a blessing beyond estimation that this most dreadful of wars has been brought to a close, ending our country's agony and saving millions of lives; with that my life's work has been done, it does not matter what befalls me.[12]

Tōgō died in prison on July 23, 1950, at the age of 67.

KORECHIKA ANAMI

Anami acted to prevent the war from ending to the very end, including three times immediately after the second *seidan* on August 14. The actions he seriously considered on the 14th would have subverted the wishes of his Emperor, the "man god" he had sworn to follow and whose words were inviolable.

A supporter of Tōjō in starting Japan's war of conquest, Anami more than any other member of the Big Six deserves credit for prolonging a lost war—and the resulting deaths of hundreds of thousands of Japanese and Asians, and tens of thousands of Allied servicemen. His popularity, far more than his prowess, caused his ascension to War Minister, a role he was ill-suited to hold.

Inside Japan's dysfunctional government, dominated by the military, Anami's power was out of proportion to his abilities. Driven by a belief in the Japanese spirit Yamato-damashii, he was oblivious to the military superiority of his enemy and immune to the suffering of his civilian countrymen.

Anami's question on August 9, 1945, offers perhaps the best insight into his deranged sense of values: "Would it not be wondrous for this whole nation to be destroyed like a beautiful flower?"

Early in the morning of August 15, Anami committed seppuku.

EMPEROR HIROHITO

The clearest indication that Hirohito assented to the commencement of Japan's war of aggression comes from his September 6, 1945, letter to his son Akihito, in which he said, "Let me say a few words about the reasons for our defeat. Our people placed too much confidence in the Empire and held England and America in contempt. Our military placed too much emphasis on spirit and forgot science." There is no expression of remorse for starting the war in the first place anywhere in these lines or in the remainder of the letter.

Emperor Hirohito supported the war and the planned final stand, Ketsu-Gō, until nearly the end, ignoring the abject suffering of His subjects. His greatest contributions came after the atomic bombs, when—impressed by the technological supremacy of his enemy—He expressed His wishes to end the war.

Ironically, it was the very same power the military imbued into their divine Emperor to unite the country and secure the subjugation of the people that essentially forced Anami, Umezu, and Toyoda to accept the Emperor's decree to end the war.

In the final months of the war, Emperor Hirohito seemed more concerned about Himself and the throne than His people. His comment to an aide on April 7, 1945, nearly a month after the onset of the

American fire-bombing campaign against Japan's cities, including the catastrophic Tokyo attack the night of March 9–10, offers proof. With all evidence to the contrary, in terms of the direction of the war, Hirohito said, "I believe the war is certainly winnable if we make our best efforts, but I am anxious about whether or not the people will be able to endure until then."

During the final days of the war, Hirohito placed great importance on securing the Imperial Regalia in His declarations to Kido on July 25 and 31, 1945, ordering the Lord Keeper of the Privy Seal to protect them "at all costs."

If not for Hirohito gaining the peaceful acceptance for the Allied occupation of Japan, the Emperor deserved to be tried as a war criminal. But while Hirohito avoided prosecution by the Allies, His myth of divinity and His power to rule Japan were permanently extinguished after the war.

On September 26, 1971, Hirohito became the first Japanese Emperor to visit the United States and meet with the president. Hirohito died at age 87, on January 7, 1989.

ERNEST J. KING

Fleet Admiral King only reluctantly voted in favor of Operation Downfall during the May 1945 meeting of the Joint Chiefs of Staff and agreed to support it in the follow-up briefing of the president on June 18. After that, he did not have a major role in advising President Truman during the final months of the war. But had the bombs not ended the war, King would have likely forced a new discussion on the advisability of Olympic in an effort to stop the invasion and continue the blockade and bombardment until Japan surrendered.

King retired from active duty just four months after Japan's surrender, on December 15, 1945. He stayed busy early in his retirement, but a stroke in 1947 led to a gradual decline in his health. King published his autobiography, *Fleet Admiral King: A Naval Record*, in 1952. He died of a heart attack on June 25, 1956; he was 77.

GEORGE C. MARSHALL

After George Washington, Marshall remains one of the most respected soldiers in American history. Marshall did not believe the atomic bomb, on its own, would be sufficient to gain Japan's capitulation, and was actively preparing to use several of them as tactical weapons to support Operation Olympic in the fall of 1945. He and King would likely have locked horns in the late summer of 1945 over the incredible Japanese buildup on Kyūshū and the rationale of an invasion under such circumstances.

In the immediate postwar era, Marshall was anything but idle. Truman tapped him as his Secretary of State in January of 1947. During the next two years, he authored a program to help rebuild a shattered Europe; the idea became known as the *Marshall Plan*. For his efforts, he won the Nobel Prize for Peace in 1953.

Truman again looked to Marshall in 1950, this time as his Secretary of Defense, during the Korean War. Marshall finally retired in the fall of 1951 and died October 16, 1959, at the age of 78.

HENRY L. STIMSON

In the lead-up to the Potsdam Conference, Stimson believed a substantial submerged group of Japanese wanted to end the war; he was wrong. He also recommended to Truman that the Japanese be given specific assurances that they could keep the Emperor. While most of his ideas found their way into the Potsdam Declaration, the one allowing the continuation of the Imperial polity did not. Not surprisingly, Stimson, upon receipt of Japan's surrender offer on August 10th, readily agreed to accept. Secretary of State Byrnes did not.

Stimson retired barely a month after the Japanese surrender, and later wrote his memoir, *On Active Service in Peace and War*, with the aid of McGeorge Bundy. It was published in 1948. On October 20, 1950, after experiencing a second heart attack, Stimson passed away at the age of 83.

JAMES F. BYRNES

Byrnes stood alone among the presidential advisers in the Oval Office on August 10 in his insistence to reject the initial surrender offer from the Japanese. As we now know, and as aptly put by historian David Robertson, "Byrnes' digging in his heels on this issue was almost certainly intended by him to apply more to the surrender of Japan than to postwar relations with the Soviet Union."[13]

Byrnes continued to serve as Truman's Secretary of State for another eighteen months until January 21, 1947, the same year he published his memoir, *Speaking Frankly*.

Four years later, in 1951, Byrnes mounted a successful bid to become the governor of South Carolina, serving one term. Byrnes passed away on April 9, 1972, at the age of 89.

WILLIAM D. LEAHY

Leahy said of the atomic bomb:

> Once it had been tested, President Truman faced the decision as to whether to use it. He did not like the idea but was persuaded that it would shorten the war against Japan and save American lives. It is my opinion that the use of this barbarous weapon at Hiroshima and Nagasaki was of no material assistance in our war against Japan. The Japanese were already defeated and ready to surrender because of the effective sea blockade and the successful bombing with conventional weapons. It was my reaction that the scientists and others wanted to make this test because of the vast sums that had been spent on the project. Truman knew that, and so did the other people involved. However, the chief executive made a decision to use the bomb on two cities in Japan.[14]

Leahy's statements about Truman, that "He did not like the idea, but was persuaded that it would shorten the war against Japan and save American lives," and that "The Japanese were already defeated and ready to surrender because of the effective sea blockade and the successful bombing with conventional weapons," have been frequently cited by revisionist historians who say the bombs weren't necessary, and that Truman was unduly influenced by his advisors—in particular Secretary of State Byrnes.

But Leahy was wrong about the Japanese being ready to surrender. The bombs prompted the extraordinary meetings and two Imperial Conferences, between August 9 and the 14, that ultimately led to the Japanese surrender—and even in those meetings the Japanese military hardliners, Anami, Umezu, and Toyoda, wanted to continue the war—or at a minimum demand four conditions to surrender. What was ultimately compelling to the Japanese, Hirohito in particular, was the fact that one plane—versus the hundreds in a conventional attack—could destroy much of a city. And, after discovering that the Americans could produce more than a single atomic bomb, there was a real chance the Americans would no longer invade Japan, making Anami's and the military's grand plans for creating a blood bath during an invasion useless. The Americans could simply continue to drop atomic bombs and never subject themselves to Japan's suicidal defenses.

Leahy continued to serve as Truman's Chief of Staff until March 21, 1949. In 1950, he published his memoir *I Was There*. Leahy died nine years later on July 20, 1959; he was 84.

HARRY S. TRUMAN

Throughout the first four months of Truman's presidency and the final days of World War II, three things motivated him: fulfilling FDR's wartime policies, first among them the unconditional surrender of the Axis powers; ending the war quickly with the least amount of American bloodshed possible; and freeing Allied POWs from their barbaric treatment at the hands of the Japanese.

Truman referenced the treatment of Allied POWs four times during the final weeks of the war: in the Potsdam Declaration (Article 10, mistreatment of our prisoners), in his national radio address on August 9, in Secretary of State Byrnes's reply to Japan's surrender offer, and in the Instrument of Surrender itself.

From the onset of his presidency, Truman proved to be a capable leader. He actively solicited input from his advisors, read every relevant thing he could, and he made his own decisions and accepted the responsibility that came with doing so—contrary to those who have characterized him as inexperienced and easily manipulated. Truman proved to be a quick study, surprising many of those closest to him.

Two years after the war, Truman divested the Army Air Forces from the Army, creating a separate and equal branch of the United States military, the Air Force, on September 18, 1947.

Less than a year later, on July 26, 1948, President Truman desegregated the United States Military. Later that year, Truman won his own term as president, defeating New York Governor Thomas E. Dewey.

Truman continued to experience a tumultuous presidency. He confronted a former ally by approving the *Berlin Airlift* on June 26, 1948, after Stalin cut off the city, which sat in the middle of the Soviet occupation zone. The American airlift finally broke the Soviet blockade eleven months later on May 12, 1949.

As Commander in Chief during the Korean War, in April of 1951, Truman fired an insubordinate General Douglas MacArthur, in perhaps the most famous civilian-military conflict in the history of the United States.

Truman published his two-volume memoir *Harry S. Truman: Year of Decisions Volume 1* and *Harry S. Truman: Years of Trial and Hope 1946–1952 Volume 2* in 1955. He died of pneumonia and multiple organ failure at the age of 88, and he is buried at the presidential library near his home in Independence, Missouri.

MAP OF OPERATION DOWNFALL, THE PROPOSED INVASION OF JAPAN

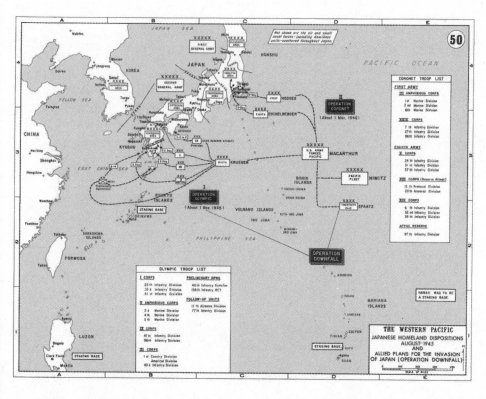

This map depicts the intended courses of attack for Operation Downfall. Operation Olympic constituted the attack on the lower left portion of Japan and Operation Coronet the upper right.

ACKNOWLEDGMENTS

The genesis for this book began in the days following 9/11. I had just returned to my alma mater, the University of Colorado, Denver to commence work on a Masters in History, with intent, after graduation, to teach high school history. My advisor thought as a starting point a class in historiography made the best sense. I chose as the topic for my first historiographic essay, *The American Decision to Drop the Atomic Bomb on Japan.*

Over the ensuing five years it took to complete my degree, one member of the history department's faculty, Professor Gabriel Finkelstein, helped me more than any other. From convincing me I had come too far, during an eighteen-month hiatus, not to finish my degree, to his seemingly endless challenges of my premises on how and why the War in the Pacific ended. Gabriel's questions forced me to do ever more research into the subject. Without his encouragement, pressure, and assistance, it's doubtful the book would have reached fruition, and for that I wish to thank him.

Over the many years I've spent researching this book, I had the good fortune of crossing paths with and interviewing dozens of World War II veterans, who served in all theaters of the war in a wide range of duties. I would like to take this opportunity to thank them all collectively for their service to their country, but I would also like to single out eight men in particular, whose interviews and diary, in one instance, offered much of the inspiration for the first chapter of *140 Days to Hiroshima.* Those men are: Captain Ed Feathers, Lieutenant Jack Alford, Second Lieutenant Homer Bourland, Corporal Elmer Burch, Corporal Ralph Darrow, Dick Field, Chuck Mahoney, and Staff Sergeant Matt Moore, all of whom flew bombing missions against Japan in B-29s and are listed in the Bibliography.

For nearly a year, from November of 2008 to October of 2009, I attended and completed all of PSI Seminars' (Clearlake Oaks, California) personal growth seminars. The firsthand experiences gained during those courses has been and continues to be an invaluable source of empowerment in my life in general and especially in my significant vocational shift from a thirty-year career in Information Technology to a professional historian and writer.

Kazuhiko Tōgō is a retired official at the Ministry of Foreign Affairs in Japan and former Ambassador to the Netherlands. He is also the grandson of Shigenori Tōgō, Japan's Foreign Minister at the onset of Japan's entry into World War II and during the final months leading to its surrender. In December of 2012, I perchance came across a reference to Mr. Tōgō, who was at the time visiting the US, where he was doing some guest lecturing at Temple University about his grandfather's role during the last months of World War II. After securing Mr. Tōgō's email address from Jeffrey Kingston at Temple, I sent a note to Kazuhiko introducing myself and explaining the focus of my research, hoping he would respond. To my surprise and delight he replied to my query a couple days later. During the ensuing seven years, Kazu has answered numerous questions about Shigenori's book, *The Cause of Japan*, (used extensively as a resource in this book), and he has also provided meaningful insights into Japanese thinking during the final months of the war and the relationships between his grandfather and the other members of Japan's Big Six. I would like to express my gratitude for his kind and thoughtful assistance.

In December 2013, I attended the National World War II Museum's annual event in New Orleans. In the course of attending, I was able to meet and spend some time with Richard B. Frank, author of *Downfall: The End of the Imperial Japanese Empire*. Frank's book *Downfall* was one of the first I read on the subject of the invasion, after visiting the Map Room in the Harry S. Truman Presidential Library in Independence Missouri in 2002. His book is widely considered one of the best sources on the topic, and I referred to it often while working on *140 Days to Hiroshima*.

In March of 2016, I was instrumental in bringing Rich to Denver as a featured speaker for a WWII event that Dr. Finkelstein and I sponsored and hosted. In the years since our first meeting, Rich has provided valuable assistance in locating important resources for this book. As I was nearing the completion of the first draft of manuscript in the summer of 2019, Rich agreed, upon my request, to be one of my historical editors. His many recommendations have unquestionably added to the quality of this volume, and for all of the assistance, I am very thankful.

Also, in December of 2013, I began a series of correspondence that has lasted to this day with Dennis (D.M.) Giangreco, at the advice of John T. Kuehn, Ph.D., military history instructor at the U.S. Army Command and General Staff College. Giangreco's original version of *Hell to Pay: Operation DOWNFALL and the Invasion of Japan, 1945-1947,* published in 2009 and the updated and expanded version in 2017, have been essential resources in understanding the American invasion plans, Japan's defensive plan Ketsu-Gō, the potential casualties associated with the invasion, and the myth of a Soviet invasion of Hokkaido, Japan. Like Rich Frank, Dennis too has lent assistance over the past six years aiding my research efforts, and his editing of the historical content, during our numerous phone calls in the past few months, included suggestions and insights that have unquestionably enhanced my book. To Dennis I owe a major debt of appreciation.

As a first-time book author and unproven literary commodity, securing representation to obtain a publishing agreement was an essential milestone. My agent, Leticia Gomez of Savvy Literary Services, was one of the first to believe in the project beyond Gabriel Finkelstein, and was responsible for gaining Diversion Books' interest and helping me negotiate the publishing agreement. I would like to acknowledge her contribution to making the book a reality.

Finally, I would also like to thank the team at Diversion Books and in particular, their editor in chief, Keith Wallman. His belief in the story, in my ability to bring it to life, guidance to a rookie writer with lots of questions, and his contributions verbally and editorially have been invaluable and greatly appreciated.

BIBLIOGRAPHY

Afflerbach, Holger and Strachan, Hew eds. *How Fighting Ends: A History of Surrender.* Oxford: Oxford University Press, 2012.

Alford, Jack, Phone interviews with author, World War II B-29 Experiences, Columbus, MS. and Littleton, CO., 7,11,14 June 2004, 2 November 2004.

Armstrong, Anne. *Unconditional Surrender: The Impact of Casablanca Policy Upon World War II.* New Brunswick: Rutgers University Press, 1961.

Ayers, Eben A. *Truman in the White House: The Diary of Eben A. Ayers,* ed. with commentary by Robert H. Ferrell. Columbia: University of Missouri Press, 1991.

Barnhart, Michael A. *Japan Prepares for Total War: The Search for Economic Security, 1919–1941.* Ithaca and London: Cornell University Press, 1987.

Beasley, W. G. *The Modern History of Japan.* New York: Frederick A. Praeger Inc., 1963.

Beauchamp, Edward R. ed. *History of Contemporary Japan Since World War II.* London: Routledge, 1998.

Bergamini, David. *Japan's Imperial Conspiracy.* New York: William Morrow and Company, Inc., 1971.

Bernstein, Barton J. *The Atomic Bomb: The Critical Issues.* Boston: Little, Brown and Company, 1976.

Bird, Kai and Lifschultz, Lawrence eds. *Hiroshima's Shadow: Writings on the Denial of History and the Smithsonian Controversy.* Stony Creek: The Pamphleteer's Press, 1998.

Bix, Herbert P. *Hirohito and the Making of Modern Japan.* New York: Harper Collins Publishers, 2000.

Borton, Hugh. *Japan's Modern Century: From Perry to 1970*, 2nd ed. New York: The Ronald Press Company, 1970.

Bourland, Homer, Phone interviews and email exchanges with author, World War II B-29 Experiences, Austin, TX. and Littleton, CO., 29, 31 May 2004, 3, 7 June 2004.

Bradley, James. *Flags of Our Fathers: Heroes of Iwo Jima.* New York: Delacorte Press, 2001.

Brooks, Lester. *Behind Japan's Surrender: The Secret Struggle That Ended an Empire.* Stamford: Carpe Veritas Books, De Gustibus Press, Ltd., 1968.

Burch, Elmer. Phone interviews and mail exchanges, World War II B-29 Experiences, Spartanburg, SC. and Littleton, CO., 23 April 2004, 11–12 June 2004, 15 October 2004, 2 November 2004, 3 December 2004.

Burrell, Robert S. *The Ghosts of Iwo Jima.* College Station: Texas A&M University Press, 2006.

Buruma, Ian. *Inventing Japan: 1853–1964.* New York: The Modern Library, 2003.

Buruma, Ian. *The Wages of Guilt: Memories of War in Germany and Japan.* New York: The Penguin Group, 1994.

Butow, Robert J. C. *Japan's Decision to Surrender.* Stanford: Stanford University Press, 1965.

Byrnes, James F. *Speaking Frankly.* New York: Harper & Brothers Publishers, 1947.

Churchill, Winston. *Triumph and Tragedy*. Boston: Houghton-Mifflin, 1953.

Cochran, Bert. *Harry Truman and the Crisis Presidency*. New York: Funk & Wagnalls, 1973.

Coffey, Thomas M. *Imperial Tragedy: The First Days and the Last, Japan's Experience of War, From the Incredible Victories to the Unthinkable Alternatives, December 1941 – August 1945*. New York: The World Publishing Company, 1970.

Coox, Alvin. *Japan: The Final Agony*. New York: Ballantine Books, 1970.

Costello, John. *The Pacific War: 1941–1945*. New York: Perennial, 1981.

Darrow, Ralph, Phone interviews, email exchanges and copies of personal diary, World War II B-29 Experiences, Atwater, CA and Littleton, CO., 23 April 2004, 6 May 2004, 8 June 2004, 2, 11 November 2004.

Daws, Gavan. *Prisoners of the Japanese: POWs of World War II in the Pacific*. New York: Quill William Morrow, 1994.

D'Este, Carlo. *Patton: A Genius for War*. New York: Harper Collins, 1995.

Dower, John W. *War Without Mercy Race and Power in the Pacific War*. New York: Pantheon Books, 1986.

Drea, Edward J. *In the Service of the Emperor*. Lincoln: University of Nebraska Press, 1998.

Drea, Edward J. *MacArthur's ULTRA: Codebreaking and the War Against Japan, 1942–1945*. Lawrence: University Press of Kansas, 1992.

Elsey, George McKee. *An Unplanned Life*. Columbia: University of Missouri Press, 2005.

Feathers, Ed. phone interviews and email exchanges with author, World War II B-29 Experiences, Pensacola, FL. and Littleton, CO., 23 April 2004, 3 June 2004, 27–28 October 2004, 2, 17 November 2004.

Feis, Herbert. *Japan Subdued: The Atomic Bomb and the End of the War in the Pacific*. Princeton: Princeton University Press, 1961.

Ferrell, Robert H. *Off the Record: The Private Papers of Harry S. Truman*. New York: Harper and Row, 1980.

Ferrell, Robert H. (ed.) *Harry S. Truman and the Bomb: A Documentary History*. Worland: High Plains Publishing, 1996.

Field, Dick, In-person interview with author, World War II B-29 Combat Experiences, Haxtun, CO., 16 October 2004.

Frank, Casey. "Truman's Bomb, Our Bomb at Foreclosure." *JD The Fletcher Forum of World Affairs* (May 1995): 131.

Frank, Richard B. *Downfall: The End of the Imperial Japanese Empire*. New York: Penguin Books, 1999.

Frank, Richard B. *Guadalcanal: The Definitive Account of the Landmark Battle*. New York: Random House, 1990.

Frank, Richard B. "Unconditional Surrender: Why Did Japan Quit?" MHQ *The Quarterly Journal of Military History*, Autumn 2015, pp. 28–37.

Fussell, Paul. "Thank God for the Atom Bomb." *The New Republic*, August 1981, p. 9.

Giangreco, D.M. "Casualty Projections for the U.S. Invasions of Japan, 1945-1946: Planning and Policy Implications." Journal of Military History, July 1997, pp. 521-82.

Giangreco, D.M. *Hell to Pay: Operation Downfall and the Invasion of Japan, 1945–1947*. Maryland: Naval Institute Press, 2009.

Giangreco, D.M. *Hell to Pay: Operation Downfall and the Invasion of Japan, 1945–1947, Updated and Expanded*. Maryland: Naval Institute Press, 2017.

Giangreco, D.M., *The Soldier from Independence: A Military Biography of Harry Truman*. Minneapolis: Zenith Press, 2009.

Groves, Leslie M. *Now it Can be Told: The Story of the Manhattan Project.* New York: Da Capo Press, 1962.

Ham, Paul. *Hiroshima Nagasaki: The Real Story of the Atomic Bombings and Their Aftermath.* London: Picador - Macmillan Publishers, 2015.

Hane, Mikiso. *Modern Japan: A Historical Survey, 3rd ed.* Boulder: Westview Press, 2001.

Harris, Sheldon H. *Factories of Death: Japanese Biological Warfare, 1932–45, and the American Cover-up.* London: Routledge, 1994.

Hasegawa, Tsuyoshi. *Racing the Enemy: Stalin, Truman, and the Surrender of Japan.* Cambridge: The Belknap Press of Harvard University Press, 2005.

Henry L. Stimson Diaries, Reel 9, Yale University Library, New Haven; memo to Truman: U. S. Department of State, Foreign Relations of the United States: Conference of Berlin (The Potsdam Conference), 1945 (Washington, D.C.: U.S. Government Printing Office, 1960), 1:888–892.

Herken, Gregg. *The Winning Weapon: The Atomic Bomb in the Cold War, 1945–1950.* New York: Alfred A. Knopf, Inc., 1980.

Hersey, John. *Hiroshima.* New York: Bantam Books, 1946.

Hiroshima (New York: Hallmark Entertainment in Association with Showtime Networks, Inc., and Adelson Entertainment, 1995), video.

Holmes, Linda Goetz. *Unjust Enrichment: How Japan's Companies Built Postwar Fortunes Using American POWs.* Mechanicsburg: Stackpole Books, 2001.

Hoshina, Zenshiro. "Secret History of the Greater East Asia War: Memoir of Zenshiro Hoshina." (Tokyo, Japan: Hara-Shobo, 1975), pp. 139–149.

Hoyt, Edwin P. *Closing the Circle: War in the Pacific: 1945.* New York: Van Nostrand Reinhold Co., 1982.

Hoyt, Edwin P. *How They Won the War in the Pacific: Nimitz and His Admirals*. New York: Weybright and Talley, 1970.

Ienaga, Saburō. *The Pacific War: World War II and the Japanese, 1931–1945*. New York: Pantheon Books, 1978.

Inside the Great Battles: Iwo Jima (New York: The History Channel, 2004), video.

Iriye, Akira. *Power and Culture: The Japanese-American War, 1941–1945*. Cambridge: Harvard University Press, 1981.

www.iwojima.com

Jansen, Marius B. ed. *The Cambridge History of Japan Vol. 5 The Nineteenth Century*. Cambridge: Cambridge University Press, 1989.

Japan's Longest Day: The Dramatic True Story of The End of WWII (Tokyo: Toho Co., Ltd. 2006), video.

Kajima, Morinosuke. *The Emergence of Japan as a World Power, 1895–1925*. Rutland: Charles E. Tuttle Co., 1968.

Kawamura, Noriko. *Emperor Hirohito and the Pacific War*. Seattle: University of Washington Press, 2015.

Kerr, E. Bartlett. *Flames Over Tokyo: The U.S. Army Air Forces' Incendiary Campaign Against Japan, 1944–1945*. New York: Donald I Fine, Inc., 1991.

King, Ernest J. *Fleet Admiral King: A Naval Record*. New York: W. W. Norton & Company, Inc., 1952.

Kort, Michael. *The Columbia Guide to Hiroshima and the Bomb*. New York: Columbia University Press, 2007.

Lawren, William. *The General and the Bomb: A Biography of General Leslie R. Groves, Director of the Manhattan Project*. New York: Dodd, Mead & Company, 1988.

Leahy, Fleet Admiral William D. *I Was There.* New York: Whittlesey House, 1950.

Leckie, Robert. *The Battle for Iwo Jima.* New York: Random House, 1967.

Leckie, Robert. *Strong Men Armed: The United States Marines vs. Japan.* New York: Da Capo Press, 1990.

Lee, Bruce. *Marching Orders: The Untold Story of World War II.* New York: Crown Publishers, Inc. 1995.

Leighton, Richard M. ed. *Global Logistics and Strategy,* V. II, Washington, D.C.: Office of the Chief of Military History, Department of the Army, 1955–1968.

LeMay, General Curtis E. and Yenne, Bill. *Superfortress: The Story of the B-29 and American Air Power.* New York: McGraw-Hill Book Company, 1988.

Lewin, Ronald. *The American Magic: Codes, Ciphers and The Defeat of Japan.* New York: Farrar Straus Giroux, 1982.

Liska, Joan Moore, Email exchanges with author, Father's diary regarding his World War II B-29 Experiences, Middletown, CT. and Littleton, CO., 22 August 2003.

MacEachin, Douglas J. *The Final Months of the War with Japan: Signals Intelligence, US Invasion Planning and the A-Bomb Decision.* Washington: Central Intelligence Agency, 1998.

Maddox, Robert James. *Weapons for Victory: The Hiroshima Decision Fifty Years Later.* Columbia: University of Missouri Press, 1995.

Maga, Timothy P. *America Attacks Japan: The Invasion That Never Was.* Lexington: The University of Kentucky, 2002.

Mahoney, Chuck, In-person interview with author, World War II B-29 Combat Experiences, Aurora, CO., 22 October 2004.

Marshall, George C., Arnold H.H., King, Ernest J. *The War Reports of General of the Army George C. Marshall, General of the Army H. H. Arnold, Fleet Admiral Ernest J. King,* First edition. Philadelphia: J. B. Lippincott Company, 1947.

McCullough, David. *Truman.* New York: Simon & Schuster, 1992.

Michno, Gregory F. *Death on the Hellships: Prisoners at Sea in The Pacific War.* Annapolis: Naval Institute Press, 2001.

Morrison, Wilbur H. *Hellbirds: The Story of the B-29's in Combat.* New York: Duell, Sloan & Pearce, 1960.

Myers, Ramon H. and Peattie, Mark R. ed. *The Japanese Colonial Empire, 1895–1945.* Princeton: Princeton University Press, 1984.

O'Brien, Phillips Payson. *The Second Most Powerful Man in the World.* New York: Dutton, 2019.

O'Connor, Raymond G. *Diplomacy for Victory: FDR and Unconditional Surrender.* New York: W.W. Norton Company, Inc., 1971.

Our Century: Iwo Jima, Hell's Volcano (New York: The History Channel, 2001), video.

Our Century: Okinawa: The Final Battle (New York: The History Channel, 2001), video.

Pape, Robert A. "Why Japan Surrendered." *International Security* 18.2 (Autumn 1993): 154–201.

Perret, Geoffrey. *Old Soldiers Never Die: The Life of Douglas MacArthur.* New York: Random House, 1966.

Polmar, Norman and Allen, Thomas B. *World War II: The Encyclopedia of the War Years, 1941–1945.* New York: Random House, 1996.

Potter, E. B. *Nimitz.* Annapolis: Naval Institute Press, 1976.

Pyle, Kenneth B. *The New Generation in Meiji Japan: Problems of Cultural Identity.* Stanford: Stanford University Press, 1969.

Rhodes, Richard. *The Making of the Atomic Bomb.* New York: Simon & Schuster, 1986.

Robertson, David. *Sly and Able: A Political Biography of James F. Byrnes.* New York: W.W. Norton & Company, 1994.

Ross, Stewart Halsey. *Strategic Bombing by the United States in World War II: The Myths and the Facts.* Jefferson: McFarland, 2002.

Schaller, Michael. *Douglas MacArthur: The Far Eastern General.* New York: Oxford University Press, 1989.

Sherry, Michael S. *The Rise of American Air Power: The Creation of Armageddon.* New Haven: Yale University Press, 1987.

Sherwin, Martin. *A World Destroyed: Hiroshima and the Origins of the Arms Race.* New York: Vintage Books, 1987.

Shinsaku Sogo, in person interviews and email exchanges with author, Personal Experience of Tokyo Fire Raid Account March 9–10, 1945, Denver, CO., 22 August 2004, 2, 11, 20 November 2004.

Sides, Hampton. *Ghost Soldiers: The Forgotten Epic Story of World War II's Most Dramatic Mission.* New York: Doubleday, 2001.

Sigal, Leon V. *Fighting to a Finish: The Politics of War Termination in the United States and Japan, 1945.* Ithaca: Cornell University Press, 1988.

Skates, John Ray. *The Invasion of Japan: Alternative to the Bomb.* Columbia: University of South Carolina Press, 1994.

Smith, Jim and McConnell, Malcolm. *The Last Mission: The Secret History of World War II's Final Battle.* New York: Broadway Books, 2002.

Stimson, Henry L. and Bundy, McGeorge. *On Active Service in Peace and War.* New York: Harper, 1948.

Stoff, Michael B. ed. *The Manhattan Project: A Documentary Introduction to the Atomic Age.* Philadelphia: Temple University Press, 1991.

Stoler, Mark A. *Allies and Adversaries: The Joint Chiefs of Staff, The Grand Alliance, and U.S. Strategy in World War II.* Chapel Hill: The University of North Carolina Press, 2000.

Storry, Richard. *The Double Patriots: A Study of Japanese Nationalism.* Westport: Greenwood Press, Publishers, 1957.

The Army Air Forces in World War II. Vol. V: *The Pacific: Matterhorn to Nagasaki, June 1944 to August 1945.* Chicago: University of Chicago Press, 1953.

The Pacific War Research Society. *Japan's Longest Day.* Tokyo: Kodansha International, 1968.

The Pacific War Research Society. *The Day Man Lost – Hiroshima, 6 August 1945.* Tokyo: Kodansha International, 1981.

The United States Strategic Bombing Survey: Japan's Struggle to End the War. Chairman's Office 1 July 1946.

The War Reports of General George C. Marshall Chief of Staff, General H. H. Arnold Commanding General Army Air Forces, and Ernest J. King Commander-in-Chief United States Fleet and Chief of Naval Operations. Philadelphia: J. B. Lippincott Company, 1947.

Thomas, James O. "Fire from the Sky." *The Retired Officer Magazine* (May 1994): 38–41.

Tibbets, Paul W. *The Return of the Enola Gay.* United States: Mid Coast, 1998.

Tillman, Barrett. *Whirlwind: The Air War Against Japan, 1942–1945.* New York: Simon & Schuster, 2010.

Tōgō, Shigenori. *The Cause of Japan*. New York: Simon and Schuster, 1956.

Toland, John. *The Rising Sun: The Decline and Fall of the Japanese Empire, 1936–1945*. Vol. 2. New York: Random House, 1970.

Truman: A Simple Man, A Legendary President (New York: HBO Home Video, 1999), video.

Truman, Harry S. *Volume One: Year of Decisions*. Garden City: Doubleday and Company, 1955.

Truman, Margaret. *Harry S. Truman*. New York: Avon Books, 1972.

Tsurumi, Shunsuke. *An Intellectual History of Wartime Japan: 1931–1945*. London: KPI, 1986.

U.S. National Archives, Record Group 77, Records of the Office of the Chief of Engineers, Manhattan Engineer District, TS Manhattan Project File '42–'46, Folder 5B (Directives, Memos, etc. to and from C/S, S/W, etc.).

U.S. National Archives, Record Group 77, Records of the Office of the Chief of Engineers, Manhattan Engineer District, TS Manhattan Project File '42–'46, folder 5D Selection of Targets, 2 Notes on Target Committee Meetings.

United States. Reports of General MacArthur: Japanese Operations in the Southwest Pacific Area. Compiled by Japanese Demobilization Bureaux Records. Vol. II. Part II. Department of the Army, 1994.

Victory in the Pacific: Death Before Surrender (Boston: *American Experience*, PBS Home Video, 2005), video.

Walker, J. Samuel. *Prompt and Utter Destruction: Truman and the Use of Atomic Bombs Against Japan*. Chapel Hill: The University of North Carolina Press, 1997.

Wilcox, Robert K. *Japan's Secret War: Japan's Race Against Time to Build its Own Atomic Bomb*. New York: Marlowe & Company, 1995.

Winters, Francis X. *Remembering Hiroshima: Was it Just?* New York: Ashgate Publishing, 2009.

Zeiler, Thomas W. *Unconditional Defeat: Japan, America, and the End of World War II*. Wilmington: Scholarly Resources Inc., 2004.

Zhukov, Georgii Konstantinovich. *The Memoirs of Marshal Zhukov*. New York: Delacorte Press, 1971.

NOTES

Whenever available, I have doubled-noted sources used in this book, i.e., the primary source followed by the secondary source where I found the information. The primary sources are quoted word for word from the secondary source. Robert J. C. Butow's book, *Japan's Decision to Surrender*, published by Stanford University Press in 1954, is a good example.

Alternatively, I have also used some very well-known secondary resources who did not provide the specific detailed descriptions of their primary sources in their footnotes or endnotes, but rather included lists of their sources. Below is a list of those authors along with a brief account of their respective works.

Brooks, Lester. *Behind Japan's Surrender: The Secret Struggle That Ended an Empire.* Stamford: Carpe Veritas Books, De Gustibus Press, Ltd., 1968, forward by Fumihiko Tōgō (Secretary and son-in-law to Shigenori Tōgō).

Lester Brooks served in the US Army in the Pacific during World War II and was stationed at Supreme Commander for the Allied Powers (SCAP) General Headquarters (GHQ), General Douglas MacArthur's headquarters for the occupation, across from the Imperial Palace in Tokyo. Brooks lists three sources in his bibliography: I. Records and Documents, II. Books, Articles, Documentaries, and III. Interviews. Under III. Interviews, Brooks conducted thirty personal interviews of eyewitnesses in 1965. That material was further expanded by: transcripts from 1965 interviews of other witnesses provided by the National Broadcasting Company (NBC); General MacArthur's Military History Section, 2 volumes of unpublished "Statements of Japanese Officials on World War II"; "Interrogations of Japanese Officials" by United States Strategic Bombing Survey (USSBS) immediately after Japan's surrender; and the Tokyo Trials—the International Military Tribunal for the Far East, which lasted more than two years and included testimony from nearly every significant figure in Japanese political and military life. "From these invaluable sources have come the actual words of the men who led the Imperial Japan in its final days."

Toland, John. *The Rising Sun: The Decline and Fall of the Japanese Empire, 1936–1945.* Volumes 1 and 2. New York: Random House, 1970. Note: Published two years earlier, Lester Brooks's book is included in Toland's bibliography.

This Pulitzer Prize–winning history of World War II chronicles the dramatic rise and fall of the Japanese empire, from the invasion of Manchuria and China to the atomic bombings of Hiroshima and Nagasaki, told from the Japanese perspective.

The Pacific War Research Society. *Japan's Longest Day*. Tokyo: Kodansha International, 1968.

The authors: Made up of fourteen members, the Pacific War Research Society is a group of Japanese historians who devoted years to the research involved in preparing *Japan's Longest Day*. The authors drew heavily on interviews with eyewitnesses of the drama that unfolded on that historic day: over one year alone was spent on interviewing and crosschecking the accounts of seventy-nine of the men who took part in the decision to surrender.

Each of the four books mentioned above were used extensively to document the dialog of Japan's leading men during the final days of the empire.

Prologue
1 Richard B. Frank, *Downfall: The End of the Imperial Japanese Empire. (Penguin Books, 1999)*, 89.
2 Frank, *Downfall*, 89.

Chapter 1: Tokyo Burn Job
1. Ernest J. King, *Fleet Admiral King: A Naval Record*. (W.W. Norton & Company, 1952), 596.
2. Barrett Tillman, *Whirlwind: The Air War Against Japan 1942-1945*. (Simon & Schuster, 2010), 135.
3. Tillman, *Whirlwind*, 135.
4. Curtis E. LeMay, and Bill Yenne, *Superfortress: The Boeing B-29 and American Airpower in World War II*. (Westholme Publishing, LLC, 1988), 130.
5. Stewart Halsey Ross, *Strategic Bombing by the United States in World War II: The Myths and the Facts*. (McFarland, 2002), 107-108.
6. Tillman, *Whirlwind*, 136-137.
7. E. Bartlett Kerr. *Flames Over Tokyo: The U.S. Army Air Forces' Incendiary Campaign Against Japan 1944-1945*. (Donald I. Fine, 1991), 5.
8. Ed Feathers, phone interviews and email exchanges with author, World War II B-29 Experiences, Pensacola, FL. and Littleton, CO., 23 April 2004, 3 June 2004, 27-28 October 2004, 2, 17 November 2004.
9. Ralph Darrow, phone interviews, email exchanges and copies of personal diary, World War II B-29 Experiences, Atwater, CA and Littleton, CO., 23 April 2004, 6 May 2004, 8 June 2004, 2, 11 November 2004.
10. Kerr, *Flames Over Tokyo*, 170-171.
11. Ibid., 171.
12. Tillman, *Whirlwind*, 147.
13. Kerr, *Flames Over Tokyo*, 178.
14. Bitter's observation and geography of Tokyo: Mark, "Black Snow and Leaping Tigers," p. 152; Tillitse, "When Bombs Rained Upon Us in Tokyo," p. 82; USSBS, *Air Raid Protection and Allied Subjects Tokyo*, p. 3; Kato, *The Lost War*, P. 210; Guillain, *I Saw Tokyo Burning*, pp. 176, 183. "Inflammability is probably the chief qualification" and features of building construction: Daniels, "Great Tokyo Air Raid," p. 117; USSBS, *Field Report Covering Air Raid Protection and Allied Subjects Tokyo*, pp. 3, 72; Edoin, *The Night Tokyo Burned*, p. 96. Incendiary munitions and their appearance: Martin, "Black Snow and Leaping Tigers," p. 155; Guillain, *I*

Saw Tokyo Burning, p. 184; Twenty-first Bomber Command Mission Report, no. 40, Consolidated Statistical Summary, "Disposition of Bombs" [hereafter XXI BC MR, no. 40.]; E. Bartlett Kerr, *Flames Over Tokyo: the U.S. Army Air Forces' Incendiary Campaign Against Japan, 1944–1945* (New York: Donald I. Find, 1991) p. 340. Frank, *Downfall*, 6-7.

15. James O. Thomas, "Fire from the Sky." *The Retired Officer Magazine* (May 1994). 40.

16. Thomas, "Fire from the Sky, 40.

17. Homer Bourland, phone interviews and email exchanges with author, World War II B-29 Experiences, Austin, TX. and Littleton, CO., 29, 31 May 2004, 3, 7 June 2004.

18. Elmer Burch, interviews and mail exchanges, 23 April 2004, 11-12 June 2004, 15 October 2004, 2 November 2004, 3 December 2004.

19. Bourland, phone interviews and email exchanges, 29, 31 May 2004, 3, 7 June 2004.

20. Bourland, phone interviews and email exchanges, 29, 31 May 2004, 3, 7 June 2004.

21. Chuck Mahoney, in person interview with author, World War II B-29 Combat Experiences, Aurora, CO., 22 October 2004.

22. Thomas, "Fire from the Sky." 41.

23. Shinsaku Sogo, interviews and email exchanges, fifteen-year-old Tokyo resident March 10, 1945. Denver, CO., August 22, 2004, October 27, 2004.

24. John Toland, *The Rising Sun: The Decline and Fall of the Japanese Empire 1936-1945.* (Random House, 1970), 759.

25. Toland, *The Rising Sun,* 759.

26. Tillman, *Whirlwind,* 149.

27. Toland, *The Rising Sun,* 760.

28. Sogo, in person interviews and email exchanges, 22 August 2004, 2, 11, 20 November 2004.

29. Toland, *The Rising Sun,* 761.

30. Ibid., 760-761.

31. Ibid., 761.

32. David Bergamini, *Japan's Imperial Conspiracy.* (William Morrow and Company, Inc., 1971), 1038-1039.

33. Tillman, *Whirlwind,* 151.

34. Accounts of Kinosuke Wakabayahi, Miwa Koshiba, Exhibit D: Edoin, *The Night Tokyo Burned*, pp. 61-62, 73-74, p. 87; Kato, *The Lost War*, p. 211 and 215; Daniels, "Great Tokyo Air Raid," p. 125; USSBS, *Air Raid Protection and Allied Subjects Tokyo*, p. 63. Guillain, *I Saw Tokyo Burning*, p. 176. Frank, *Downfall*, 13.

35. Frank, *Downfall*, 13.

36. "The entire river surface": Edoin, *The Night Tokyo Burned*, p. 100. "Staked in neat precision": Ibid., pp. 100-101. Frank, *Downfall*, 15.

37. Frank, *Downfall*, 15.

38. Medical condition of survivors: Havens, *Valley of Darkness*, p. 180; Edoin, *The Night Tokyo Burned*, pp. 103-5; Daniels, "Great Tokyo Air Raid," p. 126. "One some broad streets": Kato, *The Lost War*, p. 215; USSBS Morale Division, *The Effects of*

Strategic Bombing on Japanese Morale, Jun 47, pp. 36-37 (statement by unidentified official of the Police Bureau, Ministry of Home Affairs). Calculations of material destruction: Edoin, *The Night Tokyo Burned*, pp. 101-2, 106; USSBS, *Air Raid Protection and Allied Subjects Tokyo*, p. 1, Exhibit D, report of Archives Section of Ministry of Home Affairs; XXI BC MR, no. 40, pp. 33-38; Daniels, "Great Tokyo Air Raid," pp. 127-29; Tillitse, "When Bombs Rained on Us in Tokyo," p. 85. Frank Downfall, 16.

39. Toland, *The Rising Sun*, 764.

40. Frank, *Downfall*, 17.

41. Toland, *The Rising Sun*, 762.

42. Herbert P. Bix, *Hirohito and the Making of Modern Japan*. (Harper Collins Publishers, 2000), 491

43. Tillman, *Whirlwind*, 157-158.

44. United States Strategic Bombing Survey, Summary Report, Pacific War, Washington, D.C. July 1, 1946, 21.

45. United States Strategic Bombing Survey, Summary Report, Pacific War, 21.

Chapter 2: A Third Prime Minister in Less Than a Year

1. W. G. Beasley, *The Modern History of Japan*. (Palgrave Macmillan; 3rd edition, 2000), 102.

2. Edward Drea, *Japan's Imperial Army: Its Rise and Fall, 1853-1945*. (University of Kansas Press, 2009), 119.

3. *The Cambridge History of Japan Vol. 5 The Nineteenth Century*. (Cambridge University Press, 1989), 620.

4. Ian Burma, *Inventing Japan, 1853-1964*. (The Modern Library, 2003), 23.

5. Ian Burma, *Inventing Japan, 1853-1964*, 83.

6. Ibid., 84.

7. Shunsuke Tsurumi, *An Intellectual History of Wartime Japan: 1931-1945*, (Routledge, 2010), 29.

8. Frank, *Downfall*, 88-89.

9. Bix, *Hirohito*, 370.

10. Bergamini, *Japan's Imperial Conspiracy*, 66.

11. Ibid., 1012.

12. Ibid., 1013.

13. Ibid., 1014.

14. Ibid., 66.

15. United States Strategic Bombing Survey: Japan's Struggle to End the War, (U.S. Government Printing Office, July 1, 1946), Harry S. Truman Administration, Elsey Papers, 10.

16. United States Strategic Bombing Survey: Japan's Struggle to End the War, 10.

17. Bix, *Hirohito*, 493.

18. Diary of Colonel Ogata Kenichi, military aide-de-camp, February 14, 1945, in Nakao, Showa tenno hatsugen kiroku shusei, 2:323. Noriko Kawamura, *Emperor Hirohito and The Pacific War*. (University of Washington Press, 2015), 142.

19. Bix, *Hirohito*, 429

20. Frank, *Downfall*, 91.

21. Noriko Kawamura, *Emperor Hirohito and The Pacific War*. (University of

Washington Press, 2015), 63.

22. Michael Kort, *The Columbia Guide to Hiroshima and the Bomb.* (Columbia University Press, 2007), 359.

23. Kawamura, *Emperor Hirohito,* 149.

24. United States Strategic Bombing Survey, Summary Report, Pacific War, 19.

25. Ibid., 19.

26. Frank, *Downfall,* 92.

27. Lester Brooks, *Behind Japan's Surrender: The Secret Struggle That Ended an Empire.* (Carpe Veritas Books, 1968), 42.

28. Brooks, *Behind Japan's Surrender,* 43.

29. Shigenori Tōgō, *The Cause of Japan.* (Simon and Schuster, 1956), 279.

30. Frank, *Downfall,* 92.

31. Drea, *In the Service of the Emperor,* 203.

32. Frank, *Downfall,* 92.

33. Drea, *In the Service of the Emperor,* 203.

34. Brooks, *Behind Japan's Surrender,* 48.

35. Ibid. , 45-48.

36. Drea, *In the Service of the Emperor,* 204.

37. Toland, *The Rising Sun,* 540.

38. Frank, *Downfall,* 93.

39. Toland, *The Rising Sun,* 547.

40. Brooks, *Behind Japan's Surrender,* 53-54.

41. Drea, *In the Service of the Emperor,* 203.

42. Ibid., 93.

43. Robert J. C. Butow, *Japan's Decision to Surrender.* (Stanford University Press, 1967), 83.

44. The Pacific War Research Society. *Japan's Longest Day.* (Kodansha International, 1968), 15.

45. Brooks, *Behind Japan's Surrender,* 35.

46. Hotta, *Japan 1941,* 216.

47. Tōgō, *The Cause of Japan,* 11.

48. Bix, *Hirohito,* 420.

49. Ibid., 421.

50. Saburō Ienaga, *The Pacific War: World War II and Japanese, 1931-1945.* (Pantheon Books, 1978), 154.

51. Brooks, *Behind Japan's Surrender,* 38.

52. Frank, *Downfall,* 5.

53. Tōgō, *The Cause of Japan,* 268.

54. Ibid., 269.

55. Ibid., 269.

56. Ibid., 269.

57. Ibid., 269.

58. Ibid., 270.

59. Ibid., 270.

60. Ibid., 270.

61. Ibid., 270-271.

62. Ibid., 271.

63. Ibid., 271.

Chapter 3: A New President Gets Up to Speed

1. David McCullough, *Truman*. (Simon & Schuster, 1992), 350.

2. Carlo D'Este, *Patton A Genius for War*. (Harper Collins, 1995), 254.

3. D.M. Giangreco, *The Soldier from Independence: A Military Biography of Harry Truman*. (Zenith Press, 2009) xii.

4. McCullough, *Truman*, 346

5. Ibid., 347

6. Ibid., 347.

7. Ibid., 347.

8. Richard Rhodes, *The Making of the Atomic Bomb*. (Simon and Schuster, 1986), 621.

9. "Truman Life and Times Exhibit - Truman Presidential Museum & Library." *Truman Library: Telegram, George Kennan to James Byrnes ["Long Telegram"], February 22, 1946. Elsey Papers, Harry S. Truman Administration File. Foreign Relations – Russia (1946 – Report "American Relations with the Soviet Union") [1 of 13].*, 2017, www.trumanlibrary.org/lifetimes/senate.htm.

10. Michael B. Stoff et al., ed., *The Manhattan Project: A Documentary Introduction to the Atomic Age* (Temple University Press, 1991), 162.

11. Rhodes, *The Making of the Atomic Bomb*, 617.

12. Harry S. Truman, *Memoirs by Harry S. Truman: Year of Decisions*. Volume One. (Doubleday and Company, 1955), 17.

13. William D. Leahy, *I Was There: The Personal story of the Chief of Staff to presidents Roosevelt and Truman based on his notes and diaries made at the time*. (Whittlesey House, 1950), 347.

14. Norman Polmar and Thomas B. Allen, *World War II: The Encyclopedia of the War Years 1941-1945*. (Random House, 1996), 45-46.

15. Polmar and Allen, *World War II*. 45-46.

16. History.com Editors, "George C. Marshall," *History.com*, A&E Television Networks, 21 Aug. 2018, www.history.com/topics/george-c-marshall.

17. Polmar and Allen, *World War II*.45-46.

18. Richard B. Frank, *Guadalcanal: The Definitive Account of the Landmark Battle*. (Random House, 1990), 4.

19. https://www.history.navy.mil/browse-by-topic/people/chiefs-of-naval-operations/fleet-admiral-ernest-j–king.html

20. Truman, *Memoirs by Harry S. Truman: Year of Decisions*, 17.

21. Truman, *Memoirs by Harry S. Truman: Year of Decisions*, 18.

22. Ibid., 18.

23. Ibid., 18.

24. Ibid., 18.

25. Schulz, Luke. "Fleet Admiral William D. Leahy." *Military History of the Upper Great Lakes*, Michigan Tech, 16 Oct. 2016, ss.sites.mtu.edu/mhugl/2016/10/16/fleet-admiral-william-d-leahy/.

26. Phillips Payson O'Brien, *The Second Most Powerful Man in the World: The Life of Admiral William D. Leahy, Roosevelt's Chief of Staff*. (Dutton, 2019), 178-179.

27. Leahy, *I Was There*, 348.

28. Ibid., 348-349.

29. Truman, *Memoirs by Harry S. Truman: Year of Decisions*, 41.

30. Frank, Richard B. "Unconditional Surrender: Why Did Japan Quit?" MHQ *The Quarterly Journal of Military History*, 2015, pp. 30.

31. O'Connor, *Diplomacy for Victory*, 2-3.

32. Ibid., 3.

33. Ibid., 3

34. Ibid., 4

35. Tasker H. Bliss, "The Armistice," American Journal of International Law, XVI (1922), 520. O'Connor, *Diplomacy for Victory*, 5.

36. Raymond G O'Connor, *Diplomacy for Victory*. (W. W. Norton & Company, 1971), 6.

37. August 15, 1944, FDR Press Conferences, microfilm, roll 12, vol. 24, frames 50-51.

38. O'Connor, *Diplomacy for Victory*, 35.

39. Leahy, *I Was There*, 351-352.

40. Ibid., 352.

41. Richard Rhodes, *The Making of the Atomic Bomb.*, 623.

42. McCullough, *Truman*, 376.

43. Rhodes, *The Making of the Atomic Bomb*, 624.

45. McCullough, *Truman*, 377.

46. Rhodes, *The Making of the Atomic Bomb*, 624.

47. Truman, *Memoirs by Harry S. Truman: Year of Decisions*, 87.

48. William Lawren, *The General and the Bomb: A Biography of General Leslie R. Groves, Director of the Manhattan Project*. (Dodd, Mead & Company, 1988), 60.

49. Lawren, *The General and the Bomb*, 194.

50 Ibid., 194-195.

51 McCullough, *Truman*, 378.

52 .Truman, *Memoirs by Harry S. Truman: Year of Decisions*, 87.

53. *"James F. Byrnes."* Atomic Heritage Foundation, 2018, www.atomicheritage. org/profile/james-f-byrnes.

54. *"James F. Byrnes."* Atomic Heritage Foundation, 2018, www.atomicheritage. org/profile/james-f-byrnes.

55. *"James F. Byrnes."* Atomic Heritage Foundation, 2018, www.atomicheritage. org/profile/james-f-byrnes.

56. *"James F. Byrnes."* Atomic Heritage Foundation, 2018, www.atomicheritage. org/profile/james-f-byrnes.

57. *"James F. Byrnes."* Atomic Heritage Foundation, 2018, www.atomicheritage. org/profile/james-f-byrnes.

Chapter 4: Planning for the Invasion of Japan

1. Butow, *Japan's Decision to Surrender*, 82.

2. See *Statements*: Suezawa #62051 and Sakomizu #61979. Suezawa seems to suggest that, if any secretary objected to a decision reached by the assistant secretaries, the decision would go back to the latter before coming up for discussion at a meeting of the secretaries. Butow, *Japan's Decision to Surrender*, 82.

3. Kawamura, *Emperor Hirohito and The Pacific War*, 31.

4. Butow, *Japan's Decision to Surrender*, 82-83.

5. It was from about this time on that Matsudaira (Yasumasa), Matsutani (Makoto), Takagi (Sōkichi), Kase (Toshikazu) circle assumed importance. Early in January 1945, the four, who theretofore had worked independently of each other, began meeting together frequently so as to coordinate their activities and concentrate their efforts. After May 1945 their liaison work became especially important. Their advice as well as their information seems to have confirmed and strengthened the end the war sentiment of their superiors (Kido, Suzuki, Yonai, and Tōgō)—the men on whom the fate of the nation rested. Interview with Marquis Matsudaira and Admiral Takagi, Tokyo, July 30, 1951; interview with Colonel Matsutani, Tokyo, March 10, 1952; IMTFE: Kido, 31224–26; *Statements*: Matsudaira #61636; and Kase, Journey to the Missouri, 146–47. Butow, *Japan's Decision to Surrender*, 82-83.

6. Bix, *Hirohito and the Making of Modern Japan*, 485.

7. Kido felt "that so long as Germany remained in the war Japan would be in danger of a military coup in the event firm and positive steps were taken immediately to end the war." (See USSBS, *Japan's Struggle to End the War*, 6.) Although this argument is stronger than the one referring to Japan's treaty obligations, Kido's remarks merely explain why Japan did not seek a termination of the war *prior* to Germany's collapse but do not explain Japan's failure to be prepared to end the war *at the time of the German capitulation*. Butow, *Japan's Decision to Surrender*, 79.

8. The phrase, "self-existence and self-defense," which also appeared in the Suzuki statement of May 3, is a recapitulation of an idea expressed in the December 8, 1941, Imperial rescript declaring war: "Our Empire for its existence and self-defense has no other recourse but to appeal to arms to crush every obstacle in its path." See *Contemporary Japan*, XIV (April-December 1945), 158-59. Butow, *Japan's Decision to Surrender*, 79.

9. Toland, *The Rising Sun*, 838-839.

10. Toland, *The Rising Sun*, 839-840.

11. The International Military Tribunal for the Far East (IMTFE_ document #54483. Toland, *The Rising Sun: The Decline and Fall of the Japanese Empire*, 840.

12. Tōgō, *The Cause of Japan*, 260.

13. Butow, *Japan's Decision to Surrender*, 83.

14. Tōgō, *The Cause of Japan*, 284.

15. Butow, *Japan's Decision to Surrender*, 77.

16. Tōgō, *The Cause of Japan*, 284.

17. Ibid., 285.

18. Ibid., 267.

19. Kawamura, *Emperor Hirohito*, 141.

20 Tōgō, *The Cause of Japan*, 279.

21. Bix, *Hirohito and the Making of Modern Japan*, 506.

22. Tōgō, *The Cause of Japan*, 281.

23. Ibid., 284.

24. Butow, *Japan's Decision to Surrender*, 77.

25. Tōgō, *The Cause of Japan*. 285.

26. Ibid., 285.
27. Ibid., 285-286.
28. Ibid., 286.
29. Ibid., 266.
30. Ibid., 286.
31. Butow, *Japan's Decision to Surrender,* 84.
32. Tōgō, *The Cause of Japan,* 287.
33. Ibid., 287-288.
34. Ibid., 288.
35. Ibid., 288.
36. Ibid., 288.
37. Ibid., 288.
38. Ibid., 288.
39. Ibid., 288.
40. PBS Home Video, *Victory in the Pacific: American Experience.*
41. Summary of Redeployment Forecast, March 14, 1945. Demobilization Branch, plans and Operation Division, Army Service Forces, call no N8864. Combined Arms Research Library (CARL), Fort Leavenworth, Kansas. Kort, *The Columbia Guide to Hiroshima and the Bomb,* 241-242.
42. Mark Stoler, *Allies and Adversaries – The Joint Chiefs of Staff, The Grand Alliance, and U.S. Strategy in World War II.* (The University of North Carolina Press, 2000), 702.
43. Frank, Guadalcanal: The Definitive Account of the Landmark Battle, 614.
44. Stoler, *Allies and Adversaries,* 702.
45. John Ray Skates, *The Invasion of Japan Alternative to the Bomb.* (University of South Carolina Press, 1994), 167.
46. Ibid., 167.
47. Stoler, *Allies and Adversaries,* 702.
48. Ibid., 703.
49. Frank, *Downfall,* 117.
50. A.J. Baime, *The Accidental President: Harry S. Truman and the Four Months That Changed the World.* (Houghton Mifflin Harcourt, 2017), 217-218.
51. Frank, , 117-118.
52. Ibid., 118.
53. Ibid., 118.
54. Skates, *The Invasion of Japan Alternative to the Bomb,* 167.
55. Ibid., 167.
56. Frank, Richard B. "Unconditional Surrender: Why Did Japan Quit?" MHQ *The Quarterly Journal of Military History,* 2015, pp. 30.
57. Giangreco, *Hell to Pay: Operation Downfall and the Invasion of Japan, 1945-1947,* 54.
58. Memorandum on Ending the Japanese War, 5.30.1945. Truman Library.
59. Frank, *Downfall,* 216.
60. Ibid., 216.
61. It is impossible to determine whether the "Conclusions" were written by the chief of the Plans Coordination Bureau or by an assistant secretary representing

the cabinet. To what extent the person who drafted the "Conclusions" was coerced into doing so—and to what extent he was a free-agent—is also open to question. There can be no doubt, however, that the "Conclusions" were an afterthought, written in order to reconcile the trouble-laden content of the two appraisals with the recommendations set forth in the "Fundamental Policy." See *Statements*: Suezawa #62051, Matsudaira #60745, Sone #60999, Toyoda #57669, Sakomizu #62003 and #62016. Butow, *Japan's Decision to Surrender*, 95.

62. Toland, *The Rising Sun*, 842.

63. The possibility of winning an operational victory and of thereby obtaining terms favorable to Japan became a key point in the military's demand to continue the war through an Allied invasion of the home islands. In this connection, see *Statements*: Suezawa #62051, Amano #54480, and Toyoda #61340. Butow, *Japan's Decision to Surrender*, 95.

64. In addition to the references cited previously in connection with the Supreme Council meeting of June 6, see *Statements*: Tōgō #50304; Yoshizumi #54484; and Sakomizu #61969, #62003, #62004, and #62006. Butow, *Japan's Decision to Surrender*, 97.

65. Toland, *The Rising Sun*, 842.

66. At the Supreme Council meeting on June 6, Vice-Admiral Hoshina had said that each person present should put forth his best efforts and that if anyone failed he should be prepared to commit suicide. Although Suzuki repeated this thought to the cabinet on June 7, he was forced to retract his statements after Minister of Agriculture and Commerce Ishiguro vigorously protested. See *Statements*: Hoshina #61978; JFO MS: Ch. 28 (Sensō kansui yōkō no kettei), especially "'Sensō shidō no kihon taikō' kakugi kettei ni tai suru sōri no shoken" and "Shimomura, *Shūsenki*'" and Translations: Doc, #53440–F. Butow, *Japan's Decision to Surrender*, 99.

67. Butow, *Japan's Decision to Surrender*, 97.

68. While the secretaries were urging Tōgō to improved relations Soviet Union, Ambassador Harriman in Moscow was cabling Washington that Stalin's armies fully on the Manchurian frontier by August 8—ready to launch their attack on Japan's Kwantung army. See Millis (ed.), *The Forrestal Diaries*, 67, and Leahy, *I was there*, 383. Butow, *Japan's Decision to Surrender*, 97.

69. Tōgō, *The Cause of Japan*, 292.

70. Bix, *Hirohito*, 493.

71. Bix, *Hirohito*, 495.

72. Brooks, *Behind Japan's Surrender*, 115-116.

73. Ibid., 116.

74. Ibid., 237.

75. D. M. Giangreco, *Hell to Pay: Operation Downfall and the Invasion of Japan, 1945-1947, Updated and Expanded.* (Naval Institute Press), 76-77.

76. *Hell to Pay: Operation Downfall and the Invasion of Japan, 1945-1947, Updated and Expanded.* , 120.

77. Ibid., 77.

78. "Memorandum for the Joint Chiefs of Staff" from Admiral Leahy, enclosure to JPS 697/D, 14 June 1945, "Details of the Campaign Against Japan," RG 165, ABC

384 Japan (3 May 1944), Sec. 1-B, Entry 421, Box 428, NARA.
79. D.M. Giangreco, "President Truman and the Atom Bomb Decision: 'Preventing an Okinawa from One End of Japan to Another.'" *History News Network* (August 1, 2015). 4.
80. D.M. Giangreco and Kathryn Moore, *Dear Harry… Truman's Mailroom, 1945-1953.* (Stackpole Books, 1999), 8-9.
81. Douglas J. MacEachin, *The Final Months of the War with Japan: Signals Intelligence, U.S. Invasion Planning, and the A-Bomb Decision* (Washington, D.C.: Center for Study of Intelligence, 1998), Document 5.
82. J.C.S. (1945, June 18) Minutes of Meeting held at the White House on Monday, 18 June 18 1945 at 1530. National Archives, Washington, DC., 1.
83. American Planning Association: New York Upstate Chapter. (2014, March 21)
84. Leahy, *I Was There,* 605.
85. J.C.S. (1945, June 18) Minutes of Meeting held at the White House on Monday, 18 June 18 1945 at 1530. National Archives, Washington, DC., 2.
86. J.C.S. (1945, June 18) Minutes of Meeting held at the White House on Monday, 18 June 18 1945 at 1530. National Archives, Washington, DC., 3.
87. Frank, *Downfall,* 195.
88. J.C.S. (1945, June 18) Minutes of Meeting held at the White House on Monday, 18 June 18 1945 at 1530. National Archives, Washington, DC., 3.
89. McCullough, *Truman.* 399.
90. J.C.S. (1945, June 18) Minutes of Meeting held at the White House on Monday, 18 June 18 1945 at 1530. National Archives, Washington, DC., 4.
91. Frank, *Downfall,* 142.
92. Ibid., 142.
93. J.C.S. (1945, June 18) Minutes of Meeting held at the White House on Monday, 18 June 18 1945 at 1530. National Archives, Washington, DC., 5.
94. Frank, *Downfall,* 142.
95. J.C.S. (1945, June 18) Minutes of Meeting held at the White House on Monday, 18 June 18 1945 at 1530. National Archives, Washington, DC., 6.
96. Ibid., 6.
97. Frank, *Downfall,* 143.
98. Ibid., 143.
99. Ibid., 143.
100. J.C.S. (1945, June 18) Minutes of Meeting held at the White House on Monday, 18 June 18 1945 at 1530. National Archives, Washington, DC., 6.
101. Ibid., 6.
102. Ibid., 7.
103. Ibid., 7.
104. Frank, *Downfall,* 143.
105. J.C.S. (1945, June 18) Minutes of Meeting held at the White House on Monday, 18 June 18 1945 at 1530. National Archives, Washington, DC., 8.
106. Leahy, *I Was There,* 293.
107. General Charles E. Willoughby Article in *Military Review,* June 1946 ("Occupation of Japan and Japanese Reaction"). Written in late 1945 by Major General Charles E. Willoughby, MacArthur's top intelligence officer, the article includes a

high casualty estimate for the invasion and final defeat of Japan. Kort, *The Columbia Guide to Hiroshima and Bomb*, 160.

108. Arens, *V[Marine] Amphibious Corps Planning*, 81; and Kuribayashi quotation from Bill D. Ross, *Iwo Jima: Legacy of Valor* (New York: Vanguard Press, 1985), 62. Giangreco, *Hell to Pay*, Updated and Expanded, 226-227.

109. D. M. Giangreco, *Hell to Pay: Operation Downfall and the Invasion of Japan, 1945-47* Updated and Expanded. (Naval Institute Press, 2017), 129.

110. Grace Person Hayes, *The History of the Joint Chiefs of Staff in World War II: The War Against Japan.* (Naval Institute Press, 1982), 702.

111. Giangreco, *Hell to Pay, Updated and Expanded*, 67.

112. Ibid., 68.

113. Ibid., 70.

114. CINCAFPAC transmission C-19848, MMA. D. M. Giangreco, "Casualty Projections for the U.S. Invasions of Japan, 1945-1946: Planning and Policy Implications" in Journal of Military History, 61 (July 1997): 521-82.

115. D. M. Giangreco, "Casualty Projections for the U.S. Invasions of Japan, 1945-1946: Planning and Policy Implications" in Journal of Military History, 61 (July 1997): 521-82.

Chapter 5: Ketsu-Gō, "The Decisive Operation"

1. United States, *Reports of General MacArthur: Japanese Operations in the Southwest Pacific Area*, comp. Japanese Demobilization Bureaux Records, vol. II, Part II (Department of the Army, 1994), 584-586.

2. Giangreco, *Hell to Pay Updated and Expanded*, 28.

3. Giangreco, *Hell to Pay*, 78.

4. Suicide attack tactics: USSBS, Japanese Air Power. p. 71. Frank, *Downfall*, 184.

5. Giangreco, *Hell to Pay Updated and Expanded*, 176.

6. United States, *Reports of General MacArthur: Japanese Operations in the Southwest Pacific Area*, comp. Japanese Demobilization Bureaux Records, vol. II, Part II (Department of the Army, 1994), 641-643.

7. Nonaerial suicide weapons: "Water's Edge Surprise Attack Force," 17 Jul., SRS–484; SRMD–008, p. 275, 23 Jul. p. 5. Japanese suicide craft: Shizuo Fukui, *Japanese Naval Vessels at the End of World War II* (Annapolis: Naval Institute Press, 1991), pp. 99–102; *Hondo Kessen Junbi*, pp. 474–75; *Japanese Suicide Craft*, S–02, U.S. Naval Technical Mission to Japan, January 1946, NHC; SRS–484 17 July 45, Far East Summary, pp. 2-3. Frank, *Downfall*, 183.

8. United States, *Reports of General MacArthur: Japanese Operations in the Southwest Pacific Area*, comp. Japanese Demobilization Bureaux Records, vol. II, Part II (Department of the Army, 1994), 612.

9. Takagi, *Chiran* [air base]. Information on the compulsory aspect of the Special Attack units may be found in Tominaga Toshimi, "Kaerazuru kyūkōka" (Nose Dive to Oblivion), in *Chichi no senki*; Honda, *Shidōsha*; Mizuki Hitoshi, "Kishū sentei" (Choosing a Plane), in Kaigun Hikō Yobi Gakusei Daijūyonkikai, ed., *Aa, dōki no sakura* (A Navy Pilot Classmate), appendix, " Dōkisei no shuki" (A Classmates's Notes). For point of view diametrically opposite to the interpretation of Iguchi and Nakajim cited in note 6, see the self-criticism of professional Navy officer Yokoi Toshiyuki, "Kikusui sakusen tsui ni narazu" (The Kikusui Strategy Failed),

Taikeiyō sensō no zenbō, bessatsu chisei. Saburo Ienaga, *The Pacific War: World War II and the Japanese, 1931-1945.* (Pantheon Books, 1978), Frank, *Downfall,* 183.

10. "Kongo torubeki sensō shidō taikō" (Summary of War Measures to Be Adopted), in Takagi, Taihiyō kisen-shi, appendix. Saburo, *The Pacific War,* Frank, *Downfall,* 183.

11. United States, *Reports of General MacArthur: Japanese Operations in the Southwest Pacific Area,* comp. Japanese Demobilization Bureaux Records, vol. II, Part II (Department of the Army, 1994), 591.

12. United States, *Reports of General MacArthur: Japanese Operations in the Southwest Pacific Area,* comp. Japanese Demobilization Bureaux Records, vol. II, Part II (Department of the Army, 1994), 592.

13. Giangreco, *Hell to Pay Updated and Expanded,* 28-29.

14. Ibid., 29.

15. Ibid., 28.

16. Ibid., 170.

17. Ibid., 171.

18. Drea, *In the Service of the Emperor,* 147.

19. Timothy P. Maga, *America Attacks Japan: The Invasion That Never Was.* (The University Press of Kentucky, 2002), 4.

20. Giangreco, *Hell to Pay Updated and Expanded,* 172.

21. Marine Corps Gazette, August 1965, Vol 49, No.8.

22. United States, *Reports of General MacArthur: Japanese Operations in the Southwest Pacific Area,* comp. Japanese Demobilization Bureaux Records, vol. II, Part II (Department of the Army, 1994), 611-612.

23. Ibid., 612.

24. In this connection, see *Statements*: Toyoda #61340. Butow, *Japan's Decision to Surrender,* 99.

25. Paul Fussell, "Thank God for the Atom Bomb." *The New Republic,* August 1981.

26. United States, *Reports of General MacArthur: Japanese Operations in the Southwest Pacific Area,* comp. Japanese Demobilization Bureaux Records, vol. II, Part II (Department of the Army, 1994), 603.

27. Ibid., 605.

28. United States, U.S. Army, Headquarters, USAFFE and Eighth U.S. Army (Rear), *Homeland Operations Record: Japanese Monograph No. 17* (Office of the Chief of Military History, Dept. of the Army, 1945), 126-127.

29. United States, *Reports of General MacArthur: Japanese Operations in the Southwest Pacific Area,* comp. Japanese Demobilization Bureaux Records, vol. II, Part II (Department of the Army, 1994), 615.

30. Ibid., 668.

31. Giangreco, *Hell to Pay Updated and Expanded,* 29.

32. Fuel availability; USSBS, Japanese Air Power, pp. 24-25, 42. Some of the Imperial Army officers interrogated after the war expressed conflicting views. Two officers saw the Strategic Bombing Survey figures produced other numbers showing that the Imperial Army, at least, was in far more strained conditions. Lt. Col. Jiro Tsukushki and Lt. Col. Mikize Takemura, Report on the Survey Army Aviation Situation in the Mainland Area During and After January 1945, Doc.

No. 56826, *Statements* of Japanese Officials, CMH. Their numbers indicated that the Imperial Army had on hand 59,000 kiloliters (15,876,620 gallons) of fuel at the end of July and needed 40,000 (10,567,200 gallons) for the Ketsu operation. They anticipated absolutely no imports. Fuel production, of which only 20% gasoline and the rest alcohol and turpentine, languished at only 7,000 to 10,000 kiloliters, while monthly projected consumption ran at 12,000 to 14,000 kiloliters. By the end of December, there would be only 43,000 kiloliters on hand. Somewhat different numbers were provided by Lt. Col. Katsuo Kato, who stated that by July 1945 Imperial Army stocks totaled about 70,000 kiloliters, of which 40,000 were reserved for the decisive battle. Consumption ran about 10,000 per month, but with use of substitute fuels, this reduced to 6,000. Lt. Col. Katsuo Kato, *Statement* on Ketsu-Gō Air Operations, Doc. No. 59402, *Statements* of Japanese Officials on World War II, General Headquarters, Far East Command, Military Intelligence Section, Historical Division, CMH.
Another knowledgeable Imperial Army officer Lt. Col. Koji Tanaka, provided data that essentially supported the USSBS, but he admitted that "fuel situation was our greatest worry in the Ketsu Operation." Frank, *Downfall*, 183.
33. United States, *Reports of General MacArthur: Japanese Operations in the Southwest Pacific Area*, comp. Japanese Demobilization Bureaux Records, vol. II, Part II (Department of the Army, 1994), 632.
34. Stanley Weintraub, *The Last Great Victory: The End of World War II, July/August 1945.* (Truman Tally Books, 1995), 223.
35. Gavan Daws, *Prisoners of the Japanese: POWs of Wolrd War II in the Pacific.* (William Marrow, 1994), 322.
36. Giangreco, *Hell to Pay Updated and Expanded*, 81.
37. Updated intelligence as of August 10, 1945; Joint Intelligence Committee, "Japanese Reaction to an Assault on the Sendai Plain," JIC 218/10, 10 August 1945 (final revision August 20, 1945). The total for Kyushu includes the Tsushima Fortress, which was under the Fifty-sixth Army. Geographic file 1942–45, CCS 381 Honshu (7–19–44) Sec. 4, RG 218, Box 90, NARA. Frank, *Downfall*, 203.
38. United States, *Reports of General MacArthur: Japanese Operations in the Southwest Pacific Area*, comp. Japanese Demobilization Bureaux Records, vol. II, Part II (Department of the Army, 1994), 644.

Chapter 6: Potsdam Declaration, A Missed Opportunity
1. Toland, *The Rising Sun*, 857.
2. Ibid., 857.
3. Ibid., 857-858.
4. Notes of the Interim Committee Meeting Friday, 1 June 1945. 11:00 A.M.–12:30 P.M., 1:45 P.M.–3:30 P.M.
5. Bruce Lee, *Marching Orders: The Untold Story of World War II.* (Crown Publishers, Inc., 1995), 497.
6. Lee, *Marching Orders, 497-498.*
7. Ibid., 498.
8. Stimson's July 2 memo to Truman: Memorandum for the President, July 2, 1945, and attached "Proposed Program for Japan," Harry S. Truman Papers, Naval Aide Files, Box 4, Folder: Berlin Conference, Vol. 11, Japan, HSTL. Also

found in *FRUS*, 1945, 1:890-94. See also Sigal, *Fighting to a Finish*. p. 125. Stimson's position by the May—June period represented an evolution of his thinking. Earlier in January, Stimson had noted in his diary that John McCloy had showed him a paper from Admiral King proposing a modification of the unconditional surrender formula, which McCloy endorsed. Stimson, however, believed at that time that it would weaken the American position and wished to talk it over with Marshall (Stimson Diary, January 22, 1945). By certainly the day after the White House meeting that sanctioned Olympic, Stimson was noting in his diary that while he and Forrestal agreed with the proposed military program they believed it "would be deplorable if we have to go through with the military program with all its stubborn fighting to a finish" and that some way should be found to induce Japan to surrender. Stimson Diary, Jun 19, 1945; see also June 26-30, 1945. Frank, *Downfall*, 218.

9. McCullough, *Truman*. 405

10. Ibid., 409

11. Toland, *The Rising Sun*, 861-862.

12. McCullough, *Truman*. 406

13. MAGIC DIPLOMATIC SUMMARY NO. 1204, JULY 12, 1945 (SRS 1726). Kort, *The Columbia Guide to Hiroshima and the Bomb*, 278-279.

14. MAGIC DIPLOMATIC SUMMARY NO. 1205, JULY 13, 1945 (SRS 1727). Kort, *The Columbia Guide to Hiroshima and the Bomb*, 279-280.

15. MAGIC DIPLOMATIC SUMMARY NO. 1206, JULY 14, 1945 (SRS 1728). Kort, *The Columbia Guide to Hiroshima and the Bomb*, 280-281.

16. Leahy, *I Was There*, 394.

17. McCullough, *Truman*. 420.

18. O'Brien, *The Second Most Powerful Man in the World*, 351.

19. Hull's exchanges with Byrnes: *FRUS, 1945*, 2:1267-68; Sherwin, *A World Destroyed*, p. 225. Frank, *Downfall*, 218.

20. McCullough, *Truman*. 436

21. Leahy, *I Was There*, 395.

22. Truman, Memoirs by *Harry S. Truman:Year of Decisions*, 341.

23. McCullough, *Truman*, 414.

24. Truman, Memoirs by *Harry S. Truman: Year of Decisions*, 341.

25. Leahy, *I Was There*, 396.

26. MAGIC DIPLOMATIC SUMMARY NO. 1210, JULY 17, 1945 (SRS 1732). Kort, *The Columbia Guide to Hiroshima and the Bomb*, 283.

27. David Robertson. *Sly and Able: A Political Biography of James F. Byrnes*. (W.W. Norton & Company, 1994), 421.

28. Soviet plan for Manchuria offensive: David M. Glantz, *August Storm: The Soviet 1945 Strategic Offensive in Manchuria*, Leavenworth Paper No. 7 (Fort Leavenworth, Kansas: Combat Studies Institute, U.S. Army Command and General Staff College, 1983), pp. xvii, 1-2, 4; T.N. Deputy and Paul Martell, *Great Battles on the Eastern Front* (Indianapolis: Bobbs-Merrill, 1982), p. 241. Frank, *Downfall*, 277.

29. Toland, *The Rising Sun*, 864.

30. Leahy, *I Was There*, 398-399.

31. McCullough, *Truman*, 424.

32. Truman, Memoirs by *Harry S. Truman: Year of Decisions*, 415.

33. Ibid., 396.

34. Ibid., 396.

35. McCullough, *Truman*, 425.

36. MAGIC DIPLOMATIC SUMMARY NO. 1212, JULY 20, 1945 (SRS 1734). Kort, *The Columbia Guide to Hiroshima and the Bomb*, 283-284.

37. Tōgō, *The Cause of Japan*, 307.

38. Leahy, *I Was There*, 410.

39. McCullough, *Truman*, 428.

40. Ibid., 429.

41. Ibid., 429.

42. MAGIC DIPLOMATIC SUMMARY NO. 1214, JULY 22, 1945 (SRS 1736). Kort, *The Columbia Guide to Hiroshima and the Bomb*, 284-285.

43. Togo's message of July 21: Magic Diplomatic Summary, No. 1214, 22 July 45; SRH-086. p.2. Frank, *Downfall*, 230.

44. McCullough, *Truman*, 431-432.

45. Toland, *The Rising Sun*, 867.

46. Giangreco, *Hell to Pay*, 92.

47. McCullough, *Truman*, 436.

48. Toland, *The Rising Sun*, 867-868.

Chapter 7: The Final Countdown Begins

1. McCullough, *Truman*, 437.

2. Ibid., 442.

3. Truman, Memoirs by *Harry S. Truman: Year of Decisions*, 420.

4. U.S. National Archives, Record Group 77, Records of the Office of the Chief of Engineers, Manhattan Engineer District, TS Manhattan Project File '42 to '46, Folder 5B (Directives, Memos, etc. to and from C/S, S/W, etc.)

5. Truman, Memoirs by *Harry S. Truman: Year of Decisions*, 421.

6. McCullough, *Truman*, 441.

7. Leahy, *I Was There*, 415.

8. Toland, *The Rising Sun*, 868-869.

9. Winston Churchill, *Triumph and Tragedy*. (Houghton-Mifflin, 1953), 669-70.

10. Robert H. Ferrell, *Off the Record: The Private Papers of Harry S. Truman*. (Harper and Row, 1980), 55-56.

11. The Army Air Forces in World War II. *Vol. V: The Pacific: Matterhorn to Nagasaki, June 1944 to August 1945*. (University of Chicago Press, 1953). 712-713.

12. James Carroll, *House of War: The Pentagon and the Disastrous Rise of American Power*. (Mariner Books, 2007) 44.

13. Daws, *Prisoners of the Japanese*, 323.

14. McCullough, *Truman*, 439.

15. Casey Frank, "Truman's Bomb, Our Bomb at Foreclosure." *JD The Fletcher Forum of World Affairs* (May 1995), 263.

16. John Costello, *The Pacific War 1941-1945*. (Perennial, 1981). 586-587.

17. Costello, *The Pacific War 1941-1945*, 588.

18. George McKee Elsey. *An Unplanned Life*. (University of Missouri Press, 2005), 89.

19. Bix, *Hirohito*, 360.

20. Daws, *Prisoners of the Japanese*, 325.

21. Ibid., 363-364.

22. "If he lay on one side:" Gavan Daws, *Prisoners of the Japanese* (New York: William Morrow, 1994), p. 343. Frank, *Downfall*, 160.

23. Forrest Knox: Ibid., pp. 18, 30, 96, 343. Daws points out that the exact figures for Allied prisoners of war are hard to ascertain. He sets figures at about a total of 320,000 captured by Japan, of whom 180,000 were other Asians: Filipinos serving with Americans, Indians and Chinese serving with the British, and Indonesians serving with the Dutch. Another study by Van Waterford, *Prisoners of the Japanese in World War II* (Jefferson, N.C.: McFarland and Co., 1994), p. 146, gives numbers for POW captives at plus or minus 193,000 and deaths at 60,600. Frank, *Downfall*, 160.

24. U.S. Army POWs: Bernard M. Cohen and Maurice Z. Cooper, *A Follow-Up Study of World War II Prisoners of War* (Washington D.C.: Department of Medicine and Surgery, Veterans Administration, 1954), Table 2, p. 4. A total of 1,416 naval personnel (Navy and Marine Corps) died in Japanese captivity (versus three held by Germany). I could not, however, locate a figure for the total number of U.S. naval personnel taken prisoner by the Japanese. *History of the Medical Department of the United States Navy*, vol. 3, pp. 170-171. E. Bartlett Kerr, Surrender and Survival (New York: William Morrow, 1985), pp. 339-40, gives total U.S. POWs (Army and Navy) at 25,600, of whom 10,650 were listed as killed or died, a ratio of 42 percent. These figures probably understated the number of naval personnel taken prisoner, thus somewhat increasing the percentage of deaths. Frank, *Downfall*, 160.

25. Deaths among POWs shipped by Japan: Daws, *Prisoners of the Japanese*, p. 297. Frank, *Downfall*, 161.

26. Killing of Airmen: Daws, *Prisoners of the Japanese*, pp. 277, 321-22. Frank, *Downfall*, 161.

27. Saburō Ienaga, *The Pacific War: World War II and the Japanese, 1931-45.* (Wiley-Blackwell, 1978), 189-190.

28. *After the Battle* 26 (1979): As to deaths among *romusha*, "The Death Railway" puts the figures as between 80,000 and 100,000. The text figure is derived by subtracting the number of Allied POW dead from the total dead given in Newman, *Truman and the Hiroshima Cult*. Frank, *Downfall*, 160.

29. Tōgō, *The Cause of Japan*, 311-312.

30. Ibid., 311-312.

31. Naval-intelligence analysis of July 27: Magic Diplomatic Summary, No. 1219, 27 July 45, SRS-494. Frank, *Downfall*, 231-232.

32. Satō's message of July 27: Naval-intelligence analysis of July 27: Magic Diplomatic Summary, No. 1221, 29 July 45, Part II. Frank, *Downfall*, 232.

33. The Pacific War Research Society, *Japan's Longest Day*, 17.

34. Department of State United States of America, FOREIGN RELATIONS OF THE UNITED STATES: DIPLOMATIC PAPERS, THE CONFERENCE OF BERLIN (THE POTSDAM CONFERENCE), 1945, VOLUME II
No. 1258. Press Conference Statement by Prime Minister Suzuki printed from

"Daily Report, Foreign Radio Broadcasts, Monday, July 30, 1945" (Washington, Federal Communications Commission, Foreign Broadcast Intelligence Service, mimeographed, 1945), pp. BC 1–2. The extracts here printed are a translation of portions of a Domei transmission in romaji carried by Radio Tokyo's Greater East Asia service at 3 a.m., Eastern War Time, July 29, as monitored by the Foreign Broadcast Intelligence Service.

35. Bix, *Hirohito*, 501.

36. Truman, *Volume One: Year of Decisions*, 397.

37. Bix, *Hirohito*, 501.

38. Exchanges between Satō and Tōgō: Satō's July 15 message: Magic Diplomatic Summary, No. 1208, 16 July 45; SRH-085, pp. 10-12; Tōgō's message of July 17; Ibid., No. 1209, 17 July 45; SRH-085, pp. 12-13. Frank, *Downfall*, 239.

39. Ibid. Frank, *Downfall*, 239.

40. Bix, *Hirohito*, 502.

41. MAGIC DIPLOMATIC SUMMARY NO. 1224, AUGUST 1, 1945 (SRS 1746). Kort, *The Columbia Guide to Hiroshima and the Bomb*, 287.

42. McCullough, *Truman*, 448.

43. Toland, *The Rising Sun*, 873-874.

44. Paul W. Tibbets, *The Return of the Enola Gay*, (Mid Coast, 1998), 201.

45. Leahy, *I Was There*, 427.

46. Ibid., 428.

47. Toland, *The Rising Sun*, 873.

48. Ibid., 872.

49. McCullough, *Truman*, 449.

50. MAGIC DIPLOMATIC SUMMARY NO. 1225, AUGUST 2, 1945 (SRS 1747). Kort, *The Columbia Guide to Hiroshima and the Bomb*, 287-288.

51. Bix, *Hirohito*, 503.

52. MAGIC DIPLOMATIC SUMMARY NO. 1226, AUGUST 3, 1945 (SRS 1748). Kort, *The Columbia Guide to Hiroshima and the Bomb*, 288.

53. MAGIC DIPLOMATIC SUMMARY NO. 1228, AUGUST 5, 1945 (SRS 1750). Kort, *The Columbia Guide to Hiroshima and the Bomb*, 288-289.

Chapter 8: Hiroshima

1. Tibbets, *The Return of the Enola Gay*, 201.

2. Toland, *The Rising Sun*, 874.

3. Ibid., 875.

4. Tibbets, *Return of the Enola Gay*, 208.

5. Ibid., 208-209.

6. Ibid., 209.

7. Ibid., 210.

8. Ibid., 212-213.

9. Toland, *The Rising Sun*, 876.

10. Tibbets, *Return of the Enola Gay*, 226.

11. Ibid., 227-228.

12. Ibid., 228-229.

13. Ibid., 229.

14. Ibid., 229-230.

15. John Hershey, *Hiroshima*. (Bantam Books, 1946), 5.

16. Toland, *The Rising Sun*, 877.

17. The Pacific War Research Society, *The Day Man Lost: Hiroshima, 6 August 1945*. (Kodansha International LTD., 1981), 235.

18. "The entire northeast and eastern sides:" Headquarters Twentieth Air Force, Tactical Mission Report, Special Mission, 20 July—14 August 1945, pp. 13-14. Frank *Downfall*, 262-263.

19. Leslie R. Groves, *Now it Can be Told: The Story of the Manhattan Project*. (Da Capo Press, 1962), 316.

20. Tibbets, *Return of the Enola Gay*, 230.

21. Hershey, *Hiroshima*, 5.

22. Toland, *The Rising Sun*, 880.

23. Ibid., 885.

24. Tibbets, *Return of the Enola Gay*, 230-233.

25. Truman, *Memoirs by Harry S. Truman: Year of Decisions*, 421.

26. O'Brien, *The Second Most Powerful Man in the World*, 357.

27. The Pacific War Research Society, *Japan's Longest Day*, 21.

28. News reaches Tokyo: *Daihon'ei Rikugun-Bu* (10), p. 418; Freedman and Dockrill, "Hiroshima: A Strategy of Shock," p. 203; Statement of LT. Gen. Torashiro Kawabe, 23 Aug 48, Doc. No 61539, CMH: Butow, *Japan's Decision to Surrender*, pp. 150-51. Kawabe reported he was aware of the possibility of an atomic bomb from a briefing by Dr. Nishina **or** one of Nishina's associates. Frank, *Downfall*, 269.

29. The Pacific War Research Society, *Japan's Longest Day*, 20-21.

30. "The possible effect upon OLYMPIC operations": Joint War Plans Committee, JWPC 397 4 August 1945 (with attached copy of "Defensive Preparations in Japan," JIC), RG 218, NARA. Frank, *Downfall*, 273.

31. August 7, 1945, The diary entry of the Vice Chief of the General Staff [Translator's note: This is Torashiro Kawabe, younger brother of Masakazu Kawabe, Commander Air General Army]. Kort, *The Columbia Guide to Hiroshima and the Bomb*, 310-311.

32. Toland, *The Rising Sun*, 894.

33. Paul Ham, *Hiroshima Nagasaki: The Real Story of the Atomic Bombings and Their Aftermath*. (Picador - Macmillan Publishers, 2015), 261

34. The Pacific War Research Society. *The Day Man Lost—Hiroshima, 6 August 1945*, 18-19.

35. Foreign Relations of the United States: Diplomatic Papers, The Conference of Berlin (The Potsdam Conference), 1945, Volume II No. 1258. Press Conference Statement by Prime Minister Suzuki, Tokyo, July 28, 1945.

36. Edward R. Beauchamp, ed. *History of Contemporary Japan Since World War II*. (Routledge, 1998) 84.

37. Ham, *Hiroshima Nagasaki*, 263.

38. Francis X. Winters, *Remembering Hiroshima: Was it Just?* (Routledge, 2009), 149.

39. Effect of the atomic bomb on the royal family: Statement of Lt. Col. Masao Inaba, 13 Oct 49, Doc. Not 57692. p. 7, CMH. Frank, *Downfall*, 270.

40. Statements of Kido Koichi, statements of Japanese Officials on World War

II, General Headquarters, Far East Command, Military Intelligence Section, Historical Division (August 14, 1950), published at the Center of Military History, Washington, DC. Francis X. Winters, *Remembering Hiroshima: Was it Just?*, 134.

41. The Pacific War Research Society, *Japan's Longest Day*, 21.

42. Tōgō, *The Cause of Japan*, 315.

43. U.S. Strategic Bombing Survey (Pacific), *Interrogations of Japanese Leaders and Responses to Questionnaires*, Microfilm Publication M1654, Roll 5. Kort, *The Columbia Guide to Hiroshima and the Bomb*, 342.

44. Marshall to MacArthur exchange: OPD (WAR) [Marshall] to MACARTHUR WAR 45369; CINCAFPAC [MacArthur] to WARCOS [Marshall] C31897, CINCPAC Command Summary, Book Seven, pp. 3508-10. The exchange is also found in OPD Top Secret Incoming Msg Jul 28-Aug 17, 1945, RG 165, Box 39, NARA. Frank, *Downfall*, 274.

45. August 8 raid: 20th AF MR, no. 319-20, pp. 1-18, Consolidated Statistical Summaries. The modest size of the strike force for Yawata was due to crashes that limited the 58th Wing to only thirty-five Superfortresses. Frank, *Downfall*, 277.

46. The Pacific War Research Society, *Japan's Longest Day*, 21-22.

47. Ibid., 22.

Chapter 9: A Shift of Power, The First Imperial Intervention

1. The Pacific War Research Society, *Japan's Longest Day,*, 23.

2. August 9, 1945, The diary entries of the Vice Chief of the General Staff [Translator's note: This is Torashiro Kawabe, younger brother of Masakazu Kawabe, Commander Air General Army]. Kort, *The Columbia Guide to Hiroshima and the Bomb*, 311-312.

3. "MacArthur consistently dismissed ULTRA evidence" and Luzon: Drea, *MacArthur's Ultra*, pp. 180-85, 229-30. Frank, *Downfall*, 274-275.

4. Frank, *Downfall*, 275.

5. Ibid., 275.

6. King to Nimitz: COMINCH AND CNO TO CINCPAC ADV HQ 092205 Aug 45 (headed "KING TO NIMITZ EYES ONLY") and attached copies of CINCAFPAC to WARCOS C 31897 and OPD (WAR) to MACARTHUR WAR 45369, CINCPAC Command Summary, Book Seven, pp. 3508-10. Frank, *Downfall*, 276.

7. Kido's audience with Emperor and instructions to Suzuki: *Daihon'ei Rikugun-Bu (10)*, pp. 431-32; IMTFE Kido 31,172-74 (here the IMTFE version is fuller and clearer than *Diary of Marquis Kido* variant). Frank, *Downfall*, 289-290.

8. Suzuki's initial reaction: Statement of Sumihisa Ikeda, 23 Dec 49, Doc. No. 54479, p. 2, CMH. Suzuki's conduct over the next several days suggests Ikeda exaggerated or Suzuki, characteristically, vacillated. Frank, *Downfall*, 288.

9. Giangreco, *Hell to Pay Updated and Expanded*, 26-29.

10. Ibid., 27.

11. Japanese underestimate of Soviet attack: Glantz, *Soviet Tactical and Operational Combat*, p. 33. See also *Daihon'ei Rikugun-Bu (10)*, p. 432, which indicates the Kwantung Army initially estimated that the Soviets only intended some border incursions, but by 6:00 A.M. characterized the attack as an all-out one. The Kwantung Army, However, continued to drastically underestimate the scope of the Soviet effort. Frank, *Downfall*, 289.

12. Lester Brooks, *Behind Japan's Surrender the Secret Struggle That Ended an Empire.* (Carpe Veritas Books, De Gustibus Press, Ltd., 1968), 56.

13. The Pacific War Research Society, *Japan's Longest Day*, 24.

14. Brooks, *Behind Japan's Surrender*, 58.

15. Tōgō, *The Cause of Japan.* 316-317.

16. Costello, *The Pacific War 1941-1945*, 592.

17. Brooks, *Behind Japan's Surrender*, 56.

18. Ibid., 56.

19. McCullough, *Truman*, 459.

20. Tōgō, *The Cause of Japan.* 317-318.

21. Brooks, *Behind Japan's Surrender*, 57.

22. Winters, *Remembering Hiroshima*, 136.

23. Butow, *Japan's Decision to Surrender*, 161.

24. Brooks, *Behind Japan's Surrender*, 62.

25. Ibid., 63.

26. Tōgō, *The Cause of Japan*, 318.

27. Brooks, *Behind Japan's Surrender*, 63.

28. The Pacific War Research Society, *Japan's Longest Day*, 27.

29. Ibid., 27.

30. Ibid., 27.

31. Winters, *Remembering Hiroshima: Was it Just?*, 148.

32. The Pacific War Research Society, *Japan's Longest Day*, 27.

33. Ibid., 27-28.

34. Brooks, *Behind Japan's Surrender*, 71.

35. Ibid., 71.

36. Ibid., 71.

37. Ibid., 70-71.

38. Ibid., 68-69.

39. Ibid., 69.

40. Ibid., 70.

41. Tōgō, *The Cause of Japan*, 276.

42. Tōgō, *Tōgō Shigenori gaiko shuki*, 355-56 (all quotations). Kawamura, *Emperor Hirohito*, 164.

43. Tōgō, *The Cause of Japan*, 319.

44 Brooks, *Behind Japan's Surrender*, 72.

45. Ibid., 72.

46. Butow, *Japan's Decision to Surrender*, 168.

47. Brooks, *Behind Japan's Surrender*, 73.

48. Ibid., 68.

49. Toland, *The Rising Sun.* 913.

50. U.S. Strategic Bombing Survey (Pacific), *Interrogations of Japanese Leaders and Responses to Questionnaires*, Microfilm Publication M1655, Roll 208A. USSBS INTERROGATION NO. 531, PRIME MINISTER KANTARO SUZUKI, DECEMBER 26, 1945. Kort, *The Columbia Guide to Hiroshima and the Bomb*, 359.

51. The Pacific War Research Society, *Japan's Longest Day*, 32.

52. Zenshiro Hoshina, *Secret History of the Greater East Asia War: Memoir of Zenshiro*

Hoshina. (Hara-Shobo, 1975), 140-141.

53. The Pacific War Research Society, *Japan's Longest Day*, 33.

54. DOC. NO. 53437 FROM MEMORANDUM OF HOSHIMA, ZENSHIRO, FORMER CHIEF OF NAVAL AFFAIRS BUREAU OF NAVY MINISTRY (FROM MAY 1945 TO ABOUT NOVEMBER OF 1945). (CONFERENCE IN THE PRESENCE OF THE EMPEROR, HELD AT 2330 HOURS ON 9 AUG 45, IN THE IMPERIAL PALACE AIR RAID SHELTER.) Kort, *The Columbia Guide to Hiroshima and the Bomb*, 373-374.

55. Presentation of Anami and Umezu: Ikeda, "Minutes," p. 2; Hoshina, "Minutes," pp. 2-3. Frank, *Downfall*, 293.

56. The Pacific War Research Society, *Japan's Longest Day*, 32-33.

57. Although others have since said that this was veiled threat, Toyoda has denied that he had anything more in mind than the peculiar psychology of the Japanese fighting man which Umezu had so aptly described earlier in the day. Although the reference is to a later date, see, for example, Toyoda, *Saigo no teikoku kaigun*, 225-227. Butow, *Japan's Decision to Surrender*, 174.

58. Bix, *Hirohito*, 521.

59. The Pacific War Research Society, *Japan's Longest Day*, 34.

60. Hoshina, *Secret History of the Greater East Asia War*, 146.

61. Toland, *The Rising Sun*. 915.

62. Brooks, *Behind Japan's Surrender*, 105-108.

63. The Pacific War Research Society, *Japan's Longest Day*, 34-35.

64. Truman, *Memoirs by Harry S. Truman: Year of Decisions*, 427.

65. Bix, *Hirohito*. 516.

66. Tanaka, Nobumasa *Dokyumento Shōwa tennō, dai gokan*, P. 507. Bix, *Hirohito*. 516.

67. Yokota Kisaburō, *Tennōsei* (Rōdō Bunkasha, 1949), pp. 183-84. Bix, *Hirohito*. 517-518.

68. The Pacific War Research Society, *Japan's Longest Day*, 35.

69. Ibid., 36.

70. Frank, *Downfall*, 297.

71. Toland, *The Rising Sun*, 918.

72. For the details relating to the cabinet meeting and for the Japanese text of the Board of Information statement, see JFO. *Shūsen shiroku*, Ch. 45 (Shimomura jōhōkyoku sōsai dan to rikushō fukoku). See also the vernacular papers and the *Nippon Times* for Saturday, August 11, 1945, capped the Shimomura (Board of Information) statement with the following heading: "Total Wartime Effort Asked Japanese Nation—Overcoming of Present Crisis to Defend National Polity Urged by Shimomura." Butow, *Japan's Decision to Surrender*. 182.

73. For the Japanese text, see JFO, *Shūsen shiroku*, Ch. 45 (Shimomura jōhōkyoku sōsai dan to rikushō fukoku), and the vernacular papers for August 11, 1945. For the English text, see the *Nippon Times* for Sunday, August 12, 1945: "War Minister Exhorts Army in Stirring Call—Press Forward to Smash Enemy with Spirit of Nanko, Tokimune, Declares Message." Butow, *Japan's Decision to Surrender*. 184-185.

74. Brooks, *Behind Japan's Surrender*, 212.

75. *Boeicho Boei Kenshujo Senshi* Shitsu (War History Office, Defense Agency) *Senshi Shosho* (War History Series), No. 82, *Daihon'ei Rikugun-Bu* (10) Army Division, Imperial General Headquarters, vol. 10) (Tokyo, 1975), 456. Kort, *The Columbia Guide to Hiroshima and the Bomb*, 300-301.

76. Butow, *Japan's Decision to Surrender*. 186.

77. The Pacific War Research Society, *Japan's Longest Day*, 38.

78. Truman, *Memoirs by Harry S. Truman: Year of Decisions*, 428.

79. Past policy on release of POW stories and draft warnings: See the series in ABC 383.6 Japan (17 Aug 42), RG 165, Box 393, NARA. Frank, *Downfall*, 300.

80. Draft Marshall message: Memorandum for the President, 10 August 1945, George C. Marshall Papers, box 76, Folder 7, Marshall Library. POW estimate: JCS to MacArthur, Nimitz, Sultan, Wedemeyer, 132158 June 45, CINCPAC Command Summary, p. 2926. Truman's public statement: Statement by President, June 1, 1945, Press Release File, 1945–53, Box 1, Folder: Truman Papers, May–June 1945, 2 of 2 June 45, HSTL; Memorandum for the President, August 10, 1945, Subject: Draft Warning..., State Department, White House Central Files, HSTL. Truman annotated this memorandum "Original approved & sent to Sec[retary of] St[ate]." Frank, *Downfall*, 301.

81. "In order to save us from a score of bloody Iwo Jimas and Okinawas:" Stimson diary, August 10, 1945. The figures are computed by multiplying twenty times the of American combat deaths (8,586 that Iwo Jima and 12,520 at Okinawa) and total combat casualties (31,708 and Iwo Jima and 49,133 and Okinawa). Casualty numbers for Iwo Jima are from Garand and Strowbridge. *Western Pacific Operations*, Appendix H, and *The History of the Medical Department of the United States Navy in World War II: The Statistics of Diseases and Injuries*, Vol. 3, p. 173. The totals for Okinawas are from Appleman, Burns, Gugeler, and Stevens, Okinawa: The Last Battle, p. 473. Frank, *Downfall*, 301.

82. Leahy, *I was There*, 434.

83. Robertson, *Sly and Able*, 434-435.

84. Ibid., 435.

85. Leahy, *I was There*, 435.

86. Truman, *Memoirs by Harry S. Truman: Year of Decisions*, 429.

87. Ibid., 429.

88. Frank, *Downfall*, 302.

89. Truman restricts military operations: Bernstein, "Perils and Politics of Surrender," pp. 9-10. Message on casualties in Hiroshima: SRS-507, Magic Far East Summary, 9 August 1945, p. 5. Frank, *Downfall*, 302.

90. Atomic-bomb target recommendation: COMAF 20 to CINCPAC, COMUSAS-TAF 090326 August 45, CINCPAC Command Summary, p. 3512 (copy also in Spaatz Papers, Library of Congress, Box 24). Twining recommendation: Twining, COMGEN AF 20 to COMGEN USASTAF, 140223Z Aug 45, Spaatz Papers, Library of Congress, Box 24. On August 10, Spaatz sent a separate recommendation to Arnold for an attack on Tokyo: COMGEN USASTAF to COMGENAIR 10033 Aug 45. Frank, *Downfall*, 302-303.

91. Frank, *Downfall*, 303.

92. Truman, *Memoirs by Harry S. Truman: Volume One*, 432.

93. The Pacific War Research Society, *Japan's Longest Day*, 43.
94. Ibid., 44.
95. Ibid., 45.
96. Toland, *The Rising Sun*, 922.

Chapter 10: The Second Imperial Intervention
1. Bix, *Hirohito*, 518-519.
2. Toland, *The Rising Sun*, 925.
3. Brooks, *Behind Japan's Surrender*, 215-216.
4. Ibid., 218.
5. Toland, *The Rising Sun*, 926.
6. The Pacific War Research Society, *Japan's Longest Day*, 48.
7. Ibid., 48-49.
8. Toland, *The Rising Sun*, 928.
9. Brooks, *Behind Japan's Surrender*, 219.
10. Tōgō, *The Cause of Japan*, 324-325.
11. See Kido, "Nikki," 8/12/45; IMTFE: Kido, 31184; Tōgō, 35789; *Statements*: Matsumoto #61451 and Tōgō #50304; JFO, *Shusen shiroku*, Ch. 50 (Suzuki shushō no saishōkairon to Tōgō gaishō no kushin). Butow, *Japan's Decision to Surrender*, 194.
12. Brooks, *Behind Japan's Surrender*, 219-220.
13. Kido Koichi, *Kido Koichi nikki*, 2:1225; Tōgō, *Tōgō Shigenori gaiko shuki*, 363 (quotation). Kawamura, *Emperor Hirohito and the Pacific War*, 169.
14. Kawamura, *Emperor Hirohito and the Pacific War*, 170.
15. Tōgō, *The Cause of Japan*, 325-327.
16. Ibid., 327.
17. The Pacific War Research Society, *Japan's Longest Day*, 49.
18. Butow, *Japan's Decision to Surrender*, 195.
19. Brooks, *Behind Japan's Surrender*, 227.
20. Suzuki meets with Tōgō, Matsumoto, and Kido: *Daihon'ei Rikugun-Bu (10)*, p. 485; Statements of Lord Keeper of the Privy Seal Kido, 11 Aug 50, Doc. No. 61476, p. 13, and 14 Aug 50, Doc. No. 61541, p. 7, CMH; IMTFE Kido 31, 184–86; Butow, *Japan's Decision to Surrender*, p. 196. Kido's diary in IMTFE mentions millions of innocents, while Butow sites hundreds of thousands. In a postwar statement, Minister Okamoto in Sweden confirmed that Matsumoto had told him that his message stressing that adding terms would collapse talks proved vital to ending the war. Statement of Suemasa Okamoto, 29 Jul 50, Doc. No. 61477, pp. 4–5, CMH. Frank, *Downfall*, 309.
21. Brooks, *Behind Japan's Surrender*, 229-230.
22. Toland, *The Rising Sun*, 927.
23. Ibid., 928.
24. Yonai to Emperor: Bix, "Japan's Delayed Surrender," pp. 217-18. Frank, *Downfall*, 310.
25 Saburo Ienaga, *The Pacific War: World War II and the Japanese, 1931-1945*, (Pantheon Books, 1978), 230-231.
26. McCullough, *Truman*, 461.
27. The Pacific War Research Society, *Japan's Longest Day*, 51-52.

28. Toland, *The Rising Sun*, 929.
29. Brooks, *Behind Japan's Surrender*, 238.
30. Ibid., 239-240.
31. Tōgō, The Cause of Japan, 328.
32. Brooks, *Behind Japan's Surrender*, 241-242.
33. See *Statements*: Matsumoto #61451 and Okamoto #61477; JFO, *Shūsen shiroku*, Ch. 52. (Rengōkoku kaitōbun ni kan suru zai Suisu Kase kōshi oyobi zai Su den Okamoto kōshi no kōden sono ta). Butow, *Japan's Decision to Surrender*, 201.
34. Brooks, *Behind Japan's Surrender*, 242.
35. Ibid., 242-243.
36. Kido Nikki Kenkyu-kai, *Kido Koichi nikki: Tokyo saibanki*, 445 (all quotations). Kawamura, *Emperor Hirohito and the Pacific War*, 172.
37. Sakomizu, *Dainihon teikoku saigo no yonkagetsu*, 214-17 (quotation p. 217). Kawamura, *Emperor Hirohito and the Pacific War*, 180.
38. Toland, *The Rising Sun*, 930.
39. Brooks, *Behind Japan's Surrender*, 247-248.
40. Toland, *The Rising Sun*, 931.
41. Ibid., 931-932.
42. The Pacific War Research Society, *Japan's Longest Day*, 75.
43. Toland, *The Rising Sun*, 933.
44. Tōgō, *The Cause of Japan*, 332.
45. Frank, *Downfall*, 311-312.
46. Hull and Seeman conversation: 1325 13 August 1945, George C. Marshall Papers, Verifax 2691, Marshall Library. Frank, *Downfall*, 312-313.
47. "The President directs:" Marshall to General MacArthur and General Spaatz, WR 48689 131343 Aug 45, RG 9, Box 156, Folder 1, MacArthur Archive. Arnold directed Spaatz to attack Tokyo with the maximum number of aircraft "so as to impress Japanese officials that we mean business and our serious in getting them to accept our peace proposal without delay." Spaatz replied that Tokyo was no longer a good target "except for the atomic bomb" and dispatched his forces to other targets. Radio Teletype Conference, Aug. 14, 1945, Box 21, Spaatz Papers, Library of Congress. Frank, *Downfall*, 313.
48. Robertson, *Sly and Able*, 436-437.
49. Ibid., 437.
50. Butow, *Japan's Decision to Surrender*. 206.
51. Toland, *The Rising Sun*, 935.
52. Brooks, *Behind Japan's Surrender*, 255.
53. Ibid., 256.
54. Ibid., 256-257.
55. Toland, *The Rising Sun*, 935.
56. Brooks, *Behind Japan's Surrender*, 257.
57. Meeting of Emperor and senior officers: *Daihon'ei Rikugun-Bu (10)*, pp. 491-92, 504-5. As to Anami's expectations of Hata, see Statement of Lt. Col. Inaba, 13 Oct 49, Doc. No. 57592, p. 7, CMH. According to Inaba, Hata, prior to seeing the Emperor, said to Anami that the atomic bomb had hardly any effect on the ground one foot below the surface, and Anami urged him to relate this to the

Emperor. Inaba emphasized that the atomic bomb appeared to staff officers at Imperial Headquarters to have "shaken extremely" the Imperial family. The account in *Daihon'ei Rikugun-Bu (10)* differs from the Emperor's recollection in the *Showa Tenno Dokuhakuroku*, p. 143, where he says all three senior officers present urged him to continue the war. Both these sources are based on postwar evidence, and in this case, I believe *Daihon'ei Rikugun-Bu (10)* is more accurate because Hata's subsequent behavior on August 14 fits far better with what he later reported he told the Emperor than with the Emperor's recollections. Frank, *Downfall*, 314.

58. Toland, *The Rising Sun*, 936.

59. The Pacific War Research Society, *Japan's Longest Day*, 78.

60. Ibid., 79.

61. See Toyoda, *Saigo no teikoku kaigun*, 220-22; *Statements:* Toyoda #61340, Hasunuma #58225, Tōgō #50304; Shimomura, "The Memoirs of Mr. Shimomura at the Imperial Council, 14 August 1945" (MS); and the JFO, *Shūsen shiroku*, Ch. 54 (Dai nikai gozen kaigi to kakugi kettei). The text is also based on material obtained from Hisatsune Sakomizu during an interview in Tokyo, April 6, 1952. Butow, *Japan's Decision to Surrender*, 207.

62. Toland, *The Rising Sun*, 936.

63. The Pacific War Research Society, *Japan's Longest Day*, 79.

64. Ibid., 81-83.

65. Ibid., 83.

66. Winters, *Remembering Hiroshima: Was it Just*, 143.

67. Anami's conversation with Umezu: Statement of Sumihisa Ikeda, 16 June 50, Doc. No. 54479, p.6. CHM. Ikeda reported he heard this direct from Umezu immediately after the conversation. Given Ikeda's long and close relationship with Umezu, the possibility that Ikeda fabricated this account to shed favorable light on Umezu has to be considered (see IMTFE IKEA 36,942). But in view of Ikeda's severely critical description of Umezu's behavior in the decisive meetings ("Umezu was not a man of firm conviction"), it appears Ikeda's report is trustworthy (Statement, p. 5). Frank, *Downfall*, 316.

68. Toland, *The Rising Sun*, 938.

69. Ibid., 938.

70. Ibid., 938-939.

71. The Pacific War Research Society, *Japan's Longest Day*, 90.

72. Brooks, *Behind Japan's Surrender*, 276-277.

73. The Pacific War Research Society, *Japan's Longest Day*, 96-97.

74. Ibid., 94.

75. Ibid., 95.

76. Toland, *The Rising Sun*, 939.

77. The Pacific War Research Society, *Japan's Longest Day*, 107.

78. Meeting of Kawabe, Wakamatsu, and senior commanders: Statement of Lt. Gen. Torashirō Kawabe, 3 Dec 1948, Doc. No. 50224, CMH; IMTFE Wakamatsu 36,937-40, Wakamatsu reported that when Kawabe broached the subject of securing agreement of the senior leaders of the army, he said this was also the intention of Umezu. Frank, *Downfall*, 316-317.

79. Toland, *The Rising Sun*, 940.

80. Ibid., 940.

81. Ida has noted that only 20 percent of his colleagues agreed with him about a mass suicide on the part of the army's leaders, 10 percent advocated going underground, and 70 percent remained undecided. Butow, *Japan's Decision to Surrender*, 213-214.

82. Brooks, *Behind Japan's Surrender*, 288-289.

83. Toland, *The Rising Sun*, 942.

84. Ibid., 942.

85. Brooks, *Behind Japan's Surrender*, 291.

86. Toland, *The Rising Sun*, 943.

87. Brooks, *Behind Japan's Surrender*, 297.

88. Tōgō, *The Cause of Japan*, 336-337.

89. Toland, *The Rising Sun*, 944.

90. Brooks, *Behind Japan's Surrender*, 306-307.

91. The Pacific War Research Society, *Japan's Longest Day*, 205.

92. Toland, *The Rising Sun*, 944.

93. Ibid., 944-946.

94. Ibid., 946.

95. The Pacific War Research Society, *Japan's Longest Day*, 216-217.

Chapter 11: A Failed Coup d'État and Surrender

1. Brooks, *Behind Japan's Surrender*, 308.

2. During his absence, Hatanaka had called upon Lieutenant Colonel Takeshita in an effort to persuade the latter to intervene with his brother-in-law, War Minister Anami. After a vain attempt to get Hatanaka to reconsider, Takeshita agree to do what he could. See *Statements:* Takeshita #56366 and #50025 A. Butow, *Japan's Decision to Surrender*, 214-215.

3. The Pacific War Research Society, *Japan's Longest Day*, 220.

4. Ibid., 220.

5. Ibid., 221.

6. Ibid., 221.

7. Ibid., 223.

8. Brooks, *Behind Japan's Surrender*, 309-310.

9. Ibid., 310.

10. The Pacific War Research Society, *Japan's Longest Day*, 224-225.

11. Ibid., 226-227.

12. Ibid., 236-236.

13. Ibid., 229-230.

14. Ibid., 241.

15. Ibid., 246.

16. Ibid., 266.

17. Ibid., 268-269.

18. Ibid., 271-272.

19. Ibid., 277.

20. Ibid., 280-281.

21. Ibid., 282-283.

22. McCullough, *Truman*, 461.
23. The Pacific War Research Society, *Japan's Longest Day*, 289-290.
24. Brooks, *Behind Japan's Surrender*, 332-333.
25. The Pacific War Research Society, *Japan's Longest Day*, 296.
26. Ibid., 297-298.
27. Ibid., 303.
28. Ibid., 308.
29. Ibid., 324.
30. Ibid., 325.
31. Ibid., 326.
32. Leahy, *I Was There*, 436-437.
33. Ibid., 437.
34. McCullough, *Truman*, 463.
35. Robertson, *Sly and Able*, 438.
36. The Pacific War Research Society, *Japan's Longest Day*, 328.
37. "Like others in the room:" Michihiko Hachiya, *Hiroshima Diary*, pp. 81-82. Frank, *Downfall*, 321.
38. Donald S. Detweiler and Charles B. Burdick, eds., *War in Asia and the Pacific*, Vol 12, *Defense of the Homeland and the End of the War* (New York: Garland, 1980), 23-26. Kort, *The Columbia Guide to Hiroshima and the Bomb*, 334.
39. U.S. Department of State, *Foreign Relations of the United States, 1945: The British Commonwealth, The Far East* (Washington, D.C.: U.S. Government Printing Office, 1969), 6:670-672. Kort, *The Columbia Guide to Hiroshima and the Bomb*, 333.
40. Robertson, *Sly and Able*, 439.
41. SRS 1777, 1 September 1945. These recommendations by Okamoto are listed under the heading "Psychological and Subversive." Lee, *Marching Orders*, 548-549.
42. Nakao, *Showa tenno hatsugen kiroku shusei*, 2:414-15. Another English translation is in Large, *Emperor Hirohito and Showa Japan*, 132. Kawamura, *Emperor Hirohito and the Pacific War*, 183.
43. Edward Behr, *Hirohito: Behind the Myth*, (Villard, 1989), 8, 344. Winters, *Remembering Hiroshima*, 147.
44. Lee, *Marching Orders*, 549.
45. Ibid., 549.
46. SRS 1791, 15 September 1945. Lee, *Marching Orders*, 549.

Epilogue
1. Frank, *Downfall*, 301.
2. Lawren, *The General and the Bomb*, 238.
3. Giangreco, *Hell to Pay Updated and Expanded*, 250-251.
4. Slavinsky, *Neutrality Pact*, 180; Slavinsky, "Soviet Occupation of the Kuril," 95-114, esp. 97-98. Each of these brief Slavinsky treatments of the June 27, 1945, meeting provide details not offered in the other one. Richard B. Frank gave this assessment of their [Russia's] amphibious capabilities: "The Soviets would conduct an effective invasion of Japan if their soldiers could march across the bottom of the Sea of Japan, breathing through reeds and hauling heavy ropes pulling their artillery and tanks." See Frank, "Fall of the Japanese Empire, "Presentation at the Harry S. Truman Library and Museum, Independence, MO., July 14, 2015,

and the question-and-answer session following the D.M. Giangreco presentation, "The Hokkaido Myth: U.S., Soviet, and Japanese Plans for Invasion," United States Memorial, Washington, D.C., August 6, 2015, sponsored by the Institute for the Study of Strategy and Politics. Bothe programs are available via C-SPAN. Giangreco, *Hell to Pay Updated and Expanded*, 254.

5. Ibid., 254.
6. Ibid., 255.
7. Russel, *Project Hulu*, 39-40. Giangreco, *Hell to Pay Updated and Expanded*, 258.
8. Frank, Richard B. "Unconditional Surrender: Why Did Japan Quit?" MHQ *The Quarterly Journal of Military History*, 2015, p. 30.
9. Ibid., p. 30.
10. Ibid., p. 30.
11. Dower, *War Without Mercy Race & Power in the Pacific War*, 54.
12. Tōgō, *The Cause of Japan*, 339.
13. Robertson, *Sly and Able*, 435.
14. Leahy, *I Was There*, 441.

INDEX

ABOUT THE AUTHOR

David Dean Barrett is a military historian, specializing in World War II. He has published work in *WWII Quarterly* magazine, *U.S. Military History Review,* and *Global War Studies.* He is the Consultant/ Producer for Lou Reda Productions' two-hour documentary, tentatively titled *The Real Mighty Eighth,* which will air as a primetime global event on National Geographic in late 2020. David has been a frequent guest speaker for more than a decade on the use of the atomic bomb in the final days of WWII and the end of the Pacific War.

Mr. Barrett began his career as a professional historian late in life, after spending nearly thirty years in Information Technology. David was awarded his master's degree in history from the University of Colorado, Denver, in 2006. Six years later, in 2012, he officially entered his new profession, opening the doors of One With History, Inc. Mr. Barrett lives in Littleton, Colorado.